THE MULTINATIONAL ENTERPRISE IN TRANSITION

Selected Readings and Essays

Edited by

A. Kapoor

Graduate School of Business Administration
New York University

Phillip D. Grub

School of Government and Business Administration
The George Washington University

THE DARWIN PRESS
Princeton, New Jersey

Library of Congress Catalog Card Number: 72-161053

Printed in the United States of America

To Mathilda and Alden
and
To Agnes, who made many things possible

CONTENTS

Contributors   **ix**

Preface   **xi**

    PART I: INTRODUCTION   *1*

Chapter One: The Multinational Enterprise in Perspective   *2*
1. On the Definition of a Multinational Corporation
     Yair Aharoni   3
2. The Multinational Corporation
     Neil H. Jacoby   21
3. The Tortuous Evolution of the Multinational Corporation
     Howard V. Perlmutter   53
4. The Emergent World Economy
     Judd Polk   67
5. International Business: How Big Is It? The Missing Measurements
     Stefan H. Robock and *Kenneth Simmonds*   81

    PART II: THE FUNCTIONS: A MANAGERIAL APPROACH   *103*

Chapter Two: Organizational Structure and Management   *104*
6. Organizational Structure and the Multinational Strategy
     Lawrence E. Fouraker and *John M. Stopford*   105
7. Is Management Exportable?
     William H. Newman   119
8. International Business Management . . . Its Four Tasks
     Michael G. Duerr   137
9. The Compensation of International Executives
     Hans Schollhammer   144

Chapter Three: Marketing   *163*
10. Are Domestic and International Marketing Dissimilar?
     Robert Bartels   164
11. International Advertising Principles and Strategies
     Gordon E. Miracle   174
12. The International Storekeepers
     Stanley C. Hollander   187
13. Can You Standardize Multinational Marketing?
     Robert D. Buzzell   204
14. Multinational Product Planning: Strategic Alternatives
     Warren J. Keegan   224

Chapter Four: Accounting and Finance   *232*

15. Nationalism and the International Transfer of Accounting Skills
    Lee J. Seidler   233

16. Accounting Principles Generally Accepted in the United States
    Versus Those Generally Accepted Elsewhere
    G. G. Mueller   243

17. Some Special Accounting Problems of Multinational Enterprises
    Hanns-Martin Schoenfeld   255

18. Taxation Policy in Multinational Companies
    Albert J. Rädler   266

19. Protective Measures Against Devaluation
    H. W. Allen Sweeny   270

Chapter Five: Manufacturing   *279*

20. Industrial Competition and R and D
    P. Piganiol   280

21. Where in the World Should We Put that Plant?
    Robert B. Stobaugh, Jr.   292

22. Organizing for International Production
    Business International   305

    PART III: ENVIRONMENT AND FUTURE EVOLUTION   *323*

Chapter Six: Nationalism and the Multinational Enterprise   *324*

23. A Theoretical Model of Economic Nationalism in New
    and Developing States
    Harry G. Johnson   325

24. Nationalism and the Multinational Firm
    John Fayerweather   339

25. Analyzing Political Risks in International Business
    Franklin R. Root   354

Chapter Seven: The Multinational Enterprise and Host Governments   *366*

DEVELOPING COUNTRIES: *366*

26. International Business-Government Negotiations in Developing Countries
    A. Kapoor   367

27. Conflict and Resolution Between Foreign Direct Investors
    and Less Developed Countries
    Raymond Vernon   384

DEVELOPED COUNTRIES: *401*

28. Multinational Enterprises and Nation States
    John H. Dunning   402

29. The Multinational Enterprise and Nation States:
    the Shifting Balance of Power
    Jack N. Behrman   411

30. Issues Between the Multinational Corporation and Host Governments:
    the European Case
    J. Boddewyn   426

Chapter Eight: Evolution   *437*

31. The Multinational Corporation and Uneven Development
         Stephen Hymer   438
32. How to Divest in Latin America, and Why
         Albert O. Hirschman   445
33. International Divestment: Panacea or Pitfall?
         Jack N. Behrman   467
34. The Future of International Management
         Richard D. Robinson   490
Index   501

CONTRIBUTORS

YAIR AHARONI
Tel Aviv University

ROBERT BARTELS
Ohio State University

JACK N. BEHRMAN
University of North Carolina

J. BODDEWYN
New York University

ROBERT D. BUZZELL
Harvard University

MICHAEL G. DUERR
National Industrial Conference
    Board

JOHN H. DUNNING
University of Reading

JOHN FAYERWEATHER
New York University

LAWRENCE E. FOURAKER
Harvard University

ALBERT O. HIRSCHMAN
Harvard University

STANLEY C. HOLLANDER
Michigan State University

STEPHEN HYMER
New School for Social Research

NEIL H. JACOBY
University of California
    at Los Angeles

HARRY G. JOHNSON
London School of Economics
    and University of Chicago

A. KAPOOR
New York University

WARREN J. KEEGAN
Columbia University

GORDON E. MIRACLE
Michigan State University

G. G. MUELLER
University of Washington

WILLIAM H. NEWMAN
Columbia University

HOWARD V. PERLMUTTER
University of Pennsylvania

P. PIGANIOL
Saint Gobain Glass Company

JUDD POLK
U.S. Council of the International
    Chamber of Commerce

ALBERT J. RÄDLER

RICHARD D. ROBINSON
Massachusetts Institute
    of Technology

STEFAN H. ROBOCK
Columbia University

FRANKLIN R. ROOT
University of Pennsylvania

HANNS-MARTIN SCHOENFELD
University of Illinois

HANS SCHOLLHAMMER
University of California

LEE J. SEIDLER
New York University

KENNETH SIMMONDS
London Graduate School of
Business Studies

ROBERT B. STOBAUGH, JR.
Harvard University

JOHN M. STOPFORD
Harvard University

H. W. ALLEN SWEENY
Esso Chemical Company

RAYMOND VERNON
Harvard University

PREFACE

The multinational enterprise has had as great an impact as any other institution on the flow of goods and services in world trade. It has been said that "one of the most significant changes in international economic institutions during the last two decades has been the emergence of the multinational enterprise. Policy formulation has not yet caught up with this change." Government officials and corporate executives are attempting to cope with this new phenomenon and formulate appropriate guidelines for policy coordination and control.

The purpose of *The Multinational Enterprise in Transition* is to provide the business executive, government official, scholar, and student with a better understanding of the changing context in which business is conducted on a global basis. Thirty-six leading observers of the multinational enterprise have contributed to this book.

Particular emphasis has been placed on creating an awareness of the evolving patterns of features which uniquely characterize the multinational enterprise. In so doing, the editors have endeavored to accomplish the following objectives:

1. To present many of the key characteristics of an important and relatively new form of international business activity, namely, the multinational enterprise;

2. To describe the circumstances leading to the emergence and growth of the multinational enterprise;

3. To discuss the ways in which various areas—management, marketing, accounting, finance, manufacturing—function within a multinational enterprise;

4. To present some of the major environmental factors which influence and are influenced by the multinational enterprise;

5. To explore the likely paths of evolution of the multinational enterprise.

The multinational enterprise *is* in transition. It is a relatively new form of organization which has acquired tremendous economic power with far-reaching social, economic, and political implications that transcend national boundaries. These and other dimensions of the multinational enterprise which are the subject of growing research and debate are only beginning to be recognized by corporate and public policy makers. Understandably, policy makers are raising fundamental questions such as: For what and for whose benefit does the multinational enterprise exist? Are the costs (political, social, economic) borne by a country greater than the benefits it secures by admitting a multinational enterprise? To whom is the enterprise accountable? Is it a new entity or an old one in a new garb? How does the enterprise affect the sovereignty of a nation? What is the future of the enterprise? Important questions are also being posed on a functional level: How does the multinationality of a company affect its management style? What implications does it have for extension of corporate policies and practices across national boundaries?

The Multinational Enterprise in Transition does not pretend to offer ready-made answers to these and other complex problems. It does, however, provide the student and researcher, as well as government and business executives, with a wealth of information not presently available in an organized form in current textbooks or journals from which a better understanding of the current and emerging characteristics may be gained.

This book is organized into three parts: Introduction, the Functions of the Enterprise, Environment and Future Evolution. A reference index is also included.

In Part I, Introduction, the major question of what is or should be the definition of the multinational enterprise is discussed in detail. Subsequent selections refer to this question and offer a rich diversity of viewpoints. In addition, Part I offers an overall survey of the nature, emergence, development, and range of issues faced by the multinational enterprise in developed, developing, and centrally planned economies.

The human dimension is critical in any enterprise but particularly in the multinational enterprise, which functions within different social-cultural environments. The extent to which management recognizes the importance of cultivating a multinational attitude on the part of company executives will influence a company's effectiveness in engaging in multinational business. As the world economy displays increasing interdependence between nations, national economies —the richest one in the world (the United States of America) included — cannot formulate economic policies and programs without recognizing the interaction with the broader international economy of which it is a part. Yet more often than not nation-states make decisions without full recognition of the international economic framework.

In the concluding introductory part, a simple but fundamental question is raised: How big is international business? One discovers that the availability of data and the form in which it is gathered leave much to be desired and, as a result, policy decisions, especially by governments, are based significantly on guesswork rather than on a rational evaluation of well formulated alternatives.

In Part II, attention is directed toward the functional aspects of the multinational enterprise. It has been found that corporations which have been most successful in meeting the challenges of operating on a multinational basis have been those which possess managers with the skill for developing a multinational strategy that is capable of controlling and guiding a heterogeneous and diverse enterprise. Beginning with an analysis of organizational structure and multinational strategy, the question of whether or not management is exportable is explored in Chapter Two. Attention is then focused on developing international management, including the identification, selection, and training of managers for overseas operations, as well as the development of international expertise in the companies' domestic staff.

The rapid growth of many multinational firms has led them to select executives on a multinational basis. The concluding article of this chapter is concerned with the compensation of international executives and stresses the importance of developing a rational, company-wide executive compensation program.

The role of marketing in the multinational enterprise and the development of appropriate strategies is the focus of Chapter Three. Questions such as "Are domestic and international marketing dissimilar?" and "Can you standardize multinational marketing?" are explored along with guidelines for multinational product planning and multinational advertising strategies. Included are discussions of the changing role of international marketing managers and the growth of multinational voluntary chain systems and other international retailing ventures that are responding to the opportunities for multinational mass merchandisers.

Traditional marketing strategy has been geared to specific local markets; however, there is evidence to indicate that there are indeed benefits to be gained by developing an integrated approach to marketing strategies on a multinational basis. This is accomplished through standardization of products, packaging, and promotion as well as the development of more uniform price and credit policies which facilitate a more positive approach to over-all planning, coordination, and control as well as profitability for the multinational enterprise. Having explored these areas, the final article identifies five strategic alternatives which can assist multinational marketing managers in identifying the significant factors in determining the appropriate multinational marketing strategies.

In Chapter Four, emphasis is placed on accounting and on the financial operations of the multinational enterprise. Beginning with an article on nationalism and the international transfer of accounting skills, attention is then directed toward the accounting principles which are generally accepted in the United States as opposed to those generally accepted elsewhere in the world. Special consideration is given to the development of taxation policies which minimize the incidence of taxation while maximizing the total profits for the multinational enterprise in the long run. In the concluding article of this chapter, protective measures against devaluation are explored and some practical examples are offered.

Much controversy has arisen over management of research and development, the location of R & D centers in the multinational enterprise, and the rate at which technology flows from the parent company to its subsidiaries in other countries. Beginning with an analysis of multinational industrial competition and research and development, consideration is given to the optimization of plant location. Selecting the right company for investment of new or added production facilities is indeed a major decision. The concluding article in this section discusses the question of organizing for international production, taking into account the plans for integration of production, both across national boundaries and product lines. The development of control mechanisms in the overall planning process appears to be the key to successful management of international production, and it provides a program of integrated production and optimal use of capital resources and technology.

Part III covers two important areas—the environment and the future evolution of the multinational enterprise.

The environment is made up of many features of an historical, economic, political, social, and cultural nature, all of which are essential for understanding the broader environmental context within which the multinational enterprise functions. However, two types of environmental forces—nationalism and government relations—are of particular significance and are discussed in some length in this section.

Nationalism is a varied and complex force which expresses itself in many ways as is pointed out in Chapter Six. Restrictions on foreign ownership or on the employment of foreign nationals is an expression of nationalism. Government policies (such as expropriation) are often justified on the grounds of nationalism. The nature and growth of nationalism in developed and developing countries is discussed with particular attention to its implications for the multinational enterprise, and an approach for analyzing and forecasting political risks is presented to assist the corporate decision maker.

The importance of governments—both home and host country—in international business is discussed in Chapter Seven, with particular emphasis on the issues of conflict and potential for reconciliation between the multinational enterprise and governments. Additionally, the dynamics of interaction (negotiation) between the multinational enterprise and host governments are explored.

The second section of Part III focuses on the general question of the future evolution of the multinational enterprise. As is to be expected, there is limited agreement between the contributors on what is likely to be the path of evolution in the next decade. Some are beginning to view the multinational enterprise as a vehicle contributing to uneven development, especially between the developed and the developing countries, while other observers reflect on the need for approaches to foreign direct investment different from those which have been used to date. Fundamental differences exist between observers on the acceptability of such new approaches either for host governments or for investing companies.

The concluding articles raise several basic questions: Is economic growth necessary and/or desirable? What will be the effect on environmental pollution if a significant level of economic development actually takes place in the developing countries? Should the enterprise be more concerned not with increasing the size of the "economic pie" but rather in achieving a better distribution of the "pie" which exists at present?

The Multinational Enterprise in Transition is designed for both the student and practitioner. However, its primary market is the graduate or advanced undergraduate course in international business. The 34 articles in the book provide specific insights into many phases of operations of the multinational enterprise. As such, this book is a useful text for courses in the management of international operations. Also, it provides an excellent group of readings for case-oriented courses, and can be used as a companion book with many of the existing texts in international business.

The Multinational Enterprise in Transition provides the breadth necessary to broaden the horizons of a typically domestic business policy text and consequently offer a multinational perspective where either the text or other required readings are domestic in their orientation. This book may also be used in international economic courses providing a pragmatic viewpoint which complements the more theoretically oriented texts in this field. As such, the background of information offered the student is far greater than if only a basic text or cases are used.

While the co-editors assisted each other in the development of the book and in the selection of articles, Professor Kapoor had the primary responsibility for Parts I and III while Professor Grub was responsible for Part II.

In the preparation of this book, the authors are indebted to many of their colleagues in academia for their comments and suggestions as well as encouragement. It was indeed a formidable task to narrow the number of contributions to such a degree that would be in keeping with the framework of a single volume. While we are grateful for the assistance given us, we bear the sole responsibility for the final selections made.

Numerous individuals contributed to the completion of this book. In particular, we would like to express our appreciation to Timothy Burningham, Lynette Cunningham, Richard Davenport, Thomas Emrich, Ian Groom, Dara Khambata, John Kirby, James Ward, and Michael Weiner. We also wish to acknowledge the useful comments contributed by our colleagues and students. Most importantly, we wish to express our sincere appreciation for the cooperation of the authors—particularly those authors whose contributions were written specifically for this book—and the publishers whose works have been herewith included.

Ashok Kapoor and Phillip D. Grub
April, 1972

Part I:
Introduction

Chapter One:
The Multinational Enterprise in Perspective

1

On the Definition of a Multinational Corporation

Yair Aharoni

The rise of the multinational corporation is often cited as one of the most powerful forces operating in the world today and is the object of considerable scholarly research both in the United States and abroad.[1] Government bodies are concerned with the rise of the multinational enterprise, and some politicians see it as a threat to the nation-state.[2] Already some people are asserting that not more than 300 multinational corporations will control 90 percent of the world trade by the end of the century, while others contend that "over the next decade a few multinational corporations will, in the attitude of their management, cut loose even from one home nation and try to be rational on a global scale so as to maximize the long run welfare of the entire worldwide company."[3] Conferences have been held, and many talks given, discussing the future relationship between multinational corporations and the nation-state. It has been proposed that the development of the multinational corporation is the doom of the nation-state; others see it as a substitute for colonialism or imperialism.[4] Still others say that the multinational corporation is not really a new phenomenon, and that it existed as early as the nineteenth century. Some assert multinational corporations are all big; others disagree. Some say that the majority of multinational corporations are United States-based; others assert that about half of them are European and Japanese.[5]

In this paper I shall discuss the various definitions of multinational enterprise. In the first section, I shall define multinationality according to

Reprinted by permission, from the *Quarterly Review of Economics and Business,* Vol. II, Autumn, 1971.

some structural criterion; in the second section, I shall define it according to a yardstick of performance; and in the third section, I shall define it according to behavioral characteristics. The criteria used in discussing the foregoing definitions of multinationality parallel that used in another branch of economics in which the problem of classification is an acute one: namely, in the area of industrial organization and anti-trust policies. In the final section, a suggestion is made for what seems to this writer to be a first approximation of defining the area of inquiry.

STRUCTURAL CRITERION

NUMBER OF FOREIGN OPERATIONS

As far as the writer could ascertain, the term "multinational firm" was probably first used by David E. Lilienthal in a paper delivered before a symposium on "Management and Corporations, 1985" at the Graduate School of Industrial Administration of the Carnegie Institute of Technology in April 1960.[6] Observing that "many large and even medium-sized American firms are already operating in other countries, in one way or another," and noting that "the business activities of these multinational corporations have proliferated enormously, particularly in the past decade, it is almost certain to increase even more rapidly in the future, not only for American firms but also for those in almost all of the other industrialized nations." Lilienthal suggested the definition of "multinational corporations" as "corporations which have their home in one country but operate and live under the laws and customs of other countries as well."[7]

To Lilienthal, therefore, "multinational" simply meant a firm operating in more than one country. He hardly elaborated on the definition, or explained what types of operations should be included, or in how many countries a corporation should operate to qualify as "multinational." He did, however, make it clear that:

By operating I do not mean merely that they have a financial stake, like a portfolio investment, in business in other countries than their own; nor do I refer to sales agencies or distributions. I have particularly in mind industrial or commercial operations abroad which directly involve managerial responsibility.[8]

Lilienthal's definition stresses the structural element: the criterion for defining multinationality is the number of countries in which a firm is doing business.

OWNERSHIP

An alternative definition of multinational, still based on structural considerations, emphasizes the *ownership,* not operations, of the company. A "multinational firm" means a firm owned by persons from many nations: "multi" usually means "consisting of many," and "multinational" therefore is consisting of many nations. Indeed, Mr. Olivier Giscard d'Estaing, Director General of INSEAD, Fontainbleau, has suggested precisely this definition for "multinational firm" in his report of the Crotonville conference held by the Atlantic Council urging United States companies to become "a truly multinational enterprise by making available either the stock of your local subsidiary or of the mother company in all countries where you operate." [9]

If one wants to adhere to Mr. Giscard d'Estaing's definition, a multinational firm hardly existed at the time of his talk. Unilever, Royal Dutch Shell, and Agfa-Gevaert are the only three exceptions that come to mind of firms whose *ownership base* was distributed over more than one country. As a matter of fact, research on the behavior of both United States and United Kingdom firms whose operations are scattered in various countries unmistakably shows a clear tendency to avoid as far as possible joint ventures and a strong propensity to keep a hundred percent control of the subsidiaries abroad in the hands of the parent company (in the United States or in the United Kingdom). Thus, for example, Professor Jack Behrman of the University of North Carolina, in research on "Foreign Associates and Their Financing," found strong preference for controlling foreign subsidiaries: out of a sample of 72 United States corporations, 47 or nearly two-thirds preferred 100 percent ownership of foreign companies, and an additional 14 preferred more than 50 percent ownership. Only one company preferred a fifty-fifty arrangement, three preferred minority interest, and seven had no preference. [10]

Professor Behrman reports the same conclusions in a more recent study:

There is a definite preference among U.S. multinational enterprises for wholly-owned affiliates. During this six-and-a-half year period, the percentage of new establishments that were wholly-owned ranged from 83 per cent in Canada to 26 per cent in India, Pakistan and Ceylon . . . . The implication which may be drawn is that U. S. parents move toward a partnership only when they are pushed to do so by governmental or other constraints.

The extent to which Canadian manufacturing companies are wholly-owned is reflected in the fact that non-resident control is only slightly larger than non-resident ownership . . . . This means that only a few companies were majority-held by foreigners, and among these most would be foreign-owned by large percentages—e.g., 75 per cent or more. This inference is supported by data on 280 companies developed by Professor A. E. Safarian . . . . showing that over 70 per cent of the American-owned companies were held 100 per cent; a similar percentage was wholly-owned among affiliates of other foreign companies. Only about 5 per cent of the affiliates were minority-held. The larger-size affiliates frequently included more minority Canadian partners; the smaller companies were quite closely held.

European companies—like U. S. parents—tend to own foreign affiliates 100 per cent. U. K. companies own between 90 and 98 per cent of the earnings of their affiliates abroad . . . . This aggregate figure means that there is a very high proportion of all affiliates which are wholly-owned or that minority partners are restricted on the average to less than 10 per cent of equity.

The Australian Department of Trade and Industry reported that British affiliates are more often wholly-owned than are American affiliates in Australia. But given the large size of the U.S. affiliates, more assets are wholly-owned by American companies than by British companies. Of the 208 Australian companies studied by Professor Donald Brash which were American owned, 60 per cent were held 100 per cent and only 15 per cent were minority-owned . . . . Of 200 affiliates of U.S. manufacturing companies in Britain during 1953, nearly three-fourths were wholly-owned and only 10 per cent were less than 60 per cent owned by the U.S. parent . . . .

Foreign ownership of German industry is also heavily concentrated in the wholly-owned category. Over 60 per cent of companies with foreign participation were more than 90 per cent owned by the foreign investor; and these held over three-fourths of the foreign investment. Less than 20 per cent were minority-held by foreign companies in 1964; the percentage rose to 25 per cent in 1965."[11]

It may be added that many of the problems faced by so-called multinational firms stem from the fact that they operate in a nationalistic world. From the point of view of ownership, a corporation must be — legally at least — part of a nation. There is no way as yet to register a private business corporation outside of its national boundaries (such as under the United Nations charter). The corporation must be registered according to the laws of some state,[12] and this registration makes it subject to the laws, taxation and regulation of the same state. A United States corporation will continue to be looked upon as a United States corporation, subject to U.S. taxes and enjoying the protection of the U.S. flag even if all of its operations are carried on outside the U.S. borders. In the eyes of other countries, such a firm will be considered foreign, not multinational. It will always be suspected that it has the interests of the United States at heart, not of the host country, however hard it may try to be a "good industrial citizen" in the host country. Indeed, in the event of a crisis, this corporation will probably call for the help of its government! (Witness the experience of the oil companies in the Middle East.)[13] True, Ruthenberg hypothesized that "in the next decade a few multinational corporations will . . . cut loose even from one home nation." However, Behrman found in his research that at least in this decade:

There are no strong movements to move headquarters companies to small principalities to "de-nationalize" the multinational enterprise by placing it under a small, non-interfering government. Rather, the officials of the parent companies of both U.S. and European multinational enterprises assert that they will remain in their country of origin and, in the last analysis, will extend their allegiance to the government of that country. Of course, they prefer that this allegiance not be tested, and — if it is — hopefully not publicly.

Officials generally prefer the contradictions and conflicts of the existing multiplicity of jurisdictions and loyalties to an amorphous situation under which the multinational enterprise would be incorporated by some intergovernmental agency that would be unable to protect them or to define clearly their rights in and against sovereign states.[14]

Moreover, conceptually at least, to qualify as "multinational" under the criterion of ownership, a firm should not only have *joint ventures* abroad; the *ownership base* of the *parent* companies should be distributed among the citizens of many countries. This definition, however, creates problems both in the conceptual and operational spheres. Conceptually, it is a well-known fact that in large business corporations "ownership" is not synonymous with "control." The changes in the time-hallowed concepts of property and ownership brought about by the fact that the corporation has become the dominant medium for conducting business were analyzed in the classic work of Berle and Means,[15] and the shifts in the control and leadership patterns were chronicled in Gordon's work immediately after the Second World War. [16] The analysis of the ownership of corporations tells us very little about the distribution of power, authority, or decision-centers within the corporation.

One new and very fascinating area in moving the cluster of corporations much further on the road towards multinationality is the ownership of these corporations' shares by people of varied nationalities. Many American corporations with subsidiaries abroad have become interesting investment prospects for people from different countries, to some extent because these people became familiar with the corporation through its foreign operations. Indeed, Kirschen, Bloch, and Bassett [17] show a list of 23 U.S. corporations whose shares are quoted on at least two European stock exchanges. Seven of these (Du Pont de Nemours, Eastman Kodak, Ford, General Electric, General Motors, Goodyear Tire and Rubber, and Standard Oil of New Jersey) are quoted in four. The same authors also list nineteen European firms quoted in at least two other European countries.

The foregoing has become even more pronounced since the American corporations started to finance their worldwide operations through the Eurobond and Eurodollar market. Many of the issues of securities in this market are convertible debentures. Very often a large parcel of such convertible debentures is given in exchange for shares in a European company acquired by the American firm. If and when these debentures are converted, the shareholders of the corporation will be truly multinational, according to Giscard d'Estaing's definition. [18]

On the operational side, it is very difficult to readily find any statistical breakdown of ownership according to the nationality of the shareholders. Conceivably, many Europeans buy shares of stock listed on the New York Stock Exchange and hold shares in some large U.S. corporations. Moreover, many U.S.-based corporations have increasingly turned to the European market to tap capital through Eurodollar convertible bonds and other means to finance their foreign operations. In quite a few cases, the shares of the U.S. parent are also registered and traded on other stock exchanges. It is quite conceivable that every blue chip stock listed on the New York Stock Exchange is owned to some extent by citizens of other nations. However, the extent of this ownership is unknown, and as argued above, it certainly does not have any impact on the way the corporation conducts its business.

It is interesting to note in this respect that Nestle Alimentana, a large Swiss-based food manufacturer, has been reported to own twenty percent of Libby, McNeill and Libby, a Chicago-based food processor.[19]

NATIONALITY OF TOP MANAGEMENT

These arguments bring us to a third structural definition of the multinational firm, namely, one based on the national composition of the top decision-makers. A multinational firm, one may argue, is one whose top management is composed of nationals of various countries. Such a firm will presumably be less apt to keep the interest of one country above everything, and will have a "pure" worldwide outlook.

Thus, *Business International,* in describing the organizational structure of several dozen multinational firms, called International Flavors and Fragrances "a truly international firm," citing as evidence the fact that "it not only has manufacturing, sales, and R & D activities in many countries, but its executives are drawn without regard to nationality. The executive vice president is Dutch and is located in Holland. Other ranking officers are either Dutch or English."[20]

This definition has an intuitive appeal. It is a well-known fact that nations want their local business units to be managed by nationals and that firms operating subsidiaries in foreign countries try to employ a minimum of persons of other than the subsidiary's nationality. Wouldn't it be reasonable to expect that a truly international firm will slowly let the local managers climb up the ladder and, therefore, eventually become managed by nationals of various countries?[21] In other words, when the firm's operations are worldwide in scope and its executives are drawn from various countries, these managers will have their first allegiance to the corporation and will be promoted and moved to new managerial posts anywhere in the world. While those assertions may conceivably be true in the long run, and while certainly the composition of management is quite an important factor to be watched in the operations of corporations in the world arena, this definition seems to be lacking as a criterion for eligibility as a multinational firm on two counts: first, it is difficult to define "top management." Second, national policies may hinder the international integration suggested above.

To elaborate, we still lack a good operational definition of what we mean by top management or top decision-makers. Therefore, it will be hard to draw the line as to when the nationalities of top management should be asserted. It is interesting to note in this respect that corporations publishing figures on the composition of their labor force according to nationality (and, incidentally, only a handful of firms do so) generally publish only figures on the percentage of Americans from the total labor force abroad — a figure that is, after all, meaningless: no one expects that an American firm operating a subsidiary in Brazil will send manual workers to Brazil. The question is generally the nationality of a handful of top managers.

Furthermore, one cannot escape the fact that the world is composed of sovereign states. The mobility of managers depends to a large extent on nationalistic attitudes. (Frenchmen may be reluctant to accept a German top manager, although they might accept a Dutch one.) It is also restricted by immigration and labor laws. In the United States, for one, it would be hard to employ a top manager from Europe should this man refuse to change his nationality and apply for a United States citizenship.

ORGANIZATIONAL STRUCTURE

A final possibility of defining multinationality according to some structural characteristics is to look at the organizational structure of the company. This possibility is somewhat akin to that of the composition of the top management. Surely, one may argue, a multinational firm will structure its organization in a manner best suited to reflect its worldwide network of activities. Indeed, some companies have embarked on massive reorganization programs, reflecting the rapid expansion of foreign operations and prospects of an even greater commitment of the corporation's resources abroad in the future. There is a distinct trend within companies very active in the international investment field to realign the company's organizational responsibilities based on a worldwide concept of operations. These firms, instead of splitting-off the international operations and assigning responsibilities for their management and conduct to a separate, specialized group (generally called the international division, or the international group, or sometimes organized as a separate subsidiary such as IBM World Trade), reorganize responsibilities for the conduct of worldwide operations according to regions (as is the case with the Singer Company or Richardson-Merrell), or according to product lines (as did, for example, General Electric or Deere and Company).

The organizational structure, however, seems to be a result of a long period of experience in international operations. Dozens of firms, intuitively qualifying as multinational, still did not see fit to realign their organization to the worldwide concept. As a matter of fact, these corporations (IBM, Olin

Mathieson, Johns-Manville, and Owen-Illinois, to mention just a few) strongly believe that worldwide operations are best organized when international operations are run by specialists in a separate division.[22] It would seem an ill-choice, therefore, to classify firms as multinational on the basis of this criterion alone.

PERFORMANCE YARDSTICKS

RELATIVE-ABSOLUTE MEASURES

The performance school would define a firm as multinational according to some performance characteristics, such as earnings, sales, or assets and the number of employees, and these characteristics would sometimes be advocated as absolute, sometimes as relative. The absolute measure will classify a corporation as multinational if it has committed a certain *amount of resources* to foreign operations. The relative measure asserts that a firm is multinational if it has committed a significant *portion* of its financial, technological, and human resources to overseas operations. In other words, a company is multinational if it does business in more than one country in such a volume that its well-being and growth rest in more than one country.

There is, of course, a difference between absolute and relative measures. A company may have committed only a very small fraction of its activities to overseas operations, but because of the sheer size of the firm, this small fraction by itself is a very large absolute amount. On the other hand, a company may have committed a very large percentage of its resources to foreign activities, but being a relatively small company, this large percentage of its assets is actually a small amount.

Intuitively, the definition of performance on a relative basis is more appealing than the one based on absolute measures. After all, what we seek is some definition that will include corporations where the commitments to worldwide operations are strong enough to involve the whole organization, not corporations whose investments abroad are so small relative to their total activities that those foreign operations hardly consume any of management's time. Of course, in the foregoing suggestion, we are assuming that what we are interested in is the behavior of corporations, not necessarily the impact of foreign investments on other countries. If, on the contrary, we are interested in the latter, absolute size may be a better and more relevant criterion.

Assuming that we are interested in the relative share of resources devoted to foreign operations, several questions present themselves. First, what type of measure should be used? Second, what percentage should be considered significant?

TYPES OF MEASURES

Let us analyze more carefully four elements—namely, assets, number of employees, sales, and earnings—that give some idea of the extent of a corporation's commitment to foreign operations. The asset ratio may have some advantage if we want to include companies in an early stage of development when earnings on new investments abroad are low and sales are not built up yet. The problem of assets being influenced by the capital intensity of the production process does not present itself, or at least it is much less severe than when a cross-section analysis is made. The capital intensity in the same company is presumably the same all over the world, unless of course, the main investments abroad are in assembly plants or when the company uses more labor intensive processes abroad. In the latter case, the number of employees, too, becomes a somewhat questionable criterion.

The sales criterion creates some conceptual difficulties: should export sales be included as "foreign," or should we include only sales of products made abroad? If we use the latter approach, a very careful definition of operations should be included. For example, suppose a company ships products from the parent to a subsidiary abroad and the subsidiary only packages the products. Should the sales of the subsidiary be included? Suppose the company ships knocked-down units for assembly. Should they be included? Here again we come back to the definition of operations that we wish to qualify as "foreign operations."

Earnings seem to be the most questionable measuring rod. Not only do we face many conceptual problems of how earnings should be measured, but there are two additional problems. First, there is the fact that the rate of earnings may swing quite widely (companies may be included or excluded depending on the period in which profits are measured). Second, there is the problem of transfer pricing: in a cluster of corporations controlled by the same top management, earnings may be changed at will by changing the charges for goods and services within the cluster. Presumably, rational management will use the mechanism of transfer prices in a way that will minimize the total tax burden on the company, showing higher earnings in countries where the rate of taxation is lowest.

Finally, the problem of unit of measurement. Accounting conventions are far from being uniform, and when economic units measured in different currencies are to be combined and compared, numerous problems are created. The process of achieving homogeneity in monetary units by converting or translating accounting balances expressed in terms of various foreign currencies to the national monetary unit of the parent organization is very imperfect.

To cite one authority on the subject: "It must be recognized that international monetary conditions may exist . . . which will render the results of the translation process more misleading than informative."[23]

SIGNIFICANT PERCENTAGE?

The main problem, however, is the same encountered when structural definitions were discussed: what types of operations should be included? It is generally agreed by the authorities on the subject that it is not enough for a company to have a stake in the overseas markets to qualify as a multinational company. The operations of the company abroad must be of some specific nature that commits top management to devote some of its own time to the corporation's foreign operations. Before discussing this point further, it is useful to quote the results of a study based on the foregoing performance characteristics. Professors J. K. Bruck and F. A. Lees [24] checked the 500 top U. S. industrial companies listed in *Fortune* magazine according to a composite criterion. In other words, any company having an x percent of *either* sales, earnings, assets, or employment from abroad was considered a multinational corporation. The authors used a 50 percent cut-off in their definition, but gave data for lower cut-offs, namely 25 and 10 percent respectively. Using a 50 percent cut-off, only 7 companies in 1964 and 11 in 1965 were multinational. When the cut-off was 25 percent, 77 companies qualified in 1964 and 82 in 1965. Additionally, 122 in 1964 and 129 in 1965 had at least 10 percent of their operations overseas by the above criteria. Comparative listings for the United Kingdom and Sweden are given by Rolfe.[25]

The foregoing results would vary if another criteria, such as number of countries in which the company operates, were used. According to Behrman:

The 50 per cent criterion is excessively strict for purposes of classifying a company as being "multinational" and causes the inclusion in the group of three corporations which are not really industrial and not "multinational . . . . International Milling is in formula feeds, produced in three foreign countries. International Packers is in meat packing, largely in one foreign country, and does its business mainly by export. Anaconda is similar in that its major foreign assets are in three countries, one of which supplies about half of the company's earnings, and its structure is relatively fixed. In the sense that "multinational" implies "many-nations" and "multiple choices" in the worldwide operations of the company, these companies do not fit.[26]

Fortune magazine of September 15, 1968, gave a list of "Some Big U. S. Players in the Global Game." The first on the list is General Motors, with 24 countries in which the company has production facilities. However, its percent of assets abroad form total assets was only 15 percent, net income abroad was 7 percent of the firm's net income, and sales accounted for 14 percent (excluding Canada). Incidentally, General Motors' shares are traded in Brussels, Paris, Amsterdam, and Frankfurt. Is General Motors a multinational corporation? The performance school would probably answer "no," because some structure criteria are met, some are not. The way to find out may be, as many suggest, to look at the behavior of top management.

BEHAVIORAL CHARACTERISTICS

CORPORATE MANAGEMENT ORIENTATION

According to what I term the "behavioral school of thought," a multinational firm is one whose top management "thinks internationally." Thus, according to Peter Drucker,[27] a multinational firm is one "with corporate headquarters in the U. S., but in their organization, their business, their scope, they are worldwide . . . . Corporate top management is not concerned with any one region or territory . . . an international business demands of its management people that they think and act as international businessmen in a world in which national passions are as strong as ever." A multinational firm, therefore, is a firm whose top management thinks as international businessmen. Presumably, an international businessman is one who always weighs alternative investment possibilities on a worldwide basis and who does not discard an investment opportunity abroad simply because it is not in the United States.

The definition of a multinational business on the basis of a behavioral criterion has a strong intuitive appeal. Many executives in companies involved in a large-scale foreign operation certainly see the world[28] as the market. As Robert C. Hood, President of Ansul Chemical Co., has stated:

There are some terms that bother me a little. The term "abroad" is an example, and the term "foreign." If you adopt the point of view that you are an international company, nothing is "foreign" or "alien" or "abroad"—the world is your market and you must learn how to deal in a large market place and be an economic and social part of it.[29]

The idea that the world is one market seems to be very strong indeed in some corporations, notably those with a long and successful experience abroad. However, the use of this behavior characteristic as a screening measure, to decide which are the multinational firms and which are not, seems to involve many problems and weaknesses.

First, the definition seems to be tautological. What we are saying in effect is that a firm is multinational when its top management thinks in terms of multinational firms. The behavioral characteristics are, of course, very important, and research on the behavioral differences between the domestic and multinational firm is badly needed.[30] However, these behavorial characteristics must be the variables used to explain behavior, not an *a priori* screening measure.

Second, for obvious reasons, the definition of behavior is hardly an operational criterion for research. We must have some criterion that will enable us to decide which firms should be included when research on the behavior of the multinational firms is made. It is practically impossible to define a certain set of behavior and then interview all top management just to find out which corporations should be included in the main body of the research.

Finally, aside from the foregoing difficulties, and aside from the difficulties of defining "top management," it is almost impossible to ascertain what exactly do we mean by "thinking internationally" or "looking at the world as your market place."[31] We know so little about how decisions in big organizations are made, or what are the variables taken into account, or what is the information available to the decision-makers, that it is a sheer impossibility to find at this stage a generally agreed upon definition of international behavior.

One can brush aside all these reservations by the first assertion that if a company operates in many markets, this fact may be looked upon as an *a priori* proof that its top management behaves and thinks internationally. This line of thinking has two obvious weaknesses. First, it tends to put the cart before the horse: Such an assertion must first be proved and documented before it can be positively made. Second, a company may conceivably "think internationally" and decide as a matter of strategy *against* foreign operations. The question then becomes: Should we say that such a firm is a multinational one?

To many, the possibility of thinking internationally and rejecting foreign operations may seem startling because we become used to correlating "worldwide thinking" with "worldwide operations." However, there is a very important distinction here. Assume, for example, that a firm has some distinct advantages connected with its product *because the product is made in a certain location* and that for a long period of time the product is connected in the mind of the public with a certain location. Would it be wise for such a firm to lose this important appeal by starting foreign manufacture of the same product? Conceivably, the public may be reluctant to buy the product unless it is the "real McCoy," produced in the time-honored locations. To illustrate this point, let the reader think of such products as French Champagne, Swiss cheese, Swiss watches, Scandinavian furniture, or even a prestigious product like Rolls Royce. Can one produce French Champagne, or Swiss cheese, or any other of those products elsewhere, still retaining the image and the tremendous advantage of the location connection? Is Swiss cheese made in the United States (and it is, of course, made here) the same product as Swiss cheese made in Switzerland? For that matter, can Rolls Royce assemble cars in Brazil and still carry the same prestigious, not to say snob, appeal? In all these cases, of course, *the most rational behavior of top management who think internationally may conceivably be to refuse to manufacture or license the product abroad and to confine its world activities to exporting from the home base.*

Should one classify the French champagne manufacturer, or the Scandinavian furniture manufacturer, as multinational? Most people knowledgeable in the field would answer this question in the negative, thus discarding the behavior criterion, at least as a sole criterion. One way out of the dilemma is to add performance or structure characteristics to the behavioral elements. This, essentially, is what Professor George A. Steiner has suggested. To him "a multinational company meets at least two criteria. First, it does business in two or more countries in such volume that its well-being and growth rests in more than one country. Second, its management makes decisions on the basis of multinational alternatives."[32]

This definition, however, again raises the question of what types of operations should be considered without answering it. The question of type of operations seems to be, however, the most crucial element in the definition. After all, a definition of a phenomenon must be, first, operative and simple; second, it must be helpful in differentiation between a certain phenomenon and other phenomena. We have seen before that the behavior criterion is rough and not operational; that all performance criteria involve many definitional problems, and both the performance and structural definitions seem to encompass too many different types of operations and, therefore, of behavior. The important point is to realize that structure, performance, and behavior are *not* correlated, as was demonstrated before. Moreover, the phenomenon under discussion is a very complicated one and cannot be captured by one name. Certainly, what we are mainly interested in is the identification of the internal factors that will shape the development of a corporation as it expands its sphere of operations and seeks to identify market opportunities on a worldwide basis.

From this point of view, there are distinct differences between a company like Unilever, with manufacturing subsidiaries in dozens of countries; a company like Trans World Airlines, which also operates in dozens of countries, but with distinctly different operations; a company like Bethlehem Steel, with mining operations in seven countries, all supporting the company's manufacturing activities in the United States; a company like Gulf Oil Company, which owns and operates oil fields in several countries, transports and markets oil; and a company like Rolls Royce or Omega Watches, with manufacturing operations in one country, but export network and sales and service outlets all over the world. Whether or not we wish to call all these companies multinational, there are notable differences in the problems faced by those companies and in their solution.

Another important difference among various so-called multinational firms is the type of operations considered. Lilienthal, it will be remembered, tried to distinguish between "having a financial stake," "sales agencies or distributions," and "industrial or commercial operations abroad which directly involve managerial responsibility"; he considered only the latter multinational.[33] Behrman also talks at length about the same idea of distinguishing types of operations. To him, the distinction between multinational corporations and other investors abroad "lies in the area of control and integration of operations of the affiliates."[34] The Harvard University project was specifically designed to look only at manufacturing companies.

Multinational corporations are often alleged to be supranational or beyond government control. They are accused of being floating units which do not respond to the signaling of national development policy and emasculate the political process by removing large portions of the economic life of a country. Whether or not these assertions are true, certainly those making them refer to a United States bank with many branches overseas; to a management consultant firm operating all over the world; to Sears Roebuck's integrated and centrally controlled merchandising operations in Latin America as well as to its manufacturing operations. Multinationality is not restricted to one domain of the economic life and operations.[35]

SUGGESTED APPROACH

We have analyzed critically some possible definitions for corporations —or rather clusters of corporations controlled by one headquarters—whose operations are spread over many countries. We have shown that certain definitions stress structural elements, while others emphasize performance, and still others behavioral elements. We have seen that the three are not correlated and that each definition leads to the inclusion of some corporations active in the international field and excludes others. It seems clear that the differences are not merely a question of semantics. They seem to stem from the fact that there are several kinds of so-called "multinational companies." The realization of the heterogeneity of the field is of utmost importance if confusion is to be avoided. It is essential that researchers should be careful in defining the types of corporations to which they are referring.

It goes without saying that we are not interested in the definitions per se. The use of a clearer concept is simply a tool to help alleviate some of the uncertainties prevailing today and to get a better idea of the real differences of opinion as opposed to those based on different definitions. The definitions suggested below are based on assumptions about the areas of interest of those discussing the phenomena of the multinational corporation. It is assumed that we are interested in the decision-making mechanism of these corporations, their relations with host governments, and their role in the future.

Following Richard Robinson, it is suggested that the term "international" be used in combinations with transactions, e.g., international sales; and the term "multinational" in combination with firms.[36] The following additional definitions may be helpful:

1. **A World-Wide Corporation:** A corporation registered in several countries, doing business in these countries. The distinct feature of such a corporation is a legal one: it does not incorporate as separate legal bodies in each country under the laws of various states, but retains one corporate identity. As far as we know, such a corporation does not yet exist. As a matter of fact, there are many reasons to suspect that such a corporation will not exist for a very long time because we live in a world where national sovereignty is very important and nationalistic feelings are very strong. Countries have laws governing alien corporate registration, ownership of land, rights of importing employees, and, above all, tax laws. The definition is needed, therefore, for discussing the reason for the nonexistence of the world-wide corporation, not in explaining its behavior.

2. **A Multinational Cluster:** A group of corporations, each created in the country of operation, but all controlled by one headquarters.

3. **A Multinational Corporation:** A corporation which controls a multinational cluster. While the former term refers to the cluster as a whole, the latter is reserved for the headquarters. In order to qualify as a multinational corporation, the company should control a multinational cluster in a minimum number of countries. The number of countries must be large enough so that the multinational corporation should be involved in the international field. As a first approximation, we define multinational cluster as consisting of corporations in at least five countries. This, of course, is an arbitrary number. The number of countries may be one vector in describing different multinational corporations.

The multinational corporations should be subdivided according to three additional criteria, namely, the type of operations in which they operate.

According to their operations, corporations can be classified as:

1. **Exporters:** Companies which control a multinational cluster, the only function of which is to sell and service the products manufactured by the corporation.

2. **Importers:** Companies which control an international cluster involved in mining operations, whose function is to feed raw materials to the corporation.

3. **Transporters:** Where the international cluster consists of companies dealing with the transportation of men and goods.

4. **Petroleum:** The operational problems of the petroleum industry seem to be so unique that a separate classification of these companies is called for.

5. **Manufacturers:** Companies controlling an international cluster of manufacturing and/or assembly plants.

6. **Traders:** Companies controlling an international cluster whose main function is trading in various countries (such as Sears Roebuck Co., etc.).

According to their size, corporations can be classified as:

1. Size relative to the host country, measured in terms of total assets controlled or a similar criterion.

2. Size of the multinational cluster relative to the total operations of the corporation.

The first measure is relevant to problems of relations with the host country, and the second relates to commitment.

Corporations can also be classified according to their area of operations:

1. **Regional:** confining their multinational cluster to one region, such as Western Europe or Latin America

2. **Multiregional.**

In summary, the multinational corporation means different things to different people, and different phenomena are called by the same name. It seems essential that those interested in international business clarify their meaning when discussing the multinational corporation.

NOTES

1. A major research project is that on the multinational corporation and the nation-state carried out under the direction of Professor Raymond Vernon at Harvard University, Graduate School of Business Administration and financed by a Ford Foundation grant. Editors' Note: The first book has been released—Raymond Vernon's *Sovereignty at Bay: The Multinational Spread of U.S. Enterprises* (New York: Basic Books, 1971).

2. See Melville H. Watkins, *Foreign Ownership and the Structure of Canadian Industry* (Ottawa: Queen's Printer, 1968); Kari Levitt, *Silent Surrender: The Multinational Corporation in Canada* (New York: St. Martin's Press, 1970).

3. David Ruthenberg, *Organizational Archetypes of a Multi-National Company* (Pittsburgh: Carnegie-Mellon University Graduate School of Industrial Administration, Management Science Research Report No. 114, August 1968).

4. Kari Levitt, *Silent Surrender.*

5. See, for example, George A. Steiner and Warren M. Cannon, *Multinational Corporate Planning* (New York: The Macmillan Company, 1966); Sidney E. Rolfe, *The International Corporation,* a background report to the 22nd Congress of the International Chamber of Commerce (Paris: ICC, 1969).

6. David Lilienthal, "Management of the Multinational Corporation," in Melvin Anshen and G. L. Bach, eds., *Management and Corporations, 1985* (New York: McGraw-Hill, 1960).

7. *Ibid.*

8. *Ibid.*

9. Olivier Giscard d'Estaing in the *Report* of the Crotonville Conference held by the Atlantic Council (December 12-15, 1965), p. 67.

10. Jack N. Behrman, "Foreign Associates and Their Financing," in Raymond F. Mikesell, ed., *U. S. Private and Government Investment Abroad* (Eugene, Oregon: University of Oregon Books, 1962), pp. 77-144.

11. Jack N. Behrman, *Some Patterns in the Rise of the Multinational Enterprise* (Chapel Hill: The University of North Carolina Graduate School of Business Administration Research Paper 18, 1969), pp. 58-60. Behrman also says (p.xiii): "What distinguishes the multinational enterprise from its predecessors is the centralization of policy and the integration of key operations among the affiliates. Prior to the 1960's, save for the petroleum companies there were only a few groups which could be characterized as multinational enterprises. Among the newly formed multinational enterprises, the parent companies are largely in the United States. Europe is the home of a number of companies which may become multinational enterprises, but its direct investors have been slow to adopt this form. A few are controlled by Canadian companies, and Japan is beginning to develop a few. There are none, to my knowledge, emanating from the less developed countries."
Behrman sees the distinction between the multinational corporation and its predecessors to lie "in the area of control and integration of operations of the affiliates." However, all the figures given by Behrman relate to total direct foreign investments. This slip from an operational definition to citing figures on all direct investments without discriminating between multinational corporations and others is very common. Steiner and Cannon, op. cit., p. 2 do the same. So does Rolfe, op. cit. The only book, to my knowledge, giving statistical data only on multinational corporations is by James W. Vaupell and Joan P. Curhan, *The Making of Multinational Enterprise: A Source Book of Tables Based On a Study of 187 Major U. S. Manufacturing Corporations* (Boston: Division of Research, Graduate School of Business Administration, Harvard University, 1969).

12. The idea of the internationally chartered business corporation was suggested by Eugene Staley in his book *War and the Private Sector* (Garden City, New York: Doubleday and Company, Inc., 1935). Staley felt the creation of these corporations would help in improving the relations between business and government.

13. David H. Finnie, *Desert Enterprise: The Middle East Oil Industry in its Local Environment* (Cambridge, Mass.: Harvard University Press, 1958).

14. Behrman, *Some Patterns,* p. 121.

15. A. A. Berle and Gardiner C. Means, *The Modern Corporation and Private Property* (New York: Macmillan, 1932).

16. Robert A. Gordon, *Business Leadership in the Large Corporation* (Berkeley: University of California Press, 1961).

17. E. S. Kirschen, H. S. Bloch and W. B. Bassett, *Financial Integration in Western Europe* (New York: Columbia University Press, 1969), pp. 55-56.

18. The Eurobond market grew from $134 million in 1963 to a total issue of $4,673 million in 1968. U. S. companies borrowed in 1968, $2,235 million or 47.8 percent. A full listing of bonds and convertibles in the Eurobond market is published by Credit Suisse Bank and White, Weld & Co. See also Morgan Guaranty Trust Company, *World Financial Markets* (December 27, 1968).

19. Steiner and Cannon, *Multinational,* p. 3.

20. Business International Corporation, *Organizing for Worldwide Operations* (New York, 1965).

21. For an interesting account of the problem, see Michael G. Duerr and James Greene, *Foreign Nationals in International Management* (New York: National Industrial Conference Board, 1968).

22. See Business International Corporation, *Organizing.*

23. For a summary of the accounting problems involved, see Samuel R. Hepworth, *Reporting Foreign Operations* (Ann Arbor: University of Michigan, Bureau of Business Research, School of Business Administration, Michigan Business Studies, Vol. XII, No. 5, September 1956).

24. J. K. Bruck and F. A. Lees, "Foreign Content of U. S. Corporate Activities," *Financial Analysts Journal* (September-October 1966) and "Foreign Investments, Capital Control, and the Balance of Payments," *The Bulletin* (New York University Institute of Finance, April 1968), Appendix, Table I.

25. Rolfe, *International,* pp. 154, 175.

26. Behrman, *Some Patterns,* pp. 44-45.

27. Peter F. Drucker, *The Concept of the Corporation* (New York: The New American Library, 1964), p.244 (epilogue added for this edition). For an elaboration of Drucker's view, see *The Age of Discontinuity* (New York: Harper & Row, 1969).

28. The world, though, usually means the free world: Russia and its satellites and China are excluded.

29. Robert C. Hood, "Going Abroad: The Profit Opportunities of International Business," *American Management Association Seminar* (Washington: Government Printing Office, 1961).

30. For general suggestions, see Yair Aharoni, *The Foreign Investment Decision Process* (Boston: Harvard Graduate School of Business Administration, 1967).

31. See also Behrman, *Some Patterns.*

32. George A. Steiner, "The Nature and Significance of Multinational Corporate Planning" in Steiner and Connor, *Multinational,* p. 6.

33. Lilenthal, "Management."

34. Behrman, *Some Patterns,* p. ivx. See also Chapter 3.

35. It is interesting to note that in the last few years, at least 20 new banks were created by a group of American, British, Italian, and other European banks. As an example, the new United International Bank opened in London in 1970. Its shareholders are Crocker-Citizens; Banco di Roma; Bank of Nova Scotia; Mees and Hope; Banque Française du Commerce Exterieur; Credit du Nord; Bayerische Hypotheken- und Wechselbank; Williams and Glyn's. The more "established" international banks do not join these groups because they feel strong and experienced enough to go on their own. According to the Federal Reserve Board of Governors, U. S. banks' overseas branches had total assets of $776 million in 181 branches in 1964 and $2,665 million in 295 branches in 1967.

36. Richard D. Robinson, "Joint Ventures of Transnational Business," in *International Management Review,* Vol. 1, No. 1, 1964.

2

The Multinational Corporation

Neil H. Jacoby

The emergence of the multinational private corporation as a powerful agent of world social and economic change has been a signal development of the postwar era. This evolution has been regarded with mixed opinions by public officials of the investing and the host countries, as well as by observers of international affairs.

The multinational corporation is, among other things, a private "government," often richer in assets and more populous in stockholders and employees than are some of the national states in which it carries on its business. It is simultaneously a "citizen" of several nation-states, owing obedience to their laws and paying them taxes, yet having its own objectives and being responsive to a management located in a foreign nation. Small wonder that some critics see in it an irresponsible instrument of private economic power or of economic "imperalism" by its home country. Others view it as an international carrier of advanced management science and technology, an agent for the global transmission of cultures, bringing closer the day when a common set of ideals will unite mankind.

What motives have thrust this corporate institution into a position of world prominence? How is it characteristically managed? What effects does it produce on investing and host nations, and on international relationships and institutions? Above all, how can the policies of multinational companies and of the nations in which they operate minimize international conflicts and advance the cause of human welfare and world order?

Reprinted, by permission, from the May 1970 issue of *The Center Magazine,* Vol. III, No. 1, a publication of the Center for the Study of Democratic Institutions in Santa Barbara, California.

I

MULTINATIONAL CORPORATION DEFINED

A multinational corporation owns and manages businesses in two or more countries. It is an agency of *direct,* as opposed to *portfolio,* investment in foreign countries, holding and managing the underlying physical assets rather than securities based upon those assets.

Almost every large enterprise has foreign involvements of some kind. Whatever its home, it will probably send agents to other nations, establish representative offices abroad, import foreign materials, export some products, license foreign firms to use its patents or know-how, employ foreign nationals, have foreign stockholders, borrow money from foreign bankers, and may even have a foreigner on its board of directors. None of these circumstances, however, would make an enterprise "multinational," because none would require a substantial *direct investment* in foreign countries' assets nor entail a responsibility for *managing* organizations of people in alien societies. Only when an enterprise confronts the problems of designing, producing, marketing, and financing its products within foreign nations does it become a true multinational.

Although we define the multinational corporation by ownership and management of businesses in several nations, in reality this is generally only one stage in a process of multinationalization. Characteristically, the expanding corporation traverses the following stages:

1. Exports its products to foreign countries.
2. Establishes sales organizations abroad.
3. Licenses use of its patents and know-how to foreign firms that make and sell its products.
4. Establishes foreign manufacturing facilities.
5. Multinationalizes management from top to bottom.
6. Multinationalizes ownership of corporate stock.

Upward of one hundred thousand U.S. business enterprises are stage one exporters; many fewer have reached stages two or three; only about forty-five hundred firms are stage four multinationals. A mere handful of giant firms are approaching stages five and six.

Legally, a domestic corporation may multinationalize by establishing foreign branches, by operating wholly or partially owned subsidiaries in other countries, or by entering into joint ventures with enterprises in other countries. Whatever the legal format, it becomes a working corporate citizen within many nations. This makes the word "multinational" accurately descriptive of its character. Although business transactions are typically transnational or international in nature, no company is international in a legal sense, because it must obtain its charter from a national government.

II

RISE OF CORPORATE MULTINATIONALISM

Multinational operations by private business corporations are comparatively recent in man's history. The companies of merchant traders of medieval Venice and the great English, Dutch, and French trading companies of the seventeenth and eighteenth centuries were forerunners but not true prototypes of today's multinational corporation. They were essentially trading rather than manufacturing organizations, with comparatively little fixed investment. And they operated mainly within the colonial territories or spheres of influence of their own nations rather than under the jurisdiction of foreign sovereign states.

During the nineteenth century, foreign investment flowed extensively from Western Europe to the undeveloped areas of Asia, Africa, and the Americas, including the United States. In this age of empire-building, Victorian Britain was the great capital exporter, followed by France, the Netherlands, and Germany. Little of this capital flow was direct investment outside imperial boundaries. Although British firms made large investments in India, Canada, Australia, and South Africa, French companies deployed capital in Indochina, Algeria, and other French colonies, and Dutch firms helped to industrialize the East Indies, corporate investment was conducted mainly within the matrix of empire. When British and European capitalists helped to finance the railroads and canals of the United States, Argentina, and other countries outside of their imperial jurisdictions, they did it by purchasing the securities of American governments or corporations. Rare was the profit-seeking business corporation that ventured outside the imperial realm to make commitments in brick and mortar under an alien regime. Nevertheless, by the turn of this century American firms were producing in Britain such products as farm equipment, sewing machines, printing presses, and revolvers, and a book entitled *The American Invasion* was published in London in 1902.[1]

The earliest substantial multinational corporate investment came in the mining and petroleum industries during the initial years of the twentieth century. Nature decreed a wide geographical separation of great mineral deposits in less developed regions from important markets in the United States and Western Europe. Hence large oil companies like British Petroleum and Standard Oil Company were among the first true multinationals, and hard-mineral corporations, such as International Nickel, Anaconda Copper, and Kennecott Copper, were other early entrants. Singer, Coca-Cola, and Woolworth were early American manufacturing and merchandising multinationals; Unilever, Phillips, and Imperial Chemicals entered the foreign arena from Britain and the Netherlands. Chemical and drug companies went abroad from Germany.

Multinational corporate investment spread further in the years after World War I, spurred by rising barriers to international trade, and led by the burgeoning automobile and associated industries. General Motors and Ford acquired ownership of auto-making companies in Britain, France, and Germany. American companies making tires and rubber, plate glass, and auto accessories followed. By 1940, some six hundred American firms had invested more than half a billion dollars in factories in Britain.[2] The worldwide economic depression of the nineteen-thirties throttled this incipient movement, and foreign corporate investment languished until after World War II.

After the Second World War, the multinational corporation flowered as American firms heavily invested abroad in a wide variety of manufacturing and merchandising operations. At the end of 1950, direct foreign investment by U.S. corporations was 11.8 billion dollars, mostly committed to the petroleum and minerals industries of Canada, Latin America, and the Middle East. By the end of 1968, the figure had almost sextupled to sixty-five billion. Paralleling this explosive growth were shifts in the location and industrial structure of the investment. Two-thirds of the total, 40.6 billion, was invested in manufacturing, mercantile, and other *non*-extractive industries. Almost two-thirds, 39.1 billion, was invested in Western Europe, even though commitments in other parts of the world had also expanded greatly.

American corporations are by no means the only multinationals. Direct foreign corporate investment in the United States stood at nearly eleven billion dollars at the end of 1968, having risen by twenty-five percent during the preceding three years as more foreign businesses gained the financial means and the managerial confidence to enter the huge American market.[3] Most of this investment was made by enterprises of Britain (3.4 billion), Canada (2.6 billion), the Netherlands (1.7 billion), and Switzerland (1.2 billion), with smaller sums from France, Germany, and Japan. Long used to the presence of such firms as Shell, Lever, and Bowater, Americans became conscious of new corporate citizens like British Petroleum, Courtaulds, Pechiney, Aluminium, Massey-Ferguson, Bayer, and Toyota.

Foreign *direct* investment was only one-seventh of the total foreign investment in the United States of seventy-six billion dollars at the end of 1968. In contrast, more than half of the total U.S. investment abroad, sixty-four billion of a total of a hundred and thirty-three billion, was direct in form.[4] Increasing European and Japanese business intrusion into the American continent demonstrates, nevertheless, that throughout the industrialized world, corporate business is outgrowing national boundaries. A nineteenth-century political organization provides an archaic framework for twentieth-century economy.

American corporations led the world trend toward business multinationalism because the great size and wealth of the U.S. economy had enabled them to utilize enormous amounts of savings and because they were attracted by the relatively higher foreign rates of return to investment. U.S. capital outflow took the form of corporate *direct* investment because of the superior organization of American capital markets and the larger capabilities of American managers. With its multitude of stockholders, its ready access to equity capital and credit from efficient financial markets, its experience in allocating capital and in coordinating business operations over a continental area, its growth-and-profit orientation, and its use of advanced techniques of management, the large American corporation was far better prepared for foreign investment than the typical European enterprise, with its much smaller size, narrower market, emphasis upon security and stability, and traditional mode of management. Also, European capital markets were small and public ownership of corporate securities was limited, making it expensive for a European company to acquire external funds.

American corporate investment abroad is concentrated in the hands of the largest firms. Of a total investment of sixty-five billion dollars at the end of 1968, the five hundred largest American industrial corporations had invested more than fifty billion. A score of these firms held a third or more of their total assets in other countries; an even larger number derived more than one-third of their incomes from foreign operations. For the great majority, however, foreign operations constituted a minor segment of their businesses.

American corporate investment has penetrated deeply into the economies of a few advanced nations, such as Canada and Britain, and into those of certain raw-material producing countries in Central and South America and the Middle East. Foreign firms — primarily American — owned thirty-five percent of all Canadian mining, manufacturing, transportation, and merchandising business in 1962.[5] In Australia, foreign firms owned about one-quarter of all business corporation assets in 1965.[6] They controlled about one-fourth of Brazil's rail and electrical industries and about eighteen percent of its manufacturing.[7] British subsidiaries and joint ventures of American corporations accounted for ten percent of the industrial output of the United Kingdom and for seventeen percent of that country's exports in 1965, according to a recent study.[8]   This investment was concentrated in high-technology industries (pharmaceuticals, computers) and in industries for whose products people spend a rising fraction of their incomes as their standard of living increases (autos, cosmetics, packaged foods). American companies also owned considerable parts of the industrial apparatus of Honduras, Chile, Panama, and the Arab oil countries.

In the European countries, American corporate investme..t forms less than five percent of total business investment. What concerns Europeans, however, is the deep penetration by American companies of the high-technology sectors of their economies. In France, American firms controlled two-thirds of the photographic film, papers, farm machinery, and telecommunications industries. In Europe as a whole, they produced eighty percent of the computers, ninety-five percent of the integrated circuits, fifty percent of the semi-conductors and fifteen percent of consumer electronic products.[9] Thoughtful Europeans have been haunted by the specter of domination of their most advanced industries by American firms, relegating native enterprises to conventional tasks.

When taken globally, it has been estimated that the value of the output of all foreign affiliates of U.S. corporations was a staggering one hundred and thirty billion dollars during 1968.[10] This was four times U.S. exports of thirty-three billion in that year, showing that the preponderant linkage of the United States to other markets is foreign production rather than foreign trade. Foreign affiliates accounted for fifteen percent of the total production of nine hundred billion dollars in the non-communist world outside the United States. Thus United States industry abroad had become the third largest economy in the world, outranked only by those of the domestic United States and the Soviet Union. Moreover, foreign production of American firms has grown about ten per cent a year, twice as fast as domestic economies. Multinational corporations are rapidly increasing their shares of the world's business.

III

MOTIVES TO MULTINATIONALIZE

Direct investment in foreign manufacturing facilities is usually an alternative to exporting homemade products. Why have manufacturers endured the harder tasks and larger risks of foreign operations instead of shipping their products? Evidently, direct investment appeared to be a relatively profitable use of corporate funds.

The most frequent reason for direct foreign investment is that entrepreneurs confront foreign barriers to their exports. Nationalistic sentiment leads most nations to try to build their own industrial capabilities. By raising barriers against imports of manufactured products, they induce foreign as well as domestic firms to establish domestic industries. Large numbers of American corporations became multinationals simply in order to maintain or expand markets in Canada or in the European Economic Community that could not be as profitably served by exports.

Business firms also multinationalize because their presence as a producer in a foreign nation enables them more effectively to adapt their products to local demands. For example, during the nineteen-twenties General Motors acquired Vauxhall in Britain and Opel in Germany and opened assembly plants in fifteen foreign countries. It sought to meet consumer demand for autos in those countries that had expanded to a point where local manufacturing was more profitable than exporting from the United States.[11]

The relative attractiveness of direct investment in foreign nations had many other causes. The creation of larger free-trading regions, such as the European Economic Community and the European Free Trade Association, created opportunities to capitalize upon economies of scale that American firms were prepared to seize more quickly than their European counterparts. The rapid postwar expansion of European markets, with a spreading wave of mass consumption, opened doors to profits from the introduction of mass manufacturing and marketing methods. Another reason was that the dynamic of American business is expansion, and anti-trust laws and keen competition at home channeled the attention of corporate executives to opportunities abroad.[12] An important factor was the development of management science. Together with striking advances in communications and computer facilities, it made the management of distant operations feasible. Growing confidence in the political stability and economic strength of the advanced nations appeared to reduce the risk of foreign commitments. Also, geographical diversification of a corporation's operations into many national markets offered a means of stabilizing the growth of total earnings and thereby reducing the risk/reward ratio.

By multinationalizing, a company also acquires certain competitive advantages. It can monitor technological developments in many countries. It can borrow at low interest rates in one country to finance working capital shortages in a high-interest-rate country. It is able to adjust intra-company transfer prices in ways that reduce total corporate tax liabilities. It can move surplus funds between its multiple bases to minimize the cost of borrowed funds or to take advantage of predicted changes in the exchange rates of national currencies. Entry by American firms into Europe, for example, was facilitated by the typically large amounts of credit supplied by European bankers on a limited equity base.[13]

Manifestly, the forces behind corporate multinationalism are so potent that there is a high probability that multinational business will continue to expand relative to domestic business long into the future.

IV

MANAGEMENT PATTERNS AND PROCESSES

A multinational business corporation may adopt one of two basic organizational forms: a *world corporation* format, in which the basic business functions of finance, marketing, manufacturing, and research and development are the primary pillars of organization and domestic and foreign operations are merged; or an *international division* format, in which all foreign operations are separated from domestic in an "international division."[14] There are strengths and weaknesses in each format, and both have been used by successful firms. As firms gain experience, a wider use of the world corporation plan of organization is likely because it achieves more complete integration of foreign and domestic management.

In both types of multinational organization, the head office normally makes strategic policy decisions, such as expansion of product lines or marketing territories or capital budgets, and delegates to the managers of its foreign affiliates broad authority to operate under those policies within their respective countries. Policy control of foreign affiliates is exercised, first, through the use of annual budgets that specify planned targets to be attained and, secondly, through affiliate managers' periodical reports of progress toward the specified goals.[15] Coordinated control of policy through central staff functions, and decentralized operating responsibility with clearly defined line authority — the management technique developed within General Motors — has been the key to successful multinational management.[16] Although companies differ in the extent of the authority they vest in the managers of their foreign affiliates, it is simply not feasible to handle a many-based enterprise with a tight rein.

An important issue is the necessary or desirable extent of ownership of a foreign affiliate. Up to the present time, the predominant vehicle of direct corporate investment abroad appears to be the wholly owned subsidiary.

Thus seventy-seven percent of the net assets of American firms in the United Kingdom in 1965 were held by wholly owned subsidiaries, fourteen percent by subsidiaries more than fifty percent American-owned, and only nine percent by entities financed mainly by British firms.[17] Most American and European companies believe that sole ownership is necessary to enable them to base their operations upon objective economic factors, free from the influence of foreign partners.[18] Although one hundred percent ownership may facilitate the enforcement of corporate discipline and progress toward assigned goals, it goes against prevailing opinion in most host countries, which want a "piece of the action" for their own citizens. Host countries prefer an equity interest by local businessmen because it reduces the danger of foreign control of their economies. In addition, local partners can help to improve the affiliate's relations with the foreign government and its people. The examples of Japan and Mexico, which have admitted foreign companies only as minority owners of joint ventures, demonstrate that successful foreign investment does not require majority ownership. Although joint ventures are not free of difficulties, it is desirable — and probable — that more multinational business will assume this format in the future, despite investors' preferences for one hundred percent control. Another route to joint ownership, of course, is multinational ownership of stock in the parent company, which is also desirable to minimize international frictions.

Studies of comparative management in different countries indicate that the similarities are far greater than the differences. With appropriate adaptations to local conditions, American management technique has proved to be a hardy transplant in foreign soils. As David Lilienthal has poignantly observed, the most important managerial problems of multinational corporations are their relations with governments. The legal systems and social and economic controls of host countries often conflict with those of the home country. Interminable negotiations with government officials is the lot of the foreign manager.[19]

Managers of the foreign affiliates of multinational companies once had the reputation of being "second-stringers," sidetracked from the main line of advancement to top management. This has changed, as companies have learned the folly of entrusting markets with high profit potentials to men of less than topflight abilities. A foreign assignment now is part of the grooming process for leadership of the multinational company. Overseas placement is typically not a preconceived career goal but a step in broadening the young executive's experience.[20] Indeed, the methods of multinational companies in developing executive leadership are worthy of study by national governments desiring to reform their foreign services so that they may function effectively in an age of instantaneous communication and supersonic flight.[21]

V

EFFECTS ON LESS DEVELOPED HOST COUNTRIES

The economic, political, technological, and cultural effects of multinational corporate investment are most striking when the host country is less developed than when it is relatively advanced, for it is in the less developed lands that investment has made a strong impact on development. This conclusion emerges clearly from thirteen case studies made over a fifteen-year period by the National Planning Association, whose credentials as an objective observer are beyond question.[22] In all cases the American corporation played an innovating and catalytic role, founding new industries, transmitting technological and managerial skills as well as capital, and in many cases creating entire social infrastructures of schools, housing, health facilities, and transportation in order to conduct its business.

Sears, for example, pioneered the modern general supermarkets of Mexico, and established a large coterie of native manufacturing industries to stock its stores.[23] United Fruit Company, one of the earliest American multinationals, was the major force in developing the international trade in bananas, pioneering in every aspect of the industry, from plantation production through disease-control techniques, land and ocean transport, and sales promotion.[24] It enormously expanded the real incomes and welfare of the peoples of the six Central American republics in which it operated, while earning a profit on its investment that averaged *less* than that realized by corporate business in the United States.

International Basic Economy Corporation, organized for profit by the Rockefeller family for the purpose of introducing new industries and business methods into less developed countries, had established one hundred and nineteen subsidiaries and affiliates in thirty-three countries by the end of 1968. Its efforts were focused upon agri-business. Its subsidiaries made many innovations in the production of food and low-cost housing and in the economical distribution of food through supermarkets. Because of its heavy developmental and innovational costs, which broke the ground for later entry by local entrepreneurs, I.B.E.C.'s return on investment was subnormal.[25]

These cases illustrate the role played by the American corporation in the poor countries. Although the conduct of American business abroad has not been impeccable, the over-all record strongly encourages an extension of this mode of "foreign aid." Indeed, the constructive developmental results of private business investment led the U.S. Agency for International Development (A.I.D.) to launch private enterprise support programs in 1958, and thereafter to rely increasingly upon enterprises in carrying out developmental tasks. Stimulation of private investment was the motive behind the 1968 proposal of the Nixon Administration to establish a new public corporation for this purpose.

In the face of a generally constructive record, how may one explain the widespread denunciation of American corporations abroad by foreign politicians as well as by American critics? Charges of "exploitation," "plundering," and "greed for profits" are often made, especially in the Latin-American countries. As the authors of the study of United Fruit Company have pointed out, there has been a "striking disparity between the reputation and the performance" of the company.[26] Ignorance of the realities of private enterprise, of the hard tasks to be performed and the high risks to be run, is surely one part of the answer. For those ventures that succeed, profits may appear to be inordinately high. Yet, as Professor Raymond Vernon has remarked, "the history of such investment is littered with the bleached bones of many enterprises; and taking the failures with the successes, it is not clear that the investment has been handsomely rewarded."[27] Many companies have been obliged to deal with a range of problems vastly wider than those confronted at home. They have had to create whole communities, with their appurtenant infrastructures, out of wilderness environments, usually in countries with unstable governments and politically immature populations. It is in the light of this imperative that their occasional interference with local governments should be interpreted. The foreign company is always a convenient "whipping boy" for local politicians.

American corporate investment abroad has been gradually shifting from an earlier emphasis upon the mining, extractive, and raw-material industries toward diversified manufacturing and merchandising operations. One important consequence has been a great increase in U.S. exports of technological and managerial skills and knowledge — values to the recipient country which are unrequited. This shift should serve to reduce the frequency of charges of "foreign exploitation."

The potential contribution of private corporations to the development of poor countries is large. It depends mainly on the development of stable governments in those countries and their actions to encourage private investment. Any less developed country that offers political stability, respect for contracts, financial responsibility, and equitable taxation will attract foreign investment — and domestic as well. The remarkable evolutions of such countries as Mexico, Malaysia, and Taiwan testify to this truth. If more low-income countries adhere to codes of foreign investment that reduce political risks, private firms will quickly expand their developmental roles.

The political risks of expropriation, civil war, and inconvertibility of currencies have risen in less developed lands as a result of changed world attitudes toward intervention by one nation into the domestic affairs of another. The era of "gunboat diplomacy" has passed. When an American corporation goes abroad today, it cannot expect the U.S. government to protect its foreign properties. Since the expropriation of U.S. business properties by the Soviet government in 1917, there have been major expropriations by the governments of Mexico, Cuba, Argentina, Peru, Indonesia, and Eastern European countries involving estimated losses of som.e 2.5 billion dollars.[28] "Prompt, adequate, and effective compensation," required by international law, has rarely been paid. The American company loses, but so does the expropriating country and the region in which it is located. Thus Cuba's expropriation in 1960 probably cost Latin America some five hundred million dollars of U.S. business investment in the following two years.[29]

The A.I.D. offers insurance to American corporations against major political risks of investment in those less developed countries that receive American economic assistance. If the flow of private investment is to be expanded, this insurance should be extended to cover more risks and more countries. At the same time, the low-income countries should adopt and respect codes of foreign investment, and assure fair adjudication of disputes. The establishment of the International Center for the Settlement of Investment Disputes, in 1966, was a desirable move in this direction. By mid-1968 some fifty-seven nations had ratified the convention establishing the Center, thereby agreeing to submit to its panels of experts any disputes arising between their governments and foreign private investors.[30]

Private business investment is inherently superior to governmental aid as an instrument of development because it combines transfers of managerial and technical assistance with that of capital. General dissatisfaction with bilateral governmental aid makes it important to expand the flow of business investment.[31] While measures to limit or to insure against risks will help to enlarge this flow, they will not remove the root causes of international tensions. The foreign subsidiary of the U.S. corporation will still be charged with "exploitation" of local resources and with taking out too much profit. When it pays higher than prevailing wages and benefits to its employees, their higher living standards will provoke envy and resentment among other local citizens. Ways must be found to ameliorate this problem.

A promising approach is for the American company to agree with the foreign government on a reciprocal reinvestment program. The company would agree to reinvest a specified percentage of its profits, in return for which the host government would agree to spend (invest) specified amounts of its revenues from corporate operations on schools, health, housing, and other forms of welfare for people in the communities in which the company is operating. Disparities in living conditions would be lessened and a source of social unrest would be removed. Because the agreement would require reciprocal actions and be of mutual benefit, the American company could not be accused of "interference" with local affairs.

The political and social effects of American corporate investment in poor countries are not as clear as the economic effects. The process of development is inherently unsettling to a society. By producing shifts in the distribution of income and wealth and redistributing economic power among social classes, development creates political stresses. Often these tensions can be relieved by peaceful political reforms; not infrequently they are followed by more or less violent upheavals. Indeed, being an agent of change, the foreign corporation is seen in the developing country as a threat to privileged positions in the traditional society, and is often attacked from the Right as well as from the Left.

The superficial cultural consequences of American corporate penetration of the poor countries can be plainly seen in the ready acceptance by native peoples of soft drinks, packaged foods, brand names, advertising, electrical appliances, autos, and all the other paraphernalia of American life. At a more fundamental level, it is likely that the status and value systems, the social attitudes and behavioral patterns, the arts and the essential cultural foundations of many of these countries will also undergo profound changes. While such changes ultimately should reduce barriers to communication between peoples, and lay a common basis for a stable world order, the transition from poverty to self-sustaining development will be marked by much international friction.

VI

EFFECTS ON DEVELOPED HOST COUNTRIES

In Europe, the impact of American multinational business was on politically mature societies, technologically advanced economies, and socially integrated peoples proud of their nations' long histories of achievement. Nevertheless, the physical presence in Europe of more than three thousand American corporations with forty thousand American employees could not help but be significant.[32]

Major economic results of the American "invasion" were to stimulate the growth of production, incomes, and living standards of Britons and Europeans. American corporate investment improved the efficiency of resource allocation. It also improved the balance of international payments of host countries, which benefited both from capital inflows and also from the exports generated by the foreign-owned affiliates.[33] More subtle and profound economic effects flowed from the new competition introduced by the Americans. "Hard sell" advertising, mass-marketing techniques, price competition, packaging and branding, and continental marketing strategies were some of these new concepts. Mass production of a host of new consumer products, such as fresh frozen foods, aluminum foil, and plastic containers, was both a response and a stimulus to the rising levels of European family income. The primary thrust of the American "assault" on the Continent was to accelerate the pace of a peaceful consumer revolution.

The newcomers were, of course, criticized for their "disruption of orderly marketing," "extravagant wages and salaries," and "reckless" financial practices, primarily by those in the old business establishments whose comfortable oligopolies were threatened by the new competition. American corporate managers did, on occasion, display insensitivity to local customs in their drive for lower costs and greater efficiency. General Electric was condemned for closing a computer plant and dismissing French engineers when it consolidated its foreign computer operations for greater efficiency. Goodyear and Goodrich were met with cries of protest from French tire-makers when they doubled the traditional discounts to dealers in order to make initial penetration of the French tire market. Effective competition inevitably disturbs the status quo. As Schumpeter said long ago, it is a "process of creative destruction." Available evidence indicates that affiliates of U.S. corporations have generally earned higher rates of return on investment in both Britain and on the Continent than have local enterprises in the same industries.[34]

Although the American "invasion" was received calmly in most European countries, de Gaulle's France reacted sensitively. The French government changed its policy toward U.S. direct investment three times. After 1959, it encouraged the entry of U.S. corporations. As a result of popular disapproval of the actions of General Motors in laying off workers, of Chrysler's purchase of Simca, and of the sale to General Electric of the controlling interest in Machines Bull, American investment was severely restricted in 1963. When U.S. firms reacted by switching their investments to other Common Market countries from which they could still penetrate the French market, Premier Pompidou once again relaxed the restrictions. Any Common Market country that restricts American investment only helps its rivals.[35]

The technological consequences of the American corporate invasion received much attention from European observers. U.S. investment was concentrated in the high-technology industries of computers, electronics, aerospace, and petrochemicals, and in such fast-growing industries as car manu-facturing. American firms led or dominated those industries in many Euro-pean countries. They excelled in the innovation of products and processes. American firms spent twice as much of their sales dollars on research and development as their European competitors. They were fast-footed in con-verting laboratory findings to commercial products. Many Europeans thought they saw a growing and insurmountable "technological gap" between Europe and America.

Europeans responded vigorously to the American challenge. Their governments fostered business mergers designed to create companies able to compete with the American giants. They expanded their research and devel-opment activities supporting industry. Basic European science has always been the equal of American science. Given adequate governmental and indus-trial support and an efficient scale of business operations, there is no reason why European industrial technology should fall behind, and, when taken overall, it is not clear that it is laggard. There is now general recognition that the real "gap" between European and American business is managerial rather than technological.[36] Europeans are now taking vigorous steps to close this gap by establishing graduate schools of administration and replac-ing nepotism with meritocracy in choosing industrial leadership.

What will be the ultimate social and cultural consequences of American corporate multinationalism in Europe? Mass consumption of durable goods, supermarkets, the vanishing personal servant, the ubiquitous automobile — all are indices of the rising social and geographical mobility of Europeans, the reduction of class barriers, the equalization of personal opportunities. The multinational corporation is leading Europe toward a more egalitarian homogeneous, and democratic kind of society. While traditionalists will de-plore the gradual blurring of class and national distinctions, such segmenta-tions cannot in the end withstand the onslaught of technological and eco-nomic changes. These changes create new political attitudes, just as multi-national business has generated new economic pressures. Ultimately, they may facilitate the juncture of all Europe in an enduring political and eco-nomic union. Should this come to pass, the American multinational cor-poration, as a primary carrier of social change, will share in the credit that eluded Caesar, Charlemagne, Napoleon, and Hitler.

VII

EFFECTS ON COMMUNIST COUNTRIES

Multinational corporate business has begun to penetrate the socialist nations of Eastern Europe in novel ways, and with effects that may ultimately be even more momentous for the world than their operations within market economies. The novelty lies in cooperation between private firms and public corporations. These arrangements are called "industrial cooperation" in socialist countries, probably because "joint venture" has a capitalist ring. Typically, a Western private company agrees with an Eastern European public corporation to sell specialized machinery and equipment on instalment credit terms and to provide technical and managerial services necessary to produce certain products. The Eastern European country, in turn, agrees to provide land, buildings, and labor necessary to produce those products. The joint venture may market its output in the host country or in third countries. The Western company profits from the sale of equipment and products and is paid a fee for its technical and managerial services. The Eastern European enterprise gains valuable technological and managerial know-how, and title to specialized industrial equipment that it will later on operate by itself. While differing in legal form, the essential elements of multinational corporate investment are present—international transfers of capital, management, and technology.[37]

Such East-West industrial cooperation appears to have emerged initially in Yugoslavia during the nineteen-fifties. Now all socialist countries have industrial cooperation agreements with Western firms. Rumania had no less than nineteen in effect during 1969. For example, Renault of France had agreed with a Rumanian enterprise to build auto transmissions, partly for domestic use and partly for export. Fiat of Italy agreed during 1968 with the government of the Soviet Union to supply machinery, management, and technology to create a Russian industrial community capable of making six hundred thousand automobiles a year. Sharply rising East-West trade in capital equipment shows that the magnitude of such industrial cooperation increased during the nineteen-sixties. Mainland China has also purchased industrial plant and equipment from Western countries on long-term credit.

So far, East-West industrial cooperation has involved European and Japanese enterprises, because American firms have been barred by U.S. government rules from exporting "strategic" materials or technologies to communist countries. The result has been to divert exports from American firms to competitors in other Western countries, rather than to inhibit the development of communist countries. The Soviet Union is eager to deal with American companies able to give it access to advanced managerial and technological knowledge. The thawing of the Cold War and rising indications of U.S.-Soviet cooperation afford ground for hope that industrial cooperation between the superpowers will expand. Considering the great size of the economies, the potentialities of such economic intercourse are vast. The ultimate involvement of Mainland China in commercial intercourse with the United States is also a development holding great promise for lowering barriers to international understanding.

Socialist ideology, which precludes private ownership of fixed capital, has caused East-West industrial cooperation to take place on a basis of loans rather than equity capital. Yet cracks have appeared in this ideological barrier. The Foreign Investment Law of Yugoslavia was amended during 1967 to permit joint ventures of Yugoslavian and foreign companies to acquire ownership of domestic fixed assets.[38]

Expanding East-West industrial cooperation holds the promise of relaxing international tensions and creating an environment favorable to peace. It promotes travel and communication between the peoples of countries. It emphasizes the *common* economic goal of more efficient production and a better life for people, despite ideological and practical differences in economic systems. Technological and managerial knowledge is diffused more rapidly, accelerating gains in productivity, output, and standards of living. Because the peoples of *both* cooperating countries manifestly gain from such arrangements, there is no basis for feelings of "exploitation" of one country by the other.

VIII

EFFECTS ON INVESTING COUNTRIES

Multinational corporate investment has had important economic, political, and cultural impacts upon investing countries. Thus the United States balance of payments was in substantial deficit during most of the nineteen-sixties, and foreign long-term investment is believed to have contributed to it. An Interest Equalization Tax was imposed in 1963 to deter Americans from making foreign loans or portfolio investments. Later, voluntary and then mandatory direct controls were imposed upon direct foreign investment by U.S. corporations in an effort to reduce capital outflow and to strengthen the U.S. dollar in the world's money markets.

Whether these foreign investment controls are achieving their aims and serving American interests is doubtful. Large American multinational firms are able to raise needed capital from foreign bankers or in the Eurodollar market. The heaviest impact of U.S. controls is on smaller enterprises unable to tap these financial sources. More fundamental is the argument that any improvement in the U.S. balance of payments resulting from the controls can be temporary at best. In the long run, controls have the perverse effect of enlarging the U.S. deficit by reducing the inflow of interest and dividends from foreign affiliates below the level to which it would otherwise have risen.[39]

A basic objection to foreign investment controls is that the deficit in the U.S. balance of payments they are designed to curtail vanishes when international transactions are measured on an assets basis rather than on a liquidity basis. At present, when an American company invests in a foreign country it acquires a long-term asset in return for which it pays dollars — a short-term liability of the United States. Although the transaction enlarges the U.S. deficit on the liquidity basis, it does not change the value of assets owned in the two countries. As a result of the recent creation of Special Drawing Rights (S.D.R.'s) from the International Monetary Fund as a new form of international currency reserve, dollar liquidity has become less important. A deficit in the U.S. balance of payments on the liquidity basis should no longer be a compelling reason for restricting U.S. capital outflow, especially when, on the basis of the value of assets held, the financial position of the United States is strong and growing stronger.

IX

EFFECTS ON INTERNATIONAL RELATIONS

The foreign operations of American — and European — enterprises have generated many misunderstandings and tensions with the governments and peoples of host countries as well as with the governments of their home countries. As corporate citizens of many nations engaged in transnational business, they daily confront conflicts between national policies and divergent economic and social systems and values. As agents of technological and cultural change, they naturally provoke critical reactions from businessmen and governments, both domestic and foreign.

Foreign criticisms of U.S. corporate operations abroad have focused upon six kinds of problems: (1) "exploitation" of local manpower or natural resources, (2) conflict between U.S. national policies and the national interests of the foreign country, (3) overcentralization of managerial decision-making in American headquarters, (4) the locating of all advanced research and technical tasks in the United States, (5) insensitivity to local laws and customs, and (6) behavior that disabilizes foreign economies. All these charges should be looked at closely.

"EXPLOITATION"

The charge of "exploitation" by foreign-owned enterprises is often made in less developed countries against U.S. firms producing minerals or other basic products. It is based upon the naive idea that the foreign company "takes away" irreplaceable natural resources without providing a *quid pro quo*. What native critics commonly overlook or underestimate are the heavy risks assumed by the foreign company in searching for and developing local resources, the large losses incurred in unsuccessful ventures, and the great contribution made to their own country's material welfare by the foreign company that succeeds. After the fact, it is easy to point to "extravagant" profits being realized from a successful foreign operation and to forget the many unsuccessful ventures, uncertainties, and delays experienced in creating a profitable enterprise.

"Exploitation" of a country's natural resources, in the economic sense of obtaining them at distress prices, is possible only when monopoly prevails. As long as world markets for natural resources are effectively competitive, the terms on which a foreign company enters a country to explore for and produce its natural resources reflect a careful balancing of estimated risks and rewards. Today, any country possessing natural resources finds that exploration and development rights are eagerly sought by firms from many foreign nations. It can charge substantial bonuses for limited concessions, and heavy taxes and royalties on the production from successful concessions. Dozens of oil companies from many nations compete intensely in bidding for petroleum concessions in such countries as Libya, Nigeria, and Venezuela. The terms of entry into the foreign oil business have become so onerous that the oil-producing country typically makes about three times as much money per barrel of oil produced (from *successful* concessions) as does the oil company, although it invests no capital, incurs no expense, and takes no risk. Natural-resource agreements under current conditions are non-exploitative, whatever may have been true in the past. The host country profits from the public income generated by royalties and taxes, from the private income derived from wage payments and other expenses in the local economy, and, above all, by the acquisition of modern technology and management skills. As Professor Raymond Vernon has noted, taking the good ventures with the bad, the over-all return on American foreign investment has not been excessive.

DISPARITIES BETWEEN NATIONAL POLICIES

More serious is the allegation that the foreign affiliates of U.S. companies, being under the policy directives of their home offices, are obliged to pursue policies that serve U.S. interests rather than those of the host country. For example, it has been charged that U.S. companies limit the exports of their Canadian subsidiaries to third countries, or force them to purchase raw materials or components from their American plants instead of from Canadian suppliers.[40] More generally, it is said that the efforts of a multinational firm to maximize its *aggregate* profits do not necessarily require it to do so in a particular country.

Although conflicts do arise when there are disparities between national policies, there is no conflict between the multinational company's goal of maximizing profits in each country and over-all profit maximization when national policies are harmonized. The multinational company will serve its own interests best by investing in its subsidiaries in each country up to the point where the marginal return on capital is the same in all countries, and by allowing each of its subsidiaries freedom to enter the parent company's home market, as well as the markets of third countries, to the extent that its competitive strength permits. In a rationally managed multinational corporation, comparative costs will dictate the amount of the exports of its foreign subsidiary, just as they do in a locally owned company. Indeed, A. E. Safarian found that the foreign trade of Canadian subsidiaries of U.S. companies was actually greater relative to total sales than in independent Canadian firms in the same industries.[41]

Conflicts between the national policies of investing and host countries put the multinational corporation in a quandary. For example, U.S. policy bars exports to Communist China, whereas Canadian policy permits such trade. A Canadian subsidiary of a U.S. corporation, under instruction from its home office to obey U.S. law, clearly cannot serve Canadian interests in expanding exports. A conflict also arises when a petroleum company produces crude oil in one country and refines and markets it in another. The intra-company transfer price of crude oil from the producing to the refining subsidiary will be fixed by the parent company so as to minimize the corporation's total tax liabilities. This usually results in an apportioning of tax liabilities between the two foreign countries which is unfavorable to one of them.

Frictions arise between American multinational companies and governments over anti-monopoly laws. The U.S. government seeks to prevent foreign affiliates of American companies from engaging in such anticompetitive practices as price-fixing or market-sharing as are barred at home.[42] Host governments, on the other hand, resent the application of U.S. commercial policies to firms operating within their own boundaries, when, as has been the case up to recent years, British and European policies have been much more permissive in regard to trade practices and business combinations. Although' the U.S. government holds clear jurisdiction over a wholly owned foreign subsidiary of an American corporation, its jurisdiction over a minority-owned joint venture is less clear. In any case, the cooperation of foreign governments is needed to enforce U.S. law upon foreign affiliates of American companies.

Fortunately, anti-monopoly law enforcement has not proved to be a serious problem in international relations for two reasons. Foreign affiliates of U.S. companies have generally conducted their affairs in conformity with the more rigorous U.S. standards. Also, foreign countries have moved rapidly toward anti-monopoly policies that resemble those of the United States, so that potential conflicts are being reduced.[43] The Treaty of Rome in 1958 barred monopoly from members of the E.E.C., and it set up machinery to prevent restrictive practices.

Nearly all differences between multinational corporations and host governments can be resolved by harmonizing and rationalizing national policies, and by wider use of international organizations to determine policies on a global basis. In a rational world, the United States and Canada would pursue the same trade policy toward Communist China, one determined multilaterally in the United Nations. The tax systems of different countries would be reconciled and tax treaties would assure equitable allocations of tax liabilities arising from multinational business. Multinational business has not created disparities between national policies; it has merely thrown old disparities into bolder relief, and made urgent the task of removing them.

OVERCENTRALIZED MANAGEMENT

A third genre of complaints against the multinational corporation is that it overcentralizes management decisions in its head office, leaving only routine administration to foreign officers. An allied indictment is that it uses little foreign managerial talent in its foreign operations. In a 1965 study of this matter among the French affiliates of U.S. firms, Allan Johnstone concluded that the American multinational firms did indeed drive with a tight rein; home offices often made policy decisions without consideration of their local consequences in France.[44] However, Safarian's conclusion in respect to the Canadian subsidiaries of American firms was different: wide delegations of authority were made to the managers of Canadian subsidiaries by their American parents, which were generally *less* involved in their Canadian operations than in their American subsidiaries.[45] The stronger cultural similarities of Canada and the United States and the comparative recency of U.S. direct investment in France may have accounted for this difference. Delegated authority to the management of a foreign subsidiary usually widens through time as confidence is gained from successful experience. It would be inconsistent to argue for *full* autonomy of a foreign subsidiary, because it would preclude a transfer of management   rtise. Foreign owners cannot reasonably be expected to surrender their right ω approve major decisions of the enterprise.

The record of American companies in developing foreign management personnel is good. A 1957 study revealed that only one thousand of the thirty-five thousand supervisory, technical, and professional personnel of U.S. companies in Canada had been sent from the United States. American multinational businesses have a strong economic reason for employing local personnel to the maximum extent. The cost of a local manager is much less. While the personnel policies of American companies doubtless will continue to be a source of international friction, the evidence shows that time tends to bring wider authority to the management of foreign affiliates and a greater use of native managers.

OVERCENTRALIZED RESEARCH

A fourth criticism of American multinational companies is that they centralize scientific research and engineering activities in the United States, while relegating foreign operations to "hewing wood and drawing water." No doubt this stricture applies to some multinational companies, but it is generally refuted by the evidence. Safarian found that most of the spending on industrial research and development was concentrated in the *foreign-owned* sector of Canadian industry, and J. H. Dunning found that British subsidiaries of U.S. firms spent larger parts of their sales dollars than did British firms in the same industries. Half of the Canadian subsidiaries did perform some industrial research in Canada; that most of the remainder did not was because they had access to the technical knowledge of their parent companies.[46] As in the case of management skills, international transfer of technology is an important gain from foreign investment for a host country. A multinational corporation entering a foreign national is likely in the first stage to import its technical knowledge from its home country. Later, as local personnel are trained and local problems are identified, it usually establishes local research facilities. Normally, it has a strong incentive to do so, because foreign research costs are much lower.

INSENSITIVITY TO LOCAL BUSINESS PRACTICES

American managers of foreign subsidiaries are said to be insensitive to local business customs. Oft-cited examples are the laying off of factory workers from a Parisian refrigerator plant by General Motors in 1963, Remington Rand's similar action with a Lyons typewriter plant that same year, and the previously mentioned computer plant closed by General Electric.[47] These episodes provoked angry comment by the French press, even though the American corporations amply justified their actions as a quest for efficiency in the face of shifts in market demand. French consternation was due to the French tradition that the employer, rather than the employee, bears the manpower adjustment costs of shifts in market demands. In the United States, of course, such costs are borne by employees. The Amercian companies should have made concessions to French customs by moving less rapidly. Yet France cannot achieve greater economic efficiency without painful disturbances to its status quo.

DESTABILIZING EFFECTS

It is charged that foreign subsidiaries of the U.S. corporation often frustrate stabilization policies of the host country. Canadians complain that the fluctuations in inflows of U.S. capital into their country complicate their problems of attaining stable economic growth without inflation. They also feel vulnerable to shifts in U.S. policies governing investment outflows, such as the Interest Equalization Tax and foreign investment controls. French government officials have objected to the ability of U.S. corporate subsidiaries to escape the constraints of French national economic planning. The French government possesses formidable powers to control private investment through its ownership or control of many credit facilities. Having foreign funds available, the French affiliate of a U.S. firm can elude this control.

The Canadian complaint about uneven investment inflows is simply the other side of the U.S. problem of uneven foreign investment outflows. The efforts of private investors to profit from changing opportunities and international inequalities in investment returns lead to instability of international capital flows that poses a problem for both countries. When recognized as a *mutual* problem arising from natural economic forces, and not as an extraterritorial imposition of American laws, this problem can be resolved by consultation and harmonizing actions by the two governments. The French desire to assure that foreign private investment conforms to its national economic plans can be solved by the same means. Although the multinational corporation magnified international flows of capital and internal stabilization problems, it did not create those problems.

X

EFFECTS ON INTERNATIONAL AND TRANSNATIONAL
INSTITUTIONS

Multinational corporations have helped to create transnational financial institutions, because the large scale of their operations generated financial needs beyond the capabilities of national institutions. Notable examples are the Eurodollar market, the Eurobond market, and the multinational banking syndicate. The many billions of U.S. dollars held in Europe are actively traded, borrowed, and lent by banks and businesses in the Eurodollar market for both short- and long-term purposes. Multinational businesses frequently borrow funds by selling Eurobonds — debt securities dominated in one European currency but sold and held by investors in many countries. Transnational finance has become commonplace, as syndicates composed of British, European, and American investment bankers underwrite large corporate issues and distribute them throughout the world. The multinationalization of manufacturing and trading enterprises has been followed by the multinationalization of banking, as American and British bankers have established overseas branches and affiliates. Huge amounts of funds are transferred from one country or currency to another in the course of each business day. All these developments show that the world's business has long since outgrown national boundaries. The concepts of national currencies and exchange rates have become anachronistic in the age of multinational business.

The rise of multinational business has not yet brought much tangible change in *international* institutions. Although the scale of operations of the World Bank and the International Monetary Fund has expanded, the United Nations and its other affiliated bodies so far have not been intimately involved in multinational enterprise. Nevertheless, a new era of such involvement may be dawning. Resolutions have been introduced into the General Assembly of the United Nations for the establishment of an international government over the oceans and seabeds of the world beyond national jurisdiction. Should such an ocean regime be established, one sphere of its action would be the formation and monitoring of agreements with business enterprises for the exploration and exploitation of the incalculable riches in the oceans and seabeds.[48]

This opens up a startling prospect. For the first time in history a major part of the world's surface may become the common property of all nations and be ruled by a supranational government representing all nations.[49] For the first time a supranational government would be dealing extensively with multinational corporations — a double bypassing of national boundaries. The ultimate consequences of such a development could be profoundly significant.

XI

POLICIES TO EXPAND MULTINATIONAL BUSINESS

DE-POLITICIZATION

An important problem of multinational business concerns the *political* relationships between foreign affiliates and the governments of their parent corporations. Critics charge that the multinational corporation is an instrument of "imperialism," collaborating with its home government to enhance its national power in the world. Conversely, it is alleged that multinational companies use the economic, diplomatic, and military power of their home government to gain profits, and that American foreign policy is determined by American business interests abroad.

Manifestly, the U.S. government — as does every other national government — acts in many ways to support American private enterprise abroad. The Departments of Commerce and State negotiate treaties of commerce and friendship with foreign countries, maintain consular services, promote American exports, insure against some risks of investment in less developed countries, and support international trade fairs. U.S. governmental policies encourage private foreign investment as a means of strengthening foreign economies and reducing political instabilities. Historically, this support once went beyond economic and diplomatic measures into the realm of military action. "Trade followed the flag," and vice versa, as the naval attack on the Barbary pirates in 1801, Admiral Perry's expedition to Japan in 1850, American intervention in the Boxer Rebellion in 1900, and Marine forays into Latin-American republics demonstrate.

Since World War II there has been a radical "de-politicization" of private foreign investment. The era of dollar diplomacy is past. When an American corporation invests abroad today it carries its own risks. If it loses property by civil war or expropriation without fair compensation, it cannot expect U.S. economic or military sanctions to be applied against the offending country. The recent expropriations of American corporate property in Bolivia, Peru, and Algeria stand witness to this statement, as does the nationalization of Anaconda Copper Company's property by Chile in 1969. In no case did the U.S. government intervene. It did not even apply the Hickenlooper Amendment (shutting off economic aid) to Peru when that country seized International Petroleum Corporation's property.

Even more telling evidence that business has little influence upon U.S. policy today is found in the Middle East. One of the largest concentrations of American corporate investment is found in the petroleum industry of Arab countries around the Persian Gulf and in North Africa. Yet the U.S. government has given economic and military support to Israel, whose economic importance to the U.S. is negligible, thereby arousing bitter hostility among the Arab states and provoking threats of expropriation of the property of American oil companies.

The de-politicization of American business investment abroad is desirable because it reduces the risk of military conflict growing out of economic intercourse between nations. Private economic interests in profit are separated from national political interests in power and security. Although the risks and costs of foreign investment are higher for private entrepreneurs, the more important risks and costs of war are lower for citizens. Moreover, the knowledge that private foreign investment stands on its own feet is likely to make the behavior of both investors and host countries more responsible in the future.

CORPORATE POLICIES

Multinational corporate managers should try to understand the attitudes of host governments. Typically, they want local participation in the ownership of affiliates, management by their own nationals, indigenous research and development capabilities, wide autonomy, and freedom to export products anywhere. Although these conditions cannot fully be met if efficiency and economies of scale are to be realized, top management of the multinational company can alleviate criticism and improve international relations by adopting the following policies:

1. Publicize in the host country the costs and risks the company has assumed and the economic benefits it brings to the people.

2. Identify the interests of the company with those of the host country in every possible way. (For example, American petroleum companies have developed water resources and built modern farming communities to reduce the food deficits of North African and Middle Eastern countries.)

3. Conform to local business practices, except when efficiency clearly demands a change, and then after consultation with local authorities.

4. Decentralize authority to the managers of foreign affiliates to the maximum feasible extent, and broaden such delegations through time.

5. Perform a maximum of research and product-development activities in the host country.

6. Adopt a specific program for progressively nationalizing the personnel of foreign affiliates while reducing the number of Americans.

7. Establish stock-ownership loans for foreign employees, and list the company's securities for trading on the exchange of their countries.

Some foreign complaints about U.S. corporate investment reflect a misunderstanding of the benefits received by the host country. Other complaints have merit and call for adjustments in the behavior of American managements abroad or for intergovernmental consultative machinery. The overriding conclusion, however, is that there are no irremediable conflicts of national interest. On the contrary, private international capital flows create rising pressures to lower national barriers to a world economy, and to harmonize or unify national systems of money, taxation, transportation, commerce, and law.

NATIONAL POLICIES

Because multinational business is demonstrably beneficial to both investing and host countries and tends to strengthen the forces of world order, public policy should encourage its expansion. Nations should refrain from actions that would retard the international flow of capital, and should act to expand that flow. What should the United States do to foster multinational business?

1. The ending of domestic price inflation and a termination of the war in Vietnam would materially strengthen the U.S. economy and contribute to a stable world environment for foreign investment.

2. Harmonization of United States policies on taxation, competition, and international trade with those of other nations would remove a fertile source of friction and misunderstanding.

3. Removal of the Interest Equalization Tax and restrictions upon direct corporate investment abroad would be desirable. In addition to the reasons previously cited for taking this action, there is another reason why it is now feasible to dismantle artificial barriers to capital outflow. The general rise in domestic interest rates and investment returns during recent years has brought them up to European levels, so that American capital is no longer tempted abroad by generally higher rates of return.

4. Extension of the foreign investment guaranty program of the Agency for International Development to cover more risks and more countries would be a constructive step.

5. Reciprocal investment agreements between American corporations and the governments of less developed countries would help to diminish the disparities between living conditions of local citizens and those of foreign employees of U.S. companies.

Host countries would benefit from the expansion of multinational business by removing barriers to capital flows and creating favorable climates for investment. There are other constructive measures less developed countries might take:

1. Enact and adhere to fair codes of foreign investment that would enable the foreign company to know where it stood.

2. Liberalize its foreign exchange regulations to the maximum degree feasible in order to facilitate movements of capital and income.

3. Become associated with the Center for the Settlement of Investment Disputes so that foreign investors could be assured of an impartial forum to hear any grievances.

4. Use their comparative advantages in international trade to facilitate their development, rather than seek economic autarchy through policies of "import substitution."

The public regulation of multinational companies presents an unsolved problem. So far, they have been chartered and regulated by the respective countries in which their affiliates do business. Is national regulation enough, or should regulation by a *supranational* authority, tributary to the United Nations, supplement or supplant national regulation?

This issue is analogous to the long-discussed question of federal versus state chartering and regulation of business corporations in the United States. Bearing in mind the competition among the states for corporate fees by offering ever more liberal charters, a strong case can be made for a federal monopoly of chartering and regulation of corporations engaged in interstate commerce or commerce in more than one state. Nearly all large American corporations would be required to obtain federal charters under such a requirement. Corporate powers and government would become less diverse and more easily understood by stockholders and directors. Corporations could no longer shop around among the states to obtain the best combination of broad officer powers and low taxes and fees. By analogy, there is a strong theoretical case for supranational versus national chartering of multinational business firms.

Ideally, one may visualize a World Corporation Authority, established under the aegis of the United Nations, to charter and regulate multinational enterprises. The insoluble problem is how to develop within the United Nations a universal corporate law that would be operationally valid. With the majority of voting power in the General Assembly held by less developed countries who have little experience in corporate business and a heritage of suspicion toward foreign corporations, the likelihood of adoption of a workable corporation law appears remote. The solution of this problem awaits a reform of the United Nations.

XII

FUTURE OF THE MULTINATIONAL CORPORATION

The multinational corporation is only at the beginning of its ultimate development, and its impact upon nations and the world order. Today, few corporations are multinational in *all* dimensions. Most are national corporations that have gone abroad to do business, but retain the ownership, management, and world-view of their country of origin. Professor H.V. Perlmutter has drawn a perceptive distinction between *ethnocentric* companies, run from their home country and sending management abroad, *polycentric* companies, having strong subsidiaries operated by local management but subject to firm central control, and *geocentric* companies that have stockholders throughout the world, find management anywhere, and have a global flexibility.[50] Currently, the great preponderance of multinational firms are ethnocentric, a small minority are polycentric, and a mere handful, such as Shell, Unilever, and I.B.M., are geocentric.

Through time, native officers of subsidiaries of large multinational companies may be expected to rise to the top of the corporate hierarchy. Shares of stock in more multinationals will be traded on the security exchanges of more nations. Equity ownership will spread through many lands. Geocentric companies will become numerous, polycentric companies typical, and ethnocentric companies exceptional.

While one may foresee a further expansion of U.S. direct corporate investment abroad, it is likely that the reverse flow of foreign corporate investment into the United States may expand even faster. Rates of return to investment in the United States have risen and converged with those available abroad. The growing managerial and technical competence of European and Japanese enterprisers will lead many of them to enter the American market. Such a development would enhance domestic competition, reduce the outflow of capital, and improve the U.S. balance of payments. In the long run, multinational business may prove far more effective than international trade in equalizing interest rates, real wages, and living standards throughout the world.

The multinational corporation has evolved in response to human needs for a global instrument of economic activity, able to assemble resources and to organize production on a worldwide scale. As it evolves further in this direction, it will find itself increasingly frustrated and constrained by national governments. The outcome of this conflict will depend upon the nature of the future world order. Will it continue to be a system of nation-states, weakly joined by the United Nations? Or will it become a true world government, as men come to recognize that the present order is too unstable to survive the population explosion and the technological revolution?

The multinational corporation is, beyond doubt, the most powerful agency for regional and global economic unity that our century has produced. It is fundamentally an instrument of peace. Its transactions are transnational in nature and purpose. Its interest is to emphasize the common goals of peoples, to reconcile or remove differences between them. It cannot thrive in a regime of international tension and conflict. It is too much to hope that, through the instrumentality of multinational business, the imperatives of world economic progress will ultimately succeed in doing what the awful threat of nuclear destruction has so far failed to accomplish — to bring unity to mankind?

NOTES

1. F.A. McKenzie, *The American Invasion* (London: Grant Richards, 1902). The "invasion" was primarily of American imports rather than of American products made in Britain.
2. John H. Dunning, *American Investment in British Manufacturing Industry* (London: Allen and Unwin, 1958).
3. U.S. Department of Commerce, *Survey of Current Business* (October, 1969), p. 35.
4. *Ibid.*
5. Foreigners owned sixty-three percent of Canada's petroleum and mining industries. A.E. Safarian, *Foreign Ownership of Canadian Industry* (Toronto: McGraw-Hill, 1966).
6. D.J. Brash, *American Investment in Australian Industry* (Canberra: Australian National University Press, 1966).
7. McMillan, Gonzalez, and Erickson, *International Enterprise in a Developing Economy* (East Lansing: Michigan State University Press, 1964).
8. John H. Dunning, *The Role of American Investment in the British Economy*, Political and Economic Planning Broadsheet 507 (London: February, 1969), p. 119.
9. Jean-Jacques Servan-Schreiber, *The American Challenge* (New York: Atheneum, 1968).
10. Judd Polk, *The Internationalization of Production* (New York: U.S. Council of the International Chamber of Commerce, Inc., May 7, 1969).
11. See Frederic G. Donner, *The Worldwide Industrial Enterprise* (New York: McGraw-Hill, 1967).
12. J.N. Behrman, *Some Patterns in the Rise of the Multinational Enterprise* (Chapel Hill: University of North Carolina, Graduate School of Business Research Paper 18, 1969), pp. 6-8.
13. See Sanford Rose, "The Rewarding Strategies of Multinationalism," *Fortune,* September 15, 1968.
14. *Organizing for Worldwide Operations* (New York: Business International Corp., 1965).
15. See George A. Steiner and Warren M. Cannon, *Multinational Corporate Planning* (New York: Macmillan, 1966).

16. See Alfred P. Sloan, Jr., *My Years With General Motors* (New York: Duell, Sloan & Pearce, 1963), Chap. 4.
17. Dunning, *The Role of American Investment,* p. 126. See also J. C. Behrman, *Some Patterns,* pp. 58-60.
18. Donner, *Worldwide,* Chapter 4.
19. David Lilienthal, "The Multinational Corporation" in Anshen and Bach, eds. *Management and Corporations 1958* (New York: McGraw-Hill, 1960), Chap. 5.
20. Richard F. Gonzalez and Anant R. Neghandi, *The U.S. Overseas Executive: His Orientation and Career Patterns* (East Lansing: Michigan State University Press, 1967).
21. See E. Paul Imhof, "Selected Analogies Between the Foreign Service and the Multinational Corporation." Ms., 1969.
22. Publications in the program "United States Business Performance Abroad" since 1953 have analyzed the cases of Sears in Mexico, Grace in Peru, Creole Petroleum in Venezuela, Firestone in Liberia, Stancvac in Indonesia, United Fruit in Latin America, T.W.A. in Ethiopia, General Electric in Brazil, I.B.M. in France, Aluminium in India, U.S. Plywood in Congo, and International Basic Economy Corporation worldwide.
23. *Sears, Roebuck de México, S.A.* (Washington: National Planning Association, 1953).
24. Stacy May and Galo Plaza, *The United Fruit Company in Latin America* (Washington: National Planning Association, 1958).
25. Wayne G. Broehl, Jr., *The International Basic Economy Corporation* (Washington: National Planning Association, 1968).
26. May and Plaza, *United Fruit,* p. 239.
27. Raymond Vernon, "The Role of U.S. Enterprise Abroad," *Daedalus* (Winter, 1969), p. 1130.
28. Franklin Root, "The Expropriation Experience of American Companies," *Business Horizons* (April, 1968).
29. *Ibid.,* p. 69.
30. See International Center for Settlement of Investment Disputes, Washington, D.C., *Convention on the Settlement of Investment Dispute, in force October, 1966, First Annual Report 1966-67, Second Annual Report 1967-68.*
31. Reasons for "de-politicizing" foreign aid, by replacing bilateral with multilateral assistance and private investment, are set forth by the author in *The Progress of Peoples,* Occasional Paper, II, No. 4 (June, 1969), of the Center for the Study of Democratic Institutions, Santa Barbara, California.
32. Estimates are from Edward A. McCreary, *The Americanization of Europe* (Garden City: Doubleday, 1964).
33. Evidence for Britain is given by Dunning, *American Investment,* pp. 142-45.
34. *Ibid.,* p. 130.
35. Servan-Schreiber, *American Challenge,* Chap. 2.
36. *Ibid.,* Chap. 7. See also *Gaps in Technology,* A General Report of the O.E.C.D. (Paris: 1968).
37. See "Note on Industrial Cooperation" in *Economic Survey of Europe in 1967* (New York: United Nations, 1968), pp. 79-86.
38. See *Joint Business Ventures of Jugoslav Enterprises and Foreign Firms* (New York: Columbia University Press, and Belgrade: Institute of International Politics and Economy, 1968).
39. See *U.S. Business Abroad,* an Economic Report of the Manufacturer's Hanover

Trust Company (New York: March, 1969). The short-run effect of investment controls upon the U.S. balance of international payments depends upon the length of the recoupment period. See F. Michael Adler and G. C. Hufbaur, "Foreign Investment Controls: Object — Removal," *Columbia Journal of World Business,* III, No. 3 (May-June, 1969).

40. See Safarian, *Foreign Ownership.*
41. *Ibid.*
42. As long ago as 1911 the U.S. Supreme Court held that the Sherman Act applied to the foreign activities of American corporations. U.S. *v.* American Tobacco Company, 221 U.S. 106.
43. See Sidney E. Rolfe, *The International Corporation* (Paris: International Chamber of Commerce, May, 1969), pp. 82-88.
44. Allan Johnstone, *United States Direct Investment in France* (Cambridge: M.I.T. Press, 1965), Chap. 7.
45. Safarian, *op. cit.,* Chap. 3.
46. *Ibid.,* Chap. 6, and Dunning, *American Investment,* p. 157.
47. Johnstone, *United States,* Chap. 2.
48. See Elisabeth M. Borgese, *The Ocean Regime,* Occasional Paper, I, No. 5 (October, 1968), of the Center for the Study of Democratic Institutions, Santa Barbara, California.
49. Problems of enterprises in an ocean regime were explored at *Pacem in Maribus,* an international convocation to explore peaceful uses of the oceans and ocean floor conducted on the island of Malta in June, 1970, by the Center for the Study of Democratic Institutions, Santa Barbara, California.
50. H. V. Perlmutter, Lausanne School of Management Studies.

3
The Tortuous
Evolution of the
Multinational
Corporation

Howard V. Perlmutter

Four senior executives of the world's largest firms with extensive holdings outside the home country speak:

Company A: "We are a multinational firm. We distribute our products in about 100 countries. We manufacture in over 17 countries and do research and development in three countries. We look at all new investment projects—both domestic and overseas—using exactly the same criteria."

Company B: "We are a multinational firm. Only 1 percent of the personnel in our affiliate companies are non-nationals. Most of these are U.S. executives on temporary assignments. In all major markets, the affiliate's managing director is of the local nationality."

Company C: "We are a multinational firm. Our product division executives have worldwide profit responsibility. As our organizational chart shows, the United States is just one region on a par with Europe, Latin America, Africa, etc. in each product division."

Company D (non-American): "We are a multinational firm. We have at least 18 nationalities represented at our headquarters. Most senior executives speak at least two languages. About 30 of our staff at headquarters are foreigners."

While a claim to multinationality, based on their years of experience and the significant proportion of sales generated overseas, is justified in each of these four companies, a more penetrating analysis changes the image.

Reprinted, with permission, from the January-February 1969 issue of the *Columbia Journal of World Business*. Copyright ©1969 by Trustees of Columbia University in the City of New York.

The executive from Company A tells us that most of the key posts in Company A's subsidiaries are held by home-country nationals. Whenever replacements for these men are sought, it is the practice, if not the policy, to "look next to you at the head office" and "pick someone (usually a home-country national) you know and trust."

The executive from Company B does not hide the fact that there are very few non-Americans in the key posts at headquarters. The few who are there are "so Americanized" that their foreign nationality literally has no meaning. His explanation for this paucity of non-Americans seems reasonable enough: "You can't find good foreigners who are willing to live in the United States, where our headquarters is located. American executives are more mobile. In addition, Americans have the drive and initiative we like. In fact, the European nationals would prefer to report to an American rather than to some other European."

The executive from Company C goes on to explain that the worldwide product division concept is rather difficult to implement. The senior executives in charge of these divisions have little overseas experience. They have been promoted from domestic posts and tend to view foreign consumer needs "as really basically the same as ours." Also, product division executives tend to focus on the domestic market because the domestic market is larger and generates more revenue than the fragmented European markets. The rewards are for global performance, but the strategy is to focus on domestic. His colleagues say "one pays attention to what one understands—and our senior executives simply do not understand what happens overseas and really do not trust foreign executives in key positions here or overseas."

The executive from the European Company D begins by explaining that since the voting shareholders must by law come from the home country, the home country's interest must be given careful consideration. In the final analysis he insists: "We are proud of our nationality; we shouldn't be ashamed of it." He cites examples of the previous reluctance of headquarters to use home-country ideas overseas, to their detriment, especially in their U.S. subsidiary. "Our country produces good executives, who tend to stay with us a long time. It is harder to keep executives from the United States."

A ROSE BY ANY OTHER NAME...

Why quibble about how multinational a firm is? To these executives, apparently being multinational is prestigious. They know that multinational firms tend to be regarded as more progressive, dynamic, geared to the future than provincial companies which avoid foreign frontiers and their attendant risks and opportunities.

It is natural that these senior executives would want to justify the multi-nationality of their enterprise, even if they use different yardsticks: ownership criteria, organizational structure, nationality of senior executives, percent of investment overseas, etc.

Two hypotheses seem to be forming in the minds of executives from international firms that make the extent of their firm's multinationality of real interest. The first hypothesis is that the degree of multinationality of an enterprise is positively related to the firm's long-term viability. The "multi-national" category makes sense for executives if it means a quality of decision making which leads to survival, growth and profitability in our evolving world economy.

The second hypothesis stems from the proposition that the multinational corporation is a new kind of institution—a new type of industrial social architecture particularly suitable for the latter third of the twentieth century. This type of institution could make a valuable contribution to world order and conceivably exercise a constructive impact on the nation-state. Some executives want to understand how to create an institution whose presence is considered legitimate and valuable in each nation-state. They want to prove that the greater the degree of multinationality of a firm, the greater its total constructive impact will be on host and home nation-states as well as other institutions. Since multinational firms may produce a significant proportion of the world's GNP, both hypotheses justify a more precise analysis of the varieties and degrees of multinationality.[1] However, the confirming evidence is limited.

STATE OF MIND

Part of the difficulty in defining the degree of multinationality comes from the variety of parameters along which a firm doing business overseas can be described. The examples from the four companies argue that (1) no single criterion of multinationality such as ownership or the number of nationals overseas is sufficient, and that (2) external and quantifiable measures such as the percentage of investment overseas or the distribution of equity by nationality are useful but not enough. The more one penetrates into the living reality of an international firm, the more one finds it is necessary to give serious weight to the way executives think about doing business around the world. The orientation toward "foreign people, ideas, resources," in headquarters and subsidiaries, and in host and home environments, becomes crucial in estimating the multinationality of a firm. To be sure, such external indices as the proportion of nationals in different countries holding equity and the number of foreign nationals who have reached top positions, including president, are good indices of multinationality. But one can still behave with a home-country orientation despite foreign shareholders, and one can have a few home-country nationals overseas but still pick those local executives who are home-country oriented or who are provincial and chauvinistic. The attitudes men hold are clearly more relevant than their passports.

Three primary attitudes among international executives toward building a multinational enterprise are identifiable. These attitudes can be inferred from the assumptions upon which key product, functional and geographical decisions were made.

These states of mind or attitudes may be described as ethnocentric (or home-country oriented), polycentric (or host-country oriented) and geocentric (or world-oriented).[2] While they never appear in pure form, they are clearly distinguishable. There is some degree of ethnocentricity, polycentricity or geocentricity in all firms, but management's analysis does not usually correlate with public pronouncements about the firm's multinationality.

HOME COUNTRY ATTITUDES

The ethnocentric attitude can be found in companies of any nationality with extensive overseas holdings. The attitude, revealed in executive actions and experienced by foreign subsidiary managers, is: "We, the home nationals of X company, are superior to, more trustworthy and more reliable than any foreigners in headquarters or subsidiaries. We will be willing to build facilities in your country if you acknowledge our inherent superiority and accept our methods and conditions for doing the job."

Of course, such attitudes are never so crudely expressed, but they often determine how a certain type of "multinational" firm is designed. Table 1 illustrates how ethnocentric attitudes are expressed in determining the managerial process at home and overseas. For example, the ethnocentric executive is more apt to say: "Let us manufacture the simple products overseas. Those foreign nationals are not yet ready or reliable. We should manufacture the complex products in our country and keep the secrets among our trusted home-country nationals."

In a firm where ethnocentric attitudes prevailed, the performance criteria for men and products are "home-made." "We have found that a salesman should make 12 calls per day in Hoboken, New Jersey (the headquarters location) and therefore we apply these criteria everywhere in the world. The salesman in Brazzaville is naturally lazy, unmotivated. He shows little drive because he makes only two calls per day (despite the Congolese salesman's explanation that it takes time to reach customers by boat)."

Table 1:
Three Types of Headquarters Orientation Toward Subsidiaries in an International Enterprise

Organization Design	Ethnocentric	Polycentric	Geocentric
Complexity of organization	Complex in home country, simple in subsidiaries	Varied and independent	Increasingly complex and interdependent
Authority; decision making	High in headquarters	Relatively low in headquarters	Aim for a collaborative approach between headquarters and subsidiaries
Evaluation and control	Home standards applied for persons and performance	Determined locally	Find standards which are universal and local
Rewards and punishments; incentives	High in headquarters low in subsidiaries	Wide variation; can be high or low rewards for subsidiary performance	International and local executives rewarded for reaching local and worldwide objectives
Communication; information flow	High volume to subsidiaries orders, commands, advice	Little to and from headquarters. Little between subsidiaries	Both ways and between subsidiaries. Heads of subsidiaries part of management team
Identification	Nationality of owner	Nationality of host country	Truly international company but identifying with national interests
Perpetuation (recruiting, staffing, development)	Recruit and develop people of home country for key positions everywhere in the world	Develop people of local nationality for key positions in their own country	Develop best men everywhere in the world for key positions everywhere in the world

Ethnocentric attitudes are revealed in the communication process where "advice," "counsel," and directives flow from headquarters to the subsidiary in a steady stream, bearing this message: "This works at home; therefore, it must work in your country."

Executives in both headquarters and affiliates express the national identity of the firm by associating the company with the nationality of the headquarters: this is "a Swedish company," "a Swiss company," "an American company," depending on the location of headquarters. "You have to accept the fact that the only way to reach a senior post in our firm," an English executive in a U.S. firm said, "is to take out an American passport."

Crucial to the ethnocentric concept is the current policy that men of the home nationality are recruited and trained for key positions everywhere in the world. Foreigners feel like "second-class" citizens.

There is no international firm today whose executives will say that ethnocentrism is absent in their company. In the firms whose multinational investment began a decade ago, one is more likely to hear, "We are still in a transitional stage from our ethnocentric era. The traces are still around! But we are making progress."

HOST COUNTRY ORIENTATION

Polycentric firms are those which, by experience or by the inclination of a top executive (usually one of the founders), begin with the assumption that host-country cultures are different and that foreigners are difficult to understand. Local people know what is best for them, and the part of the firm which is located in the host country should be as "local in identity" as possible. The senior executives at headquarters believe that their multinational enterprise can be held together by good financial controls. A polycentric firm, literally, is a loosely connected group with quasi-independent subsidiaries as centers—more akin to a confederation.

European multinational firms tend to follow this pattern, using a top local executive who is strong and trustworthy, of the "right" family and who has an intimte understanding of the workings of the host government. This policy seer to have worked until the advent of the Common Market.

Executives in the headquarters of such a company are apt to say: "Let the Romans do it their way. We really don't understand what is going on there, but we have to have confidence in them. As long as they earn a profit, we want to remain in the background." They assume that since people are different in each country, standards for performance, incentives and training methods must be different. Local environmental factors are given greater weight (see Table 1).

Many executives mistakenly equate polycentrism with multinationalism. This is evidenced in the legalistic definition of a multinational enterprise as a cluster of corporations of diverse nationality joined together by ties of common ownership. It is no accident that many senior executives in headquarters take pride in the absence of non-nationals in their subsidiaries, especially people from the head office. The implication is clearly that each subsidiary is a distinct national entity, since it is incorporated in a different sovereign state. Lonely senior executives in the subsidiaries of polycentric companies complain that: "The home office never tells us anything."

Polycentrism is not the ultimate form of multinationalism. It is a landmark on a highway. Polycentrism is encouraged by local marketing managers who contend that: "Headquarters will never understand us, our people, our consumer needs, our laws, our distribution, etc. . . ."

Headquarters takes pride in the fact that few outsiders know that the firm is foreign-owned. "We want to be a good local company. How many Americans know that Shell and Lever Brothers are foreign-owned?"

But the polycentric personnel policy is also revealed in the fact that no local manager can seriously aspire to a senior position at headquarters. "You know the French are so provincial; it is better to keep them in France. Uproot them and you are in trouble," a senior executive says to justify the paucity of non-Americans at headquarters.

One consequence (and perhaps cause) of polycentrism is a virulent ethnocentrism among the country managers.

A WORLD-ORIENTED CONCEPT

The third attitude which is beginning to emerge at an accelerating rate is geocentrism. Senior executives with this orientation do not equate superiority with nationality. Within legal and political limits, they seek the best men, regardless of nationality, to solve the company's problems anywhere in the world. The senior executives attempt to build an organization in which the subsidiary is not only a good citizen of the host nation but is a leading exporter from this nation in the international community and contributes such benefits as (1) an increasing supply of hard currency, (2) new skills and (3) a knowledge of advanced technology. Geocentrism is summed up in a Unilever board chairman's statement of objectives: "We want to Unileverize our Indians and Indianize our Unileverans."

The ultimate goal of geocentrism is a worldwide approach in both headquarters and subsidiaries. The firm's subsidiaries are thus neither satellites nor independent city states, but parts of a whole whose focus is on worldwide objectives as well as local objectives, each part making its unique contribution with its unique competence. Geocentrism is expressed by function, product and geography. The question asked in headquarters and the subsidiaries is: "Where in the world shall we raise money, build our plant, conduct R & D, get and launch new ideas to serve our present and future customers?"

This conception of geocentrism involves a collaborative effort between subsidiaries and headquarters to establish universal standards and permissible local variations, to make key allocational decisions on new products, new plants, new laboratories. The international management team includes the affiliate heads.

Subsidiary managers must ask: "Where in the world can I get the help to serve my customers best in this country?" "Where in the world can I export products developed in this country—products which meet worldwide standards as opposed to purely local standards?"

Geocentrism, furthermore, requires a reward system for subsidiary managers which motivates them to work for worldwide objectives, not just to defend country objectives. In firms where geocentrism prevails, it is not uncommon to hear a subsidiary manager say, "While I am paid to defend our interests in this country and to get the best resources for this affiliate, I must still ask myself the question 'Where in the world (instead of where in my country) should we build this plant?' " This approach is still rare today.

In contrast to the ethnocentric and polycentric patterns, communication is encouraged among subsidiaries in geocentric-oriented firms. "It is your duty to help us solve problems anywhere in the world," one chief executive continually reminds the heads of his company's affiliates. (See Table 1.)

The geocentric firm identifies with local company needs. "We aim to be not just a good local company but the best local company in terms of the quality of management and the worldwide (not local) standards we establish in domestic and export production." "If we were only as good as local companies, we would deserve to be nationalized."

The geocentric personnel policy is based on the belief that we should bring in the best man in the world regardless of his nationality. His passport should not be the criterion for promotion.

THE EPG PROFILE

Executives can draw their firm's profile in ethnocentric (E), polycentric (P) and geocentric (G) dimensions. They are called EPG profiles. The degree of ethnocentrism, polycentrism and geocentrism by product, function and geography can be established. Typically R & D often turns out to be more geocentric (truth is universal, perhaps) and less ethnocentric than finance. Financial managers are likely to see their decisions as ethnocentric. The marketing function is more polycentric, particularly in the advanced economies and in the larger affiliate markets.

The tendency toward ethnocentrism in relations with subsidiaries in the developing countries is marked. Polycentric attitudes develop in consumer goods divisions, and ethnocentrism appears to be greater in industrial product divisions. The agreement is almost unanimous in both U. S.- and European-based international firms that their companies are at various stages on a route toward geocentrism but none has reached this state of affairs. Their executives would agree, however, that:

1. a description of their firms as multinational obscures more than it illuminates the state of affairs;

2. the EPG mix, once defined, is a more precise way to describe the point they have reached;

3. the present profile is not static but a landmark along a difficult road to genuine geocentrism;

4. there are forces both to change and to maintain the present attitudinal "mix," some of which are under their control.

FORCES TOWARD AND AGAINST

What are the forces that determine the EPG mix of a firm? "You must think of the struggle toward functioning as a worldwide firm as just a beginning—a few steps forward and a step backward," a chief executive put it. "It is a painful process, and every firm is different."

Executives of some of the world's largest multinational firms have been able to identify a series of external and internal factors that contribute to or hinder the growth of geocentric attitudes and decision. Table 2 summarizes the factors most frequently mentioned by over 500 executives from at least 17 countries and 20 firms.

Table 2:
International Executives View of Forces and Obstacles Toward Geocentrism in Their Firms

Forces Toward Geocentrism		Obstacles Toward Geocentrism	
Environmental	Intra-Organizational	Environmental	Intra-Organizational
1. Technological and managerial know-how increasing in availability in different countries	1. Desire to use human vs. material resources optimally	1. Economic nationalism in host and home countries	1. Management inexperience in overseas markets
2. International customers	2. Observed lowering of morale in affiliates of an ethnocentric company	2. Political nationalism in host & home countries	2. Nation-centered reward and punishment structure
3. Local customers demand for best product at fair price	3. Evidence of waste and duplication in polycentrism	3. Military secrecy associated with research in home country	3. Mutual distrust between home country people and foreign executives
4. Host country's desire to increase balance of payments	4. Increasing awareness and respect for good men of other than home nationality	4. Distrust of big international firms by host country political leaders	4. Resistance to letting foreigners into the power structure
5. Growing world markets	5. Risk diversification in having a worldwide production & distribution system	5. Lack of international monetary system	5. Anticipated costs and risks of geocentrism
6. Global competition among international firms for scarce human and material resources	6. Need for recruitment of good men on a worldwide basis	6. Growing differences between the rich and poor countries	6. Nationalistic tendencies in staff
7. Major advances in integration of international transport & telecommunications	7. Need for worldwide information system	7. Host country belief that home countries get disproportionate benefits of international firms profits	7. Increasing immobility of staff
8. Regional supranational economic & political communities	8. Worldwide appeal of products	8. Home country political leaders' attempts to control firm's policy	8. Linguistic problems & different cultural backgrounds
	9. Senior management's long term commitment to geocentrism as related to survival and growth		9. Centralization tendencies in headquarters

From the external environmental side, the growing world markets, the increase in availability of managerial and technological know-how in different countries, global competition and international customers, advances in telecommunications, regional political and economic communities are positive factors, as is the host country's desire to increase its balance-of-payments surplus through the location of export-oriented subsidiaries of international firms within its borders.

In different firms, senior executives see in various degrees these positive factors toward geocentrism: top management's increasing desire to use human and material resources optimally, the observed lowering of morale after decades of ethnocentric practices, the evidence of waste and duplication under polycentric thinking, the increased awareness and respect for good men of other than the home nationality, and most importantly, top management's own commitment to building a geocentric firm as evidenced in policies, practices and procedures.

The obstacles toward geocentrism from the environment stem largely from the rising political and economic nationalism in the world today, the suspicions of political leaders of the aims and increasing power of the multinational firm. On the internal side, the obstacles cited most frequently in U. S.-based multinational firms were management's inexperience in overseas markets, mutual distrust between home-country people and foreign executives, the resistance to participation by foreigners in the power structure at headquarters, the increasing difficulty of getting good men overseas to move, nationalistic tendencies in staff, and the linguistic and other communication difficulties of a cultural nature.

Any given firm is seen as moving toward geocentrism at a rate determined by its capacities to build on the positive internal factors over which it has control and to change the negative internal factors which are controllable. In some firms the geocentric goal is openly discussed among executives of different nationalities and from different subsidiaries as well as headquarters. There is a consequent improvement in the climate of trust and acceptance of each other's views.

Programs are instituted to assure greater experience in foreign markets, task forces of executives are upgraded, international careers for executives of all nationalities are being designed.

But the seriousness of the obstacles cannot be underestimated. A world of rising nationalism is hardly a pre-condition for geocentrism; and overcoming distrust of foreigners even within one's own firm is not accomplished in a short span of time. The route to pervasive geocentric thinking is long and tortuous.

COSTS, RISKS, PAYOFFS

What conclusions will executives from multinational firms draw from the balance sheet of advantages and disadvantages of maintaining one's present state of ethnocentrism, polycentrism or geocentrism? Not too surprisingly, the costs and risks of ethnocentrism are seen to out-balance the payoffs in the long run. The costs of ethnocentrism are ineffective planning because of a lack of good feed-back, the departure of the best men in the subsidiaries, fewer innovations, and an inability to build a high calibre local organization. The risks are political and social repercussions and a less flexible response to local changes.

The payoffs of ethnocentrism are real enough in the short term, they say. Organization is simpler. There is a higher rate of communication of know-how from headquarters to new markets. There is more control over appointments to senior posts in subsidiaries.

Polycentrism's costs are waste due to duplication, to decisions to make products for local use but which could be universal, and to inefficient use of home-country experience. The risks include an excessive regard for local traditions and local growth at the expense of global growth. The main advantages are an intensive exploitation of local markets, better sales since local management is often better informed, more local initiative for new products, more host-government support, and good local managers with high morale.

Geocentrism's costs are largely related to communication and travel expenses, educational costs at all levels, time spent in decision-making because consensus seeking among more people is required, and an international headquarters bureaucracy. Risks include those due to too wide a distribution of power, personnel problems and those of re-entry of international executives. The payoffs are a more powerful total company throughout, a better quality of products and service, worldwide utilization of best resources, improvement of local company management, a greater sense of commitment to worldwide objectives, and last, but not least, more profit.

Jacques Maisonrouge, the French-born president of IBM World Trade, understands the geocentric concept and its benefits. He wrote recently:

"The first step to a geocentric organization is when a corporation, faced with the choice of whether to grow and expand or decline, realizes the need to mobilize its resources on a world scale. It will sooner or later have to face the issue that the home country does not have a monopoly of either men or ideas . . . .

"I strongly believe that the future belongs to geocentric companies . . . . What is of fundamental importance is the attitude of the company's top management. If it is dedicated to 'geocentrism,' good international management will be possible. If not, the best men of different nations will soon understand that they do not belong to the 'race des seigneurs' and will leave the business."[3]

Geocentrism is not inevitable in any given firm. Some companies have experienced a "regression" to ethnocentrism after trying a long period of polycentrism, of letting subsidiaries do it "their way." The local directors built little empires and did not train successors from their own country. Headquarters had to send home-country nationals to take over. A period of home-country thinking took over.

There appears to be evidence of a need for evolutionary movement from ethnocentrism to polycentrism to geocentrism. The polycentric stage is likened to an adolescent protest period during which subsidiary managers gain their confidence as equals by fighting headquarters and proving "their manhood," after a long period of being under headquarters' ethnocentric thumb.

"It is hard to move from a period of headquarters domination to a worldwide management team quickly. A period of letting affiliates make mistakes may be necessary," said one executive.

WINDOW DRESSING

In the rush toward appearing geocentric, many U.S. firms have found it necessary to emphasize progress by appointing one or two non-nationals to senior posts—even on occasion to headquarters. The foreigner is often effectively counteracted by the number of nationals around him, and his influence is really small. Tokenism does have some positive effects, but it does not mean geocentrism has arrived.

Window dressing is also a temptation. Here an attempt is made to demonstrate influence by appointing a number of incompetent "foreigners" to key positions. The results are not impressive for either the individuals or the company.

Too often what is called "the multinational view" is really a screen for ethnocentrism. Foreign affiliate managers must, in order to succeed, take on the traits and behavior of the ruling nationality. In short, in a U.S.-owned firm the foreigner must "Americanize"—not only in attitude but in dress and speech—in order to be accepted.

Tokenism and window dressing are transitional episodes where aspirations toward multinationalism outstrip present attitudes and resources. The fault does not lie only with the enterprise. The human demands of ethnocentrism are great.

A GEOCENTRIC MAN—?

The geocentric enterprise depends on having an adequate supply of men who are geocentrically oriented. It would be a mistake to underestimate the human stresses which a geocentric career creates. Moving where the company needs an executive involves major adjustments for families, wives and children. The sacrifices are often great and, for some families, outweigh the rewards forthcoming—at least in personal terms. Many executives find it difficult to learn new languages and overcome their cultural superiority complexes, national pride and discomfort with foreigners. Furthermore, international careers can be hazardous when ethnocentrism prevails at headquarters. "It is easy to get lost in the world of the subsidiaries and to be 'out of sight, out of mind' when promotions come up at headquarters," as one executive expressed it following a visit to headquarters after five years overseas. To his disappointment, he knew few senior executives. And fewer knew him!

The economic rewards, the challenge of new countries, the personal and professional development that comes from working in a variety of countries and cultures are surely incentives, but companies have not solved by any means the human costs of international mobility to executives and their families.

A firm's multinationality may be judged by the pervasiveness with which executives think geocentrically—by function, marketing, finance, production, R&D, etc., by product division and by country. The takeoff to geocentrism may begin with executives in one function, say marketing, seeking to find a truly worldwide product line. Only when this worldwide attitude extends throughout the firm, in headquarters and subsidiaries, can executives feel that it is becoming genuinely geocentric.

But no single yardstick, such as the number of foreign nationals in key positions, is sufficient to establish a firm's multinationality. The multinational firm's route to geocentrism is still long because political and economic nationalism is on the rise, and, more importantly, since within the firm ethnocentrism and polycentrism are not easy to overcome. Building trust between persons of different nationality is a central obstacle. Indeed, if we are to judge men, as Paul Weiss put it, "by the kind of world they are trying to build," the senior executives engaged in building the geocentric enterprise could well be the most important social architects of the last third of the twentieth century. For the institution they are trying to erect promises a greater universal sharing of wealth and a consequent control of the explosive centrifugal tendencies of our evolving world community.

The geocentric enterprise offers an institutional and supra-national framework which could conceivably make war less likely, on the assumption that bombing customers, suppliers and employees is in nobody's interest. The difficulty of the task is thus matched by its worthwhileness. A clearer image of the features of genuine geocentricity is thus indispensable both as a guideline and as an inviting prospect.

NOTES

1. H. V. Perlmutter, "Super-Giant Firms in the Future," *Wharton Quarterly*, (Winter 1968).
2. H. V. Perlmutter, "Three Conceptions of a World Enterprise," *Revue Economique et Sociale* (May 1965).
3. Jacques Maisonrouge, "The Education of International Managers," *The Quarterly Journal of AIESEC International* (February 1967).

4

The Emergent World Economy

Judd Polk

We have heard a lot about the international corporation in recent years: from Servan-Schreiber's rather unfair popularization of the notion as an American Challenge, by which is meant menace; to the quiet and thoughtful work of John Dunning; to the pervasive Canadian concerns about the big international company, particularly, of course, American companies. This concern reached the level of an expert parliamentary commission two years ago and produced a document that was in effect a reinterpretation of Canada's economic origins and mission in terms of making use of and preventing abuse of the international company's powers. Then there is the wide-front Harvard work in progress covering the behavior of international companies in an encyclopedic way.

I think, though, that all of this work is basically a lagging reaction to the impact of the international company on the world economic scene. In fact the international company itself is a reflection rather than a source of a new phenomenon, namely the internationalization of production. The state of industrial technology—and very much including instantaneous world electronic communication and computers—has created the situation in which for the first time men have been in a position to treat the world itself as the basic economic unit in pursuing that core economic problem: making the best use of its resources.

The significance of this fact, namely (to use an awkward word), the

Reprinted, by permission. Prepared statement read before the Subcommittee on Foreign Economic Policy of the Joint Economic Committee, Congress of the United States, Ninety-first Congress, Second Session, pp. 772-779.

worldizing of our housekeeping is immediate, pervasive, distinctive, and full of possible upheavals and new departures for our foreign economic policy (and it might be argued right here for our domestic economic policy as well). I would like to devote my brief time here to the nature of these new facts and their most important policy implications. It may be helpful at the outset to mention that many of our major policy directions appear misguided when viewed from the standpoint of the best interests of the United States in an internationalized world of production.

As we inform ourselves about this supposedly new phenomenon, the international or multinational company, we pursue its implications without reference to—in fact often inconsistently with—the really new phenomenon of which it is a part, namely, the internationalization of production. The international company is old, as we have every reason to recall when standing on this ground once managed by such ancestors of our modern international company as the Hudson Bay Company and the Virginia Company of London. What is new and important is the degree of cohesion in international production. The scope of these operations inevitably implies an emergent world economy.

THE INTERNATIONALIZATION OF PRODUCTION

In the fundamental task of allocating resources to maximize or optimize yield, the question of the economic area whose resources are being allocated is crucial to the question of how best to allocate them. The emergence of a national market in contrast to regional ones in the United States is an analogous event so recent that even the youngest of us here have witnessed it at least in part. For example, we are currently in a phase of national development in which national resources are being nationally allocated in such a way that the financial capabilities, the technology, the managerial skills, and the energies of all regions of the country are contributing to the distinctive pace of development in the West and Southwest. There are many examples; this is only one to suggest the feel of the thing. Any significant use of resources in this country, whether under public or private sponsorship, be it dam or computer services, embraces and answers the question. What is the most effective national, not regional or local, use of the given funds or real resources. Yet as recently as a generation ago the nation was not the reference area for typical examinations of alternative prospective yields.

It is already the implicit suggestion, now worth putting explicitly, that our commitment to international operations in response to our communications, industrial, technological, and, I think one must add, community capability requires us to assess international, not just national competing opportunities if we are to reach a tenable resource commitment. I say community because the breadth of the borders of the community we think we belong to has a lot to do with the ultimate breadth of the real community we create for ourselves. International business expresses and consolidates a sense of international community. And the existence of our $143 billion investment stake abroad, with its product profile of $220 billion, illustrates the real force to date of the invitation, perhaps economic compulsion, to commit resources to production in an international rather than a national frame of reference.

SELF-IMPOSED BARRIERS

It is an odd fact that even though we are deeply committed—I think irreversibly—to recognizing a world economic framework in our productive decisions, we are only beginning to get familiar with the implications of world economics. Our governmental policies are often ambivalent and sometimes directly inconsistent with the international character of our producing operations. Our present program of capital controls over foreign direct investment is a case in point. The general program of tightening the reins on American investment abroad began with the Interest Equalization Tax in 1963 (passed by Congress in 1964) and culminated in mandatory control over Americans' foreign investment activities generally. A good bit of the debate over the pros and cons of these restraints, and particularly the question of whether they would help or hurt the balance of payments, was argued before this Committee and other committees of Congress. I think the Committee will recall the Administration's regular contention that the high and consistent earnings from foreign investment present a persuasive justification for it in the long run, but that particular balance of payments urgencies required some limitations in the short run. As an interested student of foreign investment, I got the impression throughout these years, and particularly in connection with the mandatory program, that the Administration's cost-benefit analysis made the decision a pretty close one. An important and perhaps even deciding consideration was more political than economic. This had to do with the regularly expressed anxieties of foreign countries over the extent of American influence—the American Challenge already mentioned —in their economic affairs as implicit in the growing strength of American investment and producing operations. And I have certainly gathered from talking to foreign friends that whatever else the restraints may or may not have done they did tend to lower the American profile at a time when many of them found the sharpness of this profile disconcerting.

Two oddities illustrate the ambivalence of our policy position. In lowering the profile by inhibiting investment we also mobilized investment to respond to Washington directives in just the way that those abroad who were anxious over the profile had as the center of their anxiety. The most notable feature of the program here is the establishment of targets for repatriation of earnings—a directive that went from Washington parent to foreign subsidiary involving the disposition of funds eventuating completely outside of the United States' jurisdiction, and in the hands of companies whose "citizenship" was strictly local, though of U.S. parentage. Neighboring Canada, ever sensitive to pressure from the South, was a case in point for a few days before Canada was exempted from the mandatory controls. One Canadian economic expert, Melville H. Watkins, referred to this period in the dramatic terms that for a moment Canada saw the power grid light up. The mobilization of any country's subsidiaries abroad raises most touchy issues and, to say the least, does not contribute to a lowering of profile.

The other oddity is somewhat similar. As I have previously testified before this Committee, the artificiality of our balance of payments reckonings, and in particular the calculation and publicization of large scale balance of payments deficits, have seemed wrong to me as an economist. Nonetheless, the objective of reducing these deficits has been the main reason throughout the '60s for the various controls over American citizens' business operations abroad. The oddity lies in the fact that one conventional and perhaps the most usual basis for calculating the alleged deficit counts all of our banking liabilities to foreigners as direct increases in the deficit *without* offset by current accumulations of short term assets. The rationale for this view turned on the fact that our assets, being private in a private system, could not be marshalled to meet our liabilities. The mandatory program demonstrated the ease with which very massive short term holdings of Americans could be marshalled.

UPDATING BALANCE OF PAYMENTS ANALYSIS

Actually, balance of payments technique has moved somewhat beyond this point. The balance of payments expert Review Committee's recommendations in 1965 led to a second calculation, a deficit on official accounts. This went part of the distance in balancing the onesidedness just mentioned. But we have now passed pretty much beyond the relevance of this kind of calculation too. Existing balance of payments techniques show up best for a kind of closed national economy related to other economies primarily by limited trade transactions, with bills for any net purchases requiring settlement in an international money. When, however, a country becomes involved as the United States has in very extensive international banking, when its producers have substantial operations all over the world in a variety of currencies, when its own currency is widely used throughout the world for all monetary purposes, then the standard highly selective trade-oriented balance of payments accounting fails to measure these international relations in any meaningful way. The old-fashioned accounting tosses up enormous deficits that are really without meaning and, at the same time, fails to note international credit movements that merit the deepest concern. The minuses and pluses of these balance of payments calculations do not reflect some useful "net" of American transactions with foreigners but rather mix transactions with foreigners together with debts and credits within the American international circle of companies and banks.

The unreality of the balance of payments was everywhere apparent in the lengthy correspondence that my organization, the United States Council of the International Chamber of Commerce, has just conducted with a group of companies on the impact of the investment controls on their operations. The Council has recently reported at length on this interesting correspondence. The report is concerned primarily with the cumulative difficulties the controls have brought in the way of maintaining the competitive soundness of companies' operating structures abroad and the disadvantageous financial arrangements forced into the corporate design. A persistent note that recurred throughout the correspondence was the sense that the national balance of payments as geographically conceived is very remote if not fictitious to American companies whose branches abroad figure significantly as buyers of exports from geographic United States and sellers of imports to it.

Beyond this, actual experience with the program has displayed to businessmen the mere bookkeeping character of the balance of payments "advantages" alleged as the raison d'etre of the controls. Under the controls the government makes a crucial distinction between liabilities of a bank's New York headquarters and those of its branches in London and Paris, and similarly between dollar funds available to a company in the United States and dollar funds available to it abroad. These largely fictitious distinctions are maintained at the cost of the noted disadvantages to business operations abroad and close to crippling disadvantages to the normal further development and continued functioning of the United States' international capital and money markets. They have also advanced the dubious arts of window dressing down to the level of company accounts.

Meanwhile the balance of payments technicians struggle to log in and out the billions, even tens of billions, in funds transferred back and forth between banks and their foreign branches. We have gotten to the stage where a weekend's banking convenience to a single group of banks can create the appearance of a deficit larger than any of the deficits registered in recent years in the struggles of the pound, the French franc, and the lira, not to mention the dollar itself.

One way of bringing greater realism to the balance of payments would be to bring into its purview the whole structure of business assets which have so changed our orientation to the world. I think members of this Subcommittee will find in the table I have appended to my remarks here that the investment information compiled by the Department of Commerce yields a most interesting and basic underlying picture of United States assets and liabilities. It would not be difficult to evolve from this sort of data a relatively complete international balance sheet, and then to devise an income statement which would, as in all classical accounting, reconcile changes in the balance sheet from the beginning to the end of the period. I think it is most likely that this approach would give a far more coherent and accurate picture of the country's basic ability to discharge its existing liabilities to foreigners as banker, as trader, and as producer. I think this effort should be made.

At the same time we should not delude ourselves that a strictly geographic accounting can successfully portray the intricacy of our involvements in the world economy. It has been noted already that Americans appear on both the domestic and foreign side of the balance of payments fence. It hasn't been noted here yet, but this Subcommittee is aware that on the monetary side an extraordinary market in non-resident dollars, commonly called the Eurodollar market, has grown up over the last 15 years. We have not yet exhausted the meanings of this new and unpredicted financial phenomenon. Looking back it seems that the Eurodollar and Eurobond markets provided a crucial link that internationalized banking in a way that reflects and gives financial expression to the growing internationalization of the world's basic producing structure.

I think we must be close to the point where we should stop worrying about whether companies A, B, and C are keeping their funds in a New York bank or its branch in London, or Paris, or Frankfurt, or Tokyo; or what the exact national distribution of the companies' equity structure may be. We are close to the point where the meaningful questions, such as whether the companies are in reasonably liquid shape or not, can be faced in dollar terms without making the separate determination in a variety of national currencies.

In the case of our highly developed national market we are not concerned with state or regional balances of payments. The financial facts from which we try to derive an impression of the state of the financial health in the country belong to the national flow of funds data. I think we are very close to the point where we could and should turn to analogous international sources and uses of funds to read the true state of international financial affairs. If we are not close to that point, one of our immediate tasks should be to determine why not.

HOW FAR HAS WORLD OUTPUT BEEN INTERNATIONALIZED?

There is nothing startling about the process of internationalization of production, which is here taken to mean simply the state of affairs that exists when an entrepreneur of one country organizes production of "his" product in another country, usually as an alternative to producing it in his country and exporting it. Students of the motives for such activity, including myself, have been surprised at the now familiar variety. In the post World War II world a common occasion for producing abroad was the barriers imposed by national authorities to imports thought to be wasteful of chronically scarce foreign exchange. The typical post-war problem was to reconstitute war-damaged-destroyed-distorted resources as the appropriate means of ultimately achieving acceptably high standards of consumption, in contrast to an alternative possibility of spending (that is squandering) precious foreign exchange merely to establish foreign sources of supply for consumers. The existence of barriers and the special situation pertaining after World War II somewhat obscured the fact that even in the absence of these special conditions economics would have provided crucial reasons in terms of higher product availabilities for international production. The same economic factors that have led to the establishment of bigger national markets in contrast to earlier regional and local markets would prevail for the still wider market possibilities that exist as national barriers are lowered or withdrawn.

We do not have precise figures on the extent to which actual international investment trends have led to the establishment of an internationalized producing and marketing system in the world. But our indicators are good enough to demonstrate emphatically that American entrepreneurs are involved in production activities abroad that result in well over $200 billion a year in sales. In the same spirit of internationalizing our perspectives, we can note here that something like a tenth of the production in geographic United States is to be associated with foreigners' investment activities. Both of these estimates of international activity are based on U.S. figures. Not covered are the investing and producing activities of other countries in foreign areas other than the United States. For these the available information is very sketchy. Nonetheless, an order of magnitude can be inferred on the basis of general considerations such as achieved levels of GNP, trade, and aggregate scraps of information on investment. I think $150 billion would be a minimal guess for this category of other (foreign) international production. Taken altogether—that is, U.S. producing activities abroad, foreigners' here, and foreigners' in other foreign countries—we get an order of magnitude of $450 billion. This figure does not take into account the product of Communist countries producing operations abroad, a figure which though presumably very limited at present may well grow.

U.S. policy for its international activities has fallen far behind the world that these activities have done so much to create. By far the most important economic fact of this generation is the rapid rise of international production.

As a basic foundational fact, what we are wanting here is a figure for a gross world product (GWP). This lack is not fatal; we can make aggregate national product figures serve the purpose. But the lack illustrates the interesting point that when we need to be considering the consequences of operating an emergent world economy on the basis of national policy perspectives, we are driven to draw a picture of those activities from figures rooted in national rather than world perspective.

A world production figure can be approximated as follows:

	Billions of dollars
U. S. GNP	$1,000
Rest of industrial "West"	1,000
Russia, Eastern Europe, and China	650
Less developed countries	350
Total	3,000

Sources: These order-of-magnitude estimates have been elicited from information on national GNP or per capita production, as provided for different areas by U.S. Department of Commerce, The International Bank, the United Nations' *Yearbook of National Accounts,* O.E.C.D. National Accounts, and Joint Economic Committee's *Soviet Economic Performance.*

The figure of $450 billion, representing international production, when read against the aggregate GWP level of about $3,000 billion, reveals that this internationalized component of aggregate world production amounts to a sixth of all activity. I think it may be accepted that at this level of relative importance internationalized activities suggest not just a special area of overlap among national economies but rather the solid underpinning of an emergent world economy.

BROAD POLICY IMPLICATIONS

As I see it there are two broad policy implications for us in this picture of world production:

1. The primary international economic interest of the United States is in

the correct international allocation of resources. What it does is to translate to the world economy the key features of competitiveness and efficiency that guide our national development. As a matter of economics, it should be noted that the production gains obtained from better allocation of resources take the place formerly held by the law of comparative advantage, i.e., national specialization, as the rationale of the gains from international trade.

2. The internationalization of production has been concentrated in the industrialized market economies. How to achieve comparably productive relations with the other third of the world, which clearly has not yet been integrated in the world economy, is a major problem, economic and political, for our future policy.

In regard to the first of these—the United States' interest in international production—the nation's primary interest and probably the only tenable basis for policy is in achieving the most productive world usage of . resources. This objective will doubtless raise many intricate issues, particularly in a world whose economic integration appears to be running distinctly ahead of its political integration. Only international perspectives are valid in a world in which the factors of production move competitively to their ever more effective uses; yet these perspectives must nonetheless be read and implemented from the limited vantage points of national governments.

The economic corollaries of the principle of the international optimizing of resource uses are exacting. Wherever resources are used in a less productive and therefore more costly way than they could be in an alternative use elsewhere, real product is sacrificed. Worse, the less efficient use cannot survive the effective range of international competition.

At the moment, we are preoccupied with some of the special international problems which have arisen in selected industries. Our sense of our long run interest gets obscured in our concern either to shore up the faulty competitive position of a given industry or to offset the comparable shoring-up actions of others.

These hearings as I understand it are designed to restore the sweep of at least a decade to our policy deliberations. With the steadily growing consolidation of production in the world as a spatial context and the basic time-accounting in terms of a decade, I think it is not open to any country—not even to this one with its incomparably variegated and developed market—to validate any use of resources, that is of manpower, machines, technique, and management, less efficient than elsewhere obtainable. As a practical matter, it is doubtful that any area of national economic life can be effectively protected against the competitive power of greater efficiency. If this were not so, the prospect for our further growth and that of other countries would be unpromising. This is the inexorable benefit, hard though its terms from time to time may be, of competition. And we have not allowed ourselves to dissipate this benefit in our national development.

For the United States the achievement of adequate perspective and conviction for the next decade of international development should come readily out of our experience with the successful merging of regional interests in a pattern of overall national development. The nature of this development and its eventuation were happily foreseen in the constitutional provision of an Interstate Commerce Clause. At least as confirmed in the nation's growing experience, the economic advantages of free movement of goods and materials and capital were seen to outweigh any local gains from interrupting that freedom of movement.

Unfortunately, on the international front we do not have that sort of constitutional assurance nor do we have the same sense of community. But we have it incipiently perhaps in the seemingly hard-won principles of international cooperation that have been in the course of building over the years since World War II. The General Agreement on Tariffs and Trade was initially a limited international treaty on trading principles preserved from the wreckage of the proposed International Trade Organization nations were unable to agree upon in 1945. The GATT carries great authority with us and with all its members, unquestionably beyond anything originally intended. Perhaps even more dramatic has been the high degree of monetary cooperation achieved in and beyond the International Monetary Fund— more dramatic because of the extreme sensitivity of sovereign states to sharing with others any degree of monetary jurisdiction.

What is called for now by our real long range economic interest is unqualified support of all international initiatives that extend rather than limit the freedom of movement of goods and capital. This policy we should approach with the assurance that when given resource commitments are challenged by lower cost operations elsewhere, this is merely the economic verdict that a better use exists here for the resources in question. It is our task to find that use.

I do not want to gloss over the truly difficult problems created by the product of apparently substandard competitors. Our national notions of allowable competition have been forged in a long struggle to incorporate concepts of decent living standards and working conditions into production. In the case of the less developed countries the desperate character of their needs can virtually be defined in terms of their failure to achieve comparable standards. The effect of international competition can and should be in the direction of making decent standards prevail. This sort of problem, very analogous to problems of fair competition within the nation, is probably among the most difficult to be resolved if a satisfactorily working world economy and its enormous productive benefits are to prevail. Difficult though the problems are, there seems to be no reason to assume that they are beyond the same means of solution that have proved effective nationally, solutions in which labor unions and social legislation have been the key elements. It should be mentioned that the free movement of goods and capital is structurally essential to the effectiveness of an economy, and as in the case of our country fair labor standards must be achieved without sacrificing the freedom essential to productivity.

In this same sense the context of a world economy suggests that the key issues for the future are likely to echo those that have proved crucial in large national economies. Here again our own history I think is a good guide and finds considerable corroboration in the experience of other developed countries. In addition to the key problem of fair labor standards, three other areas that are predictably important are: (1) the harnessing of excessive bigness and influence of companies (international antitrust); (2) the internationalizing of responsibility for monetary and credit policy (an international Federal Reserve); and (3) international tax policy. Progress in these areas is familiarly a contest between international experience and national habit and the issues will not be easily or quickly disposed of. But our international experience in each of them is growing rapidly, and I think it is far easier to be hopeful of a satisfactory outcome now than it was 25 years ago when we first faced the urgency of international solutions to the problems which had previously been played close to the national chest, so to speak.

The other of the two broad policy areas mentioned before has to do with our relations with the less developed countries and the centrally planned ones. In this overview of policy it is not possible to do justice to the host of problems that make up the package we identify as relations with the less developed countries or the intricacies of political and security problems that override our economic relations with the Communist countries. Neither of these big areas, which account for about a third of the world's output, can be excluded from the concept of an emergent world economy. Yet in neither case has the interplay of local institutions yielded a pattern of dynamic production so dramatically characteristic of the economic relations among the countries of the other two-thirds of the producing world.

In the case of the less developed countries, it should also be kept in mind that in terms of output alone international activities loom very large in the total production picture—perhaps $150 billion, or well over a third of the total $350 billion aggregate GNPs. This is a product picture in which extractive industries play a large part on the international side. In short, the LDCs constitute an area in which international activity has played a long traditional and very specialized role.

The recalcitrance of the development problem in the face of a long history of intensive relations with the more developed West suggests that the emphasis in the period ahead should be on the possibilities of new departures with new cooperative institutions that bring together the entrepreneurial skills of the international community and the developmental responsibilities of the local communities. As for the United States, its position as the most developed country and as the chief international banker of the world gives it a crucial role in the process of maintaining a net flow of investment resources adequate to bring the LDCs into a more dynamic relationship with the developed world. All studies appear to indicate that their developmental potential is consistent with that more dynamic result.

Just a word more on perspectives. In the context of the entire output of the world today, the United States, at $1,000 billion, represents about a third. This fraction is more than just a manner of showing the level of U.S. production; it expresses that production in relation to the entity it is part of. The clear implication of the international production trends we have looked at is that United States production is a part of world production. We have seen that a tenth of this U. S. production of $1,000 billion is directly to be associated with the investment of foreigners, and, similarly, about a tenth of the $2,000 billion produced outside the U.S. is to be directly associated with American investment in producing activites. But beyond these designations of product as "internationalized," our growing knowledge of the methods of international companies gives a clear sense of the internationality of the whole process.

Beyond sheer size, the international sector of world production is a very dynamic one, growing steadily at an annual rate of close to 10 percent —a pace almost double the basic economic growth rates we are familiar with in the various national economies. The implication of these rates of growth is that world production continues to be internationalized at a fairly brisk pace. Projections of the rate suggest that within a generation a majority of production will have been internationalized. Moreover if the dynamism of the international sector can be maintained, it will, as it grows, exert a more and more powerful influence on general growth rates, putting within reach fairly hopeful answers to both the capital and consumption requirements of the world's rapidly growing population.

This is all subject to a big IF—we all have reservations to make whenever the game of growth rates is being played. If only the right things are produced, if only reasonably equitable distribution is achieved—and, above all, if international politics do not force an economic fragmentation of the world.

Value Of U.S. Investments Abroad and Foreign Investment in the United States, 1959-69
(In billions of dollars)

	1950	1960	1964	1965	1966	1967	1968	1969 estimate
U.S. assets (investments abroad), total	31.5	68.0	99.1	106.3	111.8	122.7	135.3	143.4
Direct investment (book value—mainly subsidiaries of U.S. companies)	11.8	31.9	44.4	49.5	54.7	59.5	64.8	69.8
Other long-term private (market value—mainly portfolio; including investments where U.S. equity is less than 10 percent)	5.7	12.6	20.5	21.6	21.0	22.2	24.2	24.1
Total long-term private (with yields typically above 10 percent)	17.5	44.4	64.9	71.0	75.7	81.7	88.9	93.9
Short-term private	1.5	5.0	10.9	10.2	10.6	11.9	13.0	13.6
Total private	19.0	49.4	75.8	81.2	86.3	93.6	101.9	107.5
Government short-term (including monetary)	1.7	4.4	4.5	4.8	4.5	5.4	7.4	7.6
Other government (f.e. Eximbank, IBRD)	10.8	14.1	18.8	20.3	21.0	23.6	25.9	28.2
Total government	12.5	18.5	23.3	25.1	25.5	29.0	33.3	35.8
U.S. liabilities (foreign in United States), total	17.7	41.2	56.9	58.7	60.4	69.7	81.1	91.2
Direct investment	3.4	6.9	8.4	8.8	9.0	9.9	10.8	12.1
Other long-term	4.6	11.5	16.6	17.6	18.0	22.1	29.5	29.8
Total long-term	8.0	18.4	25.0	26.4	27.0	32.0	40.3	41.9
Private short-term	6.5	12.0	17.5	18.2	20.8	23.0	27.0	37.5
Government short-term	3.1	10.8	14.4	14.2	12.6	14.8	13.9	11.8
Total short-term	9.7	22.8	31.9	32.4	33.4	37.8	40.9	49.3
U.S. creditor position (assets-liabilities)	13.8	26.8	42.2	47.6	51.4	53.0	54.2	52.2

Sources: U.S. Department of Commerce, Survey of Current Business, various issues; Federal Reserve Board of Governors, Federal Reserve Bulletin, April 1970; U.S. Council of the International Chamber of Commerce.

These and doubtless many other "ifs" are all relevant. But I would say the most important one, and one directly within the political capability of the United States, is *if* the United States follows an economic policy that is impeccably international.

I think the country has reached the point in its international orientation where such a policy is in its best national interest regardless of what other countries do. This is reminiscent of the classic moment in economic history when in 1846 England repealed the Corn Laws, thereby removing protection of its agriculture and improving the international cost position of its industry. Special circumstances, including especially famine conditions, gave urgency to their decision, but it is taken historically as the moment when England recognized its fundamental industrial structure had become irreversibly international.

The United States' economy, though larger, more varied, and probably more selfsufficient than England's, is in a similarly irreversible position. One simple way to illustrate the point is to recall the growing extent to which foreign production includes the productive activities of Americans abroad; to discriminate against foreigners is to discriminate against ourselves. In a subtler but I think more meaningful sense the effective operation of the American economy depends on the world setting of which it is so large a part.

5
International Business: How Big is it? The Missing Measurements

Stefan H. Robock
Kenneth Simmonds

For many centuries, the dominant business relation between countries has been in the form of exports and imports by essentially national business firms. For the 150 years since David Ricardo, the framework for explaining trade patterns and for considering trade policies has been the doctrine of comparative advantage and the theory of international trade.

Over the last decade, there has been a growing awareness among businessmen and economists that traditional trade theory does not fully cover the current realities of business relations between countries and particularly the emergence of the multinational firm. The traditional concept of trade and its highly developed theoretical framework does not allow for and does not explain the flow of international private investment or the growth of international business operations. There has been no movement to discard economic trade theory. Instead, the impression has grown that something should probably be added to the existing theory to give a framework that explains international business in addition to trade.

The evidence is growing, however, that a little something extra may not be enough—that the international business child is bigger than the trade

Reprinted, with permission, from the May-June 1970 issue of the *Columbia Journal of World Business*. Copyright © 1970 by Stefan H. Robock and Kenneth Simmonds.

parent and still growing. While in any one year, the value of world exports (and thus imports) is much larger than the annual flows of new international direct investment, trade is no longer simply the result of national middlemen in one country interacting with importers in another. International firms have taken over, and there is every indication that international business is now the dominant factor in determining changes in the pattern of world exports as well as capital flows.

The failure of traditional trade theory to anticipate and explain the growing importance to the world economy of the internationalization of business operations stems partly from the way the question to be answered is posed. Trade theory asks the question "Why do nations trade?" This is the wrong question. Businessmen trade, and increasingly, they transfer goods across national boundaries for their own business activities without selling them outside their organization. The question should be "Why are goods and services transferred between nations?"

When this question is answered, it is clear that the decision-making unit is the business enterprise and not the nation. To be sure, decisions are heavily influenced by government actions. Nevertheless, international business decisions have become the focal point for explaining most of what happens internationally—not traditional trade concepts. Moreover, an explanation of international business actions provides an integrated account of the transfer of investment and working capital as well as the transfer of goods.

The business firm has a number of different ways open to it for supplying market demand in a foreign country. Trading or exporting is only one of the options. Depending on the circumstances, a business firm can supply foreign demand by licensing its product or processes to a foreign firm, or it may establish a production facility in a foreign market in lieu of exporting. Traditional trade theory ruled out these options by assuming that investment capital was not mobile between countries and by overlooking the importance of technological know-how, management and marketing skills as significant factors of production which could form the basis of comparative and competitive advantage.

The failure of traditional trade theory to explain today's world is also partly due to its complete omission of the whole idea behind the twentieth-century development of marketing. The Ricardian concept assumes that commodities being sold in an international market place are standard, basic, and transferable—wheat, cotton, and wine, for example. Today's firms, however, are continually adjusting many dimensions of their products against their assessments of customer wants—against the market. There is no simple standard commodity.

More and more firms are putting together marketing strategies against world markets, not just their home markets. Starting from an assessment of world markets, the decision maker tends to identify his market objectives and work backward to arrive at his location of production and distribution pattern. As the markets change, so does the pattern of activity of the international firm, and these patterns loom large in the changes in the international position of individual national economies.

THE STATISTICAL VACUUM

Even though trade theory did not anticipate the international business phenomenon, journalistic books such as Jean-Jacques Servan-Schreiber's *The American Challenge* and the intense concern in many countries about takeovers by U.S. international business firms are increasing our awareness that the phenomenon exists. But when we begin to look around for comprehensive factual information on the international business phenomenon, we find that only scattered bits and pieces are available.

There has been a dramatic change in the pattern of business between nations that can easily be seen by the man in the street; yet, without a theory to explain the development, statistical agencies have largely ignored it. The best data available are on the international private investment of U.S.-based firms, and it has become customary to use the U.S. data to illustrate what is occurring. Observers generally add a caveat that the growth of international business is not exclusively a U.S. phenomenon and point out that such European firms as Shell, Philips, and Unilever are also an important part of the new trend. But in a factual way, the over-all picture of the international business phenomenon including non-U.S.-based firms as well as U.S.-based firms has not yet become available, even in terms of only one dimension—the amount of investment involved.

There is no international agency with central responsibility and authority for the collection of data on the evolution of international business operations. The few efforts to accumulate data have been mainly tied to the orthodox trade and balance-of-payments theory. In the monetary field, the International Monetary Fund has been active in encouraging nations to improve their data collection on balance-of-payments and monetary activities, and such agencies as the United Nations, GATT, and UNCTAD have pressed for improved and expanded data on trade.

Whatever information is available on international business operations and investment, therefore, must come from the statistical programs of the different nations. These programs vary widely in coverage, in concepts and in quality of statistical information on international business. The United

States and the United Kingdom, whose business firms have two of the biggest
stakes in international business, have been expanding their statistical coverage of some aspects of international business. More limited data are available
on Canadian, Swedish, German, and Japanese firms. At the other extreme,
virtually nothing has been published on the total overseas investment of
French, Dutch, and Belgian firms.

WHY WE NEED TO KNOW

How much difference will it make and to whom whether businessmen
have a better picture of the international business phenomenon? The
monetary crises and the pressures for monetary reform are a case in point.
Much of the diagnosis of the international monetary problem blames "specu-
lators" for placing pressure on weak currencies and bringing about devaluations. Remedies are being proposed which are expected to protect the system
against the forces that emerge from the diagnosis. On the other hand, the
limited and fragmentary data available on international business suggest a
much different diagnosis. Remedies quite different from those being considered may be necessary for adjusting the monetary system to the changed
structure of the international economy.

Total foreign direct investment by international firms based in all
countries is estimated at more than $100 billion and is expanding annually
at from 10 percent to 20 percent. A large share of this investment is exposed
to the risk of foreign exchange devaluation, and the conservative treasurers
of international business firms are developing a great deal of sophistication
in forecasting the foreign exchange crises of countries in which their firms
are operating and in protecting their foreign assets from foreign exchange
risks. They may do this by using local borrowing instead of bringing in outside funds, by accelerating payments for goods and services from outside the
country, by advance repatriation of profits, and by a series of other actions
and inactions. With such a large foreign investment outstanding, prudent
and conservative financial strategies of the international business firms can
easily place a pressure equivalent to one or several billion dollars on a currency when it appears to be weakening. Thus the estimate that devaluation
might occur and the consequent business steps taken to protect against devaluation make the forecast a self-fulfilling prophecy.

It is not only international agencies that need data on international
business. How can any country develop an effective policy to influence exports and foreign exchange earnings without taking into account the decisions
of international business firms and their strategies? Yet policy makers are
only beginning to recognize the important role being played by international

business. If they want to include international business in their considerations, they will quickly discover that they have not been collecting the necessary factual information.

There are many other uses for figures on international transactions, and figures that best identify the underlying causes of change are likely to produce the best diagnoses and remedial actions. Certainly, there will be added imperfections when the world that officials see reported and against which they form their actions is harnessed to out-of-date theories that do not recognise major causes of change.

WHAT WE NEED TO KNOW

The objective of the party using the information will, of course, influence the information required. The business firm interested in allocating its efforts over global markets will require different data than the international agency concerned with the over-all stability of international transactions. National governments will want still different data for regulating the activities of international business within their individual economies. These differences in objectives, however, should not be taken too far in specifying the information any party would want. The information used by any party capable of influencing the situation will inevitably be significant to the other parties likely to be affected by the action taken.

A study of the different requirements for international business information, however, shows that they can be satisfied from a limited range of basic statistics covering operations (current accounts) and ownership (capital account) of international business. This is just as well because such statistics will have to be collected from individual firms by the governments holding jurisdiction over them, and they will have to be collected in a form that fits normal accounting procedures.

On the capital side the basic data required will be the size and source of ownership, financing and profits, and location of assets. On the operations side a minimum will be the size, location and destination of current production. For both capital and current information, comparison with past figures will disclose the pattern of change, and comparison with non-international business will disclose differences.

These are not new statistical concepts. Most countries have been collecting statistics on production, imports, exports, ownership, and investment flows. What is new, however, is the requirement to collect these statistics to show the underlying pattern of international business.

To produce these statistics it would be necessary to start with figures supplied by individual firms — the decision-making units. The following simple information would meet all these requirements if summed separately for international businesses and purely national businesses. Summation across countries for particular industries or product lines would then provide a picture of the international business pattern.

Operations	(Current a/c)

Payments to other countries—by country of source
  (foreign inputs)
    a. to affiliates
    b. to other
+ Local Purchases
+ Local Added Value
= Total Sales Value
— Sales to other countries—by country of destination
    a. to affiliates
    b. to other
= Local Sales Value

Ownership	(Capital a/c)	
Ownership	—by country of source	
Other Financing	—by country of source	
Assets	—by country of location	

A few examples of what might be shown by such information will make the proposal more concrete. A national government will be able to see wh . share of a local market is under the ˀontrol of international business, what proportion of these sales are represented by value added within the country and whether there is a significant difference between international firms and national firms in this respect. If the value added locally by international firms is small, the government might consider means of increasing the local components. On the export side, the proportion that exports represent of the ultimate sales of international firms may be deduced from international tabulations by industry. A country with a high level of exports by international firms may in fact discover that further local processing is possible. From a firm's viewpoint the same statistics would be valuable if governments were likely to use them. They would also form a basis for marketing strategy and monitoring competitors' actions. Comparison of the international pattern from year to year would disclose changes in location and destination of production by international competitors.

The simple breakdown of statistics into national and international classifications would thus provide the factual basis for many decisions. There are, however, many definitional difficulties involved in such a classification. This comes through clearly when examining the patchy efforts to date to provide data on international business.

PRIVATE DIRECT INVESTMENT

The most common way of measuring international business is to present figures on the size of international direct investment. Although definitions vary greatly from country to country,[1] direct investment generally covers only investment in which the business is controlled from abroad. The U.S. government defines this as an ownership interest in foreign enterprises of at least 10 percent. It is distinguished from portfolio investment, which brings an ownership interest but not managerial involvement. At the borderline, though, the classification becomes rather arbitrary.

Direct private investment is the easiest measure of international business activity to collect from available data. It is usually obtained by totaling annual flows of inbound investment plus profits and deducting annual outflows of capital and dividends. These cumulative totals of historical flows, however, do not show current values of assets owned. Furthermore, financing through borrowing or sale of equities locally may not be recorded. While this does not immediately appear in the traditional balance of payments, such borrowing can affect it and is an important measure of international expansion.

In describing the size of international business, one of the major limitations of direct foreign investment data is its tendency to focus only on the investments of international firms outside their home base country. If international business encompasses the global investment of multinational firms, then investments in the home country, as well as foreign investments, would have to be included. If Unilever in Holland and IBM in the United States have become truly international firms with global horizons and global strategies, the investment in their home country should be considered as international business investment. In the absence of a system for incorporating with an international agency, each business firm must have a nationality of incorporation. Yet, as a global business firm, it has its own worldwide goals and strategies, which may vary as much from those of the home country as from those of other countries.

If criteria could be established to determine when corporations become international rather than domestic firms, the resulting estimate of the total investment in international business would be many times that of total foreign direct investment and would probably represent a major share of the total business investment of the non-communist world. The best criteria would seem to be the horizons and strategy of the company rather than the share of assets or sales outside of the home country. The share of assets or sales criteria would be biased by the size of the home-country economy and market. An international firm based in the Netherlands would tend to have a large share of its assets or sales outside of the country because of the small size of the home-country economy. An international firm based in the United States, on the other hand, would probably have a relatively smaller share of assets or sales outside of the United States because the home-country market is so large.

Such an approach—to determine size and trends in the investment of globally oriented business firms including investment in the home base country—is not merely a matter of academic interest. To the extent that such firms are maximizing international goals, both home-country and foreign investment are relevant to the economic and foreign policies of nations. If XYZ company in the United States has a global strategy, it will protect its U.S. assets against a prospective devaluation of the U.S. dollar in the same way that it protects its French assets against a devaluation of the franc.

There are other omissions, too, from the usual figures for foreign direct investment. Aircraft used for international business operations are mobile pieces of capital equipment and are not classified as foreign investment. Another understatement results from special international business techniques such as those used by Japan. Japan has been intimately involved in the financing of minerals and petroleum projects in other countries, but it has made its funds available as loans to be repaid to the Japanese financing groups through the shipment of the raw materials. In recent years, Japanese firms have been financing foreign projects with loan-purchase contracts totaling billions of dollars. The Japanese pattern is not portfolio investment, and it is not direct investment in the sense that the Japanese acquire equity and have management participation. As a hybrid form, the pattern results in making capital available and in preempting a share of the output of the project. It does not fit the standard definitions, but it represents a significant form of international business activity that is not included in the usual statistics.

The foreign direct investment method of describing the size of international business has still another major limitation. It does not give appropriate recognition or emphasis to important international business activities that are not capital intensive. The international operations of hotel chains, of commercial banks and other financial institutions, of advertising, accounting and consulting firms, and many other types of commercial and service enterprises do not involve major capital investment and do not show up as an important element in the direct investment measurements of international business activities.

FOREIGN PRODUCTION

More significant than the value of investment is the size of international business operations. The traditional approach for measuring business between nations is through export and import data. Since trade is essentially between business firms (some of which may be government enterprises) rather than nations, it should be recognized that the business enterprise has options in the method it will use to supply demand in foreign markets.

The concept of "international production" has emerged to define a major option for the firm. As introduced by Judd Polk, it describes "the deliveries which one nation makes in the markets of another via the direct expedient of producing there locally, as distinguished from exporting to that market the product of facilities located at home."[2] When used in this way, however, the term is really a misnomer because it excludes home-country production of the international firms and activities that do not produce buyable export commodities. The concept of "foreign production" would appear to be more appropriate for describing the activities of international firms outside of their home country.

Foreign production, as defined here, is the phenomenon of a business enterprise in one country moving management, technology, personnel, and capital across national boundaries to produce goods and services in another country. The goods and services may be exclusively or largely for the local market. Foreign production may also result in exports back to the home country or to a third-country market. Foreign production can be of three general types: (1) market-oriented, (2) resource-oriented, and (3) production-efficiency-oriented. Each of these three types of foreign production is influenced by traditional industrial location economics.

In many situations, the business enterprise substitutes foreign production for exports because foreign market demand has grown sufficiently to justify the establishment of an economic size production unit. The motivation in such cases is frequently to achieve economies from proximity to the market. It is the same motivation as that involved in establishing regional production facilities within the U.S. market when demand in a region grows to a certain level. Foreign production can also replace exports when the foreign country imposes burdensome sanctions on imports through tariffs, taxation, or foreign-exchange constraints, and when prospective production costs in a foreign nation are significantly lower, either because of lower factor costs or special incentives.

Foreign production and exports can also be complementary. Business

Table 1: International Direct Investment by Country of Ownership: 1966
(billions of U.S. dollars)

COUNTRIES	TOTAL GNP		EXPORTS		INT'L DIRECT INVESTMENT	
	Amt.	%	Amt.	%	Amt.	%
United States	$ 743	46.5	$ 30.0	16.6	$54.6	57.4
European Economic Community (EEC)						
W. Germany	120	7.5	20.1	11.1	2.5	2.6
France	101	6.3	10.9	6.1	(5.0)	5.2
Italy	61	3.8	8.0	4.4	(1.6)	1.7
Netherlands	21	1.3	6.8	3.8	(4.2)	4.4
Belgium-Luxembourg	19	1.2	6.8	3.8	(1.2)	1.3
EEC TOTAL	322	20.1	52.6	29.2	14.5	15.2
European Free Trade Association (EFTA)						
United Kingdom	105	6.6	14.3	7.9	(16.0)	16.7
Sweden	21	1.3	4.3	2.4	0.9*	1.0
Switzerland	15	.9	3.3	1.8	(4.0)	4.2
Denmark	11	.7	2.4	1.3	n.a.	—
Austria	10	.6	1.7	.9	n.a.	—
Norway	8	.5	1.6	.9	n.a.	—
Portugal	4	.3	0.6	.3	n.a.	—
EFTA TOTAL	174	10.9	28.2	15.5	20.9	21.9
Japan	100	6.3	9.8	5.4	1.2	1.3
Canada	38	2.4	9.6	5.3	3.7	4.0
Australia	20	1.3	3.2	1.8	0.2	.2
TOTAL	158	10.0	22.6	12.5	5.1	5.5
(Other Non-Communist Countries)						
Petroleum Exporting	—	—	11.7	6.4	n.a.	—
Other	—	—	35.9	19.8	n.a.	—
TOTAL	200	12.5	47.6	26.2	n.a.	—
WORLD TOTAL:	$1,597	100.0%	$181.0	100.0%	$95.2	100%
(Non-Communist Countries)						

Note: Data in parentheses are estimates.
* 1965 figure

Sources: Total GNP: *Yearbook of National Accounts Statistics 1967,* United Nations, New York, 1968.
Exports: *Statistical Yearbook,* United Nations, 1967.

firms with a global strategy may achieve economies of scale from specialization by producing specific components in one foreign plant and supplying all other plants around the world from the output of this plant. Thus the movement of goods across national boundaries becomes foreign trade and exports even though the goods are only being transferred from one unit of the firm to another unit of the same firm. In some corporations, inter-company foreign exports occur as a result of a vertical logistics strategy for locating stages of production on a global basis. This is true of most international petroleum firms.

A large and growing share of world exports and changes in them are thus accounted for by internal product movements of the international company. The significance of this development is beginning to be noted by national governments as they attempt to formulate trade and tariff policies to achieve national balance-of-payments objectives. Patterns of many types of exports (particularly manufactures), which are assiduously analyzed and projected by such international agencies as UNCTAD, cannot provide any realistic insights into future export possibilities without taking into account trends in foreign production and the strategies of the global firms.

The transfer of goods across national boundaries, however, is only one component of the international business sector. International business activity also includes transportation, tourism, communications, private finance, services, and the sale of technology. An awareness of the size and structure of business activities being operated on the basis of international business criteria would have to include the full range of inter-nation business activities.

For some purposes, a measurement of value added would be even more appropriate than measurements of either operations or production. The value added within the national boundaries excluding the import content is of great

International Direct Investment: Australia—*Annual Bulletin of Overseas Investment,* 1966-67 Commonwealth Bureau of Census Statistics; Belgium-Luxembourg estimate based on inflows and OECD data on investments in LDC's; Canada—*Quarterly Estimates of the Canadian Balance of International Payments, Third Quarter, 1968,* Dominion Bureau of Statistics; French estimate based on OECD, DAC (68) 14, 23 April 1968 Table 1, p. 11, which shows $3.8 billion direct investment by France in the Less Developed Countries (LDC's) from 1956-66 plus another $1.2 billion invested in the U.S., EEC and other OECD countries from 1962 through 1966, as reported by the French Ministère de L'Economie et des Finances News Release No. 1045, Feb. 29, 1968, French Information Service, N.Y.; *Business Week,* Nov. 30, 1968 estimates French investment at $9 billion; Italian data are cumulative total of direct investment outflows 1958-1966 from Banca D'Italia Report for 1966 and for earlier years from Ufficio dei Cambi as reported in *European Financing of Latin American Development,* Inter-American Development Bank, Washington, D.C. (no date), p. 203; Japan—Ministry of International Trade and Industry; Netherland estimate based largely on inbound investment shown by receiving countries plus OECD estimate of flows to LDC's; Swedish data from Harald Lund, *Swedish Business Investment Abroad 1960-1965,* Federation of Swedish Industries, December 1967; Switzerland estimate from *EFTA Bulletin,* July-August 1969, p. 4; United Kingdom data from *Board of Trade Journal,* 26 January 1968 plus estimates of petroleum investment made from annual reports of Shell and British Petroleum. Banking and insurance investment are not included in official estimate because of "problem of definition"; United States data from *Survey of Current Business,* Oct. 1968; W. Germany data (does not include reinvested earnings) from Deutsche Bundesbank, *Monthly Report.*

significance to governments. Statistics on foreign operations would be misleading, for example, if they showed an increase while local added value was in fact decreasing. It is quite clear that the available data and the concepts used for their collection are most inadequate for the sorts of decisions needed to function in a world in which international business is so pervasive.

HOW BIG?

How much can be pieced together from available statistics? Can businessmen begin to answer the question: "How big is international business?" In the world as a whole, the book value of direct foreign private investment totaled a minimum of $95 billion as of the end of 1966, as shown in Table 1.[3] The leading home base country was the United States with 57 percent of the total, followed by the United Kingdom with almost 17 percent. However, these countries publish the most complete information. If more complete data were available for the other countries, the U.S. and U.K. shares would be somewhat lower. Other important home countries for international business firms are France, Canada, the Netherlands, West Germany, Switzerland, Italy, Japan, and Sweden. Switzerland is a special case in the sense that many firms from other countries have been using Switzerland as a conduit through which investment outflows are channeled. Thus the data may reflect much more activity than that of truly Swiss firms.

U.S. firms are dominant in the international business field, but they do not monopolize the field. The fact that more than 40 percent of total direct investment is accounted for by non-U.S. firms may come as a surprise to some scholars, businessmen and government officials. In the case of non-communist world exports, the U.S. share of 17 percent of the total might be considered somewhat small since the United States has almost half of the non-communist world gross national product (GNP).

Although the $95 billion figure estimated for the book value of direct investment in 1966 represents the equivalent of the total GNP of a country like Japan or the United Kingdom, it is heavily understated in a number of ways. Book value has been cumulated on the basis of historical cost or values at the time the investment was made. Including the effects of appreciation in value of fixed assets and inflation, the book value figures would probably have to be increased by from 50 percent to 100 percent.

With adjustments for understatement of book values as well as exclusion of investments in transportation equipment and such hybrid investment patterns as the Japanese loan-purchase contracts, a more realistic estimate of total direct foreign investments would probably be at least $150 billion.

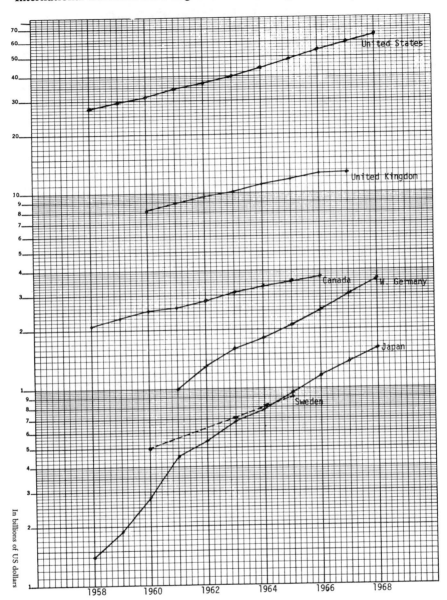

Figure 1: Growth Trends in International Direct Investment—Selected Countries

CHANGING INVESTMENT PATTERN

This picture of the international business role of different nations is only a snapshot as of one point in time. The static picture needs to be supplemented with data on trends. Data on export trends are available for most countries, but historical data on international direct investment are limited. The available information is shown in Figure 1 on a logarithmic scale, which accents growth rates rather than absolute levels.

The general picture since 1960 is that the two largest nations in international business—the United States and the United Kingdom—have not been expanding their foreign investment as fast as the other leading nations. While the United Kingdom has been lagging farthest behind, the fastest growth has come in investment from West Germany and Japan. They have recorded rapid rates of expansion although these are still computed on a small base. Furthermore, the data for West Germany do not include reinvested earnings, and the data for Japan do not include loan-purchase projects.

The trend data on international business investment must be used with caution. They suggest that the roles of Western European countries and Japan are expanding and that the present leading nations such as the United States, the United Kingdom, and Canada are losing some of their dominance. Of course, much of the rapid growth of investment by EEC countries has been within other EEC countries.

Some historical perspective adds support to the indication in the trend data that new national leadership in international business may be emerging. At the end of World War II, the international private investments of the United States, the United Kingdom, Canada, Sweden, and Switzerland remained relatively intact, except for investments in Eastern Europe and China. In contrast, Germany and Japan lost their overseas investments through wartime expropriation. Other European countries with significant foreign investments, mainly in their colonies, were not completely stripped of these investments as a result of the war, but they did lose a great deal through the independence movements in Africa and Asia.

For more than a decade after World War II, Germany and Japan concentrated on domestic reconstruction. As an aftermath of the war, investments by German and Japanese firms were not welcome in many countries. As a German observer has described the situation,

". . . German private investments abroad are minor as compared with Germany's position in the world economy.

"The reasons for Germany's small investments abroad are mainly to be found in the fact that in 1950 the German economy had to begin all over again and during its rehabilitation period had a great deal of home demand for capital and labor. In addition there are the cautious restraints due to the bitter experiences in the past of a twice repeated loss of German assets abroad and frequently not very inviting investment climate.

"Besides, many regions in the world are—partly owing to the former colonial powers' still dominating position—largely unknown to the German entrepreneurs so that for this reason the risk of investment appears to be too high to them."[4]

One might look at the patterns of different nations in international business in terms of a "stages-of-development" framework. Some nations such as the United States, the United Kingdom, and Canada had their international business takeoff several decades ago and are now reaching various degrees of maturity. Other nations have only recently reached the takeoff stage and are now in periods of rapid expansion.

The industry patterns of direct investment have also been changing. Available data suggest that the growth patterns since the end of World War II have progressed in two major phases.[5] The first extended until about 1957 and was characterized by the dominance of investment in petroleum and other raw material extraction projects. The United States, the United Kingdom, and the Netherlands invested heavily in petroleum projects in the Middle East. The United States also embarked upon new mining and petroleum projects in Canada and Latin America—principally Venezuela. The United Kingdom invested in Commonwealth countries in Asia and Oceania. Other European countries concentrated on Africa. During this period, direct investment in manufacturing was relatively small. The United States had a dominant position in the export of manufactures, and strict capital controls hindered investment flows between European countries.

A new phase in international business, which began about 1958, extends up to the present. It was characterized by a steep increase in direct investment in manufacturing and trade, directed increasingly toward Western Europe. The establishment of the EEC and EFTA greatly stimulated trade among the members of the groups and created incentives for outsiders to set up production facilities within the common market and free trade areas to avoid tariff discrimination and to take advantage of the rapid economic expansion in those markets. The comfortable export position of the United States was weakened following the recuperation and rapid expansion of manufacturing production in Western Europe and Japan.

In summary, direct foreign investment by firms of all nationalities appears to have been expanding over the last decade by at least 10 percent annually and more likely at a rate close to 15 percent annually. U.S. firms are still dominant in the field, accounting for slightly more than half of total investment, but Japan, West Germany and a few other European countries have recently begun to expand internationally at a faster rate than the average for U.S. firms. The emphasis in foreign direct investment has also shifted from raw material extraction to manufacturing.

Turning from the size of investment in international business to the size of their operations, the statistics are even fewer. While data on imports and exports are of the best quality of any international statistics, largely because of the pervasive practice of taxing trade, information on foreign production is scanty. As a result, the estimates that can be presented are highly speculative. Allowing for a wide range of error, they suggest that the phenomenon is massive in size and growing much more rapidly than exports.

The movement of goods across national boundaries as exports totaled $181 billion for the non-communist countries in 1966. Foreign production by international firms in the same year is estimated to have reached a level of about $150 billion (Table 2). The value of foreign production, in order of importance, includes manufacturing, petroleum production and refining, mining and smelting, agriculture, and the operation of public utilities.[6]

The value of foreign production is available for the manufacturing and mining operations of U.S. firms and for Swedish firms in all fields. The rest of the estimated total has been derived from national data on foreign direct investment using ratios of sales to book value as shown for U.S. business investment in foreign countries in a 1960 report of a special 1957 census of the U.S. Department of Commerce.[7] The ratios of sales to book value varied with the type of activity; manufacturing 2.2:1; petroleum 1.6:1; mining and smelting 1.0:1; agriculture, forestry, and fishing 1.3:1; and public utilities 0.6:1. Direct investment in trading offices, services, finance, hotels, and other nonproduction activities was not included in arriving at the foreign production estimate.

Most foreign production was sold within the markets of the nations in which the operations were located. But some of the value of foreign production represented components or raw materials brought in from outside of the producing country and thus were already included as some other country's exports. Some of the foreign production was exported, thus resulting in another overlap with the export data.

The extent to which foreign production goes into international trade varies greatly with the type of activity. A recent study of the foreign production of Swedish companies—mainly manufacturing—shows that 85 percent of sales was in local markets and 15 percent was exported.[8] Data for

Table 2: Product Categories of World Exports and Foreign Production

World Exports (1) (f.o.b.)			Foreign Production	
	1955	1966		1966
Food, live animals, etc.	20%	16%	Agriculture, forestry, fishing	2%
Raw materials, excluding fuels	19%	13%		
Fuels, etc.	11%	10%	Mining and smelting	5%
Manufactured goods	50%	61%	Petroleum	26%
Chemicals	(5%)	(7%)	Manufacturing	65%
Machinery, transportation equip.	(19%)	(26%)		
Other manufacturers	(26%)	(28%)	Other	2%
Total	100%	100%		
Total (billions of US$)	$93	$203		100%
				$150

1 Excludes Mainland China, Mongolia, North Korea, North Vietnam, trade between East and West Germany.

Source: Export data from *Monthly Bulletin of Statistics,* United Nations. Foreign production estimates based on same sources as for investment data described in footnotes to Table 1.

U.S. firms as of 1965 indicated that 82 percent of the sales of manufacturing plants was local and 18 percent entered into international trade.[9] In some cases, foreign manufacturing plants are established to supply the home-country market, and in other situations the foreign plants may be a base for exporting to third-country markets. But data on these important patterns are not available.

A much smaller share of the foreign production of petroleum is for local markets. The 1957 special U.S. census does not separate production and refining, showing combined local sales to be 65 percent of the total. A breakdown between production and refining would undoubtedly show that the bulk of petroleum is exported from the producing area and that most refining output is sold in local markets. In the case of mining and smelting operations, U.S. data show that in 1965 only 23 percent of the output went to local markets, 36 percent was exported to the United States, and 41 percent exported to other countries.[10]

A minimum of $45 billion overlap between exports and foreign production can be estimated, and it is probable that a large share of the overlap is movements across national boundaries among units of the same international company.

The joining of the concepts and data of exports and foreign production by international firms begins to outline a real world of inter-nation sales of goods that is far different and even more complex than the obsolete image that now underlies much, if not most, of the national decision making on trade policies. The size of sales by business firms outside their home country is much larger than that indicated by traditional export data. For the non-communist countries, foreign markets absorbed goods valued at between $250 and $300 billion in 1966, some of which were supplied by exports and some by foreign production—probably about half and half depending on how one handles the overlap.

Foreign production is growing much faster than exports. A large share of exports are movements between units of international firms across national boundaries. When governments begin to collect the necessary information, they will discover different logistics strategies for firms of different nationalities and in different industries. Within the automobile industry, the European and Japanese firms are supplying the U.S. market through exports whereas the U.S. automobile companies are primarily engaged in foreign production to supply non-U.S. markets. At the other extreme, Japanese firms are supplying foreign demand mainly through home-country manufacturing and then exporting. The foreign production activities financed or conducted by the Japanese are primarily directed toward supplying raw materials and manufacturing inputs for home-country production.

Still another aspect of the foreign production-export inter-relationship involves the product composition of exports and foreign production (Table 2). Manufactured goods are growing as a share of exports, and manufacturing activity appears to offer the greatest opportunities for expansion for international business firms. Thus an ever-increasing share of the major growth area in exports will become influenced by international business.

The most dramatic indication of the size of international business comes when the international production concept is used to show a total for international operations. This would include foreign production, home operations of international firms and intangible services as well as production of goods.

This concept gains its significance from the proposition that firms in the international category are likely to pursue an international strategy that might run contrary to the national objectives of even their home country. Performance objectives would be likely to lead to concentration on the largest and fastest growing markets, production in cost-minimizing locations, and avoidance of weakening currencies. If a large proportion of world business is able to adjust its affairs in such ways even to a small extent, international business will largely determine the international economic situation.

The basis used for classifying business as international will, of course, determine the size of the estimate. As a most imprecise basis, but to provide a rough gauge of the size of international operations, "international" may be specified as representing all firms with a minimum of 15 percent of either sales or production outside their home country. On this basis, international business would account for about $700 billion of revenues per annum. That is roughly equivalent to 40 percent of the non-communist world gross national product (1966 figures). Of course, GNP is estimated on a value-added basis and cannot be compared directly to revenues.

The top 100 U.S. companies ranked by revenue in 1968 had revenues of nearly $300 billion.[11] A majority of these firms would be classed as international. Among the next 400, with combined revenues of $225 billion, there were also many international firms. The 500 largest U.S. industrial firms, which derive more than 50 percent of their revenue from manufacturing and/or mining, had total revenues in 1968 of $405 billion.[12] Of the top 200 corporations outside the United States, a majority would also be international. Their combined revenues for 1968 were recorded at $174 billion.[13]

These estimates would automatically include international revenues for services, thus getting away from the myopic concentration on manufacturing fostered by a theory aimed at commodities. In fact, internationalism is very widespread in non-manufacturing. Commercial banking on an international scale has long engaged the interest of large British and U.S. banks. Many insurance companies have extensive international activities in direct insurance underwriting and in reinsurance. Numerous construction firms of many nationalities operate internationally. Television companies sell re-runs of their home-country productions to foreign countries. Hotel and motel chains and retail and wholesale firms have expanded their activities across national boundaries. Transportation and tourism are well entrenched as international activities. The sale of technology through licensing and royalty agreements has become a substantial source of financial flows between nations.

Presently available data, generally collected without any sensitivity to the emergence of the international business phenomenon, still give us some startling clues to the radical change that has been occurring in the structure of the world economy.

These figures are only rough estimates. They do not serve to answer the specific policy questions of international agencies, governments or the international businesses themselves. A determined effort to collect figures that depict what is really happening in the world today is needed, and it is needed with some urgency.

A prerequisite for this effort, though, would be a much wider realization that today's world no longer fits the theoretically assumed image of how imports and exports work. Countries do not export, firms do. It is little use to couch policy making on a fiction.

NOTES

1. The problem of varying national definitions of direct investment is beginning to receive attention. See *Problems of Measuring Private Capital Flows to Less Developed Countries,* Organization for Economic Cooperation and Development, Paris, 25 November 1968 (mimeo); *Rapport De La Commission Au Conseil concernant les travaux du "Groupe d'experts nationaux en statistiques de mouvements de capitaux,"* Commission Des Communautes Européennes, Brussels, 30 January 1969.

2. Joint Economic Committee, Congress of the United States, *Issues and Objectives of U.S. Foreign Trade Policy,* Washington: U.S. Government Printing Office, 1967.

3. The OECD has estimated overseas direct investments as of the end of 1966 at $89.6 billion. See *Private Direct Investment in Less Developed Countries: Capital Flows, Assets and Income,* DAC (68) 14 (Paris: OECD Mimeo, 1968). Another estimate indicates the aggregate outstanding investment was a minimum of $85 billion as of 1964. See Jack N. Behrman, *Some Patterns in the Rise of Multinational Enterprise* (Chapel Hill: The University of North Carolina Graduate School of Business Administration Research Report 18, March 1969). Behrman concludes, however, that the total was probably closer to $100 billion after adjusting for deficiencies in the available data. For 1968, he estimates outstanding direct investment "would be on the order of $125 billion."

4. Dr. Wolf Dieter Lindner, "Investment Climate and Private Investments," *Intereconomics,* No. 4 (1968).

5. "International Direct Investment by Private Enterprise in Western Europe and North America," *Economic Bulletin for Europe,* Part B—Special Studies, United Nations (November 1967).

6. In his statement before the Joint Economic Committee referred to in Note 2, Judd Polk estimates the "product associated with internationally owned and operated plants" at "perhaps $250 billion" and the share accounted for by U.S. firms to be $150 billion. Our estimate is lower because we use a lower investment estimate both for the United States and the rest of the world and a lower ratio of sales to book value of investment. In calculating the value of production we have omitted investments in the "trade" and "other" categories wherever possible. "Trade" includes wholesale trade, retail trade, and purchasing. "Other" generally includes finance and insurance, real estate, hotels, advertising agencies, motion pictures, contract construction, and other service fields. In the case of the United States, the result is that the 1966 estimate of direct investment is reduced from $55 billion to $45 billion. We have also omitted the $50 billion of product that Polk includes as associated with U.S. assets abroad other than direct investment. (See "The New World Economy," *Columbia Journal of World Business,* Jan.-Feb. 1968.) Polk uses a 2:1 sales to investment ratio, apparently based on manufacturing. We have varied the sales to book-value ratio with the type of activity.

7. U.S. Department of Commerce, *U.S. Business Investment in Foreign Countries* (1960).

8. Harald Lund, *Svenska Foretags Investeringer i Utlandet* (Stockholm: Industriforbundets Forlag, 1967).
9. "Sales of Foreign Affiliates of U.S. Firms in 1965," *Survey of Current Business* (November 1966).
10. *Ibid.*
11. *Forbes,* May 15, 1969.
12. *Fortune,* May 15, 1969.
13. *Fortune* (August 1969).

Part II:
The Functions:
A Managerial Approach

Chapter Two:
Organizational Structure and Management

6

Organizational Structure and the Multinational Strategy

Lawrence E. Fouraker
John M. Stopford

One of the landmark studies in the field of business administration is *Strategy and Structure* by A. D. Chandler, Jr. A central proposition in Chandler's book is that the strategy of diversification led to organizational problems and eventually to the emergence of a new corporate structure. The purpose of this article is to see if Chandler's proposition is useful in examining recent organizational changes in the international field.[1]

International business activity is a form of diversification that has become increasingly important for many large American companies in the last two decades. In some sense, this development may be considered a replication against which Chandler's thesis may be tested. That is, this new form of diversification should be dominated by firms with experience in managing diversified activities. Furthermore, the new diversification should lead to new problems of organization and, finally, to different structural accommodations.

MODEL

Chandler states: "Historically, the executives administering American

Reprinted, with permission, from the *Administrative Science Quarterly* (June 1968), pp. 47-64.

industrial enterprises have followed a recognizable pattern in the acquisition and use of resources."[2] This process consists of a developmental transition through several distinct phases: "Thus four phases or chapters can be discerned in the history of the large American industrial enterprise: the initial expansion and accumulation of resources; the rationalization of the use of resources; the expansion into new markets and lines to help assure the continuing full use of resources; and finally the development of a new structure to make possible continuing effective mobilization of resources to meet both changing short-term market demands and long-term market trends."[3] These four phases produced three fairly distinct organizational structures:

Type I. The organization is an extension of the interests, abilities, and limitations of its chief executive, who is often the creator and owner of the organization. This structure is generally limited to a single product line and often emphasizes one function (e.g., production) more than others. It is also constrained by the sequential decision-making pattern that characterizes a single problem solver. This is the entrepreneurial business organization, which serves as a building block for most economic models.

Type II. This is the vertically integrated, functionally coordinated enterprise. Generally such an organization continues to be limited to one or a few related product lines. The emphasis is on rational use of resources, efficiency, and coordination of functional activities.

Yet the dominant centralized structure had one basic weakness. A very few men were still entrusted with a great number of complex decisions. The executives in the central office were usually the president with one or two assistants, sometimes the chairman of the board, and the vice presidents who headed the various departments. The latter were often too busy with the administration of the particular function to devote much time to the affairs of the enterprise as a whole. Their training proved a still more serious defect. Because these administrators had spent most of their business careers within a single functional activity, they had little experience or interest in understanding the needs and problems of other departments or of the corporation as a whole.[4]

The Type II structure might be enormously efficient in the production of some classes of products, but did not produce professional management.

Type III. The accumulation of resources by a successful Type II firm often led to diversification of product lines, (1) to avoid risk, (2) to ensure continuation of the organization after the major product had completed its life cycle, or (3) to sell outside the company by some divisions due to integrated production requiring plant facilities of varying capacities at different stages.

The strategy of product diversification caused many administrative problems. The functional approach of the Type II firm required that the senior marketing executive coordinate the marketing activities for all the organization's products, even though they might utilize different forms of distribution, advertising, and sales effort. The senior production officer was confronted with similar complexity. These functional responsibilities could be delegated to subordinates, most appropriately on the basis of product assignments; but profit contribution of functional specialists could not be measured against performance, so control and comparison became even more difficult. The unavoidable problems of conflict and coordination at the lowest levels of the organization would frequently have to be passed up to the highest functional levels for adjudication. And some operating issues could not be settled there, but would have to reach the office of the chief executive.

Attempts to add product lines in such an environment could lead to organizational stasis because of the limited ability of the chief executive's office to cope with the new demands on its decision-making capacity. Management would then be confronted with a choice: either abandon the strategy of product diversification, or abandon the functional form of organization.

Many organizations chose structural reorganization. This reorganization took the form of a multidivisional product structure with many functional responsibilities delegated to the division general managers. The divisions were separated on a product basis and were relatively autonomous. Generally each division served as a profit center for control purposes; coordination and control from the central office was concentrated on finance and some general staff functions such as planning and research.

"Besides allocating decision making more effectively and assuring more precise communication and control, the new structure proved to have another advantage over the functionally departmentalized organization. It provided a place to train and test general executives."[5] This ability to produce general managers allowed the Type III organization to operate successfully in unrelated product areas.

With great diversity of products, staff, technologies, and managerial talents, the Type III decentralized organization could move simultaneously to exploit opportunities in a variety of independent areas. The management innovation of moving from a Type II structure to Type III began, in the United States, in the 1920's. As is often the case,[6] the Type III structure developed independently in several organizations; du Pont, General Motors, Standard Oil, and Sears are given special attention by Chandler. Many other organizations imitated these pioneers, with most of the transitions being delayed by the depression of the 1930's and World War II, so that many companies undertook the transition in both strategy and structure in the 1950's and 1960's.

In the Type III organization, new products can be added, or old ones dropped, with only marginal effect on the organization. Indeed, given the prospect of finite life expectancy for any commercial product, the management is committed to a strategy of research and development as a means of ensuring the continued life of the organization. This sort of activity is compatible with the diversity and independence of parts in a Type III organization. "In fact, the systematizing of strategic decisions through the building of a general office and the routinizing of product development by the formation of a research department have, in a sense, institutionalized this strategy of diversification."[7]

Since the Type III organization makes it possible to manage a variety of heterogeneous activities, it also makes it feasible for research and development activity to be incorporated in the structure. Burns and Stalker, in a study of electronic firms in England and Scotland, found that certain types of business organizations did not develop research and development departments; such activity could not normally be absorbed by their "mechanistic" structures, which closely resembled Chandler's Type II organizations.[8] The organizations that were successful in establishing research and development departments ("organic" structures) were described in terms that seem characteristic of Chandler's Type III. These results are reinforced by the field work of Lawrence and Lorsch.[9]

This connection between research and development, product innovation, and organizational structure is important for the thesis of this paper, because the innovative capacity may be an important source of competitive advantage in foreign markets. Vernon and others have argued that the United States tends to export products developed for the U.S. market that are not being produced abroad, and this monopoly position in world markets offsets high labor costs in the U.S.[10] Furthermore, at some point the organization will invest in plant and equipment abroad in order to protect its export market, particularly if that market has grown to a size that is consistent with the most efficient current productive techniques.

The result of this chain of arguments is that Type III organizations can be expected to dominate foreign direct investment. The initial structural response to this strategy of diversifying direct investment around the world is to establish an international division in the Type III organization. Such a division reports to one man. This focuses responsibility and control for foreign operations and economizes on the need for general managers with broad international experience (who are inevitably in short supply when the organization first expands its foreign operations).

The international division is at the same organizational level, and will tend to receive the same general treatment, as the product divisions. This same general treatment tends to create stresses that will make the international division a transient form. It is not a product division, but is rather less autonomous, for it depends more on the cooperation and assistance of the product divisions than they typically depend on each other. As a result, the product division manager is subjected to stresses and conflicts that are not always in the best interests of the organization. The product division manager, who is judged against domestic measures of performance, is therefore somewhat motivated to (1) fill his domestic orders before extending assistance to foreign markets; (2) assign his best employees to domestic tasks and shunt the others to the international division; (3) argue for a larger domestic share of the capital budget.

These are natural responses that may be quite costly if foreign markets are growing faster than domestic markets, which has often been the case in the postwar period. In many organizations, top management has responded to these lost opportunities in several ways. First, it has given product and functional managers more international experience and eventually more responsibility. Second, it has replaced the international division with some new organizational structure; for example, world-wide product divisions, world-partitioning geographic divisions, or some combination of these, perhaps retaining an international division for some purposes, or setting up a separate international company. Indeed some companies moved directly to these new structures, avoiding the problem of a conflict of interests between product divisions and the international division, and the possibility of a coalition of product divisions against the international division. This is most common where the vehicle for growth abroad has been merger with other organizations whose foreign interests are in different product lines.

Each of the possible alternative forms of the organization of international activities has distinct characteristics. The international division is the sole profit center for foreign operations, requiring only one general manager with international expertise. The manager of the international division and his staff become the repository of all the organization's international experience, causing problems of capital allocation, transfer pricing, and especially communication.

The world-wide product division structure avoids many of these problems by containing the areas of potential conflict within each division. The division manager is responsible for the profit performance of his product line throughout the world. This structure requires at least as many international general managers as there are product divisions operating abroad.

The geographic divisions partitioning the world also require an increased number of international general managers. The predominant characteristic is that the area divisions (of which the U.S.A. or North America is one) are headed by general managers of equal status in the structure. Each has the profit responsibility for an area, regardless of the product lines involved. Typically, this structure is associated with those organizations that have mature, standardized product lines for which marketing, rather than production or technology, is the critical variable.

The mixed structural form is a combination of two or all of the above forms, adapted to the particular needs of a firm. A food company diversifying into chemicals might retain its international division for all the food products and establish the chemical division with world-wide responsibilities.

The separate international company is usually a response to lack of success abroad or to an unwillingness on the part of top management to become more involved abroad. Typically, this move precedes the sale of all or part of the foreign operations. It should be noted that this response does not necessarily include the incorporation of the international division as a separate subsidiary, since such incorporation is normally used as a method of reducing taxes.

The structures that have been adopted to replace the international division may not be stable. As the foreign business grows and diversifies, further structural changes may be required. Operations within the U.S. require a balance between product and functional management, with area requirements relatively unimportant. However, once the organization operates abroad to a significant degree the benefits to be gained from both regional and product line control or coordination may become large. This has led a few organizations to adopt a "grid" structure, where product, area, and functional responsibilities are linked in what may be viewed as a three-dimensional organization structure. There are serious problems associated with this form, but the ability of an organization to learn to operate within such a structure may be the key to the maintenance of the flexibility of administration necessary for continued growth and prosperity abroad.

DATA

Chandler classifies the 70 largest American industrial companies in 1959 into three categories: (1) industries consisting of companies that tended to remain as Type II organizations: steel and nonferrous metal; (2) industries partially accepting the Type III structure: agricultural processing, oil, rubber, and mass merchandising; and (3) industries consisting of firms that had generally adopted the Type III structure: electrical, automobile (transportation), power machinery, and chemicals.

The last four industries have clearly played a prominent role in the economic process that we have been discussing. They are quite diversified, supporting Chandler's thesis that diversification leads to the adoption of the Type III structure.[11] They are leaders in research and development activity, supporting the Burns and Stalker propositions.[12] They are the source of most of the U.S. export strength, as indicated by Gruber and others.[13] And they are among the leaders in foreign direct investment in plant and equipment.

A crude measure of aggregate diversification is the number of manufacturing employees outside the primary industrial activity in which the firm has been classified. Of the 17 manufacturing industries of interest,[14] the five leaders are shown in Table 1. It should be noted that this is a measure of domestic diversification, and that Chandler's four industries are among the five leaders.

Table 1 also shows an aggregate measure of research and development activity provided by total employment figures for people placed in these categories by their employers. Chandler's Type III industries dominate the research and development activity of U.S. manufacturing establishments. The leading manufacturing contributors to the U.S. trade balance are also identified. Eight of the seventeen manufacturing industries had export surpluses on an industry basis; nine had deficits. Chandler's four represented 96.4 percent of the total export surplus by industry category of the U.S. in 1964. This is consistent with the Vernon position, as is the evidence that these same industries tend to follow their trade advantage with direct foreign investment as shown in Table 1.[15]

Table 1: Employment outside primary industry and in research and development; export surplus and direct foreign investment for major industries.

Industry (and SIC number)	Number of employees		Export surplus 1958–1964 (millions of dollars)†	Direct foreign investments 1959–1966 (millions of dollars)‡
	Outside primary industry 1958*	For research and development 1958*		
Transportation (37)	474,095	27,094	+493.6	4,870
Primary and fabricated metals (33-34)	342,284	—	—	1,962
Electrical (36)	265,473	36,305	+486.3	1,401
Machinery (35)	254,160	4,526	+2,063.0	2,698
Chemicals (28)	170,875	14,667	+752.7	4,130

*U.S. Bureau of the Census, *Enterprise Statistics 1958* (Washington, D.C.: Government Printing Office, 1963).

†Trade Relations Council of the U.S., *Employment, Output, and Foreign Trade of U.S. Manufacturing Industries, 1958-1964/65* (New York, 1966).

‡ U.S. Department of Commerce, *Survey of Current Business* (Washington, D.C.: Government Printing Office, various dates).

The evidence is summarized in Table 2, which relates the four industries Chandler identified as having generally accepted the Type III structure and the four activities under discussion. The numbers in the body of the table indicate the rank of the organizations in these activities among the 17 industries.

From these two tables, it seems evident that the American manufacturing company with extensive international interests is likely to be: (1) diversified in its domestic business activities; (2) Type III in organizational structure; (3) a leader in research and development; and (4) a major exporter from the U.S. These propositions can be investigated in greater detail by using relative measures and data on individual companies.

Table 2: Rank of Chandler Type III industries (out of 17) as to diversification, research and development, export surplus, and foreign investment.

	Chemical	Machinery	Electrical	Transportation
Diversification	5	4	3	1
Research and development	3	4	1	2
Export surplus	2	1	4	3
Foreign investment	2	3	5	1

Chandler distributed the 70 largest industrial companies (1959) in his three categories. Joan Curhan,[16] under the direction of Raymond Vernon, compiled a list of 170 companies that were in the 1964 or the 1965 *Fortune*[17] classifications and that had manufacturing subsidiaries in six or more foreign countries at the end of 1963 where the parent company owned 25 percent or more of the subsidiaries. The Curhan list represents most of the American-controlled manufacturing activity abroad.

Comparison of the Chandler and the Curhan lists shows that only 35 percent of Chandler's first group (predominantly Type II organizations) were also on the Curhan list. The only steel company on both lists was the most decentralized of the steel companies. In Chandler's mixed second group, 45 percent of the companies were also on the Curhan list (54 percent if merchandising was excluded from Chandler's group, as it was from the Curhan list). Chandler's third group of companies were all on the Curhan list except for one company which had gone out of existence through merger.

The mechanism by which this relationship is maintained was examined in more detail. The 170 companies of the Curhan list were sorted into the following categories: (1) Type II organizations, (2) Type III with an international division, and (3) Type III with the other forms of organized international activity that were described earlier. This sorting was done on the basis of annual reports, interviews, and secondary sources.[18] The large sample size made it inevitable that most of the information was gathered from published material. As a result, the classification reflects the formal structure and ignores possible discrepancies between the formal structure and informal control. No discrepancies were found between the analyses from published materials and the evidence gained from the interviews with a limited number of the companies. Therefore, the classification may be considered to be sufficiently accurate for the purposes of this paper. The main possible source of error is for those companies in transition between the categories, since the formal organization may often lead or lag behind actual administrative practices. This, however, was not considered a serious source of error.

The classification of each company on the basis of only a few structural forms was aimed at recording the central tendency of the structure observed. Various rules were developed to allow for the many possible minor variations in the control procedures. The most important of these rules were:

1. Foreign mining, agricultural, or service operations were not considered to be part of the manufacturing activities and were therefore ignored for the purposes of the structural classification.

2. Given an international division, the presence of one or two foreign joint-ventures reporting directly to a product division and accounting for an insignificant volume of the foreign business did not constitute a "mixed" form.

3. The international division did not have to control exports from the U.S.

4. Canadian subsidiaries were classified as part of the U.S. operations.

Each company was also classified by the two-digit Standard Industrial Classification number of its largest product line.[19] The result of these classifications is summarized in Table 3 which shows that only 18 of the 170 companies in the sample have Type II structures. This finding immediately suggests that foreign investment is dominated by Type III organizations, which is the thesis of this paper.

Table 3: Structural classification of companies by industry.

Industry SIC number	Number of companies in sample	Stage II	Stage III with international division	Stage III with other forms of international structure
20	28	5	16	7
21	1	—	1	—
22	2	—	2	—
25	1	—	1	—
26	5	1	3	1
27	1	—	1	—
28	41	1	21	19
29	8	—	2	6
30	5	—	5	—
31	1	—	1	—
32	7	1	5	1
33	8	4	2	2
34	8	1	4	3
35	19	4	9	6
36	17	1	8	8
37	11	—	4	7
38	5	—	4	1
39	2	—	1	1
Total	170	18	90	62

From Table 3 a structural index for eight industries was calculated as follows:

1. A ratio of the number of Type II companies to all Type III companies was calculated and normalized by assigning the value 1.00 to the industry with the largest proportion of Type II companies.

2. A ratio of the number of Type III companies with an international division to all Type III companies was calculated and normalized, with a value of 1.00 assigned to the industry with the highest ratio.

3. The two normalized ratios were summed to form the index which is shown in Table 4. Low values of this index indicate the predominance of Type III structures, particularly Type III with some relatively complex form of organized international activity. Low values of the index therefore indicate the relative abundance of both general management in the United States and international general management.

This method of calculating a structural index is purely arbitrary. It is clear from Table 3, however, that any index reflecting the proportions of the structures of the sample of companies within an industry will provide approximately the same ranking as that shown in Table 4.

Also to be found in Table 4 is an index of diversification as calculated by Michael Gort.[20] Gort's index is derived from a sample of 111 large manufacturing companies, drawn from the 200 largest companies in 1954. This particular index (Gort does present other measures of diversification) represents the ratio of domestic employment in the primary two-digit SIC industry divided by total domestic employment, adjusted for employment associated with vertical integration.[21] These relationships tend to be stable over time, so that they should retain some relevance for the present problem; also the time difference is in the direction required for Chandler's thesis. The eight industries in Table 4 are those for which data are available on foreign direct investment. This implies that they are the leading manufacturing industries in this respect, since the others have too little foreign direct investment to be reported separately. Gort's diversification index for SIC 33-34 is an average of his figures for those two industries, weighted by their respective employment sizes and representation on his sample.

Table 4 discloses some relationships immediately; that is, the four most diversified industries are four industries with the lowest structural index: chemicals, rubber, electrical machinery, and transportation. The four least diversified industries are four industries with the highest structural index: food, paper, primary and fabricated metals, and machinery. The Spearman coefficient of rank correlation between diversification and structure is 0.64.

This result provides additional support for Chandler's thesis that there is a relationship between diversification and structure.

Table 4 also shows the importance of foreign direct investment in plant and equipment relative to domestic direct investment in plant and equipment for the period 1959-1966. Again a relationship is apparent; that is, the four industries with the greatest relative direct foreign investment are the four most diversified (also with lowest structural index): chemicals, rubber, electrical machinery, and transportation. The four industries with the least foreign investment are the four least diversified (also with the highest structural index): machinery, primary and fabricated metal, food, paper. The coefficient of rank correlation between the relative direct investment measure and Gort's diversification index is .86; between the relative direct investment measure and the structural index it is 0.69.[22]

A relative measure of research and development activity is shown in Table 4 for 1958. The four leading research and development industries are those that are the most diversified, have the lowest structural indexes, and are the most international in their investment practices. The coefficient of rank correlation between research and structure is 0.81; between research and diversification it is .90. The relationship between research and diversification is also apparent when the analysis is made at the more detailed three-digit SIC industry level. The median specialization ratio for organizations with

Table 4: Structure and diversification; foreign investment, employment in research and development, and export/import ratio in major industries.

Industry (and SIC number)	Index of structure	Gort's index of diversification*	1959-1966 Direct foreign investment relative to domestic†	Research and development employees as percentage of central administrative employment ‡	Export/import ratio 1958-1960§
Food (20)	1.175	.933	13.2%	3.10	.79
Paper (26)	1.300	.893	16.7	2.21	.31
Chemicals (28)	0.580	.752	27.7	22.49	2.79
Rubber (30)	1.000	.697	41.3	16.46	1.19
Primary and fabricated metals (33-34)	1.545	.810	20.3	6.37	.67
Machinery (35)	1.188	.807	21.8	12.56	6.37
Electrical (36)	0.638	.667	23.7	47.00	3.85
Transportation (37)	0.364	.728	35.3	34.32	1.49

*Michael Gort, *Diversification and Integration in American Industry* (Princeton, N.J.: Princeton University, 1962), Table 8, p. 33.

†U.S. Department of Commerce, *Survey of Current Business* (Washington, D.C.: Government Printing Office, various dates).

‡U.S. Bureau of the Census, *Enterprise Statistics: 1958* (Washington, D.C.: Government Printing Office, 1963).

§Trade Relations Council of the U.S., *Employment, Output, and Foreign Trade of U.S. Manufacturing Industries, 1958-1964/65* (New York: 1966).

research and development employees is .814 in 1958, and .939 for organizations without research and development employees. The specialization ratio measures the number of manufacturing employees classified in a primary three-digit SIC industry divided by total manufacturing employment in that industry. [23]

The export/import ratio for 1958-1960 is also shown in Table 4. Here the four leading industries are the same as in the case of the trade balance (rubber ranks fifth and is replaced by machinery among the leading four). The coefficient of rank correlation between the export/import ratio and structure is 0.52. The correlation between the research and development measure and the export/import balance is .71, which is consistent with the findings of Gruber and associates.[24]

CONCLUSION

It may now begin to appear that the evidence would support *any* hypothesis about the industry characteristics of the organizations that have led the movement abroad, simply because those industries are outstanding on all relevant scales for measuring business performance. This is not the case, however. Consider the not unusual statements that it is the largest, most capital intensive and most integrated organizations that dominate foreign activity. If size is measured by assets per organization, this view is not supported by census data.[25] The rank correlation between assets per organization and the structural index is .40; between assets per organization and relative importance of foreign direct investment the correlation is .33. Gort also found that there was little association between size and diversification, as measured by the ratio of primary to nonprimary employment.[26] The correlation between the measure of size used here and Gort's diversification index is .29.

The measure of integration, taken from Gort, has a *negative* correlation with foreign activity, diversification (which agrees with his results), and decentralization for the eight internationally important industries.

Finally, the ratio of capital per production worker is negatively correlated with relative foreign activity (-.14). There is also a negative correlation between capital per production worker and the export/import ratio (-.40), as first suggested by Leontief.[27] The negative relationships carry over to the measures of structure (-.21) and diversification (-.36) used here. U.S. strength in international competition is concentrated in products with a relatively large labor content—probably the highly skilled technical labor required for product innovation and development, according to Vernon.[28]

The organizations that are left at home may be among the largest, most integrated, most capital intensive, and most profitable firms in the economy. Furthermore, they are not as likely to have problems of organization, management recruitment and training, staff-line conflicts, or of identifying what business the organization is really engaged in, or should be engaged in.

So, in the end, the question of the characteristics of the organization is a question of management's choice between sets of problems. Some business leaders have decided to make their organizations more cohesive by making them more integrated, capital intensive, and often more profitable. They have retained Type II structures, and have tended to concentrate on domestic markets. Other business leaders have undertaken the difficult task of transforming an institution, of moving from a Type II to a III structure. Many problems arise in this transition; for example, new systems of evaluation, reward, and control must be constructed. A critical aspect of the transition is teaching men to accept new roles—in this case roles as general managers. Once the organization had developed this educational capability, it could continue to diversify in an effective and efficient manner. It may be that the same pattern is being repeated in the international field: when the company has small foreign interests, it economizes on competent international management by having one man coordinate foreign activities. The growth of foreign markets and opportunities requires diversification, reorganization, and the training of many more general international managers. The organizations that have been most successful in meeting this new challenge have been those Type III organizations that had already developed the ability to produce general managers capable of controlling and guiding a heterogeneous, diverse enterprise.

NOTES

1. A. D. Chandler, Jr., *Strategy and Structure* (Garden City, N.Y.: Anchor, 1966). We have received, and greatly appreciate, the help of J. Behrman, C. R. Christensen, J. H. McArthur, B. R. Scott, and R. Vernon. This research was financed by a grant from the Ford Foundation for the study of the multinational corporation.
2. *Ibid.*, p. 478.
3. *Ibid.*, p. 479.
4. *Ibid.*, p. 50.
5. *Ibid.*, p. 385.
6. A. L. Kroeber, *Anthropology: Race, Language, Culture, Psychology, Prehistory* (Revised ed.; New York: Harcourt, Brace and Company, 1948), pp. 445-472.
7. Chandler, *Strategy*, p. 490.
8. T. Burns and G. M. Stalker, *The Management of Innovation* (London: Tavistock, 1961).
9. P. R. Lawrence and J. W. Lorsch, *Organization and Environment* (Boston, Mass.: Division of Research, Harvard Business School, 1967).

10. R. Vernon, "International Investment and International Trade in the Product Cycle," *Quarterly Journal of Economics*, 80 (May 1966) 190-207; C. P. Kindleberger, *The Dollar Shortage* (New York: Wiley, 1950); Staffan Burenstam-Linder, *An Essay on Trade and Transformation* (Uppsala, Sweden: Almqvist & Wicksell, 1961).

11. Chandler, *Strategy*, pp. 16, 17.

12. Bruns and Stalker, *Management*.

13. W. Gruber, D. Mehta, and R. Vernon, "The R&D Factor in International Trade and International Investment of United States Industries," *Journal of Political Economy*, 25 (February 1967), 20-37.

14. There are 21 two-digit Standard Industrial Classification (SIC) manufacturing industries. However, the Department of Commerce presents data for foreign direct investment on a combined basis for primary and fabricated metals industries (SIC numbers 33 and 34), excludes petroleum from manufacturing, and provides foreign trade data that omit petroleum and furniture. We have comparable data for 17 two-digit industries. These are: 20 (food), 21 (tobacco), 22 (textiles), 23 (apparel), 24 (wood products), 26 (paper), 27 (printing), 28 (chemicals), 30 (rubber), 31 (leather), 32 (stone, clay, and glass), 33-34 (primary and fabricated metal), 35 (machinery), 36 (electrical), 37 (transportation), 38 (scientific and similar instruments), 39 (misc.).

15. Vernon, "International Investment."

16. J. Curhan, private communication.

17. *Fortune*, "The 500 Largest U.S. Industrial Corporations" (June 1965 and June 1966).

18. For example, E. B. Lovell, *The Changing Role of the International Executive* (New York: National Industrial Conference Board, 1966).

19. The source of this classification was the Securities Exchange Commission, *1965 Directory of Companies Filing Annual Reports with the Securities Exchange Commission* (New York, 1966).

20. M. Gort, *Diversification and Integration in American Industry* (Princeton, N.J.: Princeton University, 1962).

21. Gort's index is based on data in U.S. Bureau of Census, *Company Statistics: 1954 Census of Business, Manufacturing, Mineral Industries* (Washington, D.C.: Government Printing Office, 1958), Table 2.

22. The structural and diversification indexes were ranked from the lowest to the highest values, so that the "most diversified" industry was given first rank on that scale.

23. U.S. Bureau of the Census, *Enterprise Statistics: 1958* (Washington, D.C.: Government Printing Office, 1963).

24. Gruber, "R&D Factor."

25. U.S. Bureau of the Census, *Statistics*.

26. Gort, *Diversification*, p. 74.

27. W. Leontief, "Domestic Production and Foreign Trade: The American Capital Position Re-examined," *Proceedings of the American Philosophical Society* 97 (September 1953), pp. 332-349.

28. Vernon, "International."

7
Is Management Exportable?

William H. Newman

The beliefs and values that underlie U.S. management ideas take numerous forms. They are not necessarily superior to those of other cultures, but they are so much a part of the U.S. environment that they are usually taken for granted. They have become reasonable assumptions. Awareness of these cultural assumptions is important for anyone seeking to transfer management concepts to, or from, a different setting.

The norms in one part of the world may be close enough to those in the "exporting" country so as not to create a problem of applicability, but occasionally the gap of one or two crucial points is sufficiently large to play havoc with a managerial plan. Such difficulties need not defeat an attempt by those who may wish to utilize U.S. management know-how abroad or to transfer the ideas of other nations to the United States. Sophisticated and imaginative analysis can, and often does, lead to selective adaptation.

In relating cultural differences to specific facets of the managerial process, the analyst is necessarily dealing with impressions rather than "hard data." He cannot describe actual U.S. behavior or culture; he must seek the premises on which U.S. management concepts are based. And, since the United States embraces a significant diversity of culture and management concepts, he is compelled to focus on the dominant, central viewpoints.

One of the more interesting dominants is the "master of destiny" psychology. Underlying much of U.S. management thought is a belief that people can substantially influence the future. A familiar saying is, "Where there's a will, there's a way," and in a somewhat lighter vein, "Every day we do difficult things; the impossible just takes a little longer." This "master of destiny" viewpoint, however, involves more than mere cockiness; it is related to several other beliefs and values.

Reprinted, with permission, from the January-February 1970 issue of the *Columbia Journal of World Business*. Copyright©1970 by the Trustees of Columbia University in the City of New York.

The typical U. S. manager believes that he exercises considerable choice in what he does and through this influences what happens to him. To be sure, he may run into "bad luck," but even here he is inclined to place at least part of the blame on himself. This belief in self-determination is in sharp contrast to a fatalistic viewpoint found in some Moslem countries. It also differs from a mystical view where events are perhaps determined by the capricious influence of spirits that must be appeased. Whatever the explanation, the critical issue is whether a person believes that events will occur regardless of what he does or whether he shares the belief that he can help shape future events.

REALISM AND HARD WORK

An important qualification in this self-determination concept is that an individual should be "realistic" in his aspirations. The Peer Gynts and the Don Quixotes are engaged in flights of fancy. Opinions may differ on what it is reasonable to undertake, and in the business world large quantities of data are gathered to predict the feasibility of a proposal. In addition to making sure that a proposed action is possible, a balancing of costs versus benefits is considered to be a part of prudent behavior. In other words, a man's belief in his mastery of his own destiny does not mean that he will endorse all sorts of idealistic schemes, such as are advanced in many reform movements throughout the world. Instead, a strong dose of pragmatic realism qualifies the objectives that are undertaken.

In the United States lore and experience underscore the necessity for hard work if objectives are to be achieved. Even if one doesn't accept the Puritan ethic that hard work is a virtue in itself, there is a strong belief that persistent, purposeful effort is necessary to achieve high goals. Hard work is not considered the only requisite for success; wisdom and luck also play their part. Nevertheless, the feeling persists that without hard work a person is neither likely to achieve nor justified in expecting to achieve his objectives.

This belief in the efficacy of hard work is by no means worldwide. Sometimes a fatalistic viewpoint makes hard work seem futile. In other instances, one needs merely to curry the favor of the right man and in still other situations hard work is regarded as unmanly.

The U.S. manager believes he is master of his own destiny partly because he and those he works with feel that commitments should be honored. A commitment to deliver materials, fix a machine or publicize a new product is not a mere statement of intention, it is a moral obligation. It is a matter of honesty; a man "keeps his word." In fact, of course, a man may be prevented from fulfilling his contract by external forces, and adjustments are made.

Nevertheless, the underlying social fabric contains a myriad of relationships in which it presumed that men will do what they say they will.

In some parts of the world it is impolite to refuse openly to do something that has been requested by another person. What a Westerner takes as a commitment may be little more than friendly conversation elsewhere. In other societies, it is understood that today's commitment may be superseded by a conflicting request received tomorrow, especially if that request comes from a highly influential person. In still other situations, agreements merely signify intention and have little relevance to capacity to perform; as long as the person tries to perform he feels no pangs of conscience or makes no special effort if he is unable to fulfill the agreement. Obviously, in these latter circumstances uncertainty is greatly increased, especially for new undertakings.

When things occur is also important. Effective use of one's own time and effective scheduling of independent activities requires a precision of timing. This concern with precise time gets reflected in daily lives in the United States; for a television program to start three minutes later than announced is a national disgrace.

Virtually all studies of comparative management have noted the wide variation in attitude toward time in various cultures. Part of the charm of Latin Americans arises from their relaxed view of the clock and the calendar. People in many other parts of the world fail to understand why the normal rhythms of life should be twisted to fit a business-imposed schedule.

The assumption that managers can determine to a large degree the future fruits of their labors has a profound effect on U.S. management concepts that are considered practical. Planning, especially long-range planning, is worth a substantial investment of energy only because of a confidence that it will really make a difference in what happens. The degree of detailed scheduling and other specific arrangements which U.S. managers consider essential if plans are to become more than vague aspirations, is justified only if a network of realistic, firm commitments can be established. Similarly, enthusiasm for decentralization rests on assumptions that men down the line share similar mores regarding self-determination, hard work, morality of commitments and the significance of time. If such mores prevail, then supervision can be general and consultative, instead of close and disciplinarian. The nature of control can become constructive feedback rather than suspicious verification.

INDEPENDENT ENTERPRISE

Most U.S. management concepts presume that joint action will be taken through an organized and structured enterprise. In fact, a substantial part of business activity, both profit and nonprofit, is legally done by corporations. The well-recognized advantages of corporations include continuity of life, ability to assemble capital, limited liabilities for the owners. Less often mentioned is the managerial role of the corporation. Actually, the organization need not operate legally as a corporation; the crucial point is that it functions as an independent enterprise—whatever its legal status. Certain characteristics identify those enterprises that are the most effective instruments for the conduct of business.

Faced with a task that requires the efforts of several people over a period of time, the U.S. manager "organizes"—i.e., he sets up an enterprise. The size and nature of the enterprise will depend on the mission, but, regardless of scope, it will quickly take on an entity of its own. It will be viewed as an institution separate from its executive and other employees. Such enterprises are believed to have a vitality and a means for coordinative action that people acting merely as individuals cannot achieve.

This concept of a whole array of man-made distinct enterprises is not understood in all cultures. Frequently an undertaking is inseparable from the individual who initiates the action; in fact, one hundred years ago this was the prevailing attitude in the United States. In other instances, major undertakings are usually associated with the church, the government or perhaps a divine ruler. Here again, the feelings about the undertaking are intermingled with attitudes toward a personality, religion or the state. History provides eloquent examples of what may be accomplished under a chauvinistic ruler or a powerful religion. U.S. management thought, in contrast, pins its faith on separate enterprises created to accomplish distinctive purposes..

For the enterprise system to work well, all employees, and especially executives, must feel a strong obligation to do their respective parts in pursuing the mission. Acceptance of employment implies a willingness to be loyal to the company. Success of the enterprise takes priority over purely personal preferences and social obligations to friends. The practical manager realizes that there are extremes beyond which such loyalty cannot be stretched. Nevertheless, a primary commitment to the good of the enterprise is an underlying premise.

The concept of primary obligation to the enterprise runs into serious difficulty in societies where each individual has an obligation to help his family (often "extended family"). In a few cultures even doing favors for one's friends takes priority over what is effective for the enterprise. The question of first loyalty can affect a spectrum of activities from employment to the extension of credit or use of company property. The issues may be quite subtle; for instance, many Latin Americans feel that they cannot rely upon a person unless they have a *simpatico* relationship with him. The result is that key transactions are likely to be influenced more by friendship than economic analysis.

Although Americans feel keenly about the obligation of an employee to his company, there is no stigma attached to terminating the relationship. "If you don't like it, you can always quit," and people do quit. Contrariwise, the employer has an implied privilege of discharging an employee. Even though in practice termination of employment is surrounded by formal and informal constraints, the initial premise is that employment is a mutually acceptable contract. As long as the contract is in effect it carries with it the loyalty obligation. However, the system achieves flexibility by facilitating honorable withdrawal.

This attitude toward terminating employment differs most noticeably from the Japanese concept of lifetime employment. In other countries switching employment is viewed with at least a suspicion. In those countries where employment is closely tied in with personal friendship, changing jobs may have all the emotional aspects of breaking a personal friendship. The central issue is whether dependability, loyalty and commitment can be a temporary and somewhat unemotional affair. The U.S. attitude is that it can be.

ETHICAL CONCEPTS

Americans expect an enterprise of any size to develop its own codes of behavior specifically designed to help achieve its mission. Objectives, policies, procedures, budgets, programs, organization structure, reports-flow, appraisal criteria, and a variety of other management tools are likely to be stated explicitly. People affected by such instruments often participate in their formulation and revision. Nevertheless, once they are established the assumption is that they will be observed. Furthermore, changes in this management system to cope with new situations are considered a normal part of life.

In societies where both internal and external actions are often done as a favor to someone, company plans and regulations are inevitably pushed into a minor position. In fact, an attempt to superimpose a rationally designed system on top of an informal one based on personal favors will add to, rather than lessen, the confusion. Similarly the Arab, whose long traditions of hospitality require him to meet visitors personally whenever they appear, may find formalized work schedules and communication systems more trouble than they are worth.

Because it is likely to be a source of potential trouble, there is a strong objection in the United States to divided interest. The feeling is that an executive should never permit himself to get into a situation where his sole consideration in any specific transaction is other than what's best for his company. Thus, most executives work for only one company at a time, and, if they should have financial or other interest in an outside company, they are expected to withdraw from any transaction involving their employer and such a company.

The receiving of gifts and even of what might be called "bribery" is customary in some countries. In fact, informal but nonetheless well-defined guides for the sharing of such contributions with other members of the organization often exist. Paying sales commissions or finders' fees to third parties is a familiar transaction in the United States, but the idea of making personal contributions to individuals who represent an enterprise violates the sense of undivided loyalty and obligation. To the extent that corruption occurs and individuals act on the basis of pay-offs rather than what is best for their enterprise, planning is difficult because unpredictable obstacles often arise; organization is difficult because one division cannot depend upon the other. The number of points at which a transaction can be held up or subverted must be minimized, and managers must introduce frequent controls (perhaps even personal inspections) to get reliable information concerning what actually transpires. U.S. management practice is simply not designed to deal with this kind of a situation.

With this unified and dependable effort presumed in the U.S. enterprise concept, organization can safely be elaborated. Duties can be divided and delegated even though they are interdependent; decentralization can be extended without fear of personal, selfish abuse; sophisticated arrangements for staff advice become possible. In planning, since both dependability and predictability are increased, managers can extend the time-span of their plans and can afford more detailed analysis of methods and schedules.

Leadership in the independent enterprise still calls for inspiring associates, but the focus of leadership shifts from personality or family to the accomplishment of a mission. An individual works for a cause, not to do a favor for a close friend. The entire control process is affected by the assumption of loyalty and undivided interest. Aside from routine audits to verify that this assumption is being observed, control can be devoted to assessing progress, difficulties and new opportunities. This information can be fed back to a variety of individuals who are already motivated to use such data for the good of the enterprise.

While instances of bribery and divided interest certainly occur in the United States and friendship may influence the placing of a big order, the fact that bribery is headline news indicates that a social norm has been violated. The idea that a man owes first allegiance to his enterprise is so common that it is rarely stated. The concept of a deliberately designed, independent enterprise—which receives loyalty and willingness to conform to its managerial system—is a major and underlying idea upon which many U.S. management concepts rest.

MERIT SELECTION OF PERSONNEL

A third cardinal belief on which U.S. management concepts are based is that individuals should be placed in jobs solely because they are the best qualified persons available. This idea is consistent with the tenet that decisions should be made objectively for the maximum good of the enterprise.

The starting point is the needs of the enterprise. The activities of an enterprise are organized into jobs with man-specifications based on the duties of each job. These specifications are used in selecting a man to fill each post. Executives who select men to fill positions are expected to make a diligent search for candidates in all likely places; if well qualified persons are not readily available this search should extend to all divisions of the enterprise as well as to outside sources.

Appointment on merit need not imply organizational inflexibility. If a particular position is being used for training purposes, the duties and the man-specifications will differ from those needed for performance of short-run operations. If suitable candidates are unavailable for a position as conceived, the organization should be redesigned to match the kind of people that can be employed. Flexibilities are introduced to promote the interests of the enterprise, not as a concession to personal indulgence.

This belief extends beyond the initial appointment. The underlying assumption is that if a man is not continuing to perform his job well, he should be replaced by someone who will. The cost to the enterprise of poor performance, especially of executives, is far greater than a man's salary: his poor performance complicates the task of people whose work inter-relates with his and may undermine the effectiveness of the entire operation.

In a number of countries the removal of a man from a recognized position involves so much loss of prestige that the action is rarely taken. This is particularly true when the appointment was made initially on the basis of family or friendship. U.S. business is not indifferent to the pain that may result from the removal of a man from his job, especially if that man in the past has rendered distinctive service. However, the feeling is that such personal obligations to a man can be met by job transfer, early retirement, dismissal compensation, or the like. Such personal recompense simply makes easier the application of the idea that a man is not entitled to remain in a position where he blocks effective performance.

MOBILITY

The U.S. tradition that a man born in a log cabin has the opportunity to become president of his country has its counterpart in business where an office boy may rise to become company president. The stress is not so much on a classless society as on a mobile, open society. There may be a managerial elite, but one achieves position in a group by personal merit rather than by birth.

Open access to all levels of management does, of course, run counter to ideas of social class which prevail in a number of countries. Fortunately, rigid class systems appear to be rapidly breaking down. Education has become the primary vehicle for achieving mobility. Even on this count, the U.S. ethic stresses ability rather than formal education; there are many company presidents who are self-made men.

An awkward issue is whether inherited ownership entitles a man to be a high executive in a company. If he is the sole owner, then ideas about private property would permit him to indulge in self-aggrandizement. However, U.S. management thought has developed on the concept that [an enterprise is independent of its owners.]In fact, very rarely does a medium- or large-size company have a sole owner. Nor can a medium-size or large enterprise be capricious in dealing with its obligations to other interest groups. Concepts of professional management of independent enterprises quickly take over. Part ownership may well affect a man's motivation and availability, and these obviously should be included among the factors to be considered in appointing executives. The theory is that ownership does not entitle a man to a position in the company, but, insofar as it adds to his ability to contribute, it does receive indirect consideration.

Horizontal movement within an enterprise is normal and not necessarily bad. It fits in with the idea that a man is not assured of life tenure in a given position. The general belief is that movement from one position to another—including the possibility of moving from line to staff and vice versa—is stimulating for the individual and encourage flexibility in company operations. These movements are often thought of as progressions to increasing responsibility, but many moves are merely adjustments to changing conditions. In companies where horizontal transfers are common practice, removal of men who are in spots where they are no longer giving top performance involves less embarrassment.

Transfers of men to other companies are also acceptable if the new post is clearly more attractive than what his previous employer can offer. No one likes to lose a well-trained man, and his present employer will probably point out the advantages of staying where he already knows the intricacies of company activity. On the other hand, the view that a man is entitled to move where his talents will be most productive has wide acceptance. Such tolerance of intercompany mobility is consistent with an attitude that executives perform a "professional" service.

This kind of mobility does not readily fit into all cultures. Where appointments are based on highly personal relationships, a movement from job to job is untenable. Where the holding of particular positions is essential to a man's status, horizontal movement is impeded. In countries like Japan, where for many years loyalty to a single company has been considered an important aspect of personal integrity, the idea of bettering oneself by transferring to another company is regarded by many as a deficiency in moral character.

In the U.S. view, executive selection on the basis of merit bears directly on the acceptance and use of authority. Its egalitarian tradition holds that the next man is "no better than I am." Neither noble birth nor advanced age bestow on an individual the right to tell other people what they should do. Nevertheless, the need for authority in a complex, interdependent operation is clearly recognized. A way out of this dilemma is to attach such authority as the system may require to various positions and then place people in these positions on the basis of their ability. Under these conditions, authority is not the personal prerogative of a particular individual (and this satisfies the egalitarian precept). Instead, it arises from the needs that an enterprise attaches to a particular job and is exercised by people objectively selected.

Many countries are not bothered by egalitarian principles, and for them this last point is not important. Nevertheless, an analogous problem may exist. It is quite possible that the authority figures in a given society will not correspond with the authority allocation necessary for effective operation of independent enterprises. In such circumstances, some means of reconciling recognized authority and selection of executives will have to be worked out.

These attitudes and premises clearly imply that organization precedes personnel selection. The argument rests on the higher value attached to a viable, efficient enterprise than to personal friendship or to hereditary class. Structure is treated as the handmaiden of strategy, and personnel are selected on the basis of that structure. Obviously, the structure must be one for which staffing is possible. If unique talent is available, the organization may be modified so that the enterprise takes full advantage of its assets. But these are only qualifications and do not alter the value scale or the basic approach.

Similarly, selection of personnel on merit has an impact on the types of control that are needed. With the stress laid on competent people motivated to carry out assigned tasks, control points shift from detailed checks of work-in-process to measurement of results. Since evaluation of "merit" becomes a vital aspect of the entire management conception, attention is focused on having this evaluation as comprehensive, objective, and as fair as possible.

OBJECTIVE ANALYSIS

A high regard for science is reflected in the U.S. approach to management. Although few managerial actions can be "scientific" in a strict sense of the word, there is a strong cultural belief that decisions should be based on objective analysis of facts. This view significantly influences the nature of data obtained and the way it is communicated throughout the organization. Such attitudes about the handling of business information are by no means fully accepted throughout the world.

Important business decisions involve substantial inputs of judgment. Often these judgments are based on intuitive feelings. The U.S. norm is that the entirely intuitive aspects of decision should be reduced to a minimum consistent with timely action. This implies that considerable effort will be devoted to assembling all the relevant information and that a rational explanation based on this information will be developed for each decision. The entire decision-making process need not be fully rational; creative ideas arise from many sources, and insights may be intuitive. Nevertheless, before becoming final, each decision should be tested against tough, factual rational analysis.

For many decisions the amount of raw data which is relevant far exceeds the capacity of a single individual to observe and appraise. Consequently, the executive who is making the decision must rely upon other people in his organization to provide an appropriate syntheses of batches of data. Sometimes this synthesis is expressed in terms of a policy or a planning premise; often it is a conclusion or an estimate prepared for the specific problem. Objective analysis requires that the decision maker consult as a normal practice all of the people who can contribute relevant, summarized information.

A factual, rational analysis of decisions is less frequently made in some countries for one or more reasons. First, personal judgment of a key executive may be the basis of a decision, and any attempt to explain it would be interpreted as a lack of confidence in the executive's judgment—by the executive himself and by others. Second, the use of "hard data" may not be customary; instead, decisions may be expressions of wisdom and/or beauty that become sullied by controversial detailed information. Third, it may be inappropriate for a senior executive to consult, at least personally, about matters on which he is already presumed to be wise. In such situations, an aura or mystique replaces objective analysis.

If data is to play a key part in decision making, it must be reliable. It is assumed that basic data will be accurately and promptly recorded. Any dishonesty in reporting such information is considered adequate cause for dismissal. The fetish for having the correct figure frequently delays final verification, and the economist's concept that cost summaries will differ for various purposes is often viewed as a bit immoral. Of course, many estimates are used, but these should be scrupulously labeled as such. Clearly the provision of accurate data is considered a matter of personal integrity.

In other countries, precise, accurate data may not be so readily available or so highly valued. It is not uncommon to keep two or three sets of financial books so that reports submitted for tax purposes differ from those used to support a bank loan. This opens the way for juggling figures for other purposes. The educational and cultural background of clerks may not have stressed accuracy. An added difficulty is that the tools for measuring market and economic phenomena may be rudimentary or nonexistent. The result is that for some decisions the kind of information the U.S. executive takes for granted does not exist.

The prevailing U.S. belief is that company information should be readily available to anyone who can use it to perform his work more effectively. The era of secrecy passed out about fifty years ago. Now, a well designed information system channels reports to all sorts of people on a regular basis. In addition, bureaucratic withholding of information to gain internal power is frowned upon. Instead, there is a general belief—often explicitly stated—that individuals needing information should go directly to its sources and are not required to go through hierarchical channels. The underlying belief is that benefits of ready availability of pertinent information outweigh the inconvenience of a competitor occasionally learning a bit more than one wishes he knew.

This idea of an open flow of data within a company contrasts sharply with the way information is handled in some countries. Sometimes a tradition of secrecy exists in which departmental information is revealed only to senior executives, and that is always done through hierarchical channels which permit considerable editing of the information that is passed along. In other circumstances, where the internal relationships are on a highly personal, non-objective basis, communication is also personalized. An executive trusts the information only if he receives it from someone with whom he is *simpatico* and has a continuing personal relationship. Even here there may be reluctance to pass along information which will hurt the other person. Finally, if a belief prevails that most people in the organization are incompetent to handle any information except that which relates to their immediate task, availability of data is often felt to be wasteful, if not dangerous.

Objective analysis in a complicated organization requires not only the availability of data; experts in various areas must be encouraged to present information and judgments which they believe are relevant. Ideally, each man is expected to form his own opinion, which may or may not agree with that of his associates and his bosses, and he has an obligation to present such views even though they may not support a popular plan of action. "Experts" in this connection include anyone who has an intimate understanding of a phase of a problem—such as salesmen, foremen or purchasing agents as well as staff specialists. Pros and cons exist for any problem, and these can be properly assessed only when each person who has something to contribute speaks his mind freely. To withhold or distort information is a form of negligence or dishonesty.

Frankness of expression does not easily fit any culture and in some cultures becomes very difficult. Great deference to people in positions of power becomes a normal manner of behavior. For a person in a subordinate position to present information and particular judgments which might not support the ideas of senior executives is unthinkable. A similar obstacle arises in Far Eastern cultures where politeness is valued above naked truth. Above all, one must not say something which embarrasses or shames another person. Where this attitude prevails, one cannot expect to get an outspoken exchange of ideas.

Such a "laying all the cards on the table" approach has a profound effect upon the planning process in an enterprise. Only in this manner can a wide dispersion of data-gathering and analysis be reconciled with wise central decisions. Long-range planning, which must involve many divisions of an enterprise if it is to be effective, is inconceivable without objective analysis. Sophisticated techniques of discounted cash-flow and operations research become metaphysical exercises without an underpinning of objective data.

Less direct but still significant are the effects on organization. For instance, requisites for decentralization include confidence in the communication system and in the evaluation techniques, both of which are built on objective data. Also, much staff work rests on the presumption of a free exchange of reliable data. Dependable facts are even more essential for control. A modern enterprise is not run like a New England town meeting where presumably all citizens participate in all decisions of the local government. Nevertheless, much of its management practice reflects a belief in wide participation in making decisions.

A SHARE IN DECISION MAKING

This participation in the planning process occurs both horizontally and vertically. The word "horizontal" is used loosely to include anyone outside the channel of command regardless of title or echelon. Generally speaking, a decision maker will be expected to consult with anyone who has information or judgment that can contribute to the quality of the decision and also with people within the company who will be significantly affected by the decision.

Vertical sharing in decision making moves beyond consultation into various degrees of decentralization. U.S. businessmen have a strong belief that localized—in contrast to centralized—decisions will be better suited to an actual operating situation and will be executed with more enthusiasm. In practice, of course, decentralization is subject to a variety of restraints, such as need for consistency or allocation of scarce resources; nevertheless, the initial presumption is in favor of decentralization and the burden of proof is on the person who wishes to centralize.

The U.S. emphasis on pushing decision making down the line stems, in part, from a belief in the high potential ability of men at all levels of the organization. The assumption is that able men can be found. With the requisite training, they will respond to increased responsibility. More than mental capacity is involved. These men will also have enough self-confidence to make decisions, and they will be willing to accept the consequences of their decisions. Not every man is a potential genius, of course. Intellectual and emotional energy, physical health, competing desires, and similar factors place limits on the capacity of each individual. But in the design of managerial systems such differences in the maximum capacity of individuals are not serious. The important consideration is that, broadly speaking, potential ability continues to run ahead of opportunities to delegate. This unused capacity makes expansion of the sharing in decision making both possible and desirable.

Other cultures often give less support to the premise that high potential is widespread. Opportunities for rigorous formal education may be limited, and social attitudes may discourage acceptance of responsibility. Especially in developing countries, capacity to comprehend a unique and changing managerial system of a specific enterprise calls for a very high degree of perception. Flexibility in accepting enterprise goals is hard to grasp.

The desire to improve one's lot—to "get ahead"—is taken for granted in U.S. management concepts. It is assumed that a man will strive to increase his financial rewards and status relative to his associates. With the important proviso that success in these terms is based on merit, the social norm is that ambition is normal and healthy and that lack of ambition is a sign of weakness.

This idea of getting ahead increases the desire to share in decision making because such participation is one of the symbols of status. The greater a man's participation in decision making, the more important is his job. In fact, the kinds of decisions that a man makes or his influence on them is a key factor in deciding the salary he receives. Consequently, as part of this whole value pattern, the ambitious individual will seek an enlarged share in decision making.

This approach presupposes competition within the enterprise. In general, it is believed that competition stimulates high performance in business as in sports. Internal competition in a company, however, may interfere with cooperative effort. To deal with this incompatibility between individual ambition and cooperation, a whole set of "ground rules" inevitably arises within each company. They seek to define when cooperation will best serve the company and how individual ambition should be expressed. The subtleties of these ground rules may be difficult to detect, but they serve an essential function of directing ambition into constructive channels.

In many countries, personal ambition is not given much encouragement or free rein. The structure of society may be sufficiently stable (or governed by other criteria) so that attempting to improve one's own status is frowned upon. In cultures that stress politeness and great respect for other persons, competitive attitudes can lead to trouble. In these circumstances, the motivational aspects implicit in U.S. management concepts must be carefully examined.

Another attitude that facilitates a high degree of decentralization is respect for all kinds of work. If a man is to be given considerable latitude in accomplishing a particular mission, he must interest himself in all activities necessary to achieve his assigned goal. For example, if the job requires personally standing in front of an open-hearth furnace, then the man is expected to stand there. The common expression is that a man must be "willing to get his hands dirty." The point is that a man must have respect for and be willing to do whatever is necessary to get the job done.

This apparently simple idea runs into difficulty in countries where various kinds of work are accorded high or low status. In some extreme instances, a man with a college degree will not concern himself directly with problems on the shop floor because he sought his degree in order to remove himself from such problems. In other instances, a man may think it is below his dignity to drive a car, compute a set of averages or visit retail shops to observe consumer buying. Perhaps more serious than physical behavior is a mental attitude which considers certain kinds of work as unworthy of careful analysis and firm supervision (this might be selling, record-keeping or physical production).

Perhaps because the United States has been subject to rapid social change during its relatively short history, or perhaps because a large part of the population stems from immigrants who came to the country with the avowed purpose of making social change, a relentless urge for improvement is part of the cultural fabric. This attitude expresses itself in various forms which affect its managerial concepts.

With technological and social change continuous in the environment, business activities cannot be immune. In fact, many people feel that anything new is progress. As with fashions, change per se is good; a familiar greeting to a friend is "What's new?" Of course, the social and psychological forces resisting change are also present, and, especially where results can be measured quantitatively, the innovator may have to demonstrate that change is, in fact, progress. The presumption is that change is desirable.

CHANGE IS NORMAL

Two beliefs associated with the desirability of change are:

1. Bringing about change requires hard work. Substantial inputs of initiative, man-hours of planning, perhaps capital investment and often painful social readjustment are necessary.

2. Participating in the change process is personally rewarding. It typically is tied up with a sense of self-fulfillment, social contribution and influence.

These attitudes toward change contrast sharply with a high reverence for tradition found in some societies. In these cultures, the values associated with practices centuries old must be respected. Not infrequently the power of a ruling group rests on the continuation of a stable structure. Here change is viewed with at least suspicion. Even in developing countries where the idea of change has acceptance, the work involved to bring it about may be unrecognized. Obviously, a managerial system based on the premise that change is normal and desirable will not easily fit a situation in which change is frowned upon or at least does not warrant much effort.

One of F. W. Taylor's basic contributions to U.S. management thought was that traditional management, in any part of a company, should be subjected to rigorous analysis. Change should not be limited to production methods and product design. Marketing, finance, the Board of Directors and every segment of a company should be examined periodically with a view toward improving its effectiveness and reducing its cost. The presumption is that new ideas, changing environment and internal development of the company will create opportunities for improvement. Consequently, challenging existing arrangements should be encouraged.

This expectation of change and improvement does not mean that a company should be in a continuous state of ferment. A workable plan, just like a successful product, has to be used long enough to reap some benefits from its design. The military commander does not change his organization's structure in the middle of a battle. The point is that no part of the business is exempt from re-examination from time to time.

This attitude runs into snags in some countries. For instance, until recently the aura surrounding a British Board of Directors virtually precluded an analysis of its operation by an outsider. In other countries where divisions of a company become, in effect, the private domain of their respective managers, change can be thwarted for long periods of time. An even more general difficulty existing in some societies is the view that the need for change reflects failure on somebody's part, and consequently pride and dignity are at stake. This is in sharp contrast with an attitude where making changes is usually attributed to "an alert and aggressive executive."

WHAT REALLY WORKS

Accompanying the endorsement of change, U.S. management practices also reflect a strong pragmatic emphasis on results. Management may endorse face-to-face communications, rational explanations, willingness to listen to suggestions, and the like, but in the end it is more impressed with what produces the most effective results. Policies, procedures, budgets, and other management techniques are similarly regarded as means. They attain value in view of the results they create.

This emphasis on what really works in terms of results achieved is a pervasive social norm. It does not say that a manager is concerned only with profits at the end of the year. He may, and does, consider social costs. The point is that whatever the goals may be, managerial process should be designed for their achievement. The underlying doctrine is that a beautiful scheme should always be tested against the hard reality of how well it works in practice.

Such pragmatic emphasis is by no means universal. Values in some societies place much greater stress on symbols of office and flourish in execution than on final results. Some Latin American executives, for example, are highly skilled in logical and dialectic discussions—so much so that they may lose sight of the object around which an argument is centered. The idea that results should be evaluated is a corollary of the importance attached to results. It also fits closely with the stress on objective analysis because an important source of information for future decisions is an accurate appraisal of past results.

While the usual schedule of audits and cross-checks exists to assure accuracy, the basic premise in management thought is that evaluation plays a constructive role. It provides a basis for special rewards and, more important, it provides "feedback" to the people doing the work and their supervisors on progress being made. At a ballgame somebody "keeps score"—it's as simple as that.

Actually in other cultures, evaluation in this sense proves to be difficult. To cite a specific instance, a U.S. executive working in the Iranian government created considerable consternation when he asked for what he thought would be a routine report on a previous assignment. Apparently, the presumption was that having delegated the task he would not check up on it unless he received a complaint about the work. Regular check-ups on progress clearly were not customary; the life of the executive was easier if he simply assumed that the assignment would be accomplished. In some Far Eastern countries, little evaluation is done so as to avoid embarrassing specific individuals. Thus, a sales contest involving the posting of individual results would be in bad taste because of the embarrassment to the people low on the list.

The high value attached to improvement permeates much management thinking in the United States. Some writers say that the major function of a manager is being an "agent of change." Clearly, a primary reason for long-range planning is to assure that the requisites for improvement and growth will be available when needed. In organizing, special staff units seek out opportunities for improvement (e.g., research and development, industrial engineering, market research, operations research, corporate planning). And decentralization is espoused because it aids a more rapid adjustment to new opportunities.

Similarly, control systems are designed not to maintain the status quo but to measure progress, detect opportunities and obstacles that call for replanning and focus attention on moving ahead. Several U.S. firms operating in Europe have grown, not because their initial plans were wise, but because their control systems (and attitude toward change) enabled them to learn quickly from experience and adjust to new inputs of observation.

The cultural premises on which management concepts are based are infinite and various. They differ from country to country and are not in every case compatible. The effective transfer of management practices from one culture to another will depend on prevailing attitudes and values and their receptivity to change. The difficulties of this type of transfer should not be exaggerated. Several approaches are available when cultural differences are significant. Non-typical individuals may be sought in the importing country who already have, or can acquire, the values necessary to make the imported technique work.

This approach has been used by petroleum refineries located in nonindustrialized countries. The imported technique can be modified to fit local conditions—e.g., full communication and participation may be restricted to special groups, "slack" may be added to production schedules, control points may be added, novel incentives may be related to attendance or output, and the like. Hybrids may be created. The imported techniques may be applied to only part of an operation while the remaining activities are "subcontracted" to local agents who follow local customs. New, creative adaptations can be designed. To cite two examples, U.S. business budgeting is a substantial modification of British government budgets and U.S. staff concepts are adaptations from the German military staff.

Perhaps most impressive is the substantial body of managerial concepts that can be transferred. Any concern over differences should not overshadow the universality of basic management processes in purposeful, cooperative endeavors, nor, with respect to those processes, the frequent—if not universal—usefulness of many managerial concepts.

8

International
Business
Management
... Its Four Tasks

Michael G. Duerr

As the American corporation expands internationally, it often faces mounting pressure on one of its most critical resources—top management's time. Problems of dealing with local tastes, business practices, and governments multiply. Sheer distance hampers communication; separately incorporated foreign subsidiaries complicate the organization chart.

Where should the top management of a company with expanding international business focus its attention so as to make the most effective use of time?

To get an indication of which tasks need a good deal of top-level attention, The Conference Board in a recent survey asked its panel* of senior international executives: "What subjects should, in your opinion, be given greater attention by top management of a company if its international business is to grow on a sound basis?"

Out of many recommendations, four key tasks for top management are mentioned most often: 1) integrating foreign and domestic operations; 2) establishing suitable control over foreign affiliates; 3) understanding and adapting to local conditions; and 4) developing international management.

Reprinted, with permission, from *The Conference Board Record* (October 1968).
*The panel is made up of U.S. executives from consumer and capital goods manufacturing, mining, and service industries. In this first survey, 166 executives responsible for their companies' international operations reported their opinions and experience. The complete findings of the survey appear in "The Problems Facing International Management," *Managing International Business,* No. 1, NICB (New York, 1968).

INTEGRATING FOREIGN AND DOMESTIC OPERATIONS

One theme which runs through many responses is the need to unite the international and domestic sides of the corporation into a "global" management team. Nearly all U.S. companies have developed as domestic companies first, with international activities in a secondary role. Despite the recent growth of international business, many executives feel that top management has yet to devise efficient ways to beam corporate resources at the world marketplace.

The task is partly organizational, but it also involves instilling an international attitude throughout the company. "The complete separation of international and domestic affairs should be looked on as only an intermediate phase," a vice president states, "and ways and means must be found to move out of this phase." Another vice president stresses top management's responsibility to "educate the whole organization, domestic as well as overseas, to think in global terms."

In several companies, international executives complain that top management is preoccupied with domestic business to the point where international operations receive little attention and an insufficient share of corporate resources. One notes: "Too often it would seem that international business is still considered a sort of stepchild . . . and in some cases even an undesirable stepchild." Another says: "If our international business is to be on a sound basis, top management must review its philosophy concerning foreign investment. Top corporate financial planning must include allocations of capital for foreign investment."

Many executives who acknowledge that their international units get a fair share of funds still see a need for top management to bring domestic resources to bear on foreign problems. According to a vice president—export, this means that managers responsible for a company's international operations must have "complete freedom to go to other divisions of the company for information, expert service, and professional assistance—no less than such divisions would render to the company's domestic operations."

Another vice president points out that where international business volume is not great enough to justify a separate international staff, the man responsible for international business "has to rely on home affairs executive colleagues for specialist assistance in their particular fields."

Similarly, another executive observes: "The top management of a medium-sized company must be aware of the necessity of the international division to draw upon the other divisions of the company for assistance. They must recognize that in order to grow on a sound basis, it requires highly competent and experienced people for these assignments—and not necessarily the person who can most readily be made available. Where an international division is not large enough to justify complete service facilities of its own, such as engineering and research, then the domestic service organization must consider the requirements of the international organization as being equally important as the domestic needs, even though international may not be currently returning comparable profits to the company."

An automobile executive stresses the need for the whole company to gear its efforts to international as well as domestic markets. "For example," he says, "the stylist must consider world tastes in design and size, and the engineer must consider the driver's power, handling, and comfort needs in other countries. Otherwise, we would end up with a one-country product in a one-world economy." And a general manager of marketing provides an illustration: "As an example, automotive test equipment as produced in the United States is in most cases unsuitable for the smaller, lower horsepower vehicles built in Europe and Japan. U.S. firms have lost out almost completely on equipment sales to these areas simply because original designs did not take local requirements into consideration."

How best to achieve foreign-domestic integration preoccupies many executives. As one vice president puts it, "In a company which has recently doubled in size as a result of mergers and which believes strongly in retaining initiative and authority at the divisional profit center level, how can we coordinate international activities and achieve a synergistic effect without arousing hostility or suspicion, or taking away from divisional profit centers activities that historically belong to them?"

The importance of this task is summed up by a chemicals executive: "Top management today must give its greatest attention to planning the use of its total resources on a global basis . . . Only by top management interest, support, and direction will a company be able to make the most judicious allocation of its manpower and its money to assure that it does in fact become an international company. Just as in the 1920's in the United States, those companies which survived were those that evolved from a local company to a national company, so in the coming decade companies that are to survive and prosper will be those which evolve from national companies to international companies."

CONTROLLING INTERNATIONAL AFFILIATES

Many participating executives say that top management must devote more attention to defining the proper amount of control that U.S. headquarters should exert over foreign subsidiaries and to determining the best means of exercising it. How much authority should be delegated to overseas managers, and how much should be retained by the parent company in the United States? What is the best way to keep foreign managers headed toward achievement of overall corporate objectives without reducing their ability to manage?

An international company's president describes the task as "establishing maximum delegation of authority to overseas management without losing necessary control." If the limits on overseas managers' authority are too rigid, a senior vice president points out, "overseas management becomes somewhat frustrated; if the limits are not fairly well defined, home office control of overall policies and procedures could be weakened to the extent that they become ineffective."

The survey reveals some disagreement as to how closely foreign subsidiaries should be controlled from the U.S. headquarters. One executive characterizes foreign operations as generally "fatter and more easy-going" than domestic operations. His current problem, he adds, is to persuade foreign subsidiary management "to use U.S. profit planning methods and to respond promptly to what these tools should reveal to them."

A president criticizes "the overzealous pursuit of the fetish of the moment—decentralization." A number of others urge the establishment of closer financial controls. A vice president recommends that top management make "a regular evaluation of all international investments to determine that they meet standard guidelines for return on capital for overseas installations." Another notes: "Better control is important. The control methods, however, should help the subsidiary manage itself and not merely provide information for the central accounting office."

Others believe that the company must become more decentralized, and that it is up to top management to find an effective way to accomplish this. "Greater authority and responsibility must be delegated to the overseas locations," one says, because "decision-making at home causes delay and inefficiency." Another urges that foreign subsidiaries be given more autonomy to increase their responsiveness to local conditions and "to free parent company management from all but policy decisions."

UNDERSTANDING AND ADAPTING TO LOCAL CONDITIONS

Another high-priority task for top management, in the opinion of many panelists, is the need to learn more about the environment in foreign countries where the company operates, so that corporate policies can be adapted accordingly. When top management does not adequately understand the local situation, they say, corporate decision-making is less efficient, and relationships with governments and businessmen in foreign countries are likely to be hampered.

"The chief executive officer, more than anyone else in the firm, should have a working hypothesis of what the world will be like; he should have an awareness of current social and political forces and make judgments as to the business environments they will shape in five, ten, and twenty years," one executive says. "International business is much more dependent on political trends and cultural attitudes around the world than is purely domestic business," another says. "Top management must be very closely attuned to the environment of many, many countries."

A vice president explains that "this means keeping up-to-date on activities in regions or countries of interest. Frequent visits should be made, and communications should be constant." Another executive states: "Top management must travel to see what is happening in each area. This takes time and is tiring, but top management must set aside enough time for it."

One reason why many international executives feel that this task if worth the time and effort is their conviction that corporate management sometimes attempts to force a U.S. solution to overseas business problems rather than adapt the solution to fit the conditions in the market. Noting that the differences in business customs between foreign countries are great, a vice president says that "many times corporate management does not understand the reason why a matter should be handled entirely differently overseas than it might be handled in the U.S.A."

Another international vice president offers an example of the difficulties caused by top management's failure to understand differences in business customs. "This lack of understanding becomes particularly noticeable during the presentation of capital appropriations requests for foreign investments," he observes. "If the top management lacks sufficient information about the market concerned, at some point in the review there is the inevitable question of why it has to be done differently from the time-honored practice in the U.S.A. At that point the international manager must go into a long-winded explanation of the differences involved, or else ask top management to accept the fact that differences do exist on the international man's say-so. Neither is satisfactory."

Several executives bring out another reason for devoting more time to understanding foreign lands. As U.S. corporations expand overseas, it becomes more important for them to maintain good relations with host country governments and with the local business community. "This presupposes complete and generous understanding of local problems and a desire to appreciate and learn how to evaluate local characteristics—not necessarily with the purpose of changing them, but to apply American methods in the form and to the extent that could be most rewarding depending on the different circumstances of each country," one said.

The vice president of a computer firm points out that "we will obviously have to give greater and greater attention to the requirements of operating in foreign countries with local interests which might not completely parallel our own. Specifically, I think we will need to look at new and better ways to cooperate with local governments and local industry in order to dispel concerns over American dominance, the technology gap, and the management gap. One of the things, for instance, that we are spending more time on is our relationships with education, because we believe that this is one area in which American companies can help."

The president of a company with extensive experience abroad empha-sizes that the motivating force in this effort must come from the top: "The top manager of a company must be concerned with all matters relating to economic and social development. He should encourage his local manage-ment and employees to participate in civic affairs and community development projects and promote and defend private enterprise interests in general as well as the business interests of the company."

DEVELOPING INTERNATIONAL MANAGEMENT

A fourth task which many panelists stress is the development of men capable of managing the company's international business. The demand for qualified international managers has grown faster than the supply, many point out, and the resulting shortage places a high priority on developing management manpower for the corporation. This includes the identification, selection, and training of managers for overseas operations and also the development of international expertise in the company's domestic staff.

"We are short of top-notch international managers," a president admits. "Adequate management personnel is scarce, and the search for and development of key personnel must call for a fair amount of top management time," says a vice president.

To one general manager, this means an "internationally-oriented manpower development program—aimed at development within the international division and the parent corporation, and sufficient hiring of outside internationally-experienced and/or interested personnel with the right balance of foreign nationals." To another, it involves "proper compensation policies, conditions which provide for fluidity for changing people within the system, and the establishment of line and staff organizational structure and policies that will insure the optimum operating effort."

A word-picture of the kind of man who is wanted comes from the vice president of a metals company: "We are all looking for 'self-starters' who can *think,* who are *simpatico,* willing to work hard, and undergo extended trips—some with much discomfort; who have a knowledge of another language or languages, or the facility and willingness to study; and who also have the ability to acquire product knowledge. Above all, diplomacy and a sense of timing are all-important."

In many companies, the focus is now on developing foreign nationals to manage overseas subsidiaries. One vice president who urges more top-management attention to this task explains: "U.S. personnel are too expensive to maintain on a continuous basis; competent, well-trained nationals must be the ultimate answer." Another vice president notes that "transfer and promotion of foreign personnel is another subject demanding more attention." A third executive places high priority on "development of a cadre of foreign nationals, both to manage local operations and to serve as a pool from which additional operations can be temporarily or permanently staffed," and he notes that this "could be done through temporary assignment of promising personnel in the parent organization." Another urges "training foreign management nationals in the United States, and possibly exposing them to actual experience in managing in the United States."

Other executives suggest training managers in both the domestic and international operations of the company, "so that international experience is not just in the international groups or divisions," as one puts it. Several explain that this helps to integrate the company, improve communications and control, and increase the understanding of foreign environments at the corporate level. "The more people who know about international business at the headquarters level," a vice president asserts, "the more effective its management."

To the extent a company can accomplish the task of developing its international management team, several executives suggest, the other tasks for top management are likely to be made easier. To the general manager of an international apparel company, managerial development is the most important of all. "I don't think it's wrong to say that virtually any type of international problem, in the final analysis, is either created by people or must be solved by people," he observes. "Hence, having the right people in the right place at the right time emerges as the key to a company's international growth. If we are successful in solving that problem, I am confident we can cope with all others . . . It follows, therefore, that the development of personnel to satisfy this need should be given the utmost priority by top management."

9
The Compensation of International Executives

Hans Schollhammer

It is generally recognized that the single, most important determinant of a firm's success is the quality of its executives. While this holds true for all business ventures, it is most clearly demonstrable in a firm's international operations. These operations are subject to a variety of social, economic, and political environmental conditions and restrictions considerably different from those that affect purely domestic business activities. Inevitably, the staffing of a firm's foreign subsidiaries and affiliates with competent and creative executives is of extreme importance. Practically all international firms follow a staffing policy which commits them to use local personnel to the maximum extent. The rationale of this policy is obvious, and most companies are successful in implementing it. A number of studies have shown, however, that most international firms staff a rather large portion of the higher and decisive management positions with nationals of the company's home base who are familiar with the parent company's policies and operating procedures, and who are the agents for the transfer of the firm's managerial and technical skills to the foreign operation.[1]

As an international firm's operations expand, it acquires in its reservoir of managerial talent *foreign* executives who again can be employed in countries other than their own. An international executive is by definition a member of one or the other group. For the purpose of this study, an executive who is a citizen of the home base of the company and who is working in one of the company's foreign subsidiaries or affiliates is referred to as a foreign service employee. An executive who is a citizen of a country other than the

Reprinted, with permission, from *MSU Business Topics* (Winter 1969), pp. 19-30, published by the Division of Research, Graduate School of Business Administration, Michigan State University.

home base of the company and who is working in a country other than his home country (for instance, a British citizen working for an American company in India) is referred to as a third country national.

It is a common notion, supported by empirical evidence,[2] that international executives receive compensation higher than that of domestic executives having similar functional responsibilities. There are a number of reasons for this situation. Primarily, it is the relative scarcity of qualified managers who can cope effectively with the increased demands which overseas position pose, such as knowledge of the local language, familiarity with local business practices, the ability to get along with people of different backgrounds, initiative, and willingness to assume greater responsibility.

OTHER FACTORS

There are other factors as well which account for the higher remuneration of international executives. One, which U.S. international firms frequently emphasize, is the reluctance with which many qualified U.S. executives accept an assignment abroad because of the inconveniences of the transfer, the frequently lower standards of living overseas, a perceived inferiority of the educational system in many foreign countries, and inadequate health services. In addition, many executives feel that being absent will not enable them to compete for a rise in the organization as effectively as if they are working in the firm's headquarters. For all these reasons, multinational firms may find it necessary to make overseas assignments attractive by offering a favorable compensation. In this connection, a number of interesting questions can be raised. What are international company policies as to the determination of the base salary for their foreign service employees and third country nationals? Are these groups treated equal? If not, what are the differentials and what determines them? What specific premiums and allowances of a recurrent as well as non-recurrent nature are paid to international executives? What factors determine these allowances or premiums? What non-financial *privileges* are granted to them?

In order to find answers to these questions, fifty large international U.S. based firms were asked to provide relevant information. Twelve of these manufacturing firms participated in the survey. All these firms have more than two foreign subsidiaries and each of the firms has at least 100 of its American employees in management positions abroad. Together, the twelve firms have 3,207 foreign service employees, not including their American employees in Canada, and 670 third country nationals.[3] The following report on the policies and practices of compensating international executives is based on information these firms provided.

DETERMINATION OF BASE SALARY

For the purpose of a uniform administration of compensation matters applicable to their international executives, all of the firms in the sample declared that they follow a set of explicitly stated policies and regulations. The main policy in this respect is that executives who accept foreign assignments should not substantially gain or lose money or property because of a transfer to an overseas operation, while at the same time minimizing related company costs. Apart from various allowances, all companies stated that they attempt to maintain the same base salary for comparable positions at home and overseas which are staffed with foreign service employees. For the determination of the base salary, which largely depends on the scope of responsibility and job content plus required background and experience, the firms use the same job evaluation plans on the foreign management positions as on the jobs at home. The base salary of third country nationals, however, is generally different from the salaries paid to foreign service employees because in their case, the going rate for comparable positions in their home country is used as a determinant of the base salary.

The companies pointed out that in general they do not transfer an executive from a higher paid position at home to a position with a lower base pay abroad, and if he is reassigned to the parent company, every effort is made to assign him to a position with responsibility and base salary at least equal to the one in his previous position and contingent on his past performance. However, the majority of the firms state that as a matter of policy, foreign assignment does not, by itself, obligate the parent company to give any individual special consideration, nor does it guarantee the reassigned executive any predetermined status in the parent organization.

Considering the various premiums and allowances which companies usually pay to their international executives while on assignment abroad, it becomes obvious that the firms' strong emphasis on the maintenance of a base pay has mainly two reasons. First, it serves as a basis for the determination and allocation of the various allowances and premiums. Second, it should eliminate salary problems at some future date when the executive is again transferred to his home base. The companies' policy of equal compensation for equal positions at home or abroad refers only to the base salary.

In addition to the base salary, international executives are generally granted a variety of allowances either for specific reasons such as the frequently higher costs of living abroad, or for more intangible ones such as severance of an established way of life, or simply as a financial inducement for qualified executives to accept an overseas assignment. The purpose of the following paragraphs is to analyze that portion of an international executive's compensation which he receives above and beyond the base pay as well as to describe and evaluate the methods which are used for determining it.

ALLOWANCES AND BONUSES

A study published in 1958, based on information by sixty-seven companies, has revealed that almost 80 percent of U.S. executives assigned to foreign subsidiaries or affiliates receive in addition to their base salary two or more separately calculated premiums or allowances. Only 3 percent of the foreign service employees (mainly employees of firms that had no more than ten executives abroad) received a single adjusted salary but no extra allowances.[4] The twelve large firms on which this study is based confirmed that the same situation still prevails. Although no two companies have exactly the same compensation system, they show considerable similarities as to four major recurrent allowances: foreign assignment allowance, cost of living allowance, housing allowance, and educational allowance.

FOREIGN ASSIGNMENT ALLOWANCE
Companies generally pay their international executives a foreign assignment allowance (sometimes referred to as an overseas premium) which is intended to be a foreign service incentive and a compensation for the inconveniences of having to live in a foreign environment, separated from an accustomed way of life, the family, friends and associates, and of having to work under more difficult conditions such as a language handicap, having greater responsibilities, and frequently less assistance. The firms determine this allowance as a percentage of the base salary, generally between 10 and 30 percent. Two-thirds of the firms pay the same percentage (in almost all cases either 15 or 20 percent of the base salary) regardless of the location. One-third of the firms vary the foreign assignment allowance either by taking into account the particular attractiveness of a certain location, and consequently allowing only 10 to 15 percent of the base salary as foreign assignment allowance, or by increasing the allowance to 25 to 30 percent in cases where the international executive has to work under unaccustomed climatic conditions, inadequate health services, lack of sanitation, and geographical isolation. Companies which set different rates pay the highest foreign assignment allowances plus hardship allowances to their employees in India and in African countries. Half of the firms grant the same foreign assignment allowance (in terms of percentage of the employee's base salary) to foreign service employees as well as third country nationals. The rest of the firms differentiate between the two groups of international executives. In the majority of cases, third country nationals are granted a somewhat lower percentage than that accorded foreign service employees.

COST OF LIVING ALLOWANCE

Since cost of living can vary greatly from one country to another (and even within a country) and since all of the international firms have a policy that the employees should neither lose nor unduly gain from an overseas assignment, it follows that they take into account the differences in the cost of living abroad in the form of a cost of living allowance. The purpose of this allowance is to enable the international executive to maintain, as nearly as possible, the same standard of living which he would have in his home country. For the individual firm it would be difficult, expensive, and time consuming to investigate the comparative cost of living level for every one of its foreign operations to which it assigns international executives. The large majority of U.S. based multinational firms use, therefore, for the determination of the cost of living allowance, the so-called local (cost of living) index, which is periodically computed by the U.S. Department of State for the many foreign cities where the U.S. government has a diplomatic or consular staff. The local index compares the cost for required goods and services as purchased locally with the cost of the same items in Washington, D.C. Firms using this index may find it appropriate to allow for differences between their foreign location and Washington, D.C. In foreign locations for which no local index has been computed by the U.S. State Department, firms may use their own formula and calculate an index, for instance, on the basis of a sample of goods and services for which the overseas employees themselves periodically report the local prices.

SALARY SPENT ABROAD

In order to come up with an equitable cost of living allowance, the companies must not only find out the foreign cost of living level as compared with the home country, but they must also determine what percentage of the base salary the employees spend for goods and services abroad. This percentage depends, of course, largely on family size and the actual pay the employee receives. According to budget studies in several foreign areas made by the Industrial Relations Counselor Service, Inc., U.S. executives abroad tend to spend only between 45 and 55 percent of their base salary in the foreign area.[5] If it is established that the cost of living in a particular foreign location is 5 percent higher than at home, an equitable cost of living allowance would amount to 5 percent of about one-half of the base salary.

FLEXIBLE ALLOWANCE

The firms which provided information for this survey determine the cost of living allowances in the manner shown in Figures 1 and 2.

Figure 1 indicates that the majority of the firms keep the determination of the cost of living allowance rather flexible due to their definitions of foreign spending. All firms (with the exception of the three using the IRCS rates) declared that they do not pay a cost of living allowance where the local cost of living index is lower than in the United States, but neither do they deduct the saving from the monthly remuneration; it is simply considered as an additional incentive to work abroad. When determining the cost of living allowance, all firms take into account the number of dependents of the foreign service employees simply by using different percentages of the spendable income as a basis for the allowance.

Figure 1: Cost of Living Allowance to Foreign Service Employees

Number of Firms	Basis of Allowance
3	Local index as computed by the U.S. State Department applied to base salary
6	Local index as computed by the U.S. State Department applied to company-determined foreign spending level (which varies from 30 percent to 85 percent of the base pay)
3	According to scale computed by Industrial Relations Counselors Service, Inc., N.Y.*

*In general, U.S. Department of State local index applied to 30-60 percent of the monthly base pay plus an adjustment, depending on how difficult it is to get the required goods and services locally.

Figure 2 : Cost of Living Allowance to Third Country Nationals

Number of Firms	Basis of Allowance
6	Cost of living allowance to third country nationals computed in the same way as for foreign service employees. Same percentages of spendable income are used.
4	Cost of living allowance depends on the cost of living index of the employee's home country. For this purpose the U.S. State Department's index of the employee's home city is divided into the local index of his present employment to obtain the relative index. Percentage of spendable income, to which the cost of living allowance is related, is the same for foreign service employees.
2	No general rule; cost of living allowance handled on an individual basis.

POLICIES EMPLOYED

Figure 2 shows that half of the firms treat third country nationals the same as foreign service employees. They provide them with a cost of living allowance as if their home country were the United States. On the basis of a policy which emphasizes neither gain nor loss because of a foreign assignment, the approach which the group of four firms uses is certainly more complicated, but it is the correct one. It is noteworthy that the incidence of a cost of living allowance to third country nationals is higher than a foreign service allowance paid to this group of international executives.

HOUSING ALLOWANCE

The purpose of a housing allowance is to compensate international executives for comparatively higher housing costs abroad. As with the determination of any other allowance, the basic problem is to find reasonably accurate data as to the cost of housing in foreign locations. In addition, it must be determined how much of his income the employee spends for housing in his home country. One possibility for the determination of shelter costs at a particular foreign location is to use again the information on housing allowances which U.S. government personnel abroad receives. They are compensated for about 90 percent of their actual housing expenditures.

A U.S. based multinational firm may use again the information on housing allowances as published by the Department of State, add 10 percent to this figure, and arrive at reasonably reliable housing expenditures at particular foreign locations. In order to determine whether a housing allowance is justified it is necessary to compare this figure with the actual expenditures of the employee at home. In the United States housing expenditures amount in general to 10-15 percent of a family's income. Therefore, under a policy of neither gain nor loss a company could expect that its foreign service employees contribute about 15 percent of the base salary as their share to the actual shelter costs. The positive difference is then the required housing allowance. In case of a negative difference (lower housing expenditures for a comparable standard of housing abroad, for example) the savings could be deducted from the foreign service allowance. Three-fourths of the firms stated that they reimburse their foreign service employees for all housing costs which are in excess of a certain percentage of the base salary (varying between 8 and 20 percent, usually 15 percent). The rest of the firms pay a general housing allowance regardless of location or actual housing costs amounting to 10 percent of the base salary of the foreign service employee. None of the companies indicated any provision for deducting a negative difference in the case where the employee's standard of housing could be maintained at lower cost than in his home country. The savings are simply considered as an additional compensation for the other hardships of a foreign assignment. The majority of the firms do not, at least not explicitly, fix an upper limit for their housing allowance. It must be recognized that under these circumstances the companies do not provide any incentive to their foreign service employees to find lower cost housing; on the contrary, it is an inducement to look for high cost housing accommodations and the status that goes with it. A few companies even encourage this by pointing out that their employees abroad are representatives of the company whose public relations may be enhanced by the status of their representatives in the community, which is in part due to their living standards.

The investigation of the companies' policies on housing allowances paid to third country nationals revealed that 40 percent of the firms use the same formula as for foreign service employees. One-fourth of the firms use a similar formula but make adjustments on an individual basis; the rest of the firms determine the housing allowance for their third country nationals by estimating the housing cost difference between the employee's home country and the new location.

Even though all companies provide their third country nationals with a housing allowance in cases of a positive difference between a predetermined amount of housing expenditures and actual costs, these practices reflect again a less fixed and much more flexible compensation policy with regard to international executives. By inquiring about the individual adjustments, two companies indicated that the percentages used for determining the housing allowances were not as favorable as the ones used for determining the housing allowance for foreign service employees — the reason being lower housing expenditure in the third country nationals' home countries.

EDUCATIONAL ALLOWANCES

Most companies are aware that one major factor affecting a manager's decision on whether he willingly accepts an overseas assignment is related to the educational possibilities for his children. To provide schooling that is comparable or better to that in the home country frequently necessitates added expenses, which the executive's firm may be willing to share in some form of educational assistance or allowance. The firms contributing to this survey reported the following practices:

1. All companies provide some form of assistance toward the cost of elementary and high school education of the children of their foreign service employees at the location of assignment. All twelve firms contribute in varying degrees to the educational fees which foreign service employees have to

pay for such education. Nine firms pay a flat amount — on the average, $300 per year for each child attending elementary or high school. One firm reimburses 75 percent of the education costs up to $800 per year per child, and another company reimburses all educational expenditures except $300, which is considered the proper contribution of the parents. Four firms declared that they do not automatically reimburse educational fees if the parents choose to send their children to an English-speaking private boarding school when adequate public schools are available locally. On the other hand, eight companies recommend that foreign service employees send their children, whenever possible, to an English-speaking school. The companies also reimburse, if applicable, additional educational expenditures such as school uniforms, textbooks, examination fees, and transportation costs to and from school.

2. Educational allowances in cases where children of foreign service employees go to colleges or universities are much more restricted. Only five out of twelve companies offer some form of assistance toward college costs, mainly in the form of an annual round trip from the U.S. college which the child attends to the foreign location of its parents.

3. Concerning an education allowance to third country nationals, seven out of the twelve firms stated that they reimburse elementary and high school costs which exceed those normally incurred in the home country for comparable education. Three companies pay 100 percent of the educational costs in case the schools which the children attend have been authorized by the company. Two of the twelve firms provide no education allowance to their third country nationals.

OTHER ALLOWANCES

Foreign assignment, cost of living, housing, and educational allowances are the major and most common payments granted to international executives in addition to their base salary. Some companies grant additional recurrent allowances such as an automobile allowance, and allowance for social or professional club memberships, and entertainment allowance, a separation allowance in case the family of the international executive does not move abroad, or special hardship allowances for particular conditions. The international executives of the twelve firms which supplied information receive between four and seven different recurrent allowances. It is thus no surprise that most personnel people find that determining the compensation of international executives is a complex, time consuming, cumbersome task.

BONUSES

Ten out of twelve companies in this survey had bonus plans. Their foreign service employees receive a bonus according to the same formula as the employees of the parent organization. The bonuses vary between 10 and 35 percent of the base salary. Third country nationals receive bonus payments in two-thirds of the cases, according to the formula used for determining the bonus of foreign service employees. One-third of the firms pay bonuses to third country nationals in accordance with the bonus scheme of the firm's subsidiary in the third country national's home country.

While an international executive's compensation is determined by his base salary and his recurrent allowances and bonuses, his actual take home pay can be influenced considerably by paying attention to tax and currency matters, which all multinational firms take into account, but in different degrees.

CURRENCY CONSIDERATIONS

All companies providing information declared that they calculate and state their foreign service employees' base salary as well as allowances in U.S. dollars. With regard to third country nationals, practices are more diversified. All three possible methods are used: stating base salary and allowances in the currency of the country of assignment, in the currency of their home country, or in U.S. dollars. Stating the international executive's compensation in dollars is obviously the advisable practice for U.S. based multinational firms for the sake of simplicity, uniformity, and comparability. A decision must be made whether the remuneration should actually be paid in U.S. dollars, in the currency of assignment, or a mixture of both. The following practices have been reported:

Five of the twelve firms pay their foreign service employees in U.S. dollars only, and the rest of the firms pay part (generally between 30 and 40 percent) in U.S. dollars and part in local currency. None of the foreign service employees are paid only in local currency. On the other hand, third country nationals receive their compensation predominantly in local currency: only two firms pay in U.S. dollars and two firms pay part in local currency and part in the currency of the third country nationals' home country. The difference in payment procedure with regard to foreign service employees and third country nationals does not necessarily indicate any discrimination to the disadvantage of the latter; this could, however, be the case with regard to those currencies which are not fully convertible and whose purchasing power depreciates rapidly, such as the currencies of some Latin American countries. Two of the companies which pay their foreign service employees only in U.S. currency said they would prefer to compensate them in part in local currency, but that the employees would resist this change. Obviously, for international executives working in a country where the currency is not freely convertible or whose exchange rate is under pressure, it is advantageous to get as much of their salary and allowances in dollars as possible; in this way they protect the value of their income and, in addition, in certain countries they may be able to exchange dollars at a premium for those expenditures for which local currency is needed. Many international companies operating in countries with currency restrictions are faced with a paradoxical situation. On the one hand, the foreign subsidiaries are generating a cash surplus but cannot exchange it into dollars and transfer it to the parent company. On the other hand, their overseas executives frequently insist on being paid in dollars instead of in local currency by the foreign subsidiary where they are working. In general, it would seem to be a defensible policy for every U.S. based multinational firm to pay a maximum of 20 percent of an international executive's base salary in dollars, and the remainder and all allowances in local currency through the organization to which he is assigned.

TAX CONSIDERATIONS

Tax considerations are of eminent importance to an international executive's compensation since in quite a number of countries the rates of personal taxation are so high that it would be unreasonable to expect an employee to serve there unless the company takes these differences into account. A policy that an executive should neither gain nor lose because of a foreign assignment leads necessarily to a solution of the personal tax question in such a way that the company deducts from the taxable salary of the employee an amount equivalent to what he would have to pay in his home country and, in turn, assumes full liability of whatever taxes he has to pay locally. This approach seems to be simple, but it is not. For instance, a U.S. based company will have to decide what it considers as taxable income or what kind of deductions it is willing to recognize. Standard deductions, for example, may do injustice to an executive who usually can claim more than merely the standard deduction. The question then is, should the company also recognize them? The investigation as to the relevant practices among twelve U.S. based international firms showed that five companies reimburse their foreign service employees for income taxes exceeding those which would have to be paid in the United States. Relevant decisions are taken on an individual basis. The rest of the firms principally deduct estimated U.S. taxes and assume full liability for any income taxes levied on foreign service employees.

This indicates that all companies shelter their foreign service employees from higher tax liabilities abroad as compared with U.S. taxes. Half of the firms let advantages derived from lower income taxes abroad accrue to their foreign service employees as an additional financial payoff of a foreign assignment. With regard to third country nationals, the seven companies which principally assume the tax liabilities for their foreign service employees and which deduct an amount closer to or equivalent to U.S. taxes, apply the same method to the compensation of the third country nationals. The rest of the companies do not follow a general rule, which again suggests a somewhat unequal treatment between the two groups of international executives.

RELOCATION EXPENDITURES

The transfer of an executive to a foreign position necessitates a variety of costs which can be classified as relocation expenditures. These expenditures are not a part of an international executive's compensation and thus seem to be of no direct concern within the framework of this study. Nevertheless, it seems justifiable to consider these expenditures, particularly since these data contribute to obtaining a complete picture as to the total cost burden caused by giving executives foreign assignments.

The main relocation expenditures for which the employee generally expects reimbursement are connected with (1) possible sale of the home and the monetary losses which it may entail, (2) the sale and storage or shipment of household effects or other items such as automobiles, (3) transportation costs to the foreign location for the executive and his family, and (4) the expenditures encountered in finding suitable housing abroad and related incidental expenses.

All firms declared that they assist their foreign service employees with the sale of their homes if they so desire. For instance, all twelve firms reimburse their employees for the necessary and unavoidable expenditures incurred by selling a home, such as commissions charged by real estate agencies, legal fees, and federal, state, or local taxes. In addition, eight out of twelve firms reimburse their foreign service employees to some extent for a financial loss incurred on the sale of their homes.

With respect to third country nationals, the firms pointed out that it happens rather infrequently that someone who owns a house is transferred and therefore arrangement for the reimbursement of related losses are made on an individual rather than on a general basis. However, the firms provide third country nationals in this respect with the same type of assistance as foreign service employees.

SHIPMENT COSTS

An employee being transferred to a foreign position expects to be reimbursed for the shipment costs of household goods and personal effects. Two-thirds of the firms pay practically 100 percent of the shipment costs for household goods and personal effects, whereas the rest of the firms stipulate a maximum (averaging about $10,000), which is so high that an employee will seldom have to pay a substantial part of the shipment expenditures out of his own pocket.

All companies also contribute to the cost of storing household goods. Nine firms stipulate no limitations in this respect, three firms pay storage costs only up to eighteen months. In addition, seven of the twelve firms also pay all expenses for shipment, insurance, import duties, and clearance charges to ship one automobile to the employee's new location. The other five firms follow a policy not to compensate for these expenditures, but to provide financial assistance in case an employee transferred to a position abroad sells his car at a loss. Most companies either supply high ranking international executives with an automobile or assist them in purchasing one.

Travel costs for the international executive and his family are also part of the relocation expenditures. Half of the firms compensate only air travel, economy or tourist class; one-fourth of the firms pay first class fares in the case of a flight of more than eight hours; one fourth of the firms allow principally first class travel.

The various relocation expenditures alone can easily amount to more than the *annual* salary of the employee who is assigned to an overseas position, and it thus shows very clearly how important it is to investigate carefully whether it is necessary to assign a foreign manager instead of a locally available executive to a particular overseas position.

FRINGE BENEFITS

Most large companies provide their executives with various benefits such as pensions, contributions to life insurance, and compensation of medical expenses. Obviously, a policy of neither gain nor loss because of a foreign assignment means that a company must grant international executives benefits comparable to those received by the parent company personnel. All firms provide their foreign service employees with life insurance covering generally two times the annual base salary. The companies pay either all or two-thirds of the insurance costs. The same benefits are also granted to third country nationals in seven out of twelve companies. Eleven of these firms reported having the same type of pension plan for their foreign service employees as for their domestic personnel. Only four companies also provide third country nationals with pension plans, which in three cases are related to the U.S. company's plan, and in one case related to a pension plan as established by the company's subsidiary in the third country national's home country.

Besides the fringe benefits which international executives generally receive in the same way as the company's domestic personnel, they frequently are granted supplementary fringe items, which can make an overseas assignment more attractive. Longer vacations, as well as periodic home leaves, are the most common in conjunction with certain financial benefits. Six out of twelve firms have special vacation schedules for their foreign service employees. For them the paid vacations are generally one week longer than if they were not working abroad. One of these six firms does not grant this same privilege to its third country nationals who get vacations according to local practice. Four firms follow the parent company's vacation schedule; for two firms the vacation period for foreign service employees is determined by local practice.

All of the U.S. based multinational firms included in this survey also grant their foreign service employees paid home leave. Only six of these firms also grant this privilege to their third country nationals; three other companies only under certain conditions (for example, the third country national's home country must be on a continent other than where he works), and three firms so far have no provision for home leave for third country nationals.

The average annual home leave period is about three weeks. In addition to the home leave, seven of twelve companies allow an additional two days for traveling. The majority of the companies require that home leave be actually spent in the employee's home country. Only three firms do not stipulate such a condition. Most of the firms also allow the regular vacation period and home leave to be taken consecutively, although two firms require that both be taken separately. Two firms do not grant the regular vacation period in the year of home leave.

CONCLUSIONS

An attempt has been made in this survey to investigate and analyze the policies of a representative sample of large U.S. based multinational firms concerning the compensation of their international executives and those major cost items which are the result of an employee's foreign assignment and which the firms are willing to absorb. These general conclusions can be drawn:

By all counts, international business activities have been expanding rapidly in recent years. This expansion has brought about a remarkable increase in the number of business executives given foreign assignments. The chief reason for this is that the transfer of an organization's technological knowledge and managerial skills to a new foreign venture depends largely on the executives who have already worked for the parent company for some time and have acquired the necessary company related know-how.

At present, U.S. based multinational firms have about 40,000 Americans in managerial positions abroad. Only ten years ago this group was estimated to number 25,000.[6] In fact, the evolution of a managerial class of international executives symbolizes most drastically the revolution which is taking place: A large segment of the business community in all developed countries is becoming more and more outward looking and is pursuing business opportunities on a global rather than a national scale. One consequence of this development is that the compensation of international executives becomes a major policy issue in a growing number of firms. Until recently even the very large multinational firms were deciding compensation questions concerning employees who were given foreign assignments on an individual basis. Today, many of these firms have manuals covering the most pertinent situations which may be encountered when assigning employees to foreign operations.

EQUITABLE REMUNERATION

Their main purpose, however, is to provide a basis for consistent and equitable remuneration. This means that the individual-centered approach to determining the compensation of an international executive is giving way to a more general, organization-centered approach, although most companies are quite prepared to grant their international executives special allowances in response to particular needs.

From the data and information presented in this survey, it becomes clear that because of a variety of necessary allowances and transfer costs, international executives are considerably more expensive than local management personnel. Of course, the individual firm establishing new operations abroad frequently has no alternative; qualified personnel are not available locally and the firm must rely on the personnel of the parent company or on personnel of well-established subsidiaries. The relative scarcity of qualified management personnel for foreign operations is certainly a sufficient reason for the higher remuneration which international executives generally receive — quite apart from the special adaptive abilities which are expected of them and other hardships of foreign assignments. As a result, all firms offer international executives a premium of about 15 percent to 25 percent of their base salary (generally the amount which they would receive for a comparable position in their home country) as a compensation for an array of elusive factors involved in an overseas position but not found in a similar position at home. In addition, it has been shown that all the firms contributing to this survey had developed rather elaborate schemes for calculating a variety of allowances, which generally are designed to compensate the international executive for higher expenditures abroad or for cost items which he would not encounter at home. Compensatory items of this nature (such as cost of living allowances, housing allowances, educational allowances, and in some cases special hardship allowances) amount in most cases to another 45-70 percent of an international executive's base salary. On the average, the recurrent compensation of a U.S. executive working abroad is roughly twice as high as the remuneration he would receive in a comparable position at home, and in certain cases this amount is three times as high.

COST ABSORPTION

In addition, the transfer of executives to a foreign operation causes a variety of relocation costs which are absorbed by the company and which, particularly in cases of a transfer to another continent, came close to, or are even in excess of, one year's salary of the employee concerned.

All top managers of multinational firms with whom this subject has been discussed agree that international executives are generally considerably more expensive than locals. They are quick to point out that, nevertheless, multinational firms have to absorb these higher costs not only because they have in many cases no other alternative, but also because they expect that work abroad will provide these executives with experience that may later be valuable to the parent company and the organization as a whole. Despite this, all companies emphasize their determination to rely to the maximum extent possible on local personnel. This leads most multinational firms to undertake a considerable training effort which ultimately allows a reduction in the number of international executives. In this respect, however, it should be kept in mind that a firm's commitment to pull out the international executive as soon as sufficiently qualified local managers are available may have positive as well as negative effects. For instance, this policy may lead, on the one hand to salary savings and may reduce a company's vulnerability against charges of remote control where nationalist sentiments are high. On the other hand, international executives may be able to show (in the interest of the company) greater resistance against certain governmental pressure than local managers who may not want to be suspected of lack of patriotism.

HIGH SALARIES

During the course of collecting empirical data on this project, a number of personnel directors of multinational firms expressed concern about the high salaries and allowances paid to employees assigned to a foreign operation. Generally they expressed regret that they were unable to do very much about it except to reaffirm their company's policy that an overseas assignment should neither lead to an undue financial gain nor a loss for persons concerned, and that local personnel should replace international personnel as soon as possible. However, in some cases, a company's high salaries and allowances to international executives are simply a remnant from a time when the international operations were limited, and thus the generous compensation to the few international executives was of little significance. As the international activities of a firm expanded and the number of foreign assignments increased, these companies neglected or found it difficult to reduce the allowances to a more reasonable level. The only solution in these cases is to use an objective approach to the calculation of cost differentials and then to reduce overseas allowances to these new justifiable levels. These difficulties also show how important it is that a company uses a rational approach to the determination of international executives' salaries and allowances even if for the time being it has only a few executives abroad.

FINANCIAL INDUCEMENTS

Some companies found that they have formidable difficulties in persuading good managers to accept foreign assignments, and thus they offer generous financial inducements. In many of these cases the high compensation to a firm's overseas personnel appears to be mainly a necessary consequence of the failure to eradicate among the firm's potential international executives the notion that they will miss opportunities for advancement at home, or that when their foreign assignment is over they may find themselves at loose ends. In these cases, a reduction of what seems to be unduly high compensation can be accomplished by proper career planning and careful attention to the reabsorption of international executives into the domestic organization. The better a company succeeds in keeping open the channels of advancement within the domestic firm for the international executive, the easier it will be to attract the organization's best men to overseas assignments at a lower cost burden than would otherwise be necessary.

TWO DISTINCT GROUPS

The increasing multinationality of many firms and their policies of selecting their international executives company-wide rather than only from the parent company's pool of managerial talent has led to two distinct groups of international executives — foreign service employees and third country nationals. Only fifteen years ago the latter group was numerically rather insignificant. In the meantime, as more and more companies became truly international in scope and philosophy, the proportion of third country nationals increased rapidly. Among the large multinational firms, about one-fourth to one third of their international executives are third country nationals. The distinction between the two groups of international executives is of no relevance from the point of view of their required activities. However, with respect to their compensation, this survey provides evidence that although in the majority of cases these executives are remunerated according to the same formula or methods, there is a certain degree of discrimination against the third country national as compared to the foreign service employee. For instance, it has been shown that some companies do not provide third country nationals with the allowances they grant to foreign service employees; in other cases, the formers' allowances are lower. Even in the cases where the two groups of executives seemingly receive the same treatment, the third country nationals actually get a lower allowance in cases where it is calculated as a percentage of the base salary of foreign service employees. The discrimination is particularly noticeable among firms with a low share of third country nationals among their international executives. The higher the percentage of third country nationals in a firm's pool of international executives, the lower is the intergroup discrimination with respect to their compensation.

This survey also provides evidence of a clear trend among the multinational firms to internationalize the upper management ranks by making an overseas assignment part of the executive career development plan. Increasingly, firms attempt to identify managerial talent of all nationalities where they are operating and then arrange cross postings at appropriate stages in their careers — an interchange which benefits the individuals concerned as well as the organization. Multinational firms which follow this route are faced with the necessity to develop centrally administered, systematic, and equitable compensation schemes which should have two main characteristics: (1) they should be based on the principle that an executive should neither gain nor lose because of a foreign assignment, and (2) they should facilitate the executive's reintegration into the parent organization or any other part of the total organization to which he may be assigned. It is hoped the information in this survey can be of use in developing a rational and equitable system for a firm's international executives.

NOTES

1. See e.g., E. R. Barlow, *Management of Foreign Manufacturing Subsidiaries* (Boston: Division of Research, Graduate School of Business Adminis-

tration, Harvard University, 1953), p. 174 ff; Thomas D. Cabot, *et al., Cooperation for Progress in Latin America* (New York: Committee for Economic Development, 1961), p. 43; Theodore Geiger, *The General Electric Company in Brazil* (New York: National Planning Association, 1961), p. 58; R. F. Gonzalez and A. R. Negandhi, *The United States Overseas Executive: His Orientations and Career Patterns* (East Lansing; Bureau of Business and Economic Research, Graduate School of Business Administration, Michigan State University, 1967).

2. See, e.g., E. R. Barlow, *op. cit.,* p. 163; E. R. Floyd, *Compensating American Managers Abroad* (New York: American Management Association, Inc., Research Study No. 31, 1958); A. Patton, "Executive Compensation Here and Abroad," *Harvard Business Review,* XL (September-October, 1962), 144 ff; G. F. Dickover, "Compensating the American Employee Abroad," *Financial Executive,* April, 1966, pp. 40-49; A. Patton and J. Lock, "Executive Compensation: Trends Here and Abroad," *The McKinsey Quarterly,* IV, No. 2 (1967) 22 ff.

3. The firms participating in this survey noted that they generally compensate their expatriates in Canada in the same way as they compensate domestic employees.

4. See Floyd, *Compensating,* p. 18.

5. See Dickover, "Compensating the American Employee," p. 46.

6. See H. and M. Krosney, *Careers and Opportunities in International Service* (New York: E. P. Dutton, Inc., 1965), p. 62.

Chapter Three:
Marketing

10
Are Domestic and International Marketing Dissimilar?

Robert Bartels

As marketing managers become increasingly involved in international marketing, and as schools of business undertake to internationalize their programs, both have queried whether there are significant differences between domestic and international marketing, and have asked whether these differences prescribe dissimilar practices and programs. Experience in international markets has shown some marketers the inadvisability of projecting domestically successful marketing strategies into foreign situations. Yet, other companies operate successfully from the premise that the world is a market in which business principles have universal applicability. That such divergent experiences and convictions persist without theoretical resolution of their apparent inconsistencies is evidence that the concept of international marketing needs further clarification. As a practice, international trading is old; as a type of modern marketing, it is a relatively new idea.

In the internationalization of marketing, as in all substantial changes in marketing practice and thought, new ideas pass through three stages in becoming accepted and established. First, a stage of *identification*. When a new idea is perceived, even before its nature is fully recognized, it is often given a name to facilitate reference and communication concerning it. The designation may be a familiar term or one newly coined. It may have temporary or lasting usage. Second, a stage of *conceptualization*,

Reprinted, by permission, from the *Journal of Marketing,* published by the American Marketing Association, Vol. 32 (July 1968).

in which definition occurs as the idea gains distinctive form and meaning. Third, a stage of *assimilation* and integration into the established body of thought. This is the process of the enlargement of thought or theory and its enrichment with new ideas.

The extension of marketing practice beyond national borders has in recent years initiated this process with respect to the terms "comparative" and "international" as applied to marketing. What had earlier been called "foreign trade" became *"international* marketing," as domestically originated techniques were applied to marketing outside the country. The arguments over the similarities and differences of marketing in the two realms have provided a degree of confusion as conceptualization progresses beyond the initial stage of identification of this broader field of marketing.

Likewise, the term *comparative* marketing has been used, designating not so much a practice of marketing but a type of analysis whereby nationally dissimilar marketing systems and practices can be compared — or more often, contrasted. The fruitlessness of simply comparing numerous differences soon became apparent and hinted at the need of a more conceptual view of the differences in marketing as practiced in different national environments. Thus, attention has turned to defining "comparative" as applied to marketing. Incorporation of the concepts, both "international" and "comparative," into marketing theory awaits further clarification of their meaning. Toward this end, the following conceptualization is offered for consideration.

WHAT IS MARKETING?

Before *"international* marketing" can have a meaning, the term *marketing* itself must be understood, for "international" only qualifies the basic process. In general, marketing connotes a process of two-fold character: technical and social.

TECHNICAL PROCESS

As a technical process, marketing consists of the application of principles, rules, or knowledge relating to the non-human elements of marketing. Non-human elements include factors such as products, price, profit, cost, and others listed in the left half of Figure 1. They include also categories such as channels, institutions, markets, buyers, and "economic man," which express economic concepts involving people, but which do not connote the full range of non-economic human behavior of the individuals occupying those roles.

Marketing has traditionally been regarded as a technical process, and marketing management as the utilization of technical means for the achievement of desired ends. Marketing technology, or marketing thought, has been elaborately developed, and the concepts and generalizations thereof have been held to have a universality transcending national boundaries and cultural differences. The technologies of turnover rates of economies of large scale operations, of length of distribution channel, and of identification of products have generally been regarded as universal, without respect to time and place.

Recognizing this universality, or presuming it, marketers have with varying success applied this technology around the world, only to learn the limitations of its applicability under certain environmental circumstances.

SOCIAL PROCESS

As a social process, marketing is a complex of interactions among individuals acting in role positions in the various systems involved in the distribution of goods and services.

This concept emphasizes the human element, the individual acting under the full range of influences, both economic and non-economic, which affiliation with the social institutions of his society imposes upon him. The categories of thought implicit in this concept of marketing are indicated in the right half of Figure 1.

Figure 1: Concepts of Marketing and Their Related Elements

Concepts of Marketing	
Technical (Non-human)	Social (Human)
Products	Social Systems
Price	Roles
Profits	Behavior
Costs	Interaction
Brands	Management
Differentiation	
Layouts	
Scales	
Channels	
Markets	
Institutions	
Flows	
Processes	

As a social process, marketing in two nations may differ markedly. While the *roles* in which individuals interact may be identical, their *expectations* and *behavior patterns* in two societies may be quite different. Marketing strategies planned for another country may differ accordingly, and similarities could be expected only to the extent that the customs, values, attitudes, and motivations of two people are alike.

Business in general and marketing in particular thus are seen to consist of two complementary aspects: the technical and the social. Managerial generalizations concerning the former appear to be more universally valid than generalizations concerning behavior and interaction in the marketing process. Applications of even presumably universally valid theories, however, may vary with the environments, thus requiring an environmental concept of marketing.

WHAT IS ENVIRONMENTALISM?

Environmentalism is a concept which relates marketing to the environment in which it is performed and holds it to be in large measure determined thereby. Marketing, of course, helps to shape the societal environment, but the environmental concept of marketing as a social process throws the emphasis in the other direction. Environmental interpretation of business is relatively new and is itself a product of the growing experience of businessmen in environments other than that of their home country. Heretofore, although marketers have always operated in a societal environment, this factor has generally been taken for granted. Patterns of behavior were learned as a part of maturation; all participants in business operated within the same legal and ethical framework; and basic uniformity characterized the diversity of the business world. This is not so in the foreign and international realms.

Merely to *perceive* environment, however, is one thing; to *conceptualize* it is another and is the essential second step in the groundwork leading to the construction of theory in international or comparative marketing. Toward this end, the abstract elements of environment — domestic and foreign — need to be identified as bases of the comparability of environments in different countries. Aid in the interpretation of environment as it affects marketing is found in several of the scholarly disciplines: geography, economics, sociology, anthropology, and psychology.

While recognizing the weakness of oversimplification, there seems to be tenability in the generalization that physical and economic environmental factors are primary determinants of the *technical* aspects of business, whereas cultural environmental factors tend to be the principal determinants of the *social* aspects of business. As suggested in Figure 2, such factors as size of country, dispersion or concentration of population, transportation and communication facilities, levels and distribution of income, and price levels are significant affectors of markets, channels, outlets, price lines, and promotion budgets. Marketing practices relating to these functions vary from country to country as the physical and economic circumstances differ.

Figure 2: Relation of Environmental Factors to Dependent Elements of Marketing

			Elements of Marketing	
			Technical	Social

National Environments	Physical and Economic	Size of:
		    Country
		    Population
		    GNP
		Level of Living
		Transportation System
		Etc.
			Products
			Price
			Profits
			Costs
			Brands
			Differentiation
			Layouts
			Scales
			Channels
			Markets
			Institutions
			Flows
			Processes	

	Societal and Social	Family School Church Economy Government Military Leisure		Social Systems Roles Behavior Interaction Government

The social aspects of marketing, on the other hand, are the more sensitive to the societal and social environments of the individuals engaged in marketing. The societal environment consists of the major institutional structure of the society and of its values on the highest level. Thus, the relationships and obligations within the family, the doctrines of the church, or the philosophy of the political regime would affect behavior of individuals as business participants. So, too, would the social environment, the influences within the lesser groups and organizations in which marketing participants act. Thus, pressures exerted through institutions which are common to all societies, but which differ in character among them, produce dissimilarities in marketing within different nations.

WHAT IS COMPARATIVE?

Identification of marketing (1) as a dual technical and social activity and (2) as a consequence of environmental circumstances leads to the next question: What is *comparative* marketing? The term "comparative" has been used in the first stage of its definition to mean simply comparison. This has been a casual uncritical usage but one which has had acceptance because of the ease with which visual comparisons or contrasts can be made by anyone observing two business systems. One country has smaller (perhaps family-oriented) retail establishments than another, buyers rather than sellers take initiative in market search and negotiation, or management decisions are made with either greater haste or greater deliberation — these facts have been cited as "comparative" evidence. The truth is that they are descriptive rather than comparative, as shown by the following illustration.

Figure 3: Model for Comparative Analysis

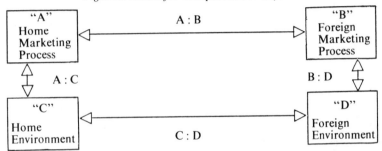

Assume that marketing and its environments are identified in two countries. As shown in Figure 3, let

A represent the marketing process in the home country,

B represent the marketing process in the foreign country,

C represent the environment of the home country, and

D represent the environment of the foreign country.

The *comparison* of marketing in two countries may be indicated by the symbols A : B. This is simply a descriptive statement, not an analytical one. So too is the relationship of C : D, which indicates a comparison of environments.

The relationships of A : C and of B : D, on the other hand, are statement of *environmentalism.* They indicate the orientation of each marketing system to its own environment, or rather to its particular complex of environments — physical, societal, social, economic, legal, and political. None of these sets of relationships, however, represents a truly comparative statement.

The *comparative* analysis in this illustration is suggested by the following equation:

$$A : C = B : D$$

This is to say that comparative study is not simply a description of either marketing or environmental differences but rather *a comparison of relationships between marketing and its environment in two or more countries.* In this context, differences which might be emphasized in simple comparisons may become similarities when related to an environmental frame of reference. It is in this sense that similarities — similarities of relationships, patterns, causes-and-effects — become more significant than bare differences to the seasoned international observer. To the extent that unexplainable differences can be replaced by explainable relationships, tentative generalizations can be postulated and theories constructed.

The translation of differences into such comparative patterns relates directly to the question of whether marketing in two countries is really "different," whether it should be organizationally segregated in the business enterprise and academically specialized in "international" functional courses contrasted with those for domestic business. An answer to this question is suggested in the distinctions here made. To the extent that either business managers or academicians *perceive* differences in foreign and domestic marketing, they will deal with them as distinct and different. To the extent that they perceive the inherent similarities, they will deal with them in more integrated marketing theory, business structure, and academic offering.

WHAT IS INTERNATIONAL?

The explanation of comparative analysis is intended to emphasize the actions and interactions of participants in the marketing process who act under the constraints of their respective societies. Their interactions constitute the business or marketing process and are generally private entrepreneurial undertakings. Cross-cultural private negotiations, however, are not the whole of international trade. In addition to the respective national environments, there is an identifiable international—or rather *inter-national*—environment affecting marketing and other business decisions. This is the environment in which trade and transactions are made *across* national borders, rather than *within* different national domains. It is created by national sovereignties on behalf of the collective interests of their nations. This international environment presents still another factor to be considered in the question of whether domestic and international marketing are different or similar.

To illustrate the character of this environment and its distinction from the national environments previously discussed, the point might be made that greater environmental differences may be found within a country than between countries. For example, differences between Manhattan and Mississippi may be more significant for marketers than those between Manhattan and Madrid. Notwithstanding the similarities of environments *within two countries,* when the national interests of two nations are involved, a special environmental circumstance may arise. Within each nation there is usually a uniform national trade policy. Among nations, the respective interests of each make constraints upon marketers which are additional to those of the societal influences upon the market participants. These constraints may be exerted upon foreigners in international trade as well as upon citizens of the constraining nation.

Figure 4: Relations of private and public sectors in the international environment

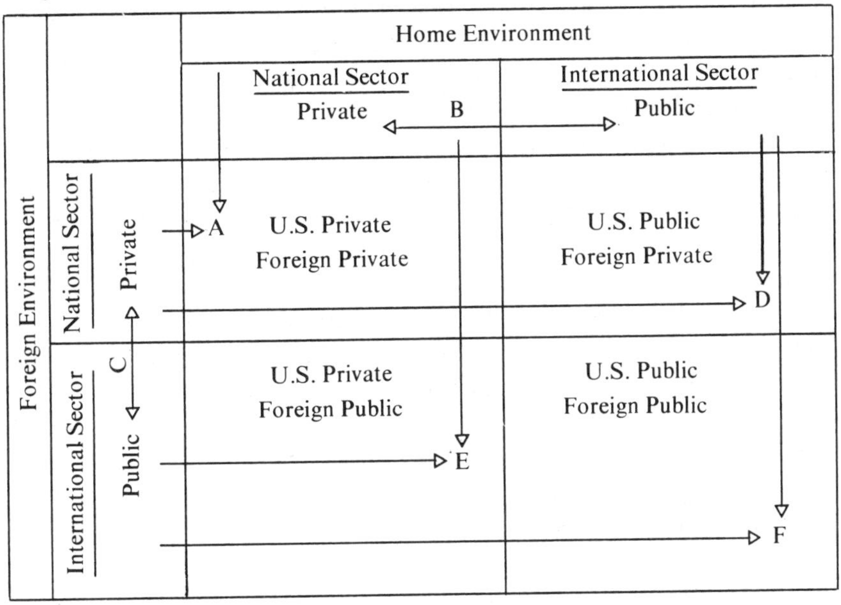

As an example, the societal environments and business systems of three countries may be so similar that, in terms of comparative analysis, there would be little differences between their domestic and international marketing. On the other hand, while one nation may permit free trading across its borders, another, to protect its national interests, may restrict imports, impose tariffs, limit currency conversion, require trade registrations, set import quality standards, and so forth. Thus, while their *national* environments may produce similarities, the environment created *between* those nations, or the *inter*-national environment, makes for dissimilarities between domestic and international marketing. This fact concerning international marketing requires consideration in both business practices and academic curricula.

Conceptually represented, the international environment is depicted in Figure 4 as areas of influence in which the national or public interests of either home or host country governments influence the private commercial relations of both their own and foreign nationals. Normal marketing transactions, indicated at point A as private-private interactions, have already been explained as subject to the national environments of each participant. The international environment is identified by the interactions lettered B, C, D, E, and F.

National interests affecting international marketing are expressed in part in relations of a government with *its own citizens* (B and C) through both encouragement and discouragement. Encouragement to exporting and direct foreign investment may be given through research, assistance, trade fairs, export credit insurance, and investment guarantees; discouragement may be given through import and export restrictions, investment restrictions, and antitrust regulation. Likewise, each country affects *foreign nationals* trading with its own citizens, as through import tariffs and other non-tariff regulations and other inducements to investment, joint venture restrictions, and the like. These relationships are denoted in blocks D and E. Finally, the international environment consists in part of the *interactions of governments* (F) which affect international marketing as through the creation of common markets and free trade areas, consummation of commercial treaties, agreement on tariffs, or the unification of antitrust laws. Together these conditions constitute an environment quite apart from the foreign national environments of individuals with whom one may trade. It is truly an international environment, and to the extent that it exists it increases the differences rather than the similarities between domestic and international marketing.

CONCLUSIONS

In relation to the question initially posed: "Are domestic and international marketing dissimilar?" the foregoing analysis leads to the following conclusions:

1. That marketing technology has universal validity and potential universal applicability.

2. That the applicability of marketing technology is dependent upon circumstances of the environments in which it is applied.

3. That the behavioral aspects of marketing, reflecting mainly cultural, societal, and social circumstances, indicate wide differences in marketing as it is carried on in different countries.

4. That notwithstanding particular behavior differences, the *relationships*

between marketing practice and environment are susceptible to generalizations in analysis termed "comparative marketing."

5. That in addition to the national environmental influences upon marketing participants in different countries, nations' interests, individually and collectively, create an inter-national environment in which the marketers operate. There is generally no equivalent to these factors within the national or domestic economy.

6. That marketing managers need to approach the international situation with expectation of both similarities and differences relative to domestic marketing, but with an understanding that both are embraced within a consistent body of marketing theory.

7. That academic marketing offerings should provide for thorough grounding in basic marketing technology, in environmental analysis both at home and abroad, and in those aspects of the international situation for which there is no equivalent in either country.

11
International Advertising Principles and Strategies

Gordon E. Miracle

Traditionally many international advertising men have maintained that the nature of the advertising task varies from market to market. In recent years the arguments have shifted and it has been fashionable to debate whether advertising themes and advertisements should be uniform or developed specifically for individual national markets. Although some are still debating this question at a fairly general level of argument, it is recognized increasingly that the issue is a phantom. The issue is not whether advertising messages and media strategy should be uniform from market to market. The real issue has to do with uniformity of procedures and criteria: when can advertising materials and ideas developed in one country be useful—or adapted for use— in another country, and when not?

It is the thesis of this article that the advertising task is essentially the same at home or abroad—namely, to communicate information and persuasive appeals effectively. The requirements of effective communication are fixed, and cannot vary with time, place, or form of communication; therefore, the same approach to communication, that is the same *approach* to the preparation of messages and selection of media, can be used in every country. It is only specific advertising messages and media strategy that sometimes must be changed from country to country. In international marketing and advertising as well as in domestic advertising, the communicator must learn

Reprinted, with permission, from *MSU Business Topics,* Autumn (1968), pp. 29-36, published by the Division of Research, Graduate School of Business Administration, Michigan State University.

about his audience, define market segments as precisely as possible, and study backgrounds and motivational influences in detail before he begins preparing an advertising campaign. In recent years advertising men in the United States and in other countries have discussed widely the degree to which ideas and advertising materials created in one country can be used in another. Eric Elinder, head of a Swedish advertising agency, has said: "Why should three artists in three different countries sit drawing the same electric iron and three copywriters write about what after all is largely the same copy for the same iron?"[1] Mr. Elinder believes consumer differences are diminishing from nation to nation and he would prefer to put top specialists to work devising a strong international campaign, which could then be presented "with insignificant national modifications rendered necessary by changes in language."[2]

Mr. Elinder and those who hold his point of view argue that sometimes the appeals, illustrations, or other features of advertisements need not be changed from market to market. They have rightly observed that in many respects, consumers in diverse markets are similar and that human nature is basically the same in most societies. Men everywhere require satisfaction of physiological and psychological needs.

However, on the other side it can be argued that a communicator should rightly take cognizance of the differences between consumers in his own country and those in other countries. They not only speak another tongue, but they adhere to other religions, philosophies, and traditions; they differ with regard to family patterns, childhood training, and the role of members in the family. The occupational hierarchy varies among nations; climate and geography and other aspects of consumers' physical environment are diverse; consumers engage in a wide variety of sports, hobbies, and other forms of amusement and entertainment. These environmental differences play an important part in shaping the demand for specific types of goods and services and in determining what promotional appeals are best. Thus while human nature and the motives of men are more or less universal, the ways in which men satisfy their needs are not. The nature of need satisfaction is determined by cultural and socio-economic conditions. Since such conditions are not the same in all countries, it may be argued that products, or the appeals, illustrations, and other advertising features used to sell them, often must differ from market to market.

The obstacles to effective communication are of the same type in both domestic and international markets, but they are magnified because of the relative heterogeneity of buyers in diverse markets. Thus the tasks of identifying and assessing the aggregate characteristics of markets, and of analyzing the individual characteristics and behavior of buyers, are more complex for world markets than for a single domestic market.

Communication with buyers in foreign markets may not be effective for a number of reasons. Of particular importance to international marketing communication are the following:

1. **The message may not get through to the intended recipient.** Either the medium may not reach the recipient, or the message may not be perceived for some reason — perhaps because the person is uninterested in the message at the moment, or other matters are more important, or other distractions may take the intended recipient's attention away from the message. Such difficulties may be due to the advertiser's lack of knowledge about which media are appropriate to reach foreign target audiences, and lack of knowledge about when to reach them (scheduling difficulties, for example).

2. **The message may not be understood in the way intended by the sender.** Because of the advertiser's lack of knowledge of the factors which influence how persons from different cultures will interpret messages, it is possible for him to prepare messages which will not be interpreted correctly — or as the advertiser intended.

3. **The message may not induce the recipient to take the action desired by the sender.** Although a message may be perceived correctly, lack of knowledge about foreign cultural factors which influence attitude formation, purchasing behavior, and so forth may cause communication to fail in producing the desired effect. Such failure may be due to the advertiser's lack of knowledge on such matters as consumer motives, reference group influence, or consumers' economic circumstances.

SYMBOLS

The successful communicator depends upon symbols as a means of establishing empathy with another person. Thus the advertiser must choose with care the symbols used in advertisements for a market.

Advertising symbols may be either: (1) verbal, such as the words in advertising copy, or (2) visual, such as the illustrations in an advertisement or television commercial. Color is one type of visual symbol. Today, in the United States, there is a continued effort to establish the effect of colors and various shades of colors on consumer behavior. It may be well for the advertiser to remember that in other cultures, colors may not have the same significance. In China, for example, light and bright colors are chosen by the young people, and plainer and deeper colors by their elders. Yellow has always been the imperial color; originally its use by the masses was prohibited, and it is still not used extensively save for religious purposes; it suggests grandeur and mystery.[3]

Because of the differences in traditions, customs, religions, and related cultural features of a foreign society, an advertiser must exercise care in selecting symbols that can convey the intended message and that do not offend the sensibilities of the audience. For example, comparing people to animals, or utilizing animals in cartoon advertisements to portray human beings may be quite unacceptable to Buddhists, who believe in reincarnation. An advertisement comparing people to animals also runs the risk of being offensive to an Arab. ("A beast is a beast and a man is a man. Allah says so.") Thus the use of animals as symbols to illustrate human behavior may not be attractive, even though understandable.

APPEALS

Appeals must be in accordance with consumer tastes, wants, and attitudes — in short, in harmony with the prevailing mentality of the market. In some countries, the use of a certain brand of lipstick or toothpaste by a well-known fashion model will enhance the product's appeal in the eyes of a working girl. But, "In Belgium (for example) it doesn't. Models are scarce and their trade is hardly considered honorable."[4]

The health appeal varies in effectiveness from country to country. Belgians are hard-working, earn a good living, and spend freely. They appreciate the good things in life. They desire comfort in clothing, heating, and home facilities. They are fun-loving and appreciate radio, television, beer, wine, and other products which add to the enjoyment in life. One observer believes that "the Belgian will hardly be found ready to buy something because it is good for him. He will buy if the taste pleases him, even if it is bad for his health."[5] Likewise, in France, the suggestion that the use of a certain toothpaste will help prevent dental caries is likely to be less effective than the same appeal in the United States, since Frenchmen are not as inclined as Americans to be concerned about the numbers of cavities in their teeth. In nearby Holland, health attitudes are quite different from those in Belgium or France. The Dutch show greater concern about their health. To the Dutch, the vitamin content and energy value of some foods are more important than taste.

For products that are identical physically but which are used differently from one market to the next — for example, cornstarch, cake mixes, instant coffee, margarine, and many other food products — the advertising message often has to be adapted for each market segment. Campbell Soup, however, in order to convey the idea of active people on the move around the world and at the same time underscore the universal appeal of Campbell Soup, commissioned the filming of a sixty-second film spot which includes a high-speed train in Japan, a market scene in Singapore, and a children's playground in Puerto Rico. It was dubbed into a number of languages, including Cantonese, Spanish, and Creole for cinema presentation in twenty countries.[6]

The list of companies that are trying to locate universal appeals for their products, which can serve as the basis for preparing prototype campaigns, is increasing. Revlon, a large manufacturer of cosmetics, is one of the best examples. "Revlon is particularly concerned that their international advertising . . . contribute to the over-all Revlon image. Latitude is granted field managers in revising individual ads or budgets; but even these must be cleared first with headquarters."[7]

J. W. Rintelin, vice-president of the Coca-Cola Export Corporation, says that his company aims for world-wide advertising uniformity, even in such exotic tongues as Swahili, Urdu, Yoruba, Ga, Twi, Ibo, Sesuto, and others. Coca-Cola has a universal thirst-quenching appeal, and "the statement that 'Coca-Cola refreshes you best' has universal significance that transcends all sectional barriers. . . . Therefore, Coca-Cola strives to achieve a similarity of messages, visual appearance, good taste, and major media selection . . . ."[8] The theme, "things go better with coke," is used in Germany as follows: "Besser geht's mit Coca-Cola."

Union Carbide markets a line of car-care products — polishes, waxes, additives for oil and gasoline, antifreeze — under its Prestone brand in European markets.[9] Before moving into Europe, however, the company and its advertising agency, Young & Rubicam, surveyed more than fifty dealers, as well as a sample of consumers in eleven countries. They studied buying habits and patterns, retail distributor practices, and many other factors in order to provide the base for a successful marketing program, including the content and nature of advertisements. As a result, they concluded that certain ideas and techniques applied previously in the United States should be appropriate for Europe. For example, in one advertisement selling car polish, run in seven languages in as many countries, Union Carbide told what salt could do to a car and offered the customer his money back if he was not satisfied with its product. Carbide and Young & Rubicam were told that European consumers would be suspicious of any product for which the maker had to offer money back if they were not satisfied. Anyway, the gloom-sayers insisted, thousands of people would buy the polish, use it, and then send back the empty can. However, the research proved correct, and the gloomy predictions were not fulfilled. The advertisement was successful in Europe just as similar advertisements have been successful in the United States. The key, of course, to ascertaining what was likely to happen in Europe was careful consumer research.

One of the most widely-heralded international themes is Esso's "Put a tiger in your tank." After considerable success in the United States, the company decided to test the slogan in Europe and Asia. Minor modifications in wording had to be made; for example, in France the word tank is *reservoir* which in the context of the phrase could be risqué, so the word *moteur* was substituted. Consumer research showed the campaign was highly successful in European countries. The theme was also appropriate in some countries in southeast Asia where the tiger is a symbol of power and luck.[10] However, in Thailand, the tiger is not a symbol of strength, and the campaign was not understood.[11]

The infusion of U.S. methods into the German "soap war" starting in 1963 has caused considerable excitement.[12] Although there are 65 producers of laundry products in Germany, three companies manufacture 90 percent of the all-purpose and delicate detergents: (1) Henkel & Cie, GmbH, an old established German company, with *Persil,* (2) Sunlicht GmbH, a subsidiary of Unilever, with *Sunil* and *Omo,* and (3) Procter and Gamble, with *Dash.* Dash rose to a position of eminence — 15 percent share of market — in two short years by using an assortment of techniques that are standard in the United States: trial samples, repetitive and motivation-oriented advertising spots replete with bright, hard-to-forget jingles. Sunlicht and Henkel adopted similar tactics quickly; nevertheless, their brands lost share of market. Generally speaking, the customary appeals of price and quality were replaced by amorphous claims of "whiter than white," "the best ever," and "the most sparkling white of my life." Price comparisons were difficult because P & G introduced "odd" sizes, forcing competitive activities more heavily into the realm of package design, display, and advertising.

ILLUSTRATIONS AND LAYOUT

Illustrations and layout are perhaps more likely to be universal than other features of advertisements. Certain types of illustrations are being used with increasing frequency in several nations. For example, advertisements for Canadian Pacific Airlines which were created in Mexico City have appeared not only in U.S. and Canadian publications but also in newspapers in such faraway places as Tokyo and Hong Kong. The advertisements originally were planned for people in cities along the company's Latin American routes, but the airline found much of the work suitable for world-wide use as well. A company spokesman said: "It's one of the best campaigns we've got going. It's too good to limit it to Latin America. A slight change in copy, and we find it does the job as well for us in Vancouver or Hong Kong.[13]

The campaign to which the Canadian Pacific Airline spokesman referred had several features which may account, at least in part, for its wide suitability. The advertisements displayed large attention-getting photographs, usually with no more than 20 percent of the space used for copy. For example, a picture of a Canada goose, a symbol of the airline, is captioned, "He knows the best routes south, so does Canadian Pacific."[14] Short and simple copy with the same message, of course, can be written for other routes.

Perhaps some forms of art work are understood universally, and hence the same illustrations sometimes may be appropriate in different markets. Revlon, to take another example, has been a leader in the production of television commercials designed for use in several nations, using Parisian models and settings. In 1962 when Filmex, Incorporated, opened its new commercial production facilities in France, Revlon International moved in as its first client. The production, representing eight days of shooting, included a series of four one-minute color commercials, earmarked for fall showing in theaters and on television in markets outside the United States. The commercials, in English and Spanish, promote lipsticks and nail enamel, face make-up, eye make-up, and facial beauty-care products. It may be surprising to find English and Spanish advertisements produced in a French-speaking country, but there are several good reasons for doing so. For one thing, the French have considerable experience and reputation as producers and users of cosmetics. Furthermore, French commercials, filmed in Parisian settings, are often more elaborate than those produced in other countries; usually the French spend much greater time and effort on each commercial than could be spent in the United States. Finally, there are economies involved in foreign production which reduce the total cost below costs in the United States.

On the other hand, cultural influences may dictate that illustrations for the same product must differ from country to country. In German magazines an advertisement for cheese might show a large foaming glass of beer with the cheese, which would whet the appetite of a Bavarian. But in France an advertisement for cheese would more appropriately substitute a glass of red wine for the beer.

COPY

There is considerable diversity of opinion with regard to the translation of copy from one language to another. On the one side are those who warn against translations. They point out that while mistakes can be made in any language, even by local copywriters, it is more likely that they will be made if advertisements are prepared in one country, translated, and inserted in international or foreign media without review by competent local linguists. One writer has listed several "famous goofs," for example:

Copywriters for General Motors found out that "body by Fisher" came out "corpse by Fisher" in Flemish. "Schweppes tonic water" was speedily dehydrated to "Schweppes Tonica" in Italy, where "il water" idiomatically indicates a bathroom.[15]

Many advertising personnel in French-speaking regions of Canada feel strongly that separate copy must be written for advertisements designed to appeal effectively to French-speaking people. Some advertising people feel that commercials which were originally in English and subsequently French-dubbed are passé, and that the few of these still being shown only give the commercials with copy created especially for a French-Canadian audience more atmosphere and more selling power.

On the other hand, a spokesman for a company selling in South America says that English copy can be translated into Spanish if it is done by a person who has: (1) good literary knowledge and command of the technical terminology of both languages, (2) a good understanding of the technical aspects of the products, and (3) copywriting ability which can recreate the persuasive tone of English copy.[16] Therefore, it appears that there is a need for a creative, not just a routine word-for-word translation.

The effects of dubbing and adapting television commercials have been studied by a commercial research organization, the Schwerin Research Corporation.[17] In one study, Schwerin tested thirty-one commercials shown in Canada. English versions were tested in Toronto and French-dubbed versions were tested in Montreal. The Schwerin competitive preference scores were used to compare the impact of the advertisements. There were two instances in which the dubbed version did even better than its English counterpart: there were eight cases in which considerable declines in effectiveness resulted. The remaining cases showed no significant difference between the effectiveness of the English and French versions of the same commercial. The losses in effectiveness occurred mainly among commercials which were very strong in English, whereas the French versions which duplicated the results of the original commercials were largely confined to examples that were not outstanding in English. It should be noted that the dubbed commercials were essentially literal translations. However, when fifteen of the same commercials were *adapted* [18] rather than translated literally, it was found that six registered a significant gain in effectiveness, nine showed no significant change, and *none* showed a significant decline. The report concluded that it is possible for television commercials originally designed for one market to obtain comparable results in a market where a different language is spoken; it also seems clear that adaptation of the commercial is preferable to literal translations.

With regard to whether or not to prepare new copy for a foreign market or to translate the English copy, it seems reasonable to conclude that an advertiser must consider whether the translated message can be received and comprehended by the foreign audience to which it is directed. Anyone with a knowledge of foreign languages realizes that it is usually necessary to be able to think in a language in order to communicate accurately. One must understand the connotations of words, phrases, and sentence structures, as well as their translated meaning, in order to be fully aware of whether or not the message will be received and how it will be understood. The same principle applies to advertising — perhaps to an even greater degree. Difficulty of communication in advertising is compounded, because it is essentially one-way communication, with no provision for immediate feedback. The most effective appeals, including organization of ideas and the specific use of language — especially colloquialisms and idioms — are those developed by a copywriter who thinks in the language and understands the consumer to whom the advertisement is directed. Thinking in a foreign language involves thinking in terms of the foreigner's habits, tastes, abilities, and prejudices; one assimilates words, customs, and beliefs.

COMPLETE ADVERTISEMENTS

Professor S. Watson Dunn of the University of Illinois has reported[19] on the results of a series of field tests to determine the extent to which the language of advertising is international, specifically, that is, to find out under what conditions an entire American advertisement would be successful in a foreign market. Five products, all low-priced convenience items which were widely used internationally, were chosen. They had all been advertised in at least one American magazine, and the appeals featured in the advertisements violated no cultural or other taboos in France and Egypt, the countries in which the test was run.

Three variations of the illustrative material and two of the headlines and copy — all of them consistent with the original creative platform — were used. One of the illustrations was the original as used in the American magazine, one was replaced with French models, and another with Egyptian models. One version of the copy and headlines consisted of an idiomatic translation into French and Arabic. The other was composed from the original by a professional copywriter of each country. The audiences consisted of a sample of middle and upper middle class consumers in the largest city in each country. Three measures of effectiveness were used for each advertisement.

The results showed surprisingly little difference in the effectiveness of the various versions. There was little evidence to support the idea that in a case such as this it is necessary to show a local model in the advertisement, or that one must attribute the message to a local (as compared with a foreign) source. There was only limited evidence that the message which is started from scratch in a foreign country is any more effective than a good refined translation from the U.S. original.

The flow of ideas and creative materials is not all one way. [20] Foote Cone & Belding GmbH, the German subsidiary of the U. S. advertising agency with that name, acquired the Silly Putty account when the product was being considered for introduction in Germany. Silly Putty can be molded into any form; left alone it flows slowly, like molasses; it can be stretched or with a sudden jerk it can be broken; it bounces higher than a rubber ball; it lifts pictures, print, and drawings from a newspaper. For sixteen years it has been sold in the United States in small, egg-shaped containers.

FCB Frankfurt started from scratch to prepare German advertising for Silly Putty; only the product came from the United States. The "European" package was prepared in nine languages. The product was introduced to retailers at the Nuremburg Toy Fair, where it proved to be a major attraction. Consumer advertising was concentrated on cinema and television. A film was designed so that it could be used in all European markets, altering only the sound track. The famous German stage and film comedian George Thomalla presented the product. He showed how Silly Putty can be stretched, how it bounces, and how it picks up photos from paper. Then a trick camera made Thomalla act out one of the qualities of Silly Putty. His face stretched and suddenly broke into two halves. Sales of Silly Putty rose rapidly in Europe. The TV spot was so successful that it was subsequently shown on U.S. television, with sound dubbed in English.

On the other hand, there are, of course, numerous examples of advertisements that are appropriate in one country but not in another. For example, an advertisement in some of India's leading newspapers showed an attractive and apparently nude young woman dousing herself liberally with talcum powder while partly hidden behind a black strip that read "Don't go wild — just enough is all you need of Binoca talc." Irate readers condemned the paper for carrying "indecent" advertising offensive to traditional standards of Indian morality.[21] The article went on to report:

The controversy reflects the sweeping changes that have taken place in the Indian advertising industry within the last few years.

Until recently, Indian advertising has been generally cautious and conservative. As one advertising man put it, "Just three years ago we probably would have sold talcum powder with a picture of the box and a bit of copy which began 'known for 75 years as the queen of talcums. . . .' "[22]

SOME GENERALIZATIONS

Generally speaking, most advertising men would agree that it is unlikely that Mr. Elinder's recommendations for "uniform advertising" can be successful for all products, for all companies, in all markets. Thus the critical questions are *when* will Mr. Elinder's approach be successful and *when not?* And, *what criteria* can be used to make a selective judgment?

The factors which influence the appropriateness of "uniform advertising" for various market segments (whether national or international) are:

1. The type of product. When there are certain universal selling points for some products — for example, razor blades, electric irons, automobile tires, ball point pens — products are sold primarily on the basis of objective physical characteristics. These objective characteristics are likely to be considered by consumers to be identical, regardless of market differences, suggesting that the same appeals will be effective in all markets.

2. The homogeneity or heterogeneity of markets. When aggregate characteristics such as income, education, and occupation are alike, individual consumer characteristics such as needs, attitudes, and customs may also be alike, thus suggesting that the advertiser use the same selling points.

3. The characteristics and availability of media. If certain media are available in one country but not in another, certain messages and materials may not be usable.

4. The types of advertising agency service available in each market segment. If in some markets only poor agency service is available, a firm may be forced to rely on centralized control of advertising, with necessary uniformities in messages and media strategy.

5. Government restrictions on the nature of advertising. Some governments prohibit certain types of messages, thereby making certain appeals or copy unlawful.

6. Government tariffs on art work or printed matter. Such expenses may offset a cost advantage achieved by centralization of the art and production functions.

7. Trade codes, ethical practices, and industry agreements. In some countries there may be a "gentlemen's agreement" among competitors: they will refrain from using certain media, such as television, an expensive medium, which in a limited market might only increase "competitive advertising."

8. Corporate organization of the advertiser. If a company is organized to conduct business on a multinational basis, and if personnel are available, uniform advertising may be feasible — for example, if a company has "controlled" subsidiaries it can often control advertising better than companies that use independent licensees to produce and market their brands abroad.

People the world over have the same needs, such as food, safety, and love. But people sometimes differ in the ways in which they satisfy their needs. Just as it is important to provide physical variations in products to meet the varying demands of diverse market segments, it is also important to tailor advertisements to meet the requirements of each market segment. But it is the demands of the market segments which are diverse, not the approach to planning and preparing marketing programs. The principles underlying communication by advertising are the same in all nations. It is only the specific methods, techniques, and symbols which sometimes must be varied to take account of diverse environmental conditions. Therefore U.S. advertisers may be well advised to export their approach to planning and preparing international advertising, but before making final decisions on copy or media they should be sure to consult personnel who know the foreign market intimately.

NOTES

1. Eric Elinder, "International Advertisers Must Devise Universal Ads, Dump Separate National Ones, Swedish Adman Avers," *Advertising Age,* November 27, 1961, p. 91. See also Erik Elinder, "How International Can European Advertising Be?" *Journal of Marketing,* (April 1965), pp. 7-11, and Erik Elinder, "How International Can Advertising Be?" in S. Watson Dunn, *International Handbook of Advertising* (New York: McGraw-Hill Book Company, 1964), pp. 59-71.
2. *Ibid.*
3. For additional examples, see Elma Kelly, "Use Symbols with Sense to Earn More Dollars," *Export Trade,* May 12, 1959, p. 15.
4. Dan E. G. Rosseels, "Consumer Habits and Consumer Advertising in the Benelux Countries," *Export Trade and Shipper,* January 28, 1957, p. 17.
5. *Ibid.*
6. "Soup Around the Globe," *Advertising Age,* November 28, 1966, p. 56.
7. *Grey Matter* (January 1966), p. 4.
8. "Languages, Goals Are International Advertisement Pitfalls: Garcia," *Advertising Age,* July 16, 1962, p. 8.
9. The following information on Union Carbide's venture into Europe was adapted from "Shining Up to a European Market," *Business Week,* May 14, 1966, pp. 190-94.
10. "Put a Tiger in Your Tank," *Marketing Insights,* November 28, 1966, p. 11.
11. Margaret Carson, "Admen in Thailand, Singapore, Find Unusual Problems, Novel Solutions," *Advertising Age,* November 27, 1967, p. 50.
12. The following information is adapted from "P & G Adds a Bit of Dash to German Marketing," *German American Trade News* (May 1966), pp. 10 ff.
13. *Advertising Age,* August 6, 1962, p. 70.

14. *Ibid.*
15. Edward M. Mazze, "How to Push a Body Abroad Without Making It a Corpse," *Business Abroad and Export Trade,* August 10, 1964, p. 15.
16. Emmet P. Langen, "How to Write Spanish Copy — Without a Yankee Accent," *Industrial Marketing* (July 1959), p. 49.
17. "The Effects of Dubbing and Adapting Television Commercials for Foreign Markets," *Schwerin Research Corporation Technical and Analytical Review,* No. 9, Summer, (1961).
18. The word "adapted" was not defined in the report.
19. S. Watson Dunn, "The International Language of Advertising" (a talk presented at the East Central Region Annual Meeting of the American Association of Advertising Agencies, Detroit, November 16-17, 1966).
20. The following is adapted from information in "Commercial for German TV Now Used in U.S. Campaign," Effective Solutions to German Marketing Problems, Case History No. 9, *German American Trade News* (December 1966), p. 14.
21. "Nude in Talc Ad Offends in India," The New York *Times,* April 29, 1967, p. 36.
22. *Ibid.,* pp. 36, 55.

12
The International Storekeepers

Stanley C. Hollander

Retailers used to talk of local, regional, and national chains. In today's merchandising world, however, the retail organization that doesn't reach across national boundaries may seem almost parochial. Woolworth stores are part of the retail landscape in Canada, Great Britain, Germany, Mexico, and more recently Spain, as well as in the United States. Sears extends throughout South and Central America, is a partner in the Canadian Simpson Sears, and has recently opened its first Spanish unit. Safeway stores are located in Canada, Great Britain, Germany, and Australia; Jewel (formerly Jewel Tea) is engaged in joint ventures in Belgium, Italy, and Spain; Walgreen owns the Sanborn drug chain in Mexico; Federated Department Stores holds a 10 percent interest in the Galerías Preciado group of Madrid; and Singer has added a German mail order house to its almost world-wide network of sewing machine and appliance outlets. The Australian K-Marts are a joint venture of Kresge and an Australian department store firm, and the J. C. Penney Company now owns an interest in Sarma, a Belgium variety chain that also has some foreign outposts in Spain.

Avon ladies call upon customers in Venezuela, Mexico, France, Canada, Spain, Italy, England, Germany, Brazil, Puerto Rico, Belgium, and

Reprinted, with permission, from *MSU Business Topics* (Spring, 1969), pp. 13-23, published by the Graduate School of Business Administration, Michigan State University.

Author's note: This article was written on the research for a project supported by the Midwest Universities Consortium for International Activities. The Michigan State University All-University Research Fund also provided assistance. Space limitations and confidentiality requirements preclude proper acknowledgement of the help and cooperation provided by business, association, academic, and government officials both in the United States and abroad. I wish to indicate a debt to the International Association of Department Stores, whose monthly *Retail Newsletter* has been used here in ways that make footnoting difficult. I have also had access to the Ressigiue collection of retailing notes and newspaper clippings at Baker Library, Harvard School of Business.

Australia. Rexall Drug, with its Tupperware and Beauty Counselor divisions, is another leader, besides Singer and Avon, in overseas direct (home) selling operations. Both Fuller Brush and Stanley Home Products also have significant although less extensive foreign divisions.[1]

Although many other American retailers could be added to the above lists, they are by no means the only storekeepers with international outlets. Among Canadian firms, the Weston group owns grocery stores in England, France, Germany, and the United States; Bata Shoe of Toronto has retailing and manufacturing subsidiaries in approximately ninety countries; and Steinberg's, a Quebec supermarket chain, has established its offshoot, Supermarches Montreal, in France. British, French, and other European trading companies, such as United Africa Company, S.C.O.A., John Holt, Ltd., and Booker McConnell Ltd., have long been significant factors in African retailing. Booker McConnell also owns drug and department stores in the Caribbean in addition to having domestic branches in England, and United Africa Company's parent, the Unilever combine, includes grocery chains in England and Germany.

Great Universal Stores, a highly diversified British organization, includes clothing and furniture stores in France, Canada, and South Africa, a department store in Hong Kong, and mail order businesses in Sweden, Austria, and Holland. Several other mail order firms, including Littlewoods (British) and Neckerman and Die Quelle (German) also have foreign ventures. A Dutch clothing dynasty, the Brenninkmeyer family, operates approximately 150 stores in Holland, Belgium, Germany, and England, and also controls the Orbach department stores in the United States. Several ties connect French and Belgian department store operators. Prisunic, the leading French variety chain, has been active as a merchant, franchisor, and joint venturer in many non-European French speaking countries. It also is a participant in the new Simago (Spanish) and Etavik-Prisunic (Greek) chains. General Shopping S.A., a Luxembourg-based investment trust with substantial Swiss interests on its board, is involved in a host of retailing and retailing-related ventures in Switzerland, Germany, Austria, France, and Spain.

Numerous other examples of internationalization could be cited. They would include South African clothing chains with branches in Britain, an Austrian grocery firm with stores in northern Italy, the French branches of a British menswear firm, German grocery stores and British TV outlets under Dutch ownership, some inter-Scandinavian ventures, and many other multinational businesses. Two unusual companies, one Swiss and the other American, have entered foreign retailing through essays in international economic assistance. Migros, a vigorous and public-spirited Swiss distributive organization, has devoted considerable effort to its Migros-Turk experiment in Istanbul. The Rockefeller family's International Basic Economy Corporation, established to apply private enterprise techniques in economic development, created successful Venezuelan, Peruvian, and Italian supermarket chains as well as less rewarding groups in Puerto Rico and Argentina.[2]

LUXURY MERCHANDISE

Most of the companies mentioned so far primarily deal in popular- and medium-priced merchandise, although what is considered medium-priced in one country may well be a luxury in another. But another interesting segment of multinational retailing handles expensive items and high-styled luxuries. This smaller segment includes some well-known jewelry shops, art galleries, show salons, and men's and women's clothing stores. In addition to the older prestige shops, a number of new foreign-sponsored boutiques, such as Rive Gauche (dresses), Pierre Cardin (menswear), Studio Haus (tableware), and Carrier Cookshops (kitchen utensils) have recently opened in New York and are spreading throughout the country.[3] Some of the luxury shops are owned by manufacturers who want the prestige of foreign labels or the attention of visiting merchants in addition to the profits the stores themselves may provide. Various patterns of multinational ownership, franchising, and licensing are used in this trade. But unlike the medium-priced organizations that sometimes consider a discreet deemphasis of any alien affiliation to be good public relations, the international dealers in luxuries almost always glory in their foreign-ness.

INTERNATIONALIZATION WITHOUT OWNERSHIP

The multinational voluntary chain systems that have burgeoned in postwar western Europe, particularly in the food trades, demonstrate how locally-owned shops may also be integrated into international networks. As of 1966-67, 36,000 stores in twelve countries participated in the SPAR chain, approximately 30,000 in ten countries belonged to the VeGe organization, approximately 20,000 in seven countries were part of VIVO, and about 14,000 were attached to the seven-country Centra group.[4] The individual grocers in these groups have affiliated with sponsoring wholesalers who provide operating assistance, managerial aid and advice, joint promotional programs, and opportunities to sell the chain's private-label merchandise. Somewhat similar arrangements tie the wholesalers together in national organizations which, in turn, link up to form the international superchains.

The international headquarters provide research and advisory services, represent their members before the Common Market and other supranational administrative agencies, and also to an increasing extent they are operating buying pools, developing international private brands, and formulating pan-European promotional programs.

Various sets of corporate chains, department store firms, retailer buying groups, and consumer cooperative societies have created a considerable number of other European and Canadian-American international buying pools and information exchange agreements. Some of these arrangements have had very little practical significance, but at least a few have developed considerable market effectiveness. Nordisk Andelsforbund, the joint purchasing agency of the various Scandinavian national consumer cooperative societies, is one of the oldest and largest of the buying pools. In 1965, its offices in California, Italy, Spain, Brazil, and Denmark bought approximately $80,000,000 worth of foodstuffs for the Scandinavian and other European cooperatives.[5] Increased competitive pressures from the expanding private sector chains and groups are forcing the non-Scandinavian European cooperatives to become more centralized and, slowly and awkwardly, to become more interested in international joint buying. At the same time, the number and effectiveness of the private purchasing pools seem likely to increase.

Franchising arrangements are analogous to the voluntary chain system in providing substantial vertical integration without ownership. Although many recent American developers of food and service trade franchises have had hopes and plans for internationalization, operating difficulties and problems in establishing satisfactory franchise relationships have so far limited the fulfillment of these hopes.[6] Some plans, however, have achieved widespread distribution. The franchised Wimpy Hamburger Bars, of American origin but developed by a British firm, are now established in much of western Europe as well as Australia and parts of Africa. And international dealer franchising programs, with varying degrees of control over the retail operation, are regularly used by American and European gasoline refiners and automobile, tire, and electrical appliance manufacturers.

INFORMATION AND ADVICE

Organizational control, through ownership, franchising and similar arrangements, is by no means the only transnational influence in retailing. Merchandising and operating ideas travel from country to country through a communications network that includes trade magazines, merchants' travels and store visits, trade association bulletins, private and governmental consultancy services, and supplier activities. The Paris office recently opened by the National Retail Merchants Association, an American organization with many foreign members, exemplifies the growing internationalization of retail trade associations. One enthusiastic participant claims the National Cash Register Company's intensive seminars for foreign retailers have influenced "four out of every five modern commercial enterprises now being started up on the five continents."[7] Any large-scale merchant who is seriously interested in change can today draw upon an almost world-wide reservoir of information and experience.

THE CHANGING PATTERN OF INTERNATIONALIZATION

Multinational retailing is not new. Venturesome merchants have often gone abroad for both merchandise and ideas. Foreign sales branches also have a long history. In the late years of the nineteenth century and the beginning of this one, for example, Dutch margarine manufacturers began making heavy investments in British grocery retailing, both American meat packers and American shoe manufacturers opened stores in Britain, British and European trading companies became heavily involved in some aspects of West African retail distribution, and the Hudson's Bay Company (still a British firm) added Canadian department store retailing to its several hundred years old fur trading business.[8] Woolworth's British operations started in 1909, and its German subsidiary began in 1926. The Nordisk Andelsforbund buying pool was founded in 1918. Singer sewing machine salesmen have been calling on foreign customers for more than 100 years. British and French capital played a part in the growth of Latin American department stores, such as Harrods of Buenos Aires and Palacio de Hierro in Mexico City. The spread of foreign-owned jewelry shops led the *New Yorker* to speak, in 1929, of "the invasion of Rue de la Paix houses."[9]

But the current pattern of multinational retailing seems to differ substantially, in degree and possibly in kind, from the past. Nationalism and revolution have closed many historic routes for international investment in storekeeping. The Castro revolution confiscated U.S.-owned outlets in Cuba, such as Sears and Woolworth. European department store, chain store and trading firms have been expelled or severely handicapped in many parts of both north and sub-Saharan Africa, and in previously colonial parts of the Far East, such as Indo-China, Indonesia, and Burma.

The big British and French trading companies now tend to believe that discretion is the better part of valor. Many of them are withdrawing from the types of local, small-scale and "back-country" retailing that can most easily pass into indigenous hands. United Africa Company repeatedly announces its intentions of phasing out all company-owned retailing except major department stores and specialized outlets such as automobile agencies. John Holt, Ltd. is similarly seeking to limit its African retailing to a few selected complex product lines. Booker McConnell Limited has recently sold its stores in both Malawi and Zambia to newly established government trading firms. Booker McConnell, however, retains a minority interest in the new ventures and will operate the stores under management contract.[10] The trading companies have tried to establish voluntary chains of indigenous merchants to offset the decline in their own retail opportunities, but these efforts have been both difficult and less than uniformly successful.

In contrast, the growth and rising prosperity of the middle classes throughout Europe and, to a lesser extent, Latin America, have created new opportunities for multinational mass merchandisers. Substantial numbers of increasingly urbanized and cosmopolitan customers now provide attractive markets for large-scale retail organizations.[11] Simultaneously, and probably because of the same prosperity and drive for industrial efficiency that have stimulated those markets, many of the old European restrictions on large retailing have been withering away. Some of the rules that curtailed chain and department store growth, such as Belgium's "Padlock Law," have been abolished. Price maintenance laws have been repealed or weakened in many countries. And the creation of common markets has naturally encouraged interest in internationalization. Paradoxically, American, and possibly also British, internal antitrust restrictions on domestic mergers seem to push into foreign expansion some especially aggressive merchants.[12]

Undoubtedly many of the international merchandising ventures that have attracted attention in the trade press are tentative and exploratory. Even as highly internationalized a firm as Sears currently receives less than 2 percent of its sales from units outside the United States and Canada. The great bulk of retail trade practically everywhere is still in the hands of domestic enterprises. But international retailing has become significant enough, embraces enough innovative and aggressive firms, and includes enough new institutional types, such as the multinational voluntaries, to warrant serious attention.

SUCCESS IS NOT EASY

All international retailing ventures are not resounding successes. Foreign markets have rebuffed many skilled merchants who had excellent achievement records in their own countries. We need not review the whole long list of aborted efforts, failures, near-failures, and limited successes. Several examples will show that survival is difficult even in stable countries where the risks of nationalization and expropriation are low.

The more or less unhappy ventures include: two GEM discount stores opened in England, but unprofitable until sold to British interests; Elmo Stores, a British grocery chain recently sold by its South African owners after several years of losses;[13] the Minimax grocery chain in Rome, which also was unprofitable for its recent owners, the E. F. MacDonald Plaid Stamp Co.;[14] Helene Curtis' now-abandoned British Studio Girl direct-selling operation;[15] the Brenninkmeyer family attempts at establishing their C & A Stores in New York;[16] up-state New York stores operated for awhile by Swears & Wells, a British firm that describes itself as the "world's largest fur retailer";[17] and a "minor but ill-starred overseas expansion into South Africa" from 1947 to 1955 on the part of the John Lewis Partnership, one of Britain's outstanding department store chains.[18]

Robert Hall's apparently stagnating Perifa clothing retailing and manufacturing joint venture in France has encountered many difficulties.[19] Test branches opened in Los Angeles by two Japanese department stores in 1959-62 had unsatisfactory histories. Seibu's unit closed after two deficit years, while Hankyu has converted its outlet into a purely wholesale business.[20] Most of the foreign merchants who have recently established outlets in Spain have found that country a relatively inhospitable host, in part because of supply problems. *The Economist* reports that Prisunic, which has allied itself with some very knowledgeable Spanish associates, is obtaining better results than most of the other newcomers.[21]

Some of the major Belgian retailers tried to establish Dutch and French subsidiaries during the late 1950's and early '60's, but relatively few of the resultant stores remain under their original ownership. The two largest enterprises, the Priba-Nederland variety chain and the highly publicized Inno-France semiself-service department stores were both finally sold to local interests. The Inno-France stores were plagued with practically all the problems that can be endemic to expatriate retailing, including poor site selection, difficulties in developing adequate cadres of middle management and junior executives, some harassment by local authorities, and adverse consumer images as well as by some difficulties of their own.[22] (One merchant, in discussing Inno-France and Priba's problems, said that French consumers consider Belgian merchandise stodgy and unstylish while the Dutch think it is flashy and unreliable. As the saying goes, "sometimes you just can't win.")

Numerous attempts at transplanting European and British style consumer cooperation to the rest of the world have also been generally unsuccessful. American and Canadian consumers have generally felt that private retailers serve as well or better than the cooperatives could, and so the cooperative societies have attracted very few members. Recent international assistance efforts to encourage retail cooperative movements in the developing countries have encouraged similar resistance. The private traders often seem able to offer lower prices or more appealing services than would be available from unsubsidized cooperatives. The private merchants also sometimes use their creditor position to discourage cooperative membership. Moreover, the members often find that retailing, with all its merchandise selection, record keeping, and sales promotion problems, is much more difficult than, say, conducting a fisherman's marketing pool or a crude agricultural milling service. Consequently, most experts now recommend that practically all other types of cooperative enterprise be encouraged in the developing countries before any serious attempt is made to foster cooperative stores.[23]

Clearly, the transfer of retail enterprise and technology from one country to another is no easy task. A few high-style clothing franchises and similar arrangements that ride on the wings of fad and fashion may enjoy instantaneous, although perhaps ephemeral, acceptance. But these are the exceptions rather than the rule. Many retailers report that their first efforts at internationalization absorbed much more time and effort than they had anticipated at the start of the venture. Safeway's overseas division, for example, didn't reach its first period of profitability until the end of 1966, after approximately five years of loss.[24] Migros-Turk provides a striking illustration of perseverance requirements. It took nine years to demonstrate any semblance of profitability in spite of cost accounting systems that substantially undervalued the Swiss contribution to its operation. Fortunately, most successful overseas programs become self-sustaining within shorter periods than that, but two, three, or four years of deficit and need for intensive top management supervision are not uncommon.

This situation leads to a policy recommendation that plans for small-scale foreign operations are generally unwise if retaining profits are the ultimate objective. United Africa Company may be making a self-serving claim when it asserts that even its big Lagos store could not be successful without the purchasing and managerial scale economies that come from being part of an even larger organization,[25] but there is certainly at least a germ of truth in that statement. One or two strategically located foreign branches may be quite satisfactory if their main purpose is to add prestige to the domestic stores or to demonstrate ways of selling a manufacturer's line. Some tax advantages may accrue from a unit or two placed in resort areas where management wants to play or to entertain its business guests. And, of course, the initial entry even in a purely retailing venture usually must be a relatively limited one. An attempt to open too many stores at once can easily founder on a shortage of managerial talent, as well as for many other causes. But the efforts required to get the first few stores underway may not be at all worthwhile unless a fairly substantial foreign subsidiary is envisaged as the long-run goal.

PROFITABILITY

These gloomy observations should not obscure the fact that international retailing can also be very profitable. Booker McConnell's annual reports show that its shopkeeping division has generally been one of the most profitable parts of the company. The 1967 report, for example, indicates that shopkeeping provided greater dollar profits and a higher after-tax return on capital than came from the company's tropical agriculture, rum and spirit, shipping, engineering, or furnace manufacturing divisions. IBEC has found overseas supermarkets more profitable than many of its nonretailing activities. Although the situation has now reversed, Woolworth of Britain was far more profitable than its parent for many years in the late 1950's and early 1960's.[26] Sears Roebuck found that funds plowed back into its Mexican subsidiary, in part because of restrictions on repatriation, yielded greater long-run returns than would have resulted from transferring the same profits to its U.S. operations.[27] A private consultant who was sent to Mexico to search for an attractive joint venture wrote back that one international retailer he studied was far too successful to welcome any other participants.[28] Many other binational and multinational retailers can also report very satisfactory results.

DIVERSITY

Both successful and unsuccessful international retailing ventures exhibit great diversity in objectives, in geographic spread, in price and merchandise policy, in organizational structure, and operating methods. Generalization about these firms, beyond noting their diversity, is difficult and hazardous. However, some tentative observations may be appropriate.

MERCHANDISE BASE

The factors that lead a customer to buy from one retailer rather than another may be designated as the first merchant's differential advantages. Analytically, it is often useful to divide these advantages or attractions into two categories: (1) the actual goods being sold, and (2) the way in which those goods are sold. Thus a merchant can differentiate himself from his competitors either by offering items and brands that are unobtainable elsewhere, and/or by offering differentiated retail services, e.g., more convenient locations, wider selections under one roof, lower prices, or more liberal credit terms. But the marketing strategy in a surprisingly large number of viable international retail organizations seems at least to start with the first alternative, differentiated merchandise.

This point can easily be overemphasized. Most dealers actually use mixtures of product and retailing attractions to draw trade. Distinguishing between product and retail service is especially difficult when the merchandise is sold on a custom-prepared basis, as in some international jewelry, clothing, and restaurant operations. In such cases, the preparation of the product is a major component of the services. Similarly, even if the international retailer has private brands, unobtainable in competitive stores, part of the appeal those brands possess may lie in the way they are sold. Do women throughout the world buy Avon cosmetics because of product attributes, because of Avon's home selling techniques are appealing, or because of some combination of the two considerations? The fact that some leading private brand merchants, such as Sears, Bata Shoe, and the international supermarket chains, are also often effective retailers of competitive as well as exclusive merchandise demonstrates their retailing, as distinguished from their product-creation, abilities.

Nevertheless, in spite of all these caveats, a very substantial proportion of all international retailers do have exclusive or somewhat different merchandise than their competitors. The international direct selling (home selling) firms, whether in the cosmetic, encyclopedia, household supply, sewing machine, or vacuum cleaner business, almost invariably have their own private brand products. Manufacturing-retailers, particularly in the clothing and shoe trades, control another important segment of international retailing that offers differentiated product lines. Besides some companies already mentioned, this sector includes the Bally, Manfield and Salamander shoe stores, Genesco's retail subsidiaries in Canada, Europe, and Latin America, the Etam lingerie chain, which operates approximately 300 stores in Britain and western Europe,[29] and many others. Most franchisors also claim some degree of actual or imputed differentiation for the merchandise their franchisees offer. This rule applies equally to franchisors in the traditional licensed trades, such as automobile, appliance, and gasoline retailing, to the ones in the newer service and restaurant fields, and to those who license high-style boutiques. In the same vein, the trading companies and other such import-export firms seem to have received much of their start in developing country retailing through an ability to supply otherwise unobtainable merchandise, although today some of these firms rely primarily on the use of European department store techniques to attract customers. And finally, many of the multinational dealers in luxuries differ from their competitors primarily in the uniqueness and distinctiveness of their wares.

LIMITED ADVANTAGES

It may well be that, given the existing costs of labor and capital in any particular country, and given the existing regulatory system which may affect store size, labor costs, locations, and store hours, foreign retailing techniques themselves can often have only limited or no advantages over the indigenous institutions. The economies of mass production and labor substitution, and the advantages of national specialization and skills may tend to show up more sharply in product design and manufacturing than in retailing. These factors would account for the emphasis on a merchandise base. And yet, as already indicated, quite a number of firms, particularly department, super-market, and variety store merchants, have found their retailing skills to be an exportable commodity. In such cases, the differential advantages are often on the demand rather than the cost side. Some adequate market segment finds the imported way of selling goods, e.g., self service or "one-stop shopping," more attractive than the services offered by local merchants.

CONTROL AND CONSISTENCY

At first glance, multinational retailing would seem to require a high degree of decentralization. Both communications difficulties and the prob-lems of adjustment to local market conditions would seem to preclude tight control from central headquarters. And many international firms are as decentralized and as flexible as one might expect. Lord Campbell, the president of Booker McConnell, Ltd., describes his firm's practices in these terms:

... having laid down guidelines of policy on social matters and management devel-opment, and having established up-to-date systems of financial ability and control, to interfere as little as possible in the day-to-day running of the business; yet at the same time we help them in every way we can with advice and assistance.[30]

The fact that some ten executives, including two directors whose pri-mary operating responsibilities are located elsewhere in the corporation, and five secretaries comprise the entire staff of Bookers Shopkeeping Holdings, the London parent entity for all the British and overseas retailing and whole-saling subsidiaries, underlines the extent of decentralization in that company. Power and authority are also widely distributed in many other firms, as well as quite naturally in most joint retail ventures, international voluntary chains, buying pools, and advisory relationships.

Indeed, practically all large-scale merchants make formal public obeisance to the idea of local autonomy. Statements about the authority invested in local management presumably contribute to the field staffs' morale. Safeway's annual reports are somewhat unusual in the emphasis that they place upon "close liaison" between the California headquarters and the foreign subsidiaries.[31] But actually many international retailers have developed surprisingly centripetal techniques and organizations. United Africa Company's notably close supervision of its Kingsway Department Stores is based on computerized stock controls at Lagos and London and a constant flow of reports from Africa to Britain. The situation has now changed, but as recently as 1950 a company publication could speak of its entire textile requirements being "ordered and controlled" in Manchester "in much the same way as those of the other merchandise departments in London."[32] A system of moving red and blue lights on the wall of the control room at Bata's Toronto headquarters to indicate the transition from normal sleeping to waking hours in every country where a subsidiary is located exemplifies the tight connection between field and central office in that company.[33]

The use of *international,* rather than truly *multinational,* organizational techniques emphasizes the centripetal nature of most parent-foreign retail subsidiary relationships. The lines of command and communication tend to connect the subsidiaries to headquarters rather than to each other. With some notable exceptions, citizens of the parent country usually fill all or almost all central office positions. Some home country executives may also be used in the field, although local management is being increasingly nationalized these days. But only a few of the most sophisticated firms, such as Bata, have developed truly multinational executive staffs in which citizens of any country may expect to be considered for assignments wherever the company operates.

Even when the formal organization structure is thoroughly decentralized, the foreign subsidiary's management may be trained to operating styles that are very similar to those of the parent company. A vice-president of one direct-selling company remarked that "we really need only a few years of close supervision to get them to behave in the way we want." A few joint directors and top officials are about the only explicit formal interlocks between the managements of the American and British Woolworth's, yet any visiting customer will be struck by the similarity between the British and American stores.

Many other successful international retailing organizations besides Woolworth exhibit at least some of the same consistency between foreign and domestic operations: In one sense this is quite surprising, in another it is quite natural. The set of advantages and skills that a merchandising firm takes abroad are usually connected to the commodities and the operating techniques that it uses at home. Diversified foreign subsidiaries are not intolerable to a retail firm that has learned to live with domestic diversity. Jewel, for example, participates in a variety of foreign joint ventures. But Jewel is basically a diversified company with home selling routes, supermarkets, discount houses, and drugstores in the United States. The foreign ventures more or less parallel Jewel's major domestic activities.

Firms whose interests are primarily domestic and homogeneous are particularly likely to feel uncomfortable with high disparate foreign subsidiaries. Two incidents in Sears Roebuck's history illustrate this point. In 1959, Sears liquidated its interests in an Australian joint venture that had started under very promising auspices only four years previously. Walton's Ltd., the Australian partner in Walton-Sears, was a well-established firm that has since proven to be one of that country's most dynamic and profitable merchants. Nevertheless, the alliance apparently was an incompatable one from the start. Walton's special skills are in purchasing and rehabilitating declining stores, while Sears is accustomed to working with units that it designs and opens on its own. Some disagreements over dividend and reinvestment policy, plus this very substantial difference in operating techniques made the subsidiary an extremely poor fit in the Sears' scheme of things.[34] The second incident is a happier one. Through an erroneous interpretation of market conditions, Sears management assumed that its first Mexican store would have to supply high-priced imports to a restricted and wealthy audience. The customer response soon changed that, as its historians say, "perhaps to Sears relief, for it is easier for Sears to be Sears than to try to be somebody else. In any event, Sears dropped its 'Fifth Avenue' airs quickly and settled down to being itself."[35]

Thus it is quite natural to find strong family resemblances between British and American Woolworths, or German and Australian Safeways, or U.S. and Brazilian Sears, or French and Greek Prisunics, or Dutch and British C. & A. clothing shops. Local tastes and preferences, of course, always show up on the store counters and shelves. Europeans tend to buy dried soups while Americans prefer canned products, but these differences are trivial. The store "personality" remains the same across national boundaries in many of the most successful firms. And to return to the original paradox, the fact that this sort of similarity can prevail across highly disparate markets is somewhat astonishing. A priori, one would expect that different markets, with different average incomes, different cultures, tastes, and traditions, would require fairly different retail styles.

THE MIDDLE CLASS AND THE WHEEL OF RETAILING

The answer to the paradox lies in the market segments that many of these firms serve. Few, if any, of the international retailers appeal to the total market in all of the countries in which they operate. Instead they cater to narrow or broad market segments that are strikingly similar from country to country. To cite an extreme case, the U.S. Army post exchange service is the biggest and most widespread international retailer in the world, yet by definition it serves the same type of customer at all of its far-flung locations.

To a substantial degree, the same thing is true of the private storekeepers. The British department stores in Nigeria, for example, were originally planned in terms of serving the resident English and European population, in a sense as a commercial, profit-making, non-discount post exchange for civilian expatriates. Today, these stores do half or more of their business with African consumers, but these domestic customers are the prosperous, urbanized, and Europeanized Africans. The Nigerian professional who has a charge account at the Lagos Kingsway store is, for many purposes, the same type of consumer as the expatriate British specialist with an account in the same store.

In some instances the target markets are at the peaks of the income pyramid. An international art dealer, a fashion couturier, or an expensive jeweler will expect to serve much the same types of cosmopolitan and wealthy customers whether his salons are in New York or Monte Carlo, London or Rio. Increasingly today, the target markets have become middle class ones. As Yoshino and others points out, the American mass merchandisers owe most of their recent international opportunities to the rising prosperity of the middle classes in many countries.[36] This increased purchasing power in the middle income brackets operates in several ways. As the quantity of goods purchased goes up, the amount of time that people want to devote to acquiring any one item, or even to acquiring the entire mix, tends to go down. Purchase time has to compete against the desire to spend time enjoying the acquisitions. The acquisition of refrigerators and automobiles permits changes in shopping patterns: fewer trips but more items at a time. All of these factors, plus increasing urbanization and suburbanization, rising labor costs, and increases in the percentage of working wives, have worked to create both the domestic and the foreign markets for supermarkets, semi-self-service department stores and discount houses.

These new types of retailing, however, have moved into many of their new markets in rather different fashion from their typical development pattern in the United States. In this country, many of these institutions have followed a pattern that M. P. McNair calls "The Wheel of Retailing."[37] Although department store history is not quite as clearcut as that of supermarkets and discount houses, all three types tended to start as relatively or extremely low priced, low margin, low prestige institutions, and all three have tended toward higher prestige, acceptability, expenses, margins, and prices with the passage of time. Conversely, in the developing countries, these imported retailing types have usually found their easiest entry at or near the top of the prestige scale, and then have reached out for wider markets.

The Migros-Turk food stores, for example, tried unsuccessfully for many years to reach some of the poorer sectors of the Istanbul population through units in low-income areas. The chain's current success is attributable to many factors, including increased experience with the Turkish market and rising living standards in Turkey. But much of the present results seems to be due to a change in emphasis, to a movement toward modern stores in upper middle class neighborhoods. Its present market is a much more appropriate one for the introduction of new retail techniques, and is an effective base from which Migros-Turk can gradually widen its influence. Prisunic went directly to the wealthier districts of Athens, a somewhat comparable even if more prosperous city than Istanbul, and caught on much more rapidly. Many other supermarket organizations in Latin America and, as noted, European style department store firms in Africa, have also undergone a "trickling-down" process rather than McNair's classic wheel pattern.

IMPACT

Conceivably one or more of the international storekeepers might some day become so large, so firmly entrenched, and so influential that they could exercise some very harmful monopoly power. But this eventuality seems very remote. For the foreseeable future, multinational retailing should benefit the consumer. The international retailing firms may never grow even to the point of dominating most domestic markets, and they probably will never have quite as much ability to transform developing economies as some of their most ardent proponents claim for them. Nevertheless, they do bring new merchandise and new techniques to the places where they operate; they can influence and encourage local suppliers; they provide competitive stimulus to the existing retail structure; and in essence, they widen the alternatives available to local consumers. Two British analysts comment that "While this (internationalization of retailing) could lead to a degree of sameness in the goods obtainable in Madrid and Margate, the range of choice for shoppers will undoubtedly grow."[38] And since the function of a retail system is to provide shoppers' choices, internationalization in retailing is thus a very healthy development.

NOTES

1. Thomas J. Murray, "The Overseas Boom in Door-to-Door Selling," *Dun's Review and Modern Industry* (November 1964), pp. 35 +.
2. Wayne G. Proehl, Jr., *United States Business Performance Abroad: The Case Study of the International Basic Economy Corporation* (Washington: National Planning Association, 1968), chap. 5.
3. Rive Gauche is actually operated by a French subsidiary of an American manufacturing firm.
4. W. H. Wilkens, *Modern Retailing: Evolution and Revolution in the West European Distributive Trades* (London: Business Publications, 1967), p. 23.
5. Thorsten Ohde, *Scandinavian Co-operative Wholesale Society* (Copenhagen: Nordisk Andelsforbund det Danske Forlag, 1960); Co-operative Wholesale Committee, Copenhagen, *Information Exchange Service,* July 4, 1966.
6. J. A. H. Curry, *et al., Partners for Profits* (New York: American Management Association, 1966), chap. 13.
7. "How NCR Boosts Foreign Sales," *Business Abroad,* June 10, 1968, p. 30.
8. Peter Mathias, *Retailing Revolution* (London: Longmans, 1967), chap. 10; J. H. Dunning, *American Investment in British Manufacturing Industry* (London: George Allen & Unwin, 1956), p. 35; R. A. Church, "The Effect of the American Export Invasion on the British Boot and Shoe Industry," *The Journal of Economic History* (June 1968), p. 251; P. T. Bauer, *West African Trade* (London: Routledge & Kegan Paul, 1963), p. 126; D. McKay, *The Honourable Company* (Toronto: McClelland and Stewart, 1966), p. 305.
9. "On and Off the Avenue," November 23, 1929, p. 95.
10. Lord Campbell, "A New Role for Private Enterprise," *International Development Review* (December 1968), pp. 17-20; also, Bauer, *op. cit.,* p. 127; J. and R. Charbonneau; *Marches et Marchands d'Afrique Noire* (Paris: Vieux Columbier, 1961), pp. 59-60; and trading company annual reports.
11. M. Y. Yoshino, "International Opportunities for American Retailers," *Journal of Retailing,* Fall, 1966, pp. 1-10; S. C. Hollander, "The Internationalization of Retailing: A Foreword," *ibid.,* Spring, 1968, pp. 3-10.
12. Harlow Unger, "Growth Ban Forces U.S. Supermarkets Overseas," The Sunday *Times* (London), May 14, 1967, p. 31.
13. "Drag on Profits," *Financial Mail* (South Africa), October 20, 1967.
14. "MacDonald (E. F.)," *Standard Listed Stock Reports* (Standard and Poors Corp., N.Y.), Vol. 35, No. 193, October 7, 1968.
15. *Moody's Handbook of Common Stocks* (1st Quarterly 1968 edition) (New York: Moody's Investors Service, Inc., 1968), p. 464.
16. "Brenninkmeyer Brooklyn Store Will Be Closed within a Few Weeks," New York *Times,* May 30, 1964, p. 21.
17. "Swears & Wells Set to Close Buffalo Branch," *Women's Wear Daily,* December 5, 1958.
18. "What Makes John Lewis Grow?" *Management Today* (March 1968), p. 61.
19. See United Merchants and Manufacturers' (Robert Hall's parent company) annual statements.
20. "Seibu Never Broke into the Black," *Women's Wear Daily,* February 28, 1964, p. 2.
21. "Spanish Retailing: Chain Store Woes," February 17, 1968, p. 67.
22. "Make Way for Le Super Marche," *Fortune,* July 1, 1966, pp. 39-40 ff; N. McInnes, "Nation of Shopkeepers," *Barrons,* November 8, 1965, p. 9; "Bel-

gium: Retailers Still Suffering from Foreign Ventures," *Marketing in Europe* (Economist Intelligence Unit), December, 1966, p. 3. For a general discussion of local harassment and executive recruitment problems, see Yoshino, *loc. cit.*

23. See: *The Role of Co-operatives in Developing Countries* (49th International Labour Conference, Report VII-1), Geneva: International Labour Office, 1964, p. 29; Margaret Digby, *Co-operatives: A Development Pamphlet* (London: Overseas Development Institute, n.d.). Also, P. T. Bauer, "Some Aspects and Problems of Trade in Africa," and Lauchlin Currie, "Marketing Organization for Underdeveloped Countries," in R. Moyer and S. Hollander, eds., *Markets and Marketing in Developing Economies* (Homewood, Illinois: Richard D. Irwin, 1968), pp. 62-66, 122.

24. "Safeway Quarter Net Falls," *Supermarket News,* May 22, 1967, p. 11.

25. "Kingsway Stores, Lagos," *United Africa Company, Ltd. Statistical and Economic Review* (September 1953), p. 11.

26. T. W. Murray, "Changing Worlds of Woolworth," *Dun's Review and Modern Industry* (November 1965), p. 46; "What's Come over Old Woolworth?" *Fortune* (January 1960), p. 216.

27. W.R. Fritsch, *Progress and Profits: The Sears, Roebuck Story in Peru* (Washington: Action Committee for International Development, 1962), p. 65.

28. R. S. Roberts, "Reports on Investment Survey of Mexico, Venezuela, Brazil and Argentina, Section 1 — Mexico and Mexico City" (October 1963), p. 52; Clearinghouse for Federal Scientific and Technical Information, Springfield, Va., Document AID 1/16/02231.

29. Derek Knee, "Trends Towards International Operations among Large-Scale Retailing Enterprises," *Rivista Italiana di Amministrazione,* No. 2 (1966), pp. 107-11, translation courtesy of Mr. Knee. See also, "Etam to Spread Operations into Canadian Field," *Women's Wear Daily,* April 2, 1951.

30. "Shopkeeping in Developing Countries," *Journal of Retailing,* Spring (1968), p. 58.

31. See reports for 1962, 1964, and 1965.

32. "Merchandise Trading in British West Africa," *United Africa Company, Ltd. Statistical and Economic Review* (September 1950), p. 3. Company officials say that approximately half the stock is now purchased at Lagos under general merchandise budgets which, of course, have been approved at headquarters.

33. "Thomas Bata: The World Is His Marketplace," magazine article reprinted by public relations department, Bata Ltd., Toronto.

34. "Sears Is Selling Its Entire Holding in Walton-Sears," *Women's Wear Daily,* October 27, 1959; "Waltons, Sears, Expansion Plan Division Cited," *ibid.,* October 28, 1959.

35. Richardson Wood and Virginia Keyser, *United States Business Performance Abroad: The Case Study of Sears, Roebuck de Mexico, S. A.* (Washington: National Planning Association, 1953), p. 51.

36. M. Y. Yoshino, *op. cit.,* pp. 2-3.

37. For comments on the Wheel pattern, see S. C. Hollander, "The Wheel of Retailing," *Journal of Marketing* (July 1960), pp. 37-42.

38. N. A. H. Stacey and Aubrey Wilson, *The Changing Pattern of Distribution* (2d ed.; Oxford: Pergammon Press, 1965), p. 386.

13
Can You Standardize Multinational Marketing?

Robert D. Buzzell

One of the most widely discussed developments of the past decade has been the emergence of *multinational* companies as important competitors in an ever-growing number of industries. As the trade barriers in Western Europe and elsewhere have diminished, more and more companies have found attractive opportunities for expansion in countries other than their traditional home markets. For some of these companies, operations abroad have become so extensive and so complex as to require significant changes in organization and operating methods. The problems confronting management in a truly multinational company are clearly different in degree, if not in kind, from those of traditional firms.

WHAT ABOUT MARKETING?

The growing importance of multinational companies has stimulated a flood of comment and advice. Conferences, seminars, and surveys have probed the distinctive financial, legal, accounting, organizational, and personnel problems of this new breed of enterprise. In all of this discussion, however, relatively little has been said about marketing.

To be sure, some advertising men have advocated the adoption of uniform advertising approaches, on the grounds that fundamental consumer motives are essentially the same everywhere. This proposition often has a

Reprinted with permission from the *Harvard Business Review*, November-December (1968). Copyright©1968 by the President and Fellows of Harvard College; all rights reserved. The author wishes to acknowledge the valuable contributions of Richard Aylmer and Jean-Louis LeCocq, who conducted interviews with executives of multinational companies under his direction during 1967. The research was conducted under a joint project of the Harvard Business School and the European Institute of Business Administration (INSEAD) and was supported by research grants of the Ford Foundation.

partisan tone, however, especially when it is put forward by executives of large advertising agencies with international networks of subsidiary and affiliate offices. More importantly, the question of advertising approaches cannot be considered realistically in isolation from other elements of a company's marketing "mix" in each market, including its product line, packaging, pricing, distribution system, sales force, and other methods of promotion.

Is it practical to consider the development of a marketing strategy, in terms of *all* of its elements, on a multinational scale? The conventional wisdom suggests that a multinational approach is *not* realistic, because of the great differences that still exist—and probably always will exist—among nations. For example, George Weissman, President of Philip Morris, Inc., has concluded that "until we achieve One World there is no such thing as international marketing, only local marketing around the world."[1] Apparently most other marketing executives agree with this view. Thus, Millard H. Pryor, Jr., Director of Corporate Planning for Singer Company, writes:

"Marketing is conspicuous by its absence from the functions which can be planned at the corporate headquarters level. . . . The operating experience of many international firms appears to confirm the desirability of assigning long-range planning of marketing activities to local managers."[2]

The prevailing view, then, is that marketing strategy is a local problem. The best strategy for a company will differ from country to country, and the design of the strategy should be left to local management in each country.

TWO-SIDED CASE

But is the answer this simple? The experiences of leading U.S.-based companies in recent years suggest that there may indeed be something to be said in favor of a multinational marketing strategy. This article is intended to outline some of the possibilities — and limitations — of an integrated approach to multinational marketing. My thesis is that although there are many obstacles to the application of common marketing policies in different countries, there are also some very tangible potential benefits. The relative importance of the pros and cons will, of course, vary from industry to industry and from company to company. But the benefits are sufficiently universal and sufficiently important to merit careful analysis by management in virtually any multinational company. Management should not automatically dismiss the idea of standardizing some parts of the marketing strategy, at least within major regions of the world.

BENEFITS OF STANDARDIZATION

As a practical matter, standardization is not a clear-cut issue. In a literal sense, multinational standardization would mean the offering of *identical* product lines at identical prices through identical distribution systems, supported by identical promotional programs, in several different countries. At the other extreme, completely "localized" marketing strategies would contain *no* common elements whatsoever. Obviously, neither of these extremes is often feasible or desirable.

The practical question is: Which *elements* of the marketing strategy can or should be standardized, and to what degree? Currently, most multinational companies employ strategies that are much closer to the "localized" end of the spectrum than to the opposite pole. If there are potential benefits of increased standardization, then they would be achieved by incorporating *more* common elements in a multinational strategy. Each marketing aspect of policy should be considered, first, in its own right, and second, in relation to the other elements of the "mix."

Let us examine the most important potential benefits of standardization in multinational marketing strategy.

SIGNIFICANT COST SAVINGS

Differences in national income levels, tastes, and other factors have traditionally dictated the need for local products and corresponding local marketing programs. The annals of international business provide countless examples, even for such apparently similar countries as the United States and Canada. Philip Morris, Inc., for example, tried unsuccessfully to convert Canadian smokers to one of its popular American cigarette brands. The Canadians apparently would rather fight; they preserved their traditional preference for so-called "Virginia-type" tobacco blends. Examples of this kind suggest that to attain maximum sales in each country, a company should offer products, as well as packages, advertisements, and other marketing elements, which are tailored to that country's distinctive needs and desires.

However, maximizing sales is not the only goal in designing a marketing strategy. Profitability depends ultimately both on sales *and* costs, and there are significant opportunities for cost reduction via standardization. The most obvious, and usually the most important, area for cost savings is product design. By offering the same basic product in several markets with some possible variations in functional and/or design features, a manufacturer can frequently achieve longer production runs, spread research and development costs over a greater volume, and thus reduce total unit costs.

The "Italian invasion": The lesson of mass production economies through standardization, first demonstrated by Henry Ford I, has been dramatically retaught during the 1960's by the Italian household appliance industry.[3]

In the mid-1950's, total combined Italian production of refrigerators and washing machines was less than 300,000 units; there were no strong Italian appliance manufacturers. In 1955, only 3 percent of Italian households owned refrigerators, and around 1 percent owned washing machines.

Starting in the late 1950's, several companies began aggressive programs of product development and marketing. Ironically, some of the Italian entrepreneurs were simply applying lessons learned from America. One member of the Fumagalli family, owners of the appliance firm, Candy, had been a prisoner of war in the United States and brought back the idea of "a washing machine in every home."

The Italian appliance firms installed modern, highly automated equipment, reinvested profits, and produced relatively simple, *standardized* products in great numbers. By 1965, refrigerator output was estimated at 2.6 million units, and washing machine output at 1.5 million units. Much of this volume was sold in Italy; home ownership of the two appliances rose to 50 percent and 23 percent, respectively. But the Italian companies were aggressive in export marketing, too; by 1965 Italian-made refrigerators accounted for 32 percent of the total French market and for 40 percent to 50 percent of the Benelux market. Even in Germany, the home market of such electrical giants as AEG, Bosch, and Siemens, the Italian products attained a 12 percent market share. The export pattern of washing machines has followed that of refrigerators; by 1965 Italian exports had accounted for 10 percent to 15 percent of market sales in most other Western European countries.[4]

The success of the Italian appliance industry has been a painful experience for the traditional leaders—American, British, and German—as well as for the smaller French companies that had previously had tariff protection. Whirlpool Corporation, which acquired a French refrigerator plant in 1962, subsequently leased the facility to a French competitor. Even Frigidaire decided, in mid-1967, to close down its refrigerator production in France.

In competition with other European appliance makers, the Italian companies have benefited from some natural advantages in terms of lower wage rates and government export incentives. But mass production of simple, standardized products has been at least equally important. And, according to *Fortune,* "refrigerators have begun to look more and more alike as national tastes in product design give way to an international 'sheer-line' style."

Turnabout at Hoover: To compete with this "Italian invasion" in appliances, some of the established manufacturers have tried new approaches.

An interesting example is the recent introduction of a new line of automatic washing machines by Hoover Ltd., the market leader in the United Kingdom. Hoover's previous automatics, introduced in 1961, were designed primarily for the British market. The company's new "keymatic" models featured:

1. An exclusive "pulsator" washing action.
2. A tilted, enamelled steel drum.
3. Hot water provided by the home's central hot-water heater.

In contrast, most European manufacturers, including the Italian producers, offered front-loading, tumble-action washers with stainless steel drums and self-contained water heaters. Either because these features were better suited to continental needs, or because so many sellers promoted them, or perhaps both, Hoover saw its position in the major continental markets gradually decline.

When the Hoover management set out to design a new product line, beginning in 1965, it decided to look for a *single* basic design that would meet the needs of housewives in France, Germany, and Scandinavia as well as in the United Kingdom. A committee including representatives of the continental subsidiaries and of the parent company, Hoover Worldwide Corporation (New York), spent many weeks finding mutually acceptable specifications for the new line.

The result, which went on sale in the spring of 1967, was a front-loading, tumble-action machine, closer in concept to the "continental" design than Hoover's previous washers, but with provisions for "hot water fill" and enamelled steel drums on models to be sold in the United Kingdom. By standardizing most of the key design elements in the new machine, Hoover was able to make substantial savings in development costs, tooling, and unit production costs.

Other economies: The potential economies of standardization are not confined solely to product design decisions. In some industries, packaging costs represent a significant part of total costs. Here, too, standardization may offer the possibility of savings. Charles R. Williams cites the case of a food processor selling prepared soups throughout Europe in 11 different packages. He observes, "The company believes it could achieve a significant savings in cost and at the same time reduce consumer confusion by standardizing the packaging."[5]

Still another area for cost savings is that of advertising. For some of the major package goods manufacturers, the production of art work, films, and other advertising materials costs millions of dollars annually. Although differences in language limit the degree of standardization that can be imposed, *some* common elements can often be used. For example, Pepsi-Cola is bottled in 465 plants and sold in 110 countries outside the United States. Part of its foreign advertising is done by films. According to one of the company's top marketing executives, "We have found that it is possible . . . to produce commercial films overseas in one market, if planned properly, for use in most (but not all) of our international markets." According to company estimates, the added cost of producing separate films for each market would be $8 million per year.[6]

All of these examples illustrate the same basic point: standardization of product design, packaging, and promotional materials *can* offer important economies to the multinational marketer. Even if these cost savings are attained at the expense of lower sales in some markets, the net effect on profits may be positive.

CONSISTENCY WITH CUSTOMERS

Quite apart from the possibilities of cost reduction, some multinational companies are moving toward standardization in order to achieve consistency in their dealings with customers. Executives of these companies believe that consistency in product style, in sales, and customer service, in brand names and packages, and generally in the "image" projected to customers, is a powerful means of increasing sales.

If all customers lived incommunicado behind their respective national frontiers, there would be no point in worrying about this matter; only diplomatic couriers and border-crossing guards would ever notice any inconsistencies in products, services, or promotion. But in reality, of course, this is not the case. The most visible type of cross-border flow is international travel by tourists and businessmen. Especially in Europe, with its relatively high income levels and short distances, the number of people visiting other countries has reached flood proportions in the 1960's, and shows no sign of abating. If the German tourist in Spain sees his accustomed brands in the store, he is likely to buy them during his visit. More important, his re-exposure to the products and their advertising may strengthen his loyalty back home or, at least, protect him from the temptation to change his allegiance to a competitor.

Then there is the flow of communications across boundaries. Magazines, newspapers, radio and television broadcasts—all including advertising—reach international audiences. For example, according to estimates by Young & Rubicam International:

German television broadcasts are received by 40 percent of Dutch homes with TV sets.

Paris Match has a circulation of 85,000 in Belgium, 26,000 in Switzerland, and substantial readership in Luxembourg, Germany, Italy and Holland.

On an average day, over 4 million French housewives tune to Radio Luxembourg; the same broadcast reaches 620,000 Belgian housewives, 30,000 in Switzerland, and 100,000 in Holland.

The possibility of reaching multimarket audiences with common advertising messages, and the risk of confusion that may result from reaching such audiences with different brand names and promotional appeals, has led some of the major consumer goods producers to explore ways and means of standardizing at least the basic elements of their European campaigns. For instance, the Nestlé Company, Inc. and Unilever Ltd., probably the most experienced multinational consumer goods firms, have both moved in the direction of more "unified" European advertising during the 1960's. When Nestlé launched "New Nescafe" in 1961-1962, for example, the same basic theme ("fresh-ground aroma") and very similar creative treatments were used not only throughout Europe, but also in other markets such as Australia. The value of this approach is, perhaps, reflected in the fact that several years ago Nescafe was the leading brand of instant coffee in every European country.

Pressures from customers: During the 1960's an additional argument for consistency in marketing strategy has emerged — the needs of the multinational *customer*. Increasingly, both consumer and industrial goods manufacturers find themselves selling to companies which themselves operate on a multinational scale. Industrial users, retail chains, and wholesalers with operations in several countries may buy centrally; even if they do not, personnel in one country often have experience in other countries, or communicate with their counterparts in these countries. In either case, there is a strong pressure on the seller to offer similar products, prices, and services in each market. Thus, IBM has standardized the services provided to customers, the duties and training of sales and service personnel, and even the organization of branch offices, on a worldwide basis. A major reason for this policy is the need to provide the same level of service to major customers, such as international banks, in each of the several countries where they do business with IBM.

In some industries, multinational customers virtually force suppliers to standardize products, prices, and terms of sale. If a better deal is available in one country than another, the customer may find it worthwhile to transship goods and will do so.

In certain industries, trade and professional associations exert a pressure toward standardization similar to that exerted by multinational customers. Engineers, chemists, doctors, computer programmers — these groups and many others hold conferences, publish journals, and exchange ideas on an international basis. One result is that companies selling products to professional and technical groups find it advantageous to standardize their offerings. This factor may even affect consumer goods; the marketing director of a major food-processing company told us that dietetic products must be sold on the same basis everywhere because "science and teaching are international anyway."

IMPROVED PLANNING AND CONTROL

Flows of people and information across national boundaries may affect multinational marketing strategy in still another way. Consider the following situation. Philips Gloeilampenfabrieken, one of the world's largest producers of electrical products, found that prices of some of its appliances in Holland were being undercut by as much as 30 percent by the company's own German subsidiary! How did this come to pass? The German subsidiary had lower costs than the Dutch plant, and sold at lower prices to meet the more intensive competition of the German appliance market. Wholesalers buying from Philips in Germany had a further incentive to sell to outside customers on account of a 7 percent export subsidy given by the German government. To complete the circle, a European Economic Community antitrust ruling prohibited manufacturers from interfering with the rights of independent distributors to export freely within the Common Market. Consequently, there was little that Philips could do except to "equalize" prices in the two countries or live with the new sourcing arrangements.[8]

Philip's experience illustrates the difficulty of orderly planning and control by top management if a subsidiary or distributor in Country A is subject to the risk of unpredictable competition from his counterparts in nearby countries, B, C, and D.

The feasibility of transshipments among markets obviously varies from one industry to another, depending on the value/weight ratio of the products. Thus, transshipping is common for such items as scientific instruments, cameras, and precision equipment, but relatively rare for major electrical appliances. Even in the food trade, however, cross-border sales have increased in volume considerably during the 1960's.

Effective control of transshipping requires harmonization of pricing policies in the multinational company. This does not necessarily mean *equalizing* prices at either the wholesale or retail levels, for if a company's prices to dealers and/or distributors are the same in all countries, then the incentive for transshipping will be eliminated. Rather, it means some adjustments and compromises for the sake of consistency in pricing at the retail and wholesale levels.

EXPLOITING GOOD IDEAS

A fourth argument for standardization is that good marketing ideas and people are hard to find, and should therefore be used as widely as possible. Moreover, good ideas tend to have a universal appeal. This point of view is held especially strongly with regard to the "creature" aspects of advertising and promotional programs. Arthur C. Fatt, Chairman of the Board and Chief Executive Officer of Grey Advertising, Inc., states:

"A growing school of thought holds that even different peoples are *basically* the same, and that an international advertising campaign with a truly universal appeal can be effective in any market. . . . If an advertiser has a significant advertising idea at work in one country, not only may it be wasteful but often 'suicidal' to change this idea just for the sake of change."[9]

The key word in this statement is "significant." It is the scarcity of really good or significant ideas that encourages standardization. It may be easy to find creative concepts of average quality in each of many different national markets, but really new or unique approaches are not so easily matched.

During the 1960's there have been several widely discussed examples of successful application of common advertising themes:

Esso's "Put a Tiger in Your Tank" campaign, with very minor changes in art and wording, has been used from Southeast Asia to Switzerland. The tiger is, of course, an internationally recognizable symbol for power.

Avis Rent-A-Car has used minor variations on its "We Try Harder" theme throughout Europe as well as in the United States.

Magazine advertisements for Playtex brassieres in many different countries feature the same "stop-action" photographic demonstration of the product's strength and dependability. Although attitudes toward undergarments vary from country to country, Young & Rubicam, Inc. (the Playtex agency) believes that there is a *segment* in each market for which this appeal is effective. But even the most ardent proponents of the theory that "good ideas are universal" recognize the need to apply the concept with care. Approaches shown to be effective in one market are *likely* to be effective elsewhere, but they do not necessarily apply across the board.

BALANCED APPRAISAL NEEDED

To summarize, then, many companies have found real benefits in a multinational approach to marketing strategy. The gains have included greater effectiveness in marketing, reduced costs, and improved planning and control. Moreover, especially in Western Europe but also in some other parts of the world, social and economic trends are working in favor of more, rather than less, standardization in marketing policies. Tourism, international communication, increased numbers of multinational customers, and other forces are all tending toward greater unification of multinational markets.

But this is just one side of the story. It would be a mistake to assume, as at least a few companies have done, that marketing programs can be transferred from one market to another without careful consideration of the *differences* which still exist. Let us turn next to that side of the picture.

COMMON BARRIERS

Despite the potential benefits of standardization, the great majority of companies still operate on the premise that each national market is different and must therefore be provided with its own, distinctive marketing program. For instance, after a careful study of the marketing policies of U.S. appliance and photographic manufacturers in Europe, Richard Aylmer concluded: "In over 85 percent of the cases observed, advertising and promotion decisions were based on *local* product marketing objectives."[10]

Why is diversity still the rule of the day in multinational marketing? In many cases, differences simply reflect *customary* ways of doing business which have evolved in an earlier period when national boundaries were more formidable barriers than they are today. But even if tradition did not play a role, it must be recognized that there are and will continue to be some important obstacles to standardization.

A comprehensive list of these obstacles would fill many pages, and would include many factors that affect only one or two industries. The most important and generally applicable factors are summarized in Exhibit 1. The rows of this exhibit represent the major *classes* of factors which limit standardization in multinational marketing strategies. The columns correspond to different elements of a marketing program, and the "cells" in the table illustrate the ways in which the various factors affect each program element. In effect, each cell represents a condition or characteristic which *may* differ sufficiently among countries, and *may* require variations in marketing strategies. As we shall see presently, the experiences of multinational companies afford numerous examples of these barriers to standardization. Let us look briefly at each of the four major factors limiting standardization that are listed in Exhibit 1.

Exhibit 1: Obstacles to Standardization in International Marketing Strategies

	Elements of Marketing Program	
Factors limiting standardization	Product design	Pricing
Market characteristics Physical environment	Climate Product use conditions	
Stage of economic and industrial development	Income levels Labor costs in relation to capital costs	Income levels
Cultural factors	"Custom and tradition" Attitudes toward foreign goods	Attitudes toward bargaining
Industry conditions Stage of product life cycle in each market	Extent of product differentiation	Elasticity of demand
Competition	Quality levels	Local costs Prices of substitutes
Marketing institutions Distributive system	Availability of outlets	Prevailing margins
Advertising media and agencies		
Legal restrictions	Product standards Patent laws Tariffs & taxes	Tariffs & taxes Antitrust laws Resale price maintenance

Distribution	Sales force	Advertising & promotion; branding & packaging
Customer mobility	Dispersion of customers	Access to media Climate
Consumer shopping patterns	Wage levels, availability of manpower	Needs for convenience rather than economy Purchase quantities
Consumer shopping patterns	Attitudes toward selling	Language, literacy Symbolism
Availability of outlets Desirability of private brands	Needs for missionary sales effort	Awareness, experience with products
Competitors' control of outlets	Competitors' sales forces	Competitive expenditures, messages
Number and variety of outlets available	Number, size, dispersion of outlets	Extent of self-service
Ability to "force" distribution	Effectiveness of advertising, need for substitutes	Media availability, costs, overlaps
Restrictions on product lines Resale price maintenance	General employment restrictions Specific restrictions on selling	Specific restrictions on messages, costs Trademark laws

MARKET CHARACTERISTICS

Perhaps the most *permanent* differences among national markets are those arising from the physical environment — climate, topography, and resources (see the top left of Exhibit 1). Climate has an obvious effect on the sales potential for many products, and may also require differences in packaging. Topography influences the density of population, and this in turn may have a strong influence on the distribution system available to a manufacturer.

The cell in Exhibit 1 labeled "Product use conditions" includes a wide variety of environmental factors affecting marketing strategies. Differences in the size and configuration of homes, for example, have an important bearing on product design for appliances and home furnishings. European kitchens are typically small by U.S. standards, and there is seldom any basement space available to apartment dwellers for laundry facilities. As a result, there is a great emphasis on compactness of design in automatic washers, for they must somehow be fitted into a small and already crowded area. As noted in the example of Hoover Ltd., given earlier, washing machines must also be equipped with self-contained water heating systems to compensate for the lack of central hot-water heaters in most continental homes.

Industrial goods manufacturers also frequently encounter differences in product use conditions: a U.S. producer of farm equipment found that one of his pieces of machinery could not be moved through the narrow, crooked streets of French and Belgian farm villages.

Concluding that there is more dissimilarity than similarity in industrial markets in Europe, a chemical industry marketing researcher writes: "(A factor) which would severely affect the market for surface coatings is the fact that materials used in building construction are vastly different in various parts of Europe. Brick, mortar, and tile are used predominantly in Southern Europe, whereas this is not the case in Northern Germany and in Benelux." [11]

Many similar examples could be cited of differences in the environment which call for variations in product design and other aspects of marketing policy.

Development stage: Differences among countries in stages of economic and industrial development (second item under "Market characteristics" in Exhibit 1) also have a profound influence on marketing strategies. Because of the wide gaps in per capita income levels, many products or models which are regarded as inexpensive staples in the United States or Western Europe must be marketed as "luxuries" elsewhere. Even among the industrialized countries income differences are substantial: appliance manufacturers such as Philco-Ford Corporation and Kelvinator of Canada, Ltd. find themselves with little choice but to position their products as deluxe, relatively high-priced items. This, in turn, implies a very different marketing strategy from that used in the United States.

For industrial products, differences in economic development are reflected in variations in relative costs of capital and labor. Thus, General Electric Company and other companies have sold numerical controls for machine tools in U.S. factories primarily on the basis of labor cost savings. The same approach may be suitable in Germany, where there is a critical shortage of labor. But in most other countries it would be far more difficult to justify numerical controls on the basis of labor substitution.

Differences in income levels may suggest the desirability of systematic price variations. As explained earlier, many companies do charge different prices in different countries, but these variations are seldom, if ever, based solely on incomes.

Consumer shopping patterns and purchase quantities, too, tend to vary with stages of economic development. In underdeveloped countries, there typically are many small retail stores, and many consumers who buy in smaller quantities than do those in highly developed nations. For instance, cigarettes and razor blades are bought one at a time in some countries. Even in England, according to one international marketing executive, "the smallest size of detergent available in U.S. supermarkets is the largest size available in the United Kingdom."

Finally, variations in wage levels may affect choices between personal selling and other forms of promotional effort. One relatively small Italian food processor has a sales force as large as that of General Foods Corporation in the United States. Presumably salesmen's salaries are proportionately less!

Cultural factors: This category is a convenient catchall for the many differences in market structure and behavior that cannot readily be explained in terms of more tangible factors. Consider, for example, the figures in Exhibit 2, which are taken from a recent survey made by the European Economic Community's Statistical Office. Why do French households consume more than 50 times as much wine as Dutch households, but only two thirds as much milk? No doubt these differences could be explained historically in terms of variations in water, soil, and so on. But for practical purposes, it is usually sufficient and certainly more efficient simply to take differences in consumption patterns and attitudes *as given,* and adjust to them.

There are many examples of cultural differences that have affected marketing success or failure. One cultural factor is the attitude of consumers toward "foreign" goods.

*Exhibit 2: Average household consumption of beverages
1963-1964 (in liters)*

Country	Milk	Wine	Beer
France	103	116	28
Germany	100	7	46
Holland	153	2	11
Italy	87	95	2

Source: *Le Monde*, weekly overseas edition, February 15-21, 1968, p. 7.

Princess Housewares, Inc., a large U.S. appliance manufacturer, introduced a line of electric housewares in the German market. The company's brand name was well known and highly regarded in the United States, but relatively unknown in Germany; and the brand had a definitely "American" sound. The company discovered that the American association was a real drawback among German consumers. According to a survey, fewer than 40 percent of German individuals felt "confident" about electrical products made in the United States, compared with 91 percent who were "confident" of German-made products.

Lack of brand awareness, coupled with suspicion of the quality of "American" products, required the company to adopt a very different marketing strategy in Germany than that employed in the United States, where both awareness and a quality image were taken for granted.

INDUSTRY CONDITIONS

A convenient framework for comparing industry and competitive conditions in different national markets is that of the "product life cycle." The histories of many different products in the United States suggest that most of them pass through several distinct *stages* over a period of years, and that marketing strategies typically change from stage to stage.

Some products are in different stages of their life cycles in different national markets. Vacuum cleaners are owned by over 75 percent of the households in Great Britain, Germany, and Switzerland, for example, but by only 10 percent of the households in Italy and 45 percent in France. Even more marked contrasts exist for some newer types of products, such as electric toothbrushes and electric carving knives, which are widely owned in the United States but virtually unknown in most other countries. Such differences in life cycle stages usually call for adaptations of "home country" marketing approaches, if not for completely separate strategies.

In late 1965 the Polaroid Corporation introduced the "Swinger" Polaroid Land camera in the United States. The Swinger, with a retail list price of $19.95, was Polaroid's first camera selling for less than $50. The introductory promotion for the new model in the United States placed very heavy emphasis on price; there was no need to explain the basic concept of "instant photography," since millions of Polaroid Land cameras had already been sold over a 17-year period. Surveys indicated that over 80 percent of U.S. consumers were aware of the name "Polaroid" and of the company's basic product features.

The Swinger was introduced in Europe during 1966. Prior to that time, Polaroid cameras had been extremely high-priced, owing in part to high tariffs, and the company's sales had been at a very low level. Distribution of Polaroid cameras and film was spotty. Most important, fewer than 10 percent of consumers were aware of the Polaroid instant photography concept.

Under these circumstances, a very different marketing strategy was needed for the Swinger in Europe. Polaroid advertising had to be designed to do a more basic educational job, since awareness of the instant picture principle could not be taken for granted. The promotional program also had to be aimed at building retail distribution, which was also taken for granted in the United States.

If products are in different stages of their life cycles in different countries, then it is tempting to conclude that marketing strategies used in the past in the more "advanced" countries should be used in other "follower" nations. There is some evidence to support this conclusion. For instance, as described earlier, the Italian appliance manufacturers have successfully employed strategies similar to those of Henry Ford in the early 1900's; similarly, Polaroid in the 1960's in Europe can profitably use many of the same approaches that it employed in America in the early 1950's. However, history does not repeat itself exactly, and past marketing strategies cannot be reapplied without some modifications.

Competitive practices: Another important industry condition, partly but not entirely related to the product life cycle, is the extent of competition in each national market. Differences in products, costs, prices, and promotional levels may permit or even require differences in the strategies used by a multinational company in various markets. Even within the European Common Market, there are still substantial variations in prices of many products, reflecting in part traditional differences in the degree of competition. A survey made in 1967 by the European Economic Community's Statistical Office showed that price variations are still substantial even within the Common

Market. Typical prices were compared for some 125 different consumer products by country; on the average, the difference between prices in the countries with the highest and lowest prices was 58 percent. Even the price of a staple item such as aspirin varied from a high of 38 cents in Germany to a low of 22 cents in Holland.

The growth of multinational companies in itself has tended to reduce traditional differences in competitive practices. For example, advertising expenditures have traditionally been lower in France than in the United States and other European countries; on a per capita basis, total French advertising outlays are around one eighth those of the United States and one third those of Germany. However, according to M. Andre Bouhebent, a top French advertising agency executive, the entry of foreign competitors is changing the situations: "When German advertisers sell in France, they have the habit of spending at the same rate (as at home), which is three times that of their French competitors. . . ."[12] As an example, *Advertising Age* noted that the German Triumph bra and girdle company spends three to four times as much as a French undergarment company to promote its product.

MARKETING INSTITUTIONS

The multinational company's opportunities in each market depend critically on the marketing institutions available in each country—including retail and wholesale outlets and advertising media and agencies. Some of the most drastic revisions in strategy made by U.S.-based companies overseas have been imposed by the lack of adequate supermarkets, retail chains, and commercial television. Differences in the number, size, and dispersion of distributive outlets call for differences in promotional methods; and differences in prevailing wholesale and/or retail margins may require vastly different price and discount structures. Some of these variations in institutional systems are related to legal regulations, especially in the area of resale price maintenance.

As in the case of competitive practices, traditional disparities in marketing institutions have narrowed considerably since 1945. For instance, one element of the "Americanization" of Europe is the spread of chains, supermarkets, and other U.S.-style institutions of distribution. In "borrowing" these methods from the United States, the Europeans add their own modifications; their supermarkets are not as large, they rely on walk-in neighborhood trade rather than on vast parking lots, their average transactions are smaller, and there are other adaptations. But there is a clear trend toward similarity in distributive systems.

The combination of continued differences in marketing institutions *now* with the prospect of greater similarities in the *future* creates some difficult problems for multinational marketers. One such problem may be timing. The experience of Princess Housewares in Germany, previously mentioned, is a case in point.

When Princess Housewares went into the German market, the company had a basic choice to make regarding channels of distribution. In the early 1960's, the predominant system of appliance distribution was independent wholesalers selling to retail stores. Small specialty retailers still dominated the market. However, department stores, mail-order firms, and discounters were growing in importance. Most of these large retailers were able to obtain *Grosshändler* (wholesaler) discounts from manufacturers, and many of them sold at substantial discounts from "suggested" retail prices. The suggested prices, in turn, were often set at artificially high levels (so-called "moon" prices) to permit the appearance of large price cuts at retail. At the same time, because of public confusion and discontent over artificial list prices and equally artificial discounts, the resale price maintenance law was under increasing attack.

Princess Housewares, as a relatively unknown brand, felt that its first task was to obtain distribution. To do this, the company decided to establish maintained prices and enforce them, so that small retailers' margins would be protected. But this put the company at a disadvantage in selling to the large discounters. It also meant that the company had to sell direct to retailers, since wholesalers could not be relied on to enforce resale prices.

In some ways, the Princess Housewares case boils down to a choice between a traditional distributive system, similar to that used in the United States in the early 1950's, and an emerging but still undeveloped system. U.S. experience suggests that the emerging system will become the dominant one. But can a manufacturer afford to be ahead of the trend?

LEGAL RESTRICTIONS

Different countries require or permit very different practices in the areas of product design, competitive practices, pricing, employment, and advertising. They also impose differing taxes and tariffs, and multinational companies often follow devious paths in the attempt to minimize the total cost effects of these levies. Obviously, such practices can be stumbling blocks for the would-be standardizer.

Some product standards, though ostensibly designed for purposes of safety, are used by governments as a device for protecting home industries. A notable case in point was the imposition of new regulations for electrical appliances by France in 1967, along with delays in issuing approvals. This was generally regarded as a deliberate move to slow down the onslaught of competition by the Italian companies and thus give the domestic industry a breathing space.

But other legal restrictions are established for more legitimate purposes. The use of a 220-volt electrical system in Europe, for example, has led to a stringent set of safety standards for such products as irons—more stringent than U. S. standards. Cord connections must be stronger, and shielding against radio interference is necessary. These requirements, in turn, dictate modifications in product design.

Resale price maintenance and other laws designed to protect small retailers still have a strong influence on distribution policies in many countries. The trend has been away from restrictions of this kind, however, and some nations, such as the United Kingdom, have virtually abolished price maintenance.

Custom and legislative regulation combine to discourage some types of advertising and promotion. Goodyear Tire & Rubber Company, for instance, demonstrated the strength of its "3T" tire cord in the United States by showing a steel chain breaking. In Germany, this visualization was not permitted because it was regarded as disparaging to the steel chain manufacturers.[13] Such exaggerated sensitivity may be amusing, but it cannot be ignored in planning advertising campaigns.

CONCLUSION

Traditionally, marketing strategy has been regarded as a strictly local problem in each national market. Differences in customer needs and preferences, in competition, in institutional systems, and in legal regulations have seemed to require basically different marketing programs. Any similarity between countries has been seen as purely coincidental.

There is no doubt that differences among nations are still great, and that these differences should be recognized in marketing planning. But the experiences of a growing number of multinational companies suggest that there are also some real potential gains in an integrated approach to marketing strategy. Standardization of products, packages, and promotional approaches may permit substantial cost savings, as well as greater consistency in dealings with customers. The harmonization of price policies often facilitates better internal planning and control. Finally, if good ideas are scarce, and if some of them have universal appeal, they should be used as widely as possible.

All of this adds up to the conclusion that both the pros *and* the cons of standardization in multinational marketing programs should be considered, and that a company's decisions should be based on estimated overall revenues and costs. Obviously, each case must be considered on its own merits — slogans and formulas are not very helpful guides to intelligent planning.

If marketing strategy is to be designed with a multinational perspective, then the firm's organization must make provision for line and staff marketing positions at appropriate levels. Space does not permit a full discussion of the organizational issues here, but it may be noted that there is a clear trend among leading companies toward establishment of marketing coordinators, international committees, and other mechanisms for at least partial centralization of marketing management. Hoover, Singer, General Electric, Eastman Kodak, and many other companies have recently made changes in this direction.

Finding the right balance between local autonomy and central coordination is not an easy task, any more than is balancing the gains of standardized marketing strategy against the needs of heterogeneous national markets. But it is an important task, with high potential profit rewards for management. Finding the best solutions to these problems should be high on the priority list for every multinational company.

NOTES

1. "International Expansion," in *Plotting Marketing Strategy, A New Orientation,* edited by Lee Adler (New York: Simon & Schuster, 1967), p. 229.
2. "Planning in a Worldwide Business," HBR (January-February 1965), p. 137.
3. See, for example, Philip Siekman, "The Battle for the Kitchen," *Fortune* (January 1964).
4. The estimates of production, exports, and so forth, cited here are given by Carlo Castellano, *L'Industria Degli Elettrodomestici in Italia,* Universita Degli Studi di Genova (Torino, 1965), or are drawn from *Marketing in Europe,* October 1966 and September 1967.
5. "Regional Management Overseas," HBR (January-February 1967), p. 89.
6. See Norman Heller, "How Pepsi-Cola Does It in 110 Countries," in *New Ideas for Successful Marketing,* edited by John S. Wright and Jac L. Goldstucker (Chicago: American Marketing Association, 1966), p. 700.
7. *When Is a Frontier Not a Frontier?* (pamphlet) Brussels (May 1966).
8. Reported in *Business Europe,* August 23, 1967, p. 1.
9. "The Danger of 'Local' International Advertising," *Journal of Marketing* (January 1967), pp. 61-62.
10. "Marketing Decision-Making in the Multinational Firm," unpublished doctoral thesis, Harvard Business School, 1968.
11. William Gerunsky, "International Marketing Research," in *Chemical Marketing Research,* edited by N. H. Giragosian (New York: Reinhold Publishing Corp.), p. 258.
12. Quoted in *Advertising Age,* August 29, 1966, p. 218.
13. *Advertising Age,* May 9, 1966, p. 75.

14
Multinational Product Planning: Strategic Alternatives

Warren J. Keegan

Inadequate product planning is a major factor inhibiting growth and profitability in international business operations today. The purpose of this article is to identify five strategic alternatives available to international marketers, and to identify the factors which determine the strategy which a company should use. Table 1 summarizes the proposed strategic alternatives.

STRATEGY ONE:
ONE PRODUCT, ONE MESSAGE, WORLDWIDE

When PepsiCo extends its operations internationally, it employs the easiest and in many cases the most profitable marketing strategy—that of product extension. In every country in which it operates, PepsiCo sells exactly the same product, and does it with the same advertising and promotional themes and appeals that it uses in the United States. PepsiCo's outstanding international performance is perhaps the most eloquent and persuasive justification of this practice.

Unfortunately, PepsiCo's approach does not work for all products. When Campbell Soup tried to sell its U.S. tomato soup formulation to the British, it discovered, after considerable losses, that the English prefer a more bitter taste. Another U.S. company spent several million dollars in an unsuccessful effort to capture the British cake mix market with U.S.-style fancy frosting and cake mixes only to discover that Britons consume their cake at

Reprinted, by permission, from the *Journal of Marketing*, published by the American Association, Vol. 33 (January 1969).

tea time, and that the cake they prefer is dry, spongy, and suitable to being picked up with the left hand while the right manages a cup of tea. Another U.S. company that asked a panel of British housewives to bake their favorite cakes discovered this important fact and has since acquired a major share of the British cake mix market with a dry, spongy cake mix.

Close to home, Philip Morris attempted to take advantage of U.S. television advertising campaigns which have a sizable Canadian audience in border areas. The Canadian cigarette market is a Virginia or straight tobacco market in contrast to the U.S. market, which is a blended tobacco market. Philip Morris officials decided to ignore market research evidence which indicated that Canadians would not accept a blended cigarette, and went ahead with programs which achieved retail distribution of U.S.-blended brands in the Canadian border areas served by U.S. television. Unfortunately, the Canadian preference for the straight cigarette remained unchanged. American-style cigarettes sold right up to the border but no further. Philip Morris had to withdraw its U.S. brands.

The unfortunate experience of discovering consumer preferences that do not favor a product is not confined to U.S. products in foreign markets. Corn Products Company discovered this in an abortive attempt to popularize Knorr dry soups in the United States. Dry soups dominate the soup market in Europe, and Corn Products tried to transfer some of this success to the United States. Corn Products based its decision to push ahead with Knorr on reports of taste panel comparisons of Knorr dry soups with popular liquid soups. The results of these panel tests strongly favored the Knorr product. Unfortunately these taste panel tests did not stimulate the actual market environment for soup which includes not only eating but also preparation. Dry soups require 15 to 20 minutes cooking, whereas liquid soups are ready to serve as soon as heated. This difference is apparently a critical factor in the soup buyer's choice, and it was the reason for another failure of the extension strategy.

The product-communications extension strategy has an enormous appeal to most multinational companies because of the cost savings associated with this approach. Two sources of savings, manufacturing economies of scale and elimination of product R and D costs, are well known and understood. Less well known, but still important, are the substantial economies associated with the standardization of marketing communications. For a company with worldwide operations, the cost of preparing separate print and TV-cinema films for each market would be enormous. PepsiCo international marketers have estimated, for example, that production costs for specially prepared advertising for foreign markets would cost them $8 million

Table 1: Multinational Product-Communications Mix: Strategic Alternatives

Strat-egy	Product Function or Need Satisfied	Conditions of Product Use	Ability to Buy Product	Recom-mended Product Strategy	Recommended Communications Strategy	Relative Cost of Adjust-ments	Product Examples
1	Same	Same	Yes	Extension	Extension	1	Soft drinks
2	Different	Same	Yes	Extension	Adaptation	2	Bicycles, Motor-scooters
3	Same	Different	Yes	Adaptation	Extension	3	Gasoline, Detergents
4	Different	Different	Yes	Adaptation	Adaptation	4	Clothing, Greeting Cards
5	Same		No	Invention	Develop New Communi-cations	5	Hand-powered Washing Machine

per annum, which is considerably more than the amounts now spent by PepsiCo International for advertising production in these markets. Although these cost savings are important, they should not distract executives from the more important objective of maximum profit performance, which may require the use of an adjustment or invention strategy. As shown above, product extension in spite of its immediate cost savings may in fact prove to be a financially disastrous undertaking.

STRATEGY TWO:
PRODUCT EXTENSION — COMMUNICATIONS ADAPTATION

When a product fills a different need or serves a different function under use conditions identical or similar to those in the domestic market, the only adjustment required is in marketing communications. Bicycles and motorscooters are illustrations of products in this category. They satisfy needs mainly for recreation in the United States but provide basic transportation in many foreign countries. Outboard motors are sold primarily to a recreation market in the United States, while the same motors in many foreign countries are sold mainly to fishing and transportation fleets.

In effect, when this approach is pursued (or, as is often the case, when it is stumbled upon quite by accident), a product transformation occurs. The same physical product ends up serving a different function or use than that for which it was originally designed. An actual example of a very successful transformation is provided by a U.S. farm machinery company which decided to market its U.S. line of suburban lawn and garden power equipment as agricultural implements in less-developed countries. The company's line of garden equipment was ideally suited to the farming task in many less-developed countries, and, most importantly, it was priced at almost a third less than competing equipment especially designed for small acreage farming offered by various foreign manufacturers.

There are many examples of food product transformation. Many dry soup powders, for example, are sold mainly as soups in Europe but as sauces or cocktail dips in the United States. The products are identical; the only change is in marketing communications. In this case, the main communications adjustment is in the labeling of the powder. In Europe, the label illustrates and describes how to make soup out of the powder. In the United States, the label illustrates and describes how to make sauce and dip as well as soup.

The appeal of the product extension communications adaptation strategy is its relatively low cost of implementation. Since the product in this strategy is unchanged, R and D, tooling, manufacturing setup, and inventory costs associated with additions to the product line are avoided. The only costs of this approach are in identifying different product functions and reformulating marketing communications (advertising, sales promotion, point-of-sale material, and so on) around the newly identified function.

STRATEGY THREE:
PRODUCT ADAPTATION — COMMUNICATIONS EXTENSION

A third approach to international product planning is to extend without change the basic communications strategy developed for the U.S. or home market, but to adapt the U.S. or home product to local use conditions. The product adaptation-communications extension strategy assumes that the product will serve the same function in foreign markets under different use conditions.

Esso followed this approach when it adapted its gasoline formulations to meet the weather conditions prevailing in foreign market areas, but employed without change its basic communications appeal, "Put a Tiger in Your Tank." There are many other examples of products that have been adjusted to perform the same function internationally under different environmental conditions. International soap and detergent manufacturers have adjusted their product formulations to meet local water conditions and the characteristics of washing equipment with no change in their basic communications approach. Agricultural chemicals have been adjusted to meet different soil conditions as well as different types and levels of insect resistance. Household appliances have been scaled to sizes appropriate to different use environments, and clothing has been adapted to meet fashion criteria.

STRATEGY FOUR: DUAL ADAPTATION

Market conditions indicate a strategy of adaptation of both the product and communications when differences exist in environmental conditions of use and in the function which a product serves. In essence, this is a combination of the market conditions of strategies two and three. U.S. greeting card manufacturers have faced these circumstances in Europe where the conditions under which greeting cards are purchased are different than in the United States. In Europe, the function of a greeting card is to provide a space for the sender to write his own message in contrast to the U.S. card which contains a prepared message or what is known in the greeting card industry as "sentiment." European greeting cards are cellophane wrapped, necessitating a product alteration by American greeting card manufacturers selling in the European market. American manufacturers pursuing an adjustment strategy have changed both their product and their marketing communications in response to this set of environmental differences.

STRATEGY FIVE: PRODUCT INVENTION

The adaptation and adjustment strategies are effective approaches to international marketing when potential customers have the ability, or purchasing power, to buy the product. When potential customers cannot afford a product, the strategy indicated is invention or the development of an entirely new product designed to satisfy the identified need or function at a price within reach of the potential customer. This is a demanding but, if product development costs are not excessive, a potentially rewarding product strategy for the mass markets in the middle and less-developed countries of the world.

Although potential opportunities for the utilization of the invention strategy in international marketing are legion, the number of instances where companies have responded is disappointingly small. For example, there are an estimated 600 million women in the world who still scrub their clothes by hand. These women have been served by multinational soap and detergent companies for decades, yet until this year not one of these companies had attempted to develop an inexpensive manual washing device.

Robert Young, Vice President of Marketing-Worldwide of Colgate-Palmolive, has shown what can be done when product development efforts are focused upon market needs. He asked the leading inventor of modern mechanical washing processes to consider "inventing backwards" — to apply his knowledge not to a better mechanical washing device, but to a much better manual device. The device developed by the inventor is an inexpensive (under $10), all-plastic, hand-powered washer that has the tumbling action of a modern automatic machine. The response to this washer in a Mexican test market is reported to be enthusiastic.

HOW TO CHOOSE A STRATEGY

The best product strategy is one which optimizes company profits over the long term, or, stated more precisely, it is one which maximizes the present value of cash flows associated with business operations. Which strategy for international markets best achieves this goal? There is, unfortunately, no general answer to this question. Rather, the answer depends upon the specific product-market-company mix.

Some products demand adaptation, others lend themselves to adaptation, and others are best left unchanged. The same is true of markets. Some are so similar to the U.S. markets as to require little adaptation. No country's markets, however, are exactly like the U.S., Canada's included. Indeed, even within the United States, for some products regional and ethnic differences are sufficiently important to require product adaptation. Other markets are moderately different and lend themselves to adaptation, and still others are so different as to require adaptation of the majority of products. Finally, companies differ not only in their manufacturing costs, but also in their capability to identify and produce profitable product adaptations.

PRODUCT-MARKET ANALYSIS

The first step in formulating international product policy is to apply the systems analysis technique to each product in question. How is the product used? Does it require power sources, linkage to other systems, maintenance, preparation, style matching, and so on? Examples of almost mandatory adaptation situations are products designed for 60-cycle power going into 50-cycle markets, products calibrated in inches going to metric markets, products which require maintenance going into markets where maintenance standards and practices differ from the original design market, and products which might be used under different conditions than those for which they were originally designed. Renault discovered this latter factor too late with the ill-fated Dauphine, which acquired a notorious reputation for break-down frequency in the United States. Renault executives attribute the frequent mechanical failure of the Dauphine in the United States to the high-speed turnpike driving and relatively infrequent U.S. maintenance. These turned out to be critical differences for the product, which was designed for the roads of France and the almost daily maintenance which a Frenchman lavishes upon his car.

Even more difficult are the product adaptations which are clearly not mandatory, but which are of critical importance in determining whether the product will appeal to a narrow market segment rather than a broad mass market. The most frequent offender in this category is price. Too often, U.S. companies believe they have adequately adapted their international product offering by making adaptations to the physical features of products (for example, converting 120 volts to 220 volts) but they extend U.S. prices. The effect of such practice in most markets of the world where average incomes are lower than those in the United States is to put the U.S. product in a specialty market for the relatively wealthy consumers rather than in the mass market. An extreme case of this occurs when the product for the foreign market is exported from the United States and undergoes the often substantial price escalation that occurs when products are sold via multi-layer export channels and exposed to import duties. When price constraints are considered in international marketing, the result can range from margin reduction and feature elimination to the "inventing backwards" approach used by Colgate.

COMPANY ANALYSIS

Even if product-market analysis indicates an adaptation opportunity, each company must examine its own product/communication development and manufacturing costs. Clearly, any product or communication adaptation strategy must survive the test of profit effectiveness. The often-repeated exhortation that in international marketing a company should always adapt its products' advertising and promotion is clearly superficial, for it does not take into account the cost of adjusting or adapting products and communications programs.

WHAT ARE ADAPTATION COSTS?

They fall under two broad categories — development and production. Development costs will vary depending on the cost effectiveness of product/communications development groups within the company. The range in costs from company to company and product to product is great. Often, the company with international product development facilities has a strategic cost advantage. The vice-president of a leading U.S. machinery company told recently of an example of this kind of advantage:

We have a machinery development group both here in the States and also in Europe. I tried to get our U.S. group to develop a machine for making the elliptical cigars that dominate the European market. At first they said "who would want an elliptical cigar machine?" Then they gradually admitted that they could produce such a machine for $500,000. I went to our Italian product development group with the same proposal, and they developed the machine I wanted for $50,000. The differences were partly relative wage costs but very importantly they were psychological. The Europeans see elliptical cigars every day, and they do not find the elliptical cigar unusual. Our American engineers were negative on elliptical cigars at the outset and I think this affected their overall response.

Analysis of a company's manufacturing costs is essentially a matter of identifying potential opportunity losses. If a company is reaping economies of scale from large-scale production of a single product, then any shift to variations of the single product will raise manufacturing costs. In general, the more decentralized a company's manufacturing setup, the smaller the manufacturing cost of producing different versions of the basic product. Indeed, in the company with local manufacturing facilities for each international market, the additional *manufacturing* cost of producing an adapted product for each market is zero.

A more fundamental form of company analysis occurs when a firm is considering in general whether or not to pursue explicitly a strategy of product adaptation. At this level, analysis must focus not only on the manufacturing cost structure of the firm, but also on the basic capability of the firm to identify product adaptation opportunities and to convert these perceptions into profitable products. The ability to identify preferences will depend to an important degree on the creativity of people in the organization and the effectiveness of information systems in this organization. The latter capability is as important as the former. For example, the existence of salemen who are creative in identifying profitable product adaptation opportunities is no assurance that their ideas will be translated into reality by the organization. Information, in the form of their ideas and perceptions, must move through the organization to those who are involved in the product development decision-making process; and this movement, as any student of information systems in organizations will attest, is not automatic. Companies which lack perceptual and information system capabilities are not well equipped to pursue a product adaptation strategy, and should either concentrate on products which can be extended or should develop these capabilities before turning to a product adaptation strategy.

SUMMARY

The choice of product and communications strategy in international marketing is a function of three key factors: (1) the product itself defined in terms of the function or need it serves; (2) the market defined in terms of the conditions under which the product is used, including the preferences of potential customers and the ability to buy the products in question; and (3) the costs of adaptation and manufacture to the company considering these product-communications approaches. Only after analysis of the product-market fit and of company capabilities and costs can executives choose the most profitable international strategy.

Chapter Four:
Accounting and Finance

15
Nationalism and the International Transfer of Accounting Skills

Lee J. Seidler

In a discussion of how nationalistic activities interfere with the transfer of accounting skills between countries, it is appropriate to reiterate the desirability of such transfers.

The role of accounting in the efficient functioning of developed economies has been clearly explained. Accounting controls are a virtual necessity to the operation of the large economic enterprises which are a basic feature of the developed economies, capitalist or socialist. Financial accounting skills —performance measurement and the attestation function—are similarly necessary to the functioning of the capital markets in developing countries. The major reforms in financial reporting undertaken in countries such as France and Germany, in order to assist a broadening of their domestic capital markets, indicates a more acute perception of the latter function in recent years.

While accounting has long been accepted as a normal appurtenance of the already developed economy, its role in improving the state of the less developed countries has been less widely recognized. Economic development is dependent on the marshalling of greater amounts of capital for investment purposes. For various reasons—not necessarily good or bad—the major role in accumulating this investment capital in developing countries has been assumed by governments. More sophisticated tax systems, usually based on income, are required to produce the necessary revenues. Accounting

Reprinted, with permission, from *The International Journal of Accounting, Education and Research*, Vol.5, #1 (Fall 1969).

skills play a key role in the functioning of such tax systems. Capital budgeting techniques provide the information for a more efficient allocation for these investment funds. Equitable systems for price control and the allocation of scarce foreign exchange resources require reasonable cost accounting. The growth of large industries requires more sophisticated accounting, data processing, and management information systems. As in the developed countries, new capital markets require auditing skills and income measurement abilities.

TRANSFER WHICH ACCOUNTING?

If it is accepted that accounting skills are relatively advanced in the developed countries and that the developing countries have need of such skills, it is not unreasonable to suggest an appropriate transfer of these skills. In the discussion which follows, it will become apparent that the accounting skills contemplated for transfer are those which might broadly be classified as "Anglo-American."

In the past, both the French civil-law oriented accounting model and the British accounting traditions were each spread to many countries, principally through the vehicle of colonialism, and particularly in the French case, through cultural affinity. As noted below, the strongest vehicle for the current international dissemination of accounting information is the multinational corporation and its associated activities. The vast majority of such enterprises have their most significant ties to the United States or the united Kingdom. The investors in these two countries, where the shares of these corporations are generally traded, have for many decades required audited financial statements, with the result that U.S.- and U.K.- based independent accountants have developed world-wide practices. The French-Continental school of accounting has not received any similar current encouragement. There may be some argument that the Anglo-American accounting tradition is not the best one for transfer to the developing countries, but for practical purposes, it is the one which is available.

TRANSFERRING ACCOUNTING SKILLS

Skills of a technical nature appear to cross international borders with relative ease.[1] Such skills are generally free from cultural or political labels, and hence they avoid the type of barriers which more commonly affect disciplines with a social orientation.

Accounting skills would appear, from a superficial examination, to have a similar nonpolitical, noncultural orientation, which would enable them also to pass from country to country free of nationalistic influences. Unfortunately, this is not the case. Traditionally, in the Anglo-American countries with their common-law heritage, it has been assumed that accounting should be developed by accountants, independent of legal direction or coercion. While this may have been true in earlier, less complex times, at present, in both the United States and the United Kingdom, the law, particularly through taxation and capital market regulation, exerts a very sharp influence over accounting techniques. In most of the countries outside of the Anglo-American sphere, legal prescription of accounting methodology and techniques has always been the rule. This fact is especially true in those countries which have derived their business and commercial systems from the French example. There, commercial laws invariably include extensive regulation of financial reporting and bookkeeping. In countries with this civil law approach to accounting, the introduction of new, improved, or changed accounting techniques requires revisions in the law, a significant barrier to change.

FISCAL ETHNOCENTRISM

Often more troublesome than legal problems is a form of nationalism which might be labeled "Fiscal Ethnocentrism." Although the power of the former colonialists to control directly the governmental structure of most of the developing countries has largely disappeared, suspicions of their ability and desire to continue to manipulate control are strong. There appears to be a distinct tendency, in certain instances, for the developing countries to reject ideas coming from the developed countries simply because of their historical origins.

Another aspect of this problem centers on the fundamental nature of accounting. Accounting measurements, while they present the appearance of exactitude, are of course conditioned by the circumstances under which they are made. At the same time, much of the use of accounting results is closely bound to the user's instinctive conditioning to the assumptions, biases, or other distortions which may be inherent in his particular accounting system. An American financial analyst develops an instinctive ability to evaluate the "quality" of the reported earnings of an American corporation, but he lacks the perception to view the statements of a French company with equal acuity. Similarly, while the cost accounting system of a manufacturer in a developing country may be antiquated or inaccurate by our standards, it is the one that he understands, and one with which he feels familiar. A new system, although more conceptually valid, may involve a painful relearning process.

Allied with these influences is the problem that accounting theories are based on certain assumptions about human behavior and managerial goals.

For example, American managerial accounting techniques and concepts, such as responsibility accounting, are based on the assumption that attempts to increase both individual discretion and responsibility in large organizations will be acceptable to both management and employees. This is usually the case in the United States, where drives for achievement and advancement are strong. When these ideas are suggested in societies, such as those of many of the developing countries where the total of economic wealth is conceived to be static, the inherently competitive aspects of decentralization and responsibility accounting may be quite unattractive. In many societies life consists of gaining a viable position and consolidating it. Betterment or advancement requires that one risk the loss of a part or all of that which has been gained. Employees may not desire additional, or indeed any, responsibility at the price of possible failure. Correspondingly, in such countries paternalistic managers often feel that placing a responsibility on supervisors is in some sense an imposition on the employees given the responsibility.

Thus, in countries where these tendencies are strong, such as in the highly paternalistic business environment of the middle eastern and the Mediterranean countries, many of our concepts of managerial accounting may be both unacceptable and unworkable.

ACCOUNTING SKILLS ARE BADLY PACKAGED

Another barrier to the easy transfer of accounting skills stems from the unfortunate way in which these skills are packaged. Only a small portion of the skills is written. Indeed, it has been virtually an article of faith for some accountants that generally accepted accounting principles have not, or even cannot, be completely recorded. At present, only a small portion of the sum total of our accounting skills may be found in written form. A major part of the total education of an accountant is still received through direct oral communication with more experienced accountants or teachers. Certainly, this has been one of the rationalizations for the retention of the experience requirement for the CPA certificate.

Thus, the transfer of accounting skills is highly dependent on personal contact between teacher and student. It is obvious that in the international dimension the requirement for face-to-face contact between those possessing skills and those desiring them constitutes a significant barrier.

Even to the extent that accounting skills can be found in written form, language problems and the difficulties of translation are major problems. Accounting terminology is difficult to translate, not only because many languages lack an accounting vocabulary, but more important, because accounting terminology is in many respects a shorthand for rather complex concepts. Thus, while one may literally translate words such as *asset* and *income* from one language to another, a workable translation requires a *definition* of the term and the assumptions under which it is used. In this connection, it is interesting to note that translations of accounting texts often appear to be somewhat longer than the original work. Translations must be made by a translator who is skilled in accounting — and in the accounting of the countries of both languages. Such translations are very time-consuming, and they usually require the allocation of large amounts of time of the all too few accounting professors in the developing countries. In Turkey, for example, the translation of Paton and Littleton took four years of one of the country's best accounting professor's time. By the time the job was completed, a revised edition in English was already available.

These barriers should not suggest that international transfers of accounting skills are impossible. There are, in fact, a number of successful examples. The active accounting professions in most of the former British colonies testify to the success of the international efforts of the British accounting profession. These transfers, of course, were accomplished largely in the absence of language problems. The wide acceptance of American accounting principles in Mexico is a case where the language barriers have largely been overcome, but unfortunately this latter type of transfer is all too rare. In many cases the barriers discussed above have been quite effective.

TRANSFER AGENTS

There are a number of different vehicles for accomplishing the international transfer of accounting skills. Exchanges of both students and professors are effective on a limited scale, but such programs suffer from high cost and, particularly in the case of the students, from their high propensity to remain in the United States.

Some skill, of course, can be translated by books, particularly to English speaking countries. In other countries, such as Mexico where translation to the local language is relatively easily accomplished, books play an important role. For many years, the Spanish version of Finney and Miller, the well known American textbook, has been the largest selling accounting text in Mexico. In Japan, books received under U.S. programs after World War II appear to have had a significant influence over Japanese accounting. Aggressive book publishers in Mexico and Argentina have had a major role in spreading accounting skills throughout South America. In the case of the Mexican books, these skills appear to be largely American-oriented.

INTERNATIONAL ACCOUNTING FIRMS

Historically, however, the most effective vehicle for the international transfer of accounting skills has been the international accounting firms. The American accounting profession, for example, was started in great measure by representatives of British firms sent to this country. The titles of many American accounting firms include names such as Waterhouse, Peat, and Touche, all of whom were early presidents of British Institutes of Chartered Accountants.

Today, the international accounting firms remain probably the most effective vehicle for the transfer of Anglo-American accounting skills to other countries. Their principal influence is exerted when they hire, train, and utilize local nationals to practice the Anglo-American accounting skills. One finds relatively few Americans employed in the overseas offices of the firms, although there is a rather large number of British nationals. In general, and particularly in the case of South America, local nationals constitute the largest group of employees of these accounting firms. Local participation is not restricted to employee levels; there are a number of local partners in all the accounting firms.

The reasons for the predominant use of local talent in these offices probably stem more from practical realities and economic considerations than from altruism. The compensation expectations of Americans going overseas are typically so inflated that the cost of local talent, even considering substantial training expenditures, is invariably less than that of importing Americans. The expectations of British personnel tend to be considerably lower than that of Americans, and their willingness to go overseas generally quite a bit greater, thus explaining their relatively larger numbers.

Regardless of the degree of idealism involved, the operations of the international accounting firms have made them the largest developers of local accounting manpower and hence local accounting skills. As in the United States, there is substantial fallout from the international accounting firms; that is, many employees leave to take jobs with local companies or to establish their own accounting practices, thus spreading the skills further through the economy.

Sometimes by design, and at other times because of economic considerations or local restrictionism, the international operations of the accounting firms take many forms, ranging from direct operation of foreign offices which are treated as components of the parent firm to simple representation agreements with local firms. The former type of arrangement produces much more effective integration and hence more intensive training of local personnel.

In most such cases, a reasonable number of American personnel are present, thus increasing the exposure of the locals to American practice.

In the typical case where an international firm is merely represented by a local firm, the ties are less tight and the resulting acquaintance with American accounting more superficial. The local firm probably devotes most of its resources to servicing local clients, unrelated to the international firm. With only a limited interest in the profit of the local firm, the international firm will be less willing to invest significant resources to train the local staff. In terms of "enforcing" its own accounting standards, the international firm has little authority over its correspondent.

Thus, when an international firm is merely represented by a local firm, as contrasted to having its own office in the foreign country, the transfer of accounting skills flows at a substantially lower level. On the other hand, local accounting firms usually deal more extensively with purely local businesses. Thus, what skills are transferred to the local firm may be more likely to be spread to the local business community.

Slowly, but increasingly, the international offices of international firms have found a market for "American style" accounting services with local businesses. Some of this local practice development has been a result of the semicoercive efforts of international development organizations such as the World Bank and the Inter-American Development Bank, which typically require local loan applicants to provide American-style audited financial statements. In other cases, local clients have gradually perceived the value of the services. Regardless of the method, the result is to further spread both financial and managerial accounting skills into the local economies.

Additional transfers of accounting skills and attitudes occur in those countries such as Venezuela, where one finds participation by the representatives of the international accounting firms in local professional accounting associations. In yet other countries, staff and partners of the international firms often teach at local universities.

NEW NATIONALISTIC RESTRICTIONS

With the continued international expansion of American corporations and the derivative demand for services from the international accounting firms, it might be expected that the mechanism described above would function increasingly well. Unfortunately, the international expansion of the Anglo-American-based international accounting firms appears to be generating a reaction in a number of countries. Recent years have seen the enactment or intensification of legislation or restrictions designed to limit the freedom of practice upon accountants in many countries, including Peru, Chile, Venezuela, and Mexico. Legislation which at best appears threatening has been or will be passed shortly in Greece and Japan.

Restrictions against the practice of accounting by foreigners are, of course, nothing new. More than two dozen countries have traditionally had some degree of such restriction, although in many cases the practice restrictions remained on the books unenforced or easily circumvented. In recent years, however, there appears to have been an increase in the number of countries having passed or proposed new restrictions on international accounting. The new restrictions vary in severity. Those of Chile contain a residence requirement and the necessity of an additional signature on the auditor's opinion by a member of the Chilean *Colegio*. Foreigners may now, however, receive the necessary title of *contador*. Peru requires majority ownership and staffing by locals. At the extreme, Mexico completely prohibits the practice of accounting within the country by foreigners.

It should not be assumed that such restrictive efforts are confined solely to the developing countries. One of the strongest efforts to restrict practice rights of foreign accountants is currently being undertaken by the *Nederlands Instituut van Registeraccountants* (NIVRA). New laws in Holland appear to restrict audits of companies to members of NIVRA. NIVRA members are, however, forbidden to be in partnership with accountants outside of Holland.

The motivation for the restrictions imposed on foreign accountants seems to vary considerably. In some of the developing countries, particularly, there appears to be a mixture of emotional nationalism combined with economic factors. In Peru, for example, one of the groups attempting to win an election in the Peruvian professional organization ran on a platform which called for nationalization of the profession and throwing off "the chains of imperialism." The imperialists were depicted, in election literature, as the major international accounting firms.

In some countries the international restrictions are at least partially the result of local quarrels. In Chile, for example, we find the usual rivalry between university-educated and practice-educated accountants, with both attempting to exclude the other from practice. If, as is anticipated, a degree from a Chilean university becomes a requirement for accounting practice, then most foreigners will be effectively precluded from practice. The Netherlands also provides an example of mixed emotions in restrictionism. There is obviously an element of economic restrictionism in NIVRA's actions; a few large and well developed Dutch accounting firms would prefer to exclude the competition of foreign firms. In addition, however, there appears to be a genuine belief on the part of the Dutch that a partner in an accounting firm should be able to take full responsibility for the actions of all his partners and, reason the Dutch, how can one do so if the partner is thousands of miles away in another country?

In many cases, practice restrictions can be avoided by engaging in a representation agreement with a local accounting firm. As noted above, such agreements provide a lesser degree of control by the international accounting firm, and often, less coordination and quality control. Obviously the restrictions against international accounting firms are not significantly different in nature from those which countries have often attempted to institute against other types of foreign businesses. The consequences of the restrictions are also similar; the local country gains—or regains—possession of the business, often at a cost in efficiency and benefits. In the case of professional practice the possibilities of exploitation or expropriation of the national wealth, such as exist with mineral resources, are virtually nil. Since in the vast majority of cases the foreign skills are far better than those offered by the local accountants, the restricting country appears to suffer in general in order to provide supposed benefits to the small segment of its population which practices accounting.

OTHER NATIONALISTS

One major country generally requires foreigners to become citizens or to declare their intent to become citizens in order for them to receive the local accounting certificate. That country also usually requires education in a local university as a prerequisite for obtaining certification. It rarely allows reciprocity to qualified accountants of other countries, regardless of the stature of their home profession, unless they have satisfied the local requirements.

The country described in these sentences is, of course, the United States. Unfortunately, on any reasonable scale of nationalism and national restrictions, the U.S. must rank high. At present, forty-six states require U.S. citizenship or intent to obtain U.S. citizenship as a prerequisite to becoming a CPA; only California, Kentucky, Indiana, and Washington do not have citizenship requirements. Foreign accountants are usually permitted to practice accounting under their own titles, but this freedom is, obviously, of dubious economic value. Recently, the American Institute of CPA's has instituted a class of International Associates under which foreigners, *if educated in the United States,* may achieve a membership status in the AICPA after passing the uniform exam. This option is of some benefit to foreign students in the United States, but it is quite obviously not the equivalent of allowing foreigners to practice as CPA's in the United States or to actually obtain the certificate.

Thus, the United States is a member in good standing of that group of countries that restricts international accounting practice. When the international accounting firms have attempted to obtain some relief from restrictionist practices in other countries, they have found that the locals were well acquainted with U.S. actions and have utilized them as a rationale for their own restrictions.

CONCLUSION

It is apparent that the international transfer of accounting skills is heavily affected by nationalism, originating both in the United States and foreign countries. To the extent that these efforts are found on the part of the developing nations they appear to provide little benefit to the local country but they may well do substantial harm. When found in developed countries, such as the Netherlands, it is doubtful that anyone other than the accountants involved is seriously affected.

It is when accounting nationalism is found in the United States, as it is, that it appears to do the most harm. Nationalism on our part hurts American accountants, the accountants in the developing countries, and the developing countries themselves. To the extent that we display nationalistic tendencies ourselves, we provide a potent rationalization for nationalists in other countries who are endeavoring to enact restrictive legislation. As demonstrated above, this legislation is largely self-defeating from the standpoint of the developing economy, since it cuts off a vital flow of talent and managerial skills which these economies need so badly. A foreign student, who would study accounting in the United States and hope to return with the skills to his home country, is denied the right to take home the professional recognition of the CPA. Many foreign students are thus discouraged from studying accounting in the United States, and their countries are denied the benefit of the skills they might obtain.

It is therefore doubly encumbent upon the remaining forty-six jurisdictions in the United States to move as rapidly as possible to delete the anachronistic citizenship requirements for the CPA. The United States should no longer be a symbol of nationalism in international accounting.

NOTE

1. Conrad Arensberg and Arthus Niehoff, *Introducing Social Change: A Manual for Americans Overseas* (Chicago: Aldine Publishing Company, 1964), p. 62.

16
Accounting Principles Generally Accepted in the United States Versus those Generally Accepted Elsewhere

G. G. Mueller

Substantial evidence exists to support the claim that material differences characterize generally-accepted accounting principles as applied in various countries.[1] While these differences are significant for a number of individual concepts and practices, they should not obscure the equally important observation that there are also a great many similarities between the generally-accepted accounting principles of different countries. The differences, however, are the source of frequent and substantive problems in accounting practice.

With a steadily increasing volume of international business and investments, national differences in accounting principles have a growing impact. From a practical point of view, these national differences cause difficulties in at least these areas:

1. Reporting for international subsidiaries whose financial statements are to be consolidated or combined with United States parent-company statements.

Reprinted, with permission, from *The International Journal of Accounting, Education and Research*, Spring (1968). Support from the Price Waterhouse Foundation for the preparation of this article is gratefully acknowledged.

2. Reporting for international subsidiaries which lie beyond the consolidation or combination requirements—separate reports being required by the United States parent company.

3. Reporting for independent companies located in countries other than the United States where the statements are for local use and a standard United States form of opinion is to be furnished.

4. Reporting for independent companies in countries outside the United States where the statements and the opinions are likely to be read and used in the United States, e.g., for SEC filings, use by bankers, and possible acquisitions or general publication in English to stockholders in the United States.

This paper has as its main purpose the empirical evaluation of the complexities of varying accounting principles among different countries. While it is recognized that conceptual considerations are only one aspect of the over-all problem, a better perspective should be possible by limiting the focus of the discussion.

ECONOMIC AND BUSINESS ENVIRONMENTS
DIFFER AMONG VARIOUS COUNTRIES

Experience and observation tell us that the business environment normally varies from one country to the next. Indeed, some parts of an overall business environment may well differ between individual regions of a single country. On the other hand, there are instances where two or more countries have essentially the same environmental conditions. This reduces to the proposition that the dimensions of a business environment are primarily economic in nature whereas borders of a country are drawn because of political factors. Thus, political boundaries are not necessarily the only or the best lines of distinction for differing business environments.

What separates one business environment from another? Primarily, there are four marks of separation:

1. **States of economic development:** A highly developed economy provides an environment different from an undeveloped economy. In an African country, workers at a plant had to walk three hours twice each day to get to and from work. An AID program provided them with bicycles, after which they quit work. Possession of a bicycle was the sole motive for their accepting employment in the first place.

2. **Stages of business complexity:** Business needs as well as business output are functions of business complexity. An example of this is that West Germany in a recent year imported approximately DM 600 million (net) of industrial know-how in the form of Research and Development services outside Germany.

3. **Shades of political persuasion:** Political tendencies clearly affect business environments. Among the better known international examples are the expropriations of private property by central governments in South America and the Near and Far East. Forms of social legislation also affect business environments directly.

4. **Reliance on some particular system of law:** Differences between common law and code law are widely known. There are other differences as well. Detailed companies legislation may inhibit or protect business, as the case may be. The United States has rather stringent unfair trade and antitrust laws. The legal systems of some European countries tolerate market share agreements and cartel arrangements.

Using principally these four elements of differentiation, a quick analysis of business environments existing in different countries can be undertaken. This yields, in the author's opinion, ten distinct sets of business environments. Each differs from all others in at least one important respect. The ten are:

1. **United States/Canada/The Netherlands:** There is a minimum of commercial or companies legislation in this environment. Industry is highly developed; currencies are relatively stable. A strong orientation to business innovation exists. Many companies with widespread international business interests are headquartered in these countries.

2. **British Commonwealth (Excluding Canada):** Comparable companies legislation exists in all Commonwealth countries and administrative procedures and social order reflect strong ties to the mother country. There exists an inter-twining of currencies through the so-called "sterling block" arrangement. Business is highly developed but often quite traditional.

3. **Germany/Japan:** Rapid economic growth has occurred since World War II. Influences stemming from various United States military and administrative operations have caused considerable imitation of many facets of the United States practices, often by grafting United States procedures to various local traditions. The appearance of a new class of professional business managers is observable. Relative political, social, and currency stability exists.

4. **Continental Europe (Excluding Germany, The Netherlands, and Scandinavia):** Private business lacks significant government support. Private property and the profit motive are not necessarily in the center of economic and business orientation. Some national economic planning exists. Political swings from far right to far left, and vice versa, have a long history in this environment. Limited reservoirs of economic resources are available.

5. **Scandinavia:** Here we have developed economies, but characteristically slow rates of economic and business growth. Governments tend toward social legislation. Companies acts regulate business. Relative stability of population numbers is the rule. Currencies are quite stable. Several business innovations (especially in consumer goods) originated in Scandinavia. Personal characteristics and outlooks are quite similar in all five Scandinavian countries.

6. **Israel/Mexico:** These are the only two countries with substantial success in fairly rapid economic development. Trends of a shift to more reliance on private enterprise are beginning to appear; however, there is still a significant government presence in business. Political and monetary stability seem to be increasing. Some specialization in business and the professions is taking place. The general population apparently has a strong desire for higher standards of living.

7. **South America**[2]**:** Many instances are present of significant economic underdevelopment along with social and educational underdevelopment. The business base is narrow. Agricultural and military interests are strong and often dominate governments. There is considerable reliance on export/import trade. Currencies are generally soft. Populations are increasing heavily.

8. **The Developing Nations of the Near and Far East**[2] **:** Modern concepts and ethics of business have predominantly Western origins. These concepts and ethics often clash with the basic oriental cultures. Business in the developing nations of the Orient largely mean trade only. There is severe underdevelopment on most measures, coupled with vast population numbers. Political scenes and currencies are most shaky. Major economic advances are probably impossible without substantial assistance from the industrialized countries.

9. **Africa (Excluding South Africa)**[2] **:** Most of the African continent is still in the early stages of independent civilization and thus little or no native business environment presently exists. There are significant natural and human resources. Business is likely to assume a major role and responsibility in the development of African nations.

10. **Communist Nations:** The complete control by central government removes these countries from any further interest for the purpose of this article.

The above categorization suggests that each country does not necessarily have a separate and distinct environment for its business. It also suggests a manageable way of viewing the existing differences.

One additional general observation on business environments seems worthwhile. In the ten categories listed above, little likelihood of change may be expected in the near future. Of course, details and specifics constantly change in the economic surroundings of business. But the overall philosophy and character that distinguish the ten separate cases seem rather well established, perhaps for as long as a quarter of a century. Therefore, relative stability appears to be one of the properties of different business environments. This means two things: (1) business concepts and practices, including accounting concepts and practices, do not necessarily require rapid changes if they are based on environmental conditions, and (2) business environments are probably more difficult to change than is sometimes assumed.

ACCOUNTING AND THE
ECONOMIC-BUSINESS ENVIRONMENT

In society, accounting performs a service function. This function is put in jeopardy unless accounting remains, above all, practically useful. Thus, it must respond to the ever-changing needs of society and must reflect the social, political, legal, and economic conditions within which it operates. Its meaningfulness depends upon its ability to mirror these conditions.

The history of accounting and accountants reveals the changes which accounting consistently undergoes. At one time accounting was little more than a recording system for certain banking services and tax collection plans. Later it responded with double-entry bookkeeping procedures to meet the needs of trading ventures. The industrialization and division of labor made possible cost and management-type accounting. The advent of modern corporations stimulated periodic financial reporting and auditing. Most recently, accounting has revealed a greater social awareness by assuming public-interest responsibilities together with the providing of decision information for the larger public-securities markets and management-consulting functions. Accounting is clearly concerned with its environment. Its developmental processes are often compared with that of common law.

From an environmental point of view, various developments in society affect accounting. What else would have caused, for instance, the very serious preoccupation of United States accountants with the needs of United States security analysis? Similar influences are present in recent U.S. efforts concerning lessor and lessee accounting, accounting for business combinations, and the wholesale extension of accounting to international business problems.

But accounting also affects its environment. Many economic resources are allocated to specific business uses on the basis of relevant accounting information. In some measure, national economic policies are formulated on the contents or message of corporate financial statements, and unions often base wage demands on similar information. Rate cases of regulated companies are based primarily on accounting data, and so are most antitrust cases initiated by governmental agencies. Therefore, accounting both reflects environmental conditions and influences them.

Dudley E. Brown touches on the relationship of accounting to its environment in his review of *Corporate Financial Reporting in a Competitive Economy*, by Henry W. Bevis:

The financial accounting and reporting of any corporation are subject to a variety of external influences. A larger number of common approaches to accounting and reporting problems can be found in a given industry or other relatively homogeneous group of corporations than in all of industry, but the internal relationship of its operations and programs with external influences will continue to make each corporation different from every other.

The necessity that corporate financial accounting and reporting be sufficiently unrestricted to respond readily to change should be kept in mind . . . the principle of full and fair disclosure must remain the keystone of successful corporation-stockholder and corporate-society relationships.[3]

THE ISSUE OF DIFFERENT ACCOUNTING PRINCIPLES

If we accept that (1) economic and business environments are not the same in all countries and that (2) a close relationship exists between economic and business environments and accounting, it follows that a single set of generally-accepted accounting principles cannot be useful and meaningful in all situations. This conclusion admits the possibility of some honest and well-founded differences in accounting principles that find general acceptance in certain national or geographic-area circumstances.

Let us postulate for a moment that accounting principles generally accepted in the United States were enforced in all countries of the free world. This would create an international uniformity which would have some intellectual appeal and would ease many problems in international accounting practices and international financial reporting.

At the same time, such uniformity would lack meaning. It would have to assume that business conditions are the same in all parts of the free world and that the same stage of professional, social, and economic development has been reached everywhere. This is certainly not the case. In fact, enforced international uniformity on the basis of the United States accounting principles alone would probably lead to misinformation or inaccurate results in many instances. The same types of calamity which have characterized so many U.S. foreign aid problems in the past would result.

Nevertheless, the issue of international differences in accounting principles does not resolve itself into a complete laissez-faire approach. A strong theoretical argument can be made for consistency of generally-accepted accounting principles between those countries or geographic areas where economic and business environments are substantially similiar. In other words, from a theoretical viewpoint, generally accepted principles in the United States should be the same as those in Canada, but may differ in some respects from those used in South America or Pakistan or India. The business and economic environments of the United States and Canada are very similiar; the respective environments of the United States and India are very dissimilar.

ENVIRONMENTAL CIRCUMSTANCES AND APPROPRIATE ACCOUNTING PRINCIPLES

Reference to environmental conditions is subjective. It is not possible, therefore, to develop a conclusive list of those circumstances which permit or require differing accounting principles from one country or area to the next, but some of the circumstances affecting the determination of appropriate accounting principles in an international framework can be identified. Such circumstances include:

1. **Relative stability of the currency of account:** If a currency is quite stable over time, historical cost accounting is generally indicated. Significant currency instability calls for some form of price index adjustment, with the form of adjustments depending largely on the type of indexes available and reliable.

2. **Degree of legislative business interference:** Tax legislation may require the application of certain accounting principles. This is the case in Sweden where some tax allowances must be entered in the accounts before they can be claimed for tax purposes; this is also the situation for LIFO inventory valuations in the United States.

Furthermore, varying social security laws may affect accounting principles. Severance pay requirements in several South American countries illustrate this.

3. **Nature of business ownership:** Widespread public ownership of corporate securities generally requires different financial reporting and disclosure principles from those applicable to predominantly family or bank-owned corporate equities. This is in essence a difference because public and closely

held companies do not need to capitalize small stock distributions at market value whereas publicly held companies do.

4. **Level of sophistication of business management:** Highly refined accounting principles have no place in an environment where they are misunderstood and misused. A technical report on cost variances is meaningless unless the reader understands cost and accounting well. A sources and uses of funds statement should not be prepared unless it can be read competently.

5. **Differences in size and complexity of business firms:** Self-insurance may be acceptable for a very large firm where it is obviously not for a smaller firm. Similarily, a large firm mounting an extensive advertising campaign directed at a specific market or season may be justified in deferring part of the resultant expenditure, whereas smaller programs in smaller firms may need to be expensed directly.

Comparable conclusions apply to complexity. Heavy and regular Research and Development outlays by a United States corporation may require accounting recognition, especially when long-range projects are involved. Incidental development costs of a firm producing only oil additives in Mexico normally have no such requirement.

6. **Speed of business innovations:** Business combinations became popular in Europe only a few years ago. Before that, European countries had little need of accounting principles and practices for this type of business event. Very small stock distributions occur most generally in the United States. Again, this produces differences in accounting principles. Equipment leasing is not practiced in a number of countries with consequent absence of a need for lease accounting principles.

7. **Presence of specific accounting legislation:** Companies acts containing accounting provisions are found in many countries. While these acts change over time (for example, there were new acts recently in both Germany and the United Kingdom), their stipulations must be observed when in force and legally binding. The German act requires setting aside certain earnings as a "legal reserve." It also stipulates when and how consolidated financial statements are to be prepared. The British act defines how the term "reserve" is to be used in accounting. Many other examples of this type exist.

8. **Stage of economic development:** A one-crop agricultural economy needs accounting principles different from a United States-type economy. In the former, for instance, there is probably relatively little dependence on credit and long-term business contracts. Thus, sophisticated accrual accounting is out of place and essentially cash accounting is needed.

9. **Type of economy involved:** National economies vary in nature. Some

are purely agricultural, while others depend heavily on the exploitation of natural resources (oil in the Near East, gold and diamonds in South Africa, copper in Chile, etc.). Some economies rely mainly on trade and institutions (Switzerland, Lebanon), whereas still others are highly diversified and touch on a great variety of economic and business activities. These are reasons for different principles regarding consolidations, accretion or discovery of natural resources, and inventory methods, among others.

10. **Growing pattern of an economy:** Companies and industries grow, stabilize, or decline. The same applies to national economies. If growth and expansion are typical, the capitalization of certain deferred charges is more feasible than under stable or declining conditions. Stable conditions intensify competition for existing markets, requiring restrictive credit and inventory methods. Declining conditions may indicate write-offs and adjustments not warranted in other situations.

11. **Status of professional education and organization:** In the absence of organized accounting professionalism and native sources of accounting authority, principles from other areas or countries may be needed to fill existing voids. The process of adaptation, however, will be unsuccessful unless it allows for circumstantial factors of the type identified here.

12. **General levels of education and tool processes facilitating accounting:** Statistical methods in accounting and auditing cannot be used successfully where little or no knowledge of statistics and mathematics exists. Computer principles are not needed in the absence of working EDP installations. The French general accounting plan has enjoyed wide acceptance in France because it is easily understood and readily usable by those with average levels of education and without sophisticated accounting training.

The reader will recognize that several of the factors listed above may apply to a national situation as well as the international scene. This is not surprising since national variations in accounting concepts and practices are increasingly analyzed in terms of their respective environmental backgrounds, particularly in the United States. A relationship seems to exist between accounting flexibility within a country and among countries or areas. The topic of such a possible relationship, however, falls beyond the scope of this paper.

SOME EXAMPLES

As a limited test of the applicability of the list of environmental circumstances referred to in the preceding section, several different accounting principles are related to this list in order to evaluate at least some of the underlying environmental relationships. A complete diagnosis of this type would be a substantial undertaking and is not attempted here.

DIFFERENT CIRCUMSTANCES RESULTING IN
DIFFERENT ACCOUNTING PRINCIPLES

Investments in marketable securities are generally carried at the lower of cost or market, stock exchange quotations being used as indications of "market." A different principle needs application where no national stock exchange exists, for example, in Guatemala.

Severance payments are normally at the option of the employer and thus are customarily expensed at the time of payment. If severance payments of material amounts are required by law, however, they should be accrued in some fashion before the actual severance occurs.

In the United States, owners' equity is recorded, classified, and reported as to source. Interest in dividend potential is one reason for this. It results in basic distinctions between contributed capital, retained earnings, and capital from other sources.

On the other hand, a single owners' equity principle of legal capital dominates accounting in some European countries, e.g., Germany. This is based on a balance-sheet accounting orientation to creditor protection.

SIMILAR CIRCUMSTANCES RESULTING IN (LARGELY UNEXPLAINED)
DIFFERENT ACCOUNTING PRINCIPLES

The circumstances of inventory valuations are highly similar in the United States and the United Kingdom. In the lower of cost or market test, "market" means essentially replacement value in the United States and net realizable future sales value in the United Kingdom.

Despite close similarities of circumstances, deferred income tax "liabilities" are generally recognized in the United States and only sparingly recognized in Canada. Deferred tax accounting is not a generally-accepted accounting principle in Canada.

Accounting terminology varies internationally to a considerable degree without good reason. United States and United Kingdom usage of the terms "reserve" and "provision" differs, French use of the term "depreciation" differs from that in other European countries, and "goodwill" means nearly all things to all people. This is largely unexplainable.

CHANGE IN ACCOUNTING PRINCIPLES

For the time being, meaningful international uniformity of generally-accepted accounting principles should have full regard for differences existing in the environments in which accounting operates. While complete differentiation for each politically recognized country is undesirable and unwarranted, fundamentally different conditions between different countries or areas conceptually call for separate recognition.

Assuming that this can be achieved, a most important mandate of accounting is to respond to any changes in environmental conditions as soon as they occur. Accounting can actually further the cause of change since it has, as we have seen, some influence on its environment in addition to reacting to its environment. Therefore, identification with desirable efforts toward change and quick and full response to accomplished change are probably the primary leverage factors available to accounting in resolving justifiable international differences in generally-accepted accounting principles.

Three practical examples illustrate the force of change in accounting. First, the revised German companies law enacted in 1965 contains several financial disclosure provisions which are definitely patterned after United States SEC requirements. As Germany moves closer to a corporate business society that has much in common with the United States business society, tested SEC-type legislation would seem to be a valid response to the changes occurring.

Second, more comprehensive general financial-disclosure requirements are evidence in the United Kingdom via the widely discussed 1964 London Stock Exchange memorandum as well as the recent new companies legislation. For some time the Swiss business press has carried repeated strong appeals for greater disclosure in the financial statements of Swiss companies. These and similar admonitions for wider general disclosures seem to be a consequence of widening securities markets in the countries concerned. Here again, an environmental condition has changed and accounting should respond.

Third, there is a notable increase in consolidated financial reporting on the part of larger corporations in countries outside of North America. In many instances, consolidated financial statements are presented even though applicable laws do not require such presentations. The cause of this move toward greater use of consolidated financial reports undoubtedly lies in the ever growing extent of intercorporate investments and the steady growth of portfolio investments beyond the domicile countries of respective investors. The companies affected may have changed somewhat, but the far greater change has occurred in the environment of their operations.

In summary, a particular responsibility which accounting has in relation to change seems to exist. Awareness of this responsibility and concentrated efforts in connection with it are theoretically the most effective ways in which accounting principles between countries can be brought into greater harmony.

CONCLUSIONS

The three main conclusions of this paper are:

1. **United States generally-accepted accounting principles should not be enforced arbitrarily in other countries.** There is a theoretical incompatibility between the economic and business environments prevailing in different countries, and an arbitrary imposition of any single set of generally-accepted accounting principles would run counter to environmental differences which exist.

Only where environments are alike or similar can meaningful results be achieved by the use of a particular single body of accounting principles. At the same time, the overall theoretical framework of accounting itself needs to be general and permit analysis in terms of applicable environmental circumstances.

2. **Complete international diversity of accounting principles is undesirable and unnecessary.** The author has attempted to define ten different areas in which comparable environmental conditions exist and which therefore would gain from a particular approach to generally-accepted accounting principles. The ten-fold classification is highly subjective; nevertheless, it demonstrates a frame of reference with regard to limited international diversity of accounting principles.

Free international exchange and cooperation with regard to accounting principles would avoid unnecessary duplication in accounting research and provide the latest accounting know-how for application when conditions demand it.

3. **Accounting is dynamic and operates in an atmosphere of change.** Even though the basic character of a given business environment seems slow to change, the continuing evolution of the accounting discipline affords means toward more international harmony in generally-accepted accounting principles. Efforts to change unnecessary international diversities in accounting in response to changing economic and business conditions appear to hold greater promise, in theory, than legislation or another form of enforcement of dictated international accounting uniformity.

NOTES

1. For instance, *Professional Accounting in 25 Countries* (American Institute of Certified Public Accountants, 1964).
2. These areas are obviously treated very generally; exceptions exist for a few given countries.
3. Dudley E. Brown, *Financial Executive* (January 1966), p. 50.

17
Some Special
Accounting Problems
of Multinational
Enterprises

Hanns-Martin Schoenfeld

INTRODUCTION

A continuously increasing engagement of medium-sized and large companies in foreign countries gives rise to several difficult problems in accounting. These problems exist for all enterprises with operations abroad; they are, however, of particular importance to those with foreign subsidiaries. Regardless of the percentage of capital owned it is often unavoidable to develop consolidated balance sheets for determination of uniform overall evaluation and decision data. This fact, together with the absence of internationally accepted accounting principles, has led to some individual solutions by large companies (e.g. Philips). In addition, attempts to standardize accounting principles are being made jointly by professional organizations of many countries;[1] presently neither these nor others suggested by academic groups are likely to gain worldwide or even regional acceptance in the near future. Therefore, multinational enterprises are to a large degree dependent on the legal, tax, economic, and educational systems of economies for the most part nationally oriented. Any change in their accounting system might have repercussions on all other systems and, therefore, will require complex adaptations and considerable time for its accomplishment. Even more important is the fact that, historically, today's accounting system resulted from nationally oriented thoughts of the academic and professional community of their respec-

Reprinted, with permission, from *Management International Review*, Vol. 9, Nos. 4-5, 1969.

tive countries.[2] The overly critical attitude towards accounting systems of other countries together with the deeply rooted belief in the superiority of one's own system give evidence for this. The fact is frequently overlooked that most accounting systems were not consciously developed as systems, but are the results of the sometimes erratic historic development of accounting thought and related ideas. All systems, therefore, tend to be incomplete, partially inconsistent, and hardly any one can be identified as being superior. Since no system is adapted to the needs of multinational enterprises, and local financial statements have to conform with existing regulations, a solution is required which will provide all necessary decision data. Therefore, an attempt will be made to investigate the needs of such enterprises as well as the possibilities and restrictions for an interim solution.

NATIONAL RESTRICTIONS

LEGAL AND PROFESSIONAL INFLUENCES

National accounting principles and procedures are either regulated by law (Germany) or through statements of professional organizations (e.g., American Institute of Certified Public Accountants); in the latter case, additional regulations by the Security and Exchange Commission (regulation S-X) must be complied with if stock certificates are to be traded at the Stock Exchange. Legal regulations show a tendency to remain unchanged for longer periods of time whereas "authoritative" professional opinions seem to be more dynamic and are adapted faster to the needs of business (amended by the recommendations of the Accounting Principle Board of the AICPA in the U.S.). Both systems, however, reflect basically different attitudes with respect to government intervention in private business. Any attempt to mutually adjust these systems will involve basic political principles which go far beyond the area of accounting.

The German and the American accounting systems—selected as examples in this paper — can also be used to exemplify other major differences. Both attempt to accomplish a certain uniformity in accounting[3]; in Europe this implies uniformity in a formal (uniform charts of accounts) as well as in a material sense through valuation regulations. In the United States the formal uniformity is stressed to a lesser degree and applies only to government regulated industries (e.g., air lines). The major emphasis is on adherence to "generally accepted accounting principles" such as general rules for valuation, the matching principle, etc.

Major differences also exist in financial statement certification by public accountants. An unqualified certificate in the U.S. states that the financial statements represent the financial position of the company "fairly," whereas the German certificate is given, if statements and records are merely "in accordance with legal requirements." The far more comprehensive U.S. certificates have recently given rise to questions concerning its implied meaning and the ensuing liability of CPA's.

In evaluating these two systems, the following points must be mentioned. In spite of the fact that both adhere to the historical cost principle, major differences can be noticed in *inventory valuation* (the U.S. system is far more flexible permitting LIFO, FIFO, average cost, etc.)[4]; other differences can be observed in the *treatment of treasury stock,* the definition of what constitutes stock of a subsidiary, the disclosure of retained earnings (in Germany part of the earnings must be transferred to a statutory reserve), and in the *requirements to show individual items* (German corporation law positively defines balance sheet items, whereas the more flexible doctrine of materiality governs this situation in the U.S.). Another difference can be seen in the fact that in the U.S. *deferred taxes* are shown, while in Germany such an item is not required.[5]

Other differences can be found in *supplementary statements*. In the U.S. a fund statement is usually part of the annual report; it is prepared in a format showing only long-term items and thus results in a statement of net change in working capital. *Training expenses* as well as *research and development expenses* are disclosed in greater detail since the public (and particularly financial analysts) attach great importance to these "invisible" assets—a point of view brought about by fast technological development in the last decade. Because of the fact that *leasing* is used frequently, not only to acquire assets but also to facilitate certain financing transactions, these items are disclosed in detail. German reports, however, concentrate on *capital relations with subsidiaries,* payments to board members, etc., as a result of legal requirements. Even though some of the above examples are of minor importance and adjustments could be made easily, the real differences are far greater because these are traceable to attitudes toward stockholders and the general public which cannot be dealt with by simply adjusting regulations.

ECONOMIC AND FINANCIAL INFLUENCES

Goals of economic policy not only vary between countries according to different environmental conditions but change also over time. It is, therefore, only reasonable to expect this situation to continue in the future. Also, governmental aid to various industries will remain a necessity. This aid has been forthcoming in Germany through employment loans, credit guarantees, low interest government credits, etc.; in the U.S., oil depletion allowances, negotiated mail rates for carriers, etc. are typical examples. Frequently, eligibility for such aid is determined on the basis of accounting data and statistical information which in turn is compiled using the existing accounting system. It therefore appears questionable whether government authorities will accept data changes which would result from internationalizing accounting systems. Resistance to change appears to be even stronger from this quarter than in the private sector—although the private sector is subject to the same tradition dependent way of thinking. Every change in the accounting system will at least influence the balance sheet format; changes in valuation methods will realign the asset and capital structure as well as traditional financial ratios and, therefore, might require a different evaluation procedure for loans to private firms (the lower equity share of European firms with present methods substantiates this assessment).

TAX INFLUENCES

Taxation in most countries is based directly on accounting data; accounting in turn is strongly influenced by the taxation system. Published balance sheets in Germany constitute the lowest limit for legally required tax balance sheets; in the U.S. such as interdependence does not exist. The disclosure of deferred income taxes, however, influences annual profits. In both countries tax guidelines and regulations determine depreciation policy, methods and amounts. The same holds true for inventory valuation as evidenced by recurring discussions about the taxation of fictitious (inflationary) profits resulting from certain methods of inventory evaluation; the Swedish inventory valuation system represents another example. Over and beyond financial statements tax regulations shape accounting procedures, since it is only in compliance with these requirements that proof for tax deductability is established. Any change of the accounting system, therefore, might influence the taxation procedures and, more important, tax revenues. For this reason, internal revenue service authorities will be inclined to delay such adjustments.

OTHER INFLUENCES

In addition to the aforementioned there are many other influences, some of which deserve special attention. Since the accounting system has the sole purpose of providing comprehensible information for various groups of users inside and outside the firm, *education* to a large extent determines how data will be understood and interpreted. Changes, therefore, can be made only after laying proper educational foundations to assure continued understanding; this has been amply demonstrated by experiences in developing countries as well as in highly industrialized nations with sophisticated accounting systems. Another restriction is imposed by the prevalent *technology*. The widespread application of electronic data processing equipment permits a much more detailed data breakdown without additional cost; at the same time it requires specialized accounting procedures with respect to data collection, recording, storage, and transmission. Such procedures are not always readily accepted as being in accordance with sound accounting principles—a trend which could be observed in several countries. This suggests that technology, among other factors, in large part determines the direction and speed of development for entire national accounting systems. It also gives rise to the question whether at the present time (in view of the vast technological differences between nations) a single system can be devised which at any time and in any location will meet all standards for accounting reliability and disclosure. Last, but not least, the development of *accounting thought* needs to be mentioned. Depending on environmental conditions, this development varies considerably, e.g., from developing countries, to countries with a liberal capitalistic system, and in countries where governmental intervention and socialist tendencies are prevalent. As a result, accounting theory often focuses on points which are of only local interest. Evidence of this is provided by the present argument about conglomerate companies in the U.S., the off-and-on discussion concerning inflationary accounting procedures in several countries, and the emphasis on private enterprise accounting data for national planning in developing nations.

SPECIAL PROBLEM: INFLATION

At present a major problem requiring solution is the fact that the theoretical model behind all accounting systems assumes stability of currency values—a condition which in most countries has been contradicted by reality at least since World War II. Since this problem has not been recognized everywhere at the same time and to the same degree, varying theoretical and practical solution proposals have emerged. It started with the organic balance sheet theory by Schmidt,[6] who demanded a periodic adaption of the asset valuation to market prices, and continued with the practical application of an index valuation in France.[7] Other examples are the use of replacement values in the consolidated balance sheet of the Philips Corporation[8] and the voluntary publication of subsidiary balance sheets in Brazil, reflecting market values in addition to historical values.[9] Today the use of multicolumnar balance sheets is under study in the U.S., which would disclose historical cost, realizable values, and reproduction values. The latter approach fully reflects price influences from purchasing and selling markets and at the same time leaves the decision to the user of the financial statements as to which valuation to employ for his particular analysis. This proposal favors the use of specific revaluations instead of using a general price index. The question of how to appropriately and reliably determine market prices, however, remains unsolved.

At this time an internationally acceptable solution based on any one or several of these approaches does not appear to be feasible because:

a) Internal revenue service authorities seem reluctant to rule on the treatment of inflationary profits arising from revaluation and

b) The problem of auditing and certifying market prices is unsolved, since evidence for the correctness of such valuations is often insufficient.

ACCOUNTING NEEDS OF MULTINATIONAL ENTERPRISES

An accounting system for multinational enterprises has to satisfy several requirements at the same time. These are:

1. Providing financial statements for consolidation;

2. Providing financial statements for information and decision purposes, that are understandable

a) in the country in which a particular subsidiary is operating and

b) in the country in which the holding company has to make financial decisions involving more than one country.

To fulfill the requirements for consolidation, uniform labeling and content of accounts must be assured; this can well be accomplished through additional subaccounts or other records. Major difficulties, however, arise in translating foreign currency values.

Securing understandability presents a multi-level problem. First of all, understandability has to be guaranteed within the national environment. Since taxation, legal matters, governmental aid, government subsidized loans, etc. are limited to the realm of one economic system, nationally accepted procedures must be adhered to. The same holds true for efficiently using local employees who have been trained within the national system; adherence to national accounting standards also facilitates — at least within certain limits — the performance comparison with local competitors; such an evaluation is indispensable because comparison with subsidiaries operating in countries with different environmental conditions does not always yield satisfactory results, particularly since, presently, a large number of managerial decisions (pricing, financing, etc.) are dependent on national environmental constraints and therefore have to be based on pertinent relevant data.

To assure understandability of accounting data in the decision center of the home office presents more difficult problems due to the fact that only part of all pertinent variables are contained in the accounting data and that environmental decision parameters are not necessarily the same, as in, for instance, the U.S., Brazil or other countries. Overall accounting reports, however, have to be supplied as a decision basis in order to facilitate full consideration of the special situation of a multinational enterprise. Therefore, translation and consolidation of data become an absolute necessity. The recent development seems to suggest, however, that this cannot be satisfactorily accomplished through translation. For this reason (among several others) major multinational corporations have established regional headquarters; such an organizational arrangement decreases the number of national balance sheets to be consolidated and enables regional management to give full consideration to non-accounting data. As a result, the translation of financial statements is simplified — yet, the problems involved, though fewer in number, continue to exist.

TRANSLATION OF FINANCIAL STATEMENTS

In order to better assess the problems of financial statement translation, the most frequently used methods need to be analyzed. As a prerequisite, it must be assumed that account contents have been standardized by multinational enterprises through the application of internal subclassifications which do not violate national accounting principles. The prevalent translation method used in the U.S. is based on the AICPA Accounting Research Bulletin No. 43, Chapter 12; this generally accepted source recommends the following procedure:

1. Long-term items are to be translated using historical exchange rates (effective at the time of the original transaction);[10]

2. Short-term items are to be translated using exchange rates effective at the date of the financial statement;

3. Profit and loss items are to be translated using weighted averages for the period (except depreciation items which are to be translated using historical exchange rates). Realized exchange profits and losses, and unrealized exchange losses affect the overall profit, whereas unrealized exchange profits have to be stated separately in a suspension account (unless used to compensate related unrealized losses).

This method approaches translation only for the purpose of compiling raw data for consolidated balance sheets; it perpetuates all the disadvantages of the historical cost methods. Therefore, Hepworth[11] recommends a slightly different translation method. It requires:

1. Items with monetary character (including long-term receivables and payables) are to be translated using the current exchange rate to assure up-to-date presentation of financial commitments.

2. Physical items are to be translated using the historical (date of acquisi-

tion) exchange rate; the same rate is to be applied for accrued and deferred items (which originated in the past) and equity to assure the maintenance of original capital shares.

3. Profit and loss items should, theoretically, be translated using the exchange rate of the transaction date (with the exception of depreciation and disposition of accrued and deferred items); for practical reasons, a weighted average exchange rate might be used. All exchange profits and losses (realized and unrealized) have to be shown (as separate items).

Both translations accomplish their purpose only if translated items represent a small share of the total consolidated balance sheet. If major parts of the operations are located in foreign countries, the aforementioned methods do not prevent a distortion of the financial situation. If inventory items, for instance, are shown in some countries on a FIFO basis and in others LIFO is used, neither of the translations provides for valuation adjustments, which situation is aggravated by varying inflationary tendencies. In addition, no adjustments are made for discrepancies caused by various tax-influenced depreciation methods. Moreover, results of differing financing policies (assuming principles of short-term financing in countries with high inflation rates by necessity differ from those in countries with stable currency) are not shown separately in consolidated statements. It is, therefore, not surprising that translation methods applied in practice differ considerably.[12] In view of this, Mueller[13] concludes that translations should not be undertaken in cases in which meaningful consolidated statements cannot be obtained.

Finally, problems arise in selecting translation exchange rates if convertibility is restricted, because more than one exchange rate (black market) exists. The official exchange rate frequently does not reflect properly the purchasing power relation; multinational enterprises, then, are confronted with the dilemma of choosing either a deficient or an illegal rate.

SUGGESTIONS FOR AN INTERMEDIATE SOLUTION

Considering all the above facts, present hopes are slim of accomplishing worldwide uniformity in accounting principles. Nevertheless, multinational enterprises have to devise methods of financial reporting in order to simultaneously accomplish the following aims:

1. Comply with all legal and tax regulations in all countries in which operations are located;

2. Guarantee understandability for efficient operation of their accounting systems and generate locally valid information and decision data;

3. Use procedures permitting consolidation of financial statements of all

subsidiaries with those of the home office to provide publishable information and valid internal decision data.

Obviously, existing problems defy accomplishment of all aims by means of a single financial statement. Therefore, it appears to be necessary to compile several parallel statements, thus fulfilling separate requirements with each. Necessary statements are the following:

1. **National financial statements** drawn up on the basis of nationally accepted accounting principles, thus guaranteeing understandability within the national economy. The operation of an accounting system for this purpose does not require additional employee education; resulting statements are sufficient to inform the public as well as stockholders in the respective countries. Also, a comparison with competitors operating under the same environmental conditions is thereby facilitated, and management receives information which is relevant to the national economic system.

2. **Translated financial statements** provide the basis for consolidation. Compliance with accounting principles as well as translation methods accepted in the country of the home office are necessary. Frequently, for purposes of informing stockholders and the general public, several of these statements have to be provided using the generally accepted accounting principles of all countries in which a large number of stockholders reside. Their main purpose consists in consolidation and publication; therefore, compliance with accepted accounting principles takes precedence over adjustments reflecting the true economic situation of the multinational enterprises. Consequently, statements can be used for decision making in a limited way only.

3. **Financial statements reflecting the economic situation of the enterprise** can only be provided separately; these are — by and large — for internal use only; therefore, it is not necessary to adhere to legal regulations and/or accepted accounting principles. Instead, over and above uniform contents of accounts, uniform valuation methods for assets of all subsidiaries must be used (LIFO, FIFO, and other valuations have to be readjusted to the same basis); moreover, accelerated depreciation adopted solely to exhaust all legal tax advantages should be converted to write-downs reflecting the true consumption of assets. In order to neutralize inflation-caused national financing policies, separation of corresponding assets and liabilities might be advisable. For translation, methods best suited for the particular multinational enterprise can be developed. If market or replacement values are utilized for this purpose, major changes in financial ratios will result (since revaluation increases equities whereas period profits are less affected); as a result, comparisons with typical national financial ratios become impossible.

The resulting financial statements appear to be the only acceptable data basis for decisions involving the entire multinational enterprise or large portions thereof.[14]

4. **Tax statements** must be compiled wherever required by national regulations.

At the present time it seems impossible to avoid the cumbersome procedure using three or four different sets of financial statements, if a multinational enterprise wants to provide all necessary information required for divergent purposes. This only emphasizes the urgent need for developing internationally acceptable principles (or at least gradually to change national regulations toward this goal) to simplify international accounting. As a major step, empirical research within national enterprises is required to gain a better understanding of all problems involved; this is particularly important since at present, opinions vary widely as to advantages and disadvantages of existing national systems. Only after that condition is met can the development of meaningful accounting principles having worldwide acceptance reach the stage of feasibility. If, however, steps are not taken soon, the welter of individual accounting principles, each developed for one enterprise only, will be perpetuated; this will, at least, seriously affect the national and international credibility of financial statements.

NOTES

1. The following examples illustrate the situation: International Congress of Accountants (since 1904), Inter-American Accounting Conferences (since 1949), Asian and Pacific Accounting Conventions (since 1957), Union Europeenne des Experts Comptables, Economiques et Financiers (since 1951). At the same time efforts to provide an inventory of accounting procedures in the U.K., Canada, and the U.S. are carried on by several international committees. This may represent a first step towards international uniformity.
2. The importance of accepted thought patterns (or "truth") for the scientific community and the resulting development of new ideas are stressed by such diverse sources as Fleck, L., *Entstehung und Entwicklung einer Wissenschaft* (Basel: Tatsacher, 1935) and Kuhn, T.S., *The Structure of Scientific Revolutions* (Chicago, 1962).
3. Mueller, G. G., *International Accounting* (New York, 1967, pp. 88-115).
4. Valuation of current assets at lower of cost or market, though the same principle, shows considerable differences. In Switzerland, i.e., these values can be reduced by up to 60 per cent (AICPA, *Professional Accounting in 25 Countries* (New York, 1964), p. 18. In Germany an "anticipated decrease in market prices" already permits a further write-down, whereas in the U.S. such a procedure must be based on evidence instead of expectation (Niehus, R.J., "Stock Corporation Law Reform in Germany and the Public Accountant," *The International Journal of Accounting,* Vol. 1, No. 2, 1966, p. 35). It should be noted further that market value means essentially replacement value in the U.S. and net realizable future sales value in the U.K. Other discrepancies of this kind apply to terms such as "reserve," "provision," "good will," etc. (for details see Mueller,

G. G., "Accounting Principles Generally Accepted in the United States Versus Those Generally Accepted Elsewhere," *The International Journal of Accounting,* Vol. 3, No. 2 (1968), p. 101.

5. For further details see Schoenfeld, H. M., and Holzer, H. P., "Bilanzen der amerikanischen Industrie," *Grundlagen der Bilanzierung, Gliederung und Bewertung,* ZfB, Vol. 35 (July, 1965), pp. 472-506, and Mueller, G. G., *op cit.,* Chapter 5.

6. Schmidt, F., *Organische Tageswertbilanz,* 4. ed. (Wiesbaden, 1951).

7. Klinkel, H., *Die Bewertung in der französischen Jahresbilanz* (Wiesbaden, 1961), and also Schoenfeld, H. M. and Holzer, H. P., "The French Approach to the Post-War Price Level Problem," *The Accounting Review,* Vol. 37, No. 2 (April, 1963), pp. 382-388.

8. Goudeket, A., "An Application of Replacement Value Theory," *Journal of Accountancy* (July, 1960), pp. 37-47.

9. Mueller, G. G., *op. cit.,* p. 145.

10. Accounting Principles Board Opinion No. 6 permits the translation of long-term debts at current rates.

11. Hepworth, S. R., *Reporting Foreign Operations* (Ann Arbor, Michigan: Bureau of Business Research, University of Michigan, 1956).

12. This is particularly mentioned in "Accounting Practices in Fluctuating Currency Countries," *Business International Management Monograph No. 4* (New York, 1963).

13. Mueller, G. G., *op. cit.,* pp. 194-198.

14. In view of these aims, the Philips solution assumes particular importance as a pilot study; even if the determination of replacement cost remains to be a very much disputed issue, the determination of individual principles for multinational financial statements appears to be a major step forward.

18

Taxation Policy in Multinational Companies

Albert J. Rädler

Taxation policy in a multinational company should be regarded as those considerations and measures which, by minimizing the incidence of taxation in the field of foreign connections, in the long run maximize the total profits of a multinational company, which means that maintenance and growth of the company are ensured by the taxation aspect. This taxation policy in the multinational company represents a continuous process which must always adjust itself to new data. In addition to new business management trends in the international economy and developments within the company itself, new data of this type include, in particular, changes in the taxation laws and practice of the states concerned.

International taxation policy takes in, essentially, four fields of decision: the choice of location, the choice of legal form, the choice of method of finance and finally the choice of clearing prices. But these four fields cannot be kept firmly apart; rather, they interact; e.g., the choice of location can have repercussions on the legal form or method of finance, while conversely the choice of type of finance can determine the location and the legal form.

The importance of the taxation factor in choosing a location is directly dependent on the flexibility of the intended branch's location. Thus, in primary production firms the possible effect of taxation policy on the location is relatively slight. In contrast to this, the greatest flexibility of location is shown by those branches of industry or those business functions which are not restricted in advance to particular locations by reason of natural factors. Good examples of this are international shipping and also holding company

Reprinted, with permission, from *Management International Review,* Vol. 9, Nos. 4-5 (1969).

and sales functions. Here, taxation has in practice become one of the most important factors for the location.

Between these two groups of companies or company functions, one flexible, the other tied with regard to their location, stands the normal industrial manufacturing firm. In the international field, it is precisely for this type that taxation policy has increased in importance in the last few years. This is to be attributed to the fact that not only the new economic blocks like the E.E.C. and E.F.T.A., but also, even though under greater difficulties, the Central American and Latin American free trade area, are growing economically ever closer together and thereby production costs within the individual blocks are becoming more and more similar. The result is that for the choice of the optimal location differences in taxation and in investment allowances assume greater and greater weight. Recently, the European Commission expressed its concern that individual E.E.C. member states attempt to outbid each other in the granting of regional subsidies. This means that the existing tax advantages of locations are being fully exploited within the E.E.C., particularly by multinational companies from outside states.

The optimal choice of location also means that, where sensible from a taxation point of view and possible from an organizational point of view, the setting up of permanent premises or of a permanent agency equivalent to the latter should be avoided. Purely from a tax point of view, the optimal solution for a newly established industrial firm often consists of siting the manufacturing company in one of the special development areas and, if the profits thus obtained do not also remain tax-free in the department area for at least a few years, conducting sales business through a special sales company, for example with a location in Switzerland.

Closely bound up with the question of the location is — particularly in companies with a flexible location — the choice of legal form. The first question involved here is the basic one: permanent establishment or legally independent subsidiary company?

Special tax problems can arise if several branches, i.e., permanent premises or subsidiary companies, are situated in one country. A situation of this type is, for example, very possible with large-scale multinational companies with a strongly differentiated production program where for organizational reasons every home works has built independent branches abroad. It can also arise through attracting foreign participation or by branches in several countries having been brought in by one partner in a merger. A particular deficiency of double taxation agreements is the fact that they have not so far looked at inter-multinational company relationships—

very timidly in defining anyone's personal scope and not at all in other cases. Finally, the choice of legal form also involves consideration of the taxation possibilities for concentration processes over the border.

In *financing* branches abroad taxation problems arise both in the question of whether the multinational company's own or outside funds should be used and in that of how and where the latter should be applied. The question of finance from outside is important both for subsidiary companies and for permanent business; on the other hand, the question of whether the company's own funds should be introduced in the form of capital resources or company loans usually arises only for subsidiary companies. The utilization of financial sources outside the multinational company for building branches abroad is primarily a question of business management, although the tax expert must give his opinion. But the taxation factor can come first when, for example, we are concerned with using funds from the Euromarket or with other ways of avoiding coupon tax.

Tax considerations are often decisive in determining whether the capital made available by the multinational company itself to a subsidiary company abroad is to reach the latter as regular capital resources or in the form of company loans. Even though in recent years in the international field the trend towards lessening double taxation of company profits has been weakening, in most states interest payments from recognized company loans receive considerably better tax relief than dividends of a subsidiary company. Another field of taxation policy in its financial aspect is the fixing of policy for paying out dividends in the case of individual multinational companies. Finally, tax factors can also play an important role in financing sales, especially for long-term outlays exported abroad.

The most difficult point in international taxation policy is probably the choice of clearing prices. Usually there are no firm points of guidance as to whether the clearing prices chosen — for deliveries of goods, services, loans, handing over capital goods on a leasing basis, handing over intangible assets, industrial copyrights, know-how etc. — will stand up to scrutiny by the finance authorities. Reference to the so-called arm's length rule usually does not lead much further, since to an ever-increasing extent similar or even comparable deliveries or services are carried out only within the one multinational company.

Hence the answer to such cases can only lie in the casuistic assessment of the facts on a business management basis (e.g., using generally accepted rules of calculation). In my view the American guidelines to Sec. 482 I.R.C. are an important step forward in this respect. It is true that such guidelines do, on the one hand, restrict the multinational company's freedom in laying down clearing prices, but on the other hand they do guarantee that the arrangement chosen, insofar as it remains within the guidelines, is recognized by the tax authorities. A precondition here is, of course, that the finance authorities of all countries involved keep to the same guidelines. The working-out of guidelines like these will probably dominate developments in international taxation in the seventies.

19
Protective Measures against Devaluation

H. W. Allen Sweeny

The cliché "a world of opportunity" has taken on literal significance for almost every major corporation in America. From the middle of 1960 to the middle of 1965, 2,161 United States companies undertook some 5,700 business activities abroad. In dollar terms, private foreign investment now approximates $14 billion a year, an annual increment 27 percent greater than the total amount of direct foreign investment of American companies only fifteen years ago. United States business has gone international on an extraordinary scale! And there is evidence that the pace of foreign expansion will continue to increase in spite of current temporary cutbacks in response to the Administration's balance of payments program.

The financial executive involved in the affairs of an overseas affiliate of an international corporation is confronted with a whole new range of problems. In general, his basic functions will not differ significantly from those of his domestic counterpart. In specific areas, however, his role abroad is perhaps more demanding and almost certainly more vital to the success of the enterprise. To see why this is so, we will look at two of the most common and difficult problems of international business—devaluation and exchange controls—and relate them directly to the challenges and opportunities they present to the financial executive abroad.

ANTICIPATION IS CRITICAL

Devaluation, as any student of current events is now well aware, takes place when a government officially modifies the rate of exchange between its local currency and gold or U.S. dollars. Although devaluation has always been a major concern of the foreign investor, the dramatic fall of the British pound and some twenty other currencies over the last few months has

Reprinted, with permission, from the *Financial Executive* (January 1968).

brought the problem to an all-time high in prevalence and relevance to the international businessman.

During the course of these recent events, many companies have now profitably—in all senses of the word—learned that managers can do a great deal to minimize the adverse financial effects when devaluations are spotted in advance. Obviously, management cannot always be clairvoyant in these matters. However, the recent British experience illustrates that the likelihood of a devaluation does correlate with certain basic trends in a country's economic situation. For example, prolonged unfavorable trade balances or excessive deficits in government spending portend devaluation. Other common signs are rapid internal inflation and excessive currency emissions.

To appraise economic and social forces and government influences and to interpret their effect upon the business is the responsibility of the financial executive. This function of economic interpretation is crucial in the anticipation of a devaluation. We have, therefore, the first instance where the financial executive's responsibilities take on a critical dimension in the success of the foreign enterprise.

Though the role of anticipation is critical, it becomes effective only when it leads to action. The scope and thrust of what these actions might be will become more clear if we turn to a simplified discussion of exactly how devaluation affects the financial results of a foreign investment. Devaluation, as indicated previously, takes place when a government officially modifies the rate of exchange between its local currency and U.S. dollars or gold. For example, the British devalued the pound from $2.80 to $2.40 on November 18. From November 18, therefore, .42 pounds were required to purchase one U.S. dollar rather than .36. In general terms, the effect of such devaluation on a company's financial position is dependent upon:

1. The company's local-currency working-capital position at the time of devaluation.

2. The level of current dollar assets or liabilities held by the company at the time of devaluation.

3. Pricing strategies to protect dollar margins on goods in inventory at the time of a devaluation.

4. Longer-term pricing strategies to insure adequate recovery of depreciation expenses relating to original dollar investments.

TABULATING DEVALUATION

Some simple hypothetical figures will more clearly illustrate the above statements. To explore the financial effect of devaluation on working capital, assume, as shown in Table 1, that the EZI Corporation has current assets (exclusive of inventories), and long-and short-term liabilities in local currency in the amounts shown in the first column. The equivalent U.S. dollar values at an assumed exchange rate of 10 to 1 are shown in the second column. At this point, let us further assume a devaluation of 16.7 per cent. The third column shows the revised dollar value of local currency taking into account the effect of devaluation. The fourth column shows that the dollar value of assets has deteriorated. On the other hand, the dollar equivalent of all liabilities in local currency has been reduced. In this particular illustration the proportion of assets to liabilities is such that the loss on assets is greater than the reduction in liabilities. There is a net loss in dollars to the company. If the proportionate relationship between the assets and liabilities were reversed (i.e., liabilities were in excess of assets), a gain would have occurred.

Table 2 illustrates the effect that the level of dollar assets or liabilities has in this situation. In this case, the value of all balance sheet items and the rate of devaluation are identical to those shown in Table 2. It will be noted, however, that the bank loans are now assumed to be in U.S. dollars. Consequently, the corporate liability in dollars for this item remains unchanged despite devaluation. This, in turn, lowers the overall reduction in liabilities that can be used to offset the loss arising from the deterioration in the equivalent dollar value of assets. Thus the foreign exchange loss is greater. The loss would have been less had there been assets in U.S. dollars. The level and kind of dollar items on a company's balance sheet at the time of devaluation are obviously of great importance.

Table 1: EZ1 Corporation. Financial Effect of Devaluation on Working Capital

	1	2	3	4
		U.S. Dollar	U.S. Dollar	
	Local Currency	Value at 10	Value at 12	Gain/(Loss)
ASSETS				
Cash	1,000,000	100,000	83,333	(16,667)
Accounts Receivable	3,000,000	300,000	250,000	(50,000)
Other Current Assets	500,000	50,000	41,667	(8,333)
TOTAL	4,500,000	450,000	375,000	(75,000)
LIABILITIES				
Current Liabilities	750,000	75,000	62,500	12,500
Bank Loans	1,000,000	100,000	83,333	16,667
Reserves & Other	250,000	25,000	20,833	4,167
TOTAL	2,000,000	200,000	166,666	33,334
	Loss on Assets		(75,000)	
	Reduction in Liabilities		33,334	
	Loss Due to Devaluation		(41,666)	

*Table 2: EZI Corporation. Importance of Dollar Items
on Financial Effect of Devaluation*

	1 Local Currency	2 U.S. Dollar Value at 10	3 U.S. Dollar Value at 12	4 Gain/(Loss)
ASSETS				
Cash	1,000,000	100,000	83,333	(16,667)
Accounts Receivable	3,000,000	300,000	250,000	(50,000)
Other Current Assets	500,000	50,000	41,667	(8,333)
TOTAL	4,500,000	450,000	375,000	(75,000)
LIABILITIES				
Current Liabilities	750,000	75,000	62,500	12,500
Dollar Bank Loan	1,000,000	100,000	100,000	—0—
Reserves & Other	250,000	25,000	20,833	4,167
TOTAL	2,000,000	200,000	166,666	16,667
	Loss on Assets		(75,000)	
	Reduction in Liabilities		16,667	
	Loss Due to Devaluation		(58,333)	

The effect of devaluations on the value of a company's goods in inventory and the implications for short-range pricing strategy are explored in Table 3. As indicated in this table, it is assumed that at the time of devaluation the EZI Corporation has on hand inventories with the total value shown. The equivalent values in dollars before and after the assumed devaluation of 20 per cent are indicated. The last item indicates the potential loss as a result of devaluation. It will be noted that at the time of devaluation the loss is only a *potential* one inasmuch as the effect of devaluation can be offset by selling-price increases. If the sales margin in dollars that existed prior to devaluation can be maintained, the loss can be avoided altogether. (In some instances, an even greater margin may be required than before to compensate for a higher tax bite.)

PRICING STRAGEGY

The implications of devaluation in relation to long-range pricing strategy are examined in Tables 4 and 5. Table 4 shows figures relating to a simplified case of investment in fixed assets for the EZI Corporation. In the first column the dollar investment and the associated annual depreciation charges are shown. The second column indicates the local-currency equivalents of both these items at an assumed exchange rate of 10 to 1 existing prior to devaluation.

In Table 5, a simplified profit and loss statement of EZI Corporation is shown. Local-currency revenues and operating expenses, excluding depreciation, are shown and translated into dollar equivalents at an exchange of 12 to 1, the exchange rate that exists, as in the other case, after the assumed 16.7 per cent devaluation. By looking at depreciation charges, it can be seen that if the amount for this expense in local currency is translated into dollars at the devalued rate of 12 to 1, an inadequate amount of depreciation cost will be taken in this period to recover the full amount of the company's original dollar investment. Over the long term, failure to recover the dollar investment can spell disaster. The problem can best be identified by accounting for financial results in both local currency and dollars. The problem can be offset only be continuing efforts to increase local-currency revenues. These increases must maintain the relationship of dollar depreciation costs to sales revenues in dollars contemplated at the time the investment was made.

The effects of devaluation and accounting for them involve complexities beyond the scope of this article. Keeping in mind the concepts illustrated in the simple examples above, let us now consider the role of the financial executive.

WORKING CAPITAL DEFENCES

Much of what a company must do to protect itself from the effects of devaluation becomes rather obvious given a broad conceptual understanding of the problem. The financial executive must provide this understanding. Because understanding is so important and the problem less common, he literally may need to "interpret" the financial effects of devaluation to management. Preferably, he will do so in a simple and clear a manner as possible. Perhaps this need be no more complicated than the approach used in Tables 1-5.

As a corollary, he will "report." This seems obvious, but this function overseas includes the formulation and implementation of accounting policies that frequently translate profit and loss statements and balance sheets into dollars. As we saw with EZI Corporation, failure to reflect the effects of devaluation in financial reporting can lead to an overstatement of profits and disguise decapitalization. Failure to interpret these effects meaningfully can foster corporate confusion and inaction. Therefore, the financial executive, with his understanding of the problem, is in a strategic position to urge and implement policies which will protect his company from devaluation. Much of what must be done actually involves action under his direct responsibility.

Table 3: EZI Corporation. Financial Effect of Devaluation on Inventories

	Value of Inventory
Local Currency	18,000,000
U.S. Dollar Value at 10	1,800,000
U.S. Dollar Value at 12	1,500,000
Potential Loss*	(300,000)

*Loss can be avoided by increasing local-currency selling prices for products in inventory to the extent necessary to maintain previous dollar margin.

Table 4: EZI Corporation. Financial Effect of Devaluation

	1 U.S. Dollar Value	2 Local Currency Value at 10
Assumed Investment in Fixed Assets	5,000,000	50,000,000
Depreciation at 10% a Year	500,000	5,000,000

Table 5: EZI Corporation. Effect of Devaluation Depreciation Costs

Depreciation Effects	1 Local Currency	2 U.S. Dollar Value
Gross Operating Margin	36,000,000	3,000,000
Less:		
Operating Expenses Excluding Depreciation	24,000,000	2,000,000
Depreciation Charges*	5,000,000	500,000
Profit Before Tax	7,000,000	500,000
Taxes	1,200,000	100,000
Profit After Tax	5,800,000	400,000
Dollar Equivalent of Local Currency Profits	$\frac{\$5,800,000}{12}$	483,333
True Dollar Profits — Relating Depreciation Costs to Original Investment in Dollars		400,000
Effect of Devaluation		83,333

*The dollar equivalent of local currency depreciation charges at the new devalued rate of exchange $\frac{\$5,000,000}{12}$ equals \$416,667, an inadequate charge in relation to original investment of \$5,000,000 to be depreciated over ten years.

Thus, to protect his company's local-currency working-capital position and minimize dollar obligations, he will:

1. Keep cash balances low and intensify efforts to reduce cash float throughout the company's operation.

2. Keep a bank account in dollars or some other stable currency when possible.

3. Pay import or other types of dollar obligations promptly.

4. Maximize local-currency borrowing and, as a general policy, stay in debt. (Note the classical ratio of $2.00 of current assets to $1.00 of liabilities may have little application overseas.)

5. Obtain extended terms from suppliers and from the government for the payment of taxes.

6. Contract in local currencies for future obligations.

7. Purchase forward against short-term hard-currency obligations. (In essence, the purchase of exchange "futures" bets company funds on the rate and timing of a devaluation. This is risky, but can be profitable. The better the company's information on the key indicators of a devaluation, the less the risk.)

ADDITIONAL PROTECTIVE POLICIES

As the examples from the EZI Corporation further suggest, protective measures beyond those of a peculiarly financial nature will be necessary. To see that these are taken, the financial executive, evaluating and consulting with his management, will urge corporate policies which:

1. Reduce the levels of the company's local-currency accounts receivable and, when warranted, foster the use of devices, such as cash discounts, to keep them low.

2. Keep selling prices adjusted to levels that will offset devaluation. As Tables 3 and 5 indicate, this is a necessary step, but often a difficult one because of competition or price controls. Sometimes this can be accomplished by means of long-term sales contracts in dollars or geared to dollar indices.

3. Return earnings quickly and promptly to the U.S. shareholder by means of interim dividends.

4. Encourage selling efforts in hard-currency export markets.

5. Encourage the rapid investment of any long-term excess funds in property that tends to increase its value in local currency in proportion to devaluation. Classic examples are land, buildings, and automotive equipment.

6. Review periodically the local-currency "book value" of fixed assets. Devaluations rapidly and dramatically obsolesce fixed-asset values carried at

their original cost in local currency. Also, as was shown in Table 5, local-currency depreciation costs which are related to historic asset values lead to an overstatement of local-currency earnings, which can very likely be over-taxed. A formal accounting revaluation of fixed assets can provide a solution to this problem. Formal asset revaluations, while not allowed in the U.S., are sometimes possible in other countries. At best, such a revaluation may be acceptable for tax purposes and eliminate a company's tax payments on overstated profits. Even when this is not possible, revaluation can be used as a device to have a company's official local-earnings reports reflect a more accurate picture of its real profitability.

Up to this point we have been concerned with the problems that devaluation presents to the financial executive abroad. Let us turn next to the closely related problems of exchange controls.

EXCHANGE CONTROLS

Exchange controls take many forms, but usually involve restrictions on the exit of funds from a country for the repatriation of earnings for fees or for imports. As is the case with devaluation, anticipation of exchange controls is a key to effective action. (The economic and political trends signalling either are frequently identical.) We have already seen that the responsibility for the appraisal and interpretation of these economic and political trends rests with the financial executive. Thus, once again, the financial executive has a key role from the beginning in this second major problem area of international business.*

As important as it is, this function of advance interpretation serves only as a base point for action. The financial executive's next responsibility is evaluating and consulting with his management to insure the effectiveness of policies and procedures to remit dollars to U.S. shareholders or creditors.

The first step will be to inventory those funds that his company will want to remit. These can be grouped into three general categories:

1. Goods and Services, which includes payments for such items as administrative charges from headquarters, research or consulting fees, imports of all kinds, and dollar salaries of U.S. expatriate personnel.

2. Loans, which includes payments for liquidation of principle and interest.

3. Equity, which includes dividend payments (or return of branch office profits) and repatriation of capital.

From these general categories, the financial executive will cull those transactions of specific interest to his company and undertake action to in-

*I am indebted to my colleague, Allan Harrison, for the material in this particular section.

sure remittance protection. To do this for each category, he will do the following:

GOODS AND SERVICES

Obtain import licenses and exchange rights for imports

Work with government authorities to qualify his company's imports at official or more preferable rates of exchange

Document foreign obligations by letters of credit and drafts

Establish formal legal contracts to support research or consulting agreements

LOANS

Officially file and register all dollar (or other foreign currency) loan documents with the appropriate exchange authorities

Secure official assurances to liquidate loans and meet interest payments

EQUITY

Officially register the company's equity in the local affiliate

Secure rights to remit dividends and if possible the right to return equity funds

Even though these actions will not always meet with success, the greater failure would be not to have made the effort at all.

The corporate and financial strategies for devaluation and exchange controls discussed above are by no means exhaustive, and the implementation of even those suggested is not always suitable or possible. Indeed, under extremely onerous foreign exchange conditions, a company may find itself operating under somewhat the same premises as Damon Runyon's famous character, Harry the Horse, who, on his way to the race track, hoped to break even because he could use the money.

The higher profit incentive for a foreign investment carries with it a greater risk. The company that fails to manage such risks creatively does not belong in foreign operations. The financial executive is not only responsible but uniquely qualified to see that his company avoids such a failure.

Chapter Five:
Manufacturing

20

Industrial Competition and R and D

P. Piganiol

Like many short English words, the word "gap" conveys highly complex ideas. I believe that, in an industrial context, it denotes not only the differences between the United States and Europe, but perhaps also the cleavages that divide scientists, financiers, and industrialists, plus probably the separations that exist between "R & D" strategy and "financial" strategy with which R & D are sometimes incompatible.

A comprehensive discussion of all the topics suggested by the above paragraph would by no means be a simple undertaking. I shall therefore confine myself to a few basic points, if only to ensure that I and my readers are all speaking the same language. I propose to deal with a representative sprinkling of case studies, without, however, any assurance of being thoroughly acquainted with them, for seldom is it known what an industrialist's original purpose was, what his actual difficulties were, nor which contributing factors decisively affected his policies.

Consequently, the hypotheses stated below are to be regarded as a strictly personal interpretation, and not as reflecting any profound reality concerning industries. However, as they stand, these case studies are deserving of a certain amount of reflection on our part.

THE RISKS IN R & D

First of all, I wish to remind the reader that research must not be confused with development. While it is highly convenient to lump these items together under the handy formula of "R & D," the differences between them remain nonetheless basic.

Reprinted, with permission, from *European Business* (January, 1968).

To begin with, in opposition to development, research is not expensive. European firms must take cognizance of this fact. It is almost always feasible even for an average-sized firm to undertake valid research. The attendant conditions for this will be examined later.

The picture becomes entirely different when development itself is involved—that is, when a firm that has its research results in hand, and is interested in industrializing them, undertakes the work necessary for the defining of its production tools.

The average cost of this latter operation is approximately one hundred times greater than the cost of the relevant research. This fact holds especially for chemical industries, slightly less so for other fields.

Although it is possible in most industries to perform low-cost research, the transition from research to development is an operation that can compromise an industry's future by exposing it to risks that are exceedingly heavy.

At this stage in the procedure, there arise the real problems that distinguish contemporary Europe from modern-day America, problems that set the two continents apart. It is at this same stage that we must ponder the optimum techniques to be implemented in order to make the development of European industries possible.

The differences in costs and risks are by no means the only differences. The related material means are also quite different. Basically, research is founded on a knowledge of the range and prospects of a given science at a given moment, whereas development depends on a knowledge of the available techniques and their potentialities.

Whether the problems involve research programs or development programs, the decision-makers must be men who are thoroughly familiar with the state of knowledge and the state of the techniques.

This may well be the most crucial question. The mapping out of a program and the making of a decision presuppose primarily observation of the prospects and a reflecting about the potentialities. Unfortunately, the reflecting is done by men whose terminology and particular insight into matters do not coincide with those of the financiers. However, scientists and technicians, as one group, and financiers, as the other group, can reach a mutual understanding if they discuss profit-earning capacity, for here they possess a common terminology.

But in the assessing of potentialities, they do not always manage to arrive at a common language, and this situation lies at the base of the considerable difficulties that are experienced.

So, even though research and development can be lumped together, it must be clearly borne in mind that these two phases involve two sets of attitudes and two sets of risk levels.

It should likewise be borne in mind that an entire sector of industrial research is concerned simply with improvements, which fact in no way excludes an extremely high scientific level, that a second sector is concerned with substitutions — for example, the replacing of one chemical process by another — and that a third sector is specifically geared to innovation.

This brings us to the three types of industrial competition:

1. The first type, which is related to *product improvement,* is a form of competition involving price and quality. The issue here is how to manufacture a better product than one's neighbor, and at a lower price.

2. The second type, related to *substitution,* is more far-reaching, since it often involves a transformation in techniques, hence an improvement in production costs, and occasionally in quality. However, it can also involve a policy change with regard to raw materials, in chemical processing, for example. This amounts to an insertion in the overall industrial context, which is far more complex than is generally realized.

3. The third type of competition, *innovation,* is literally a capturing of positions on the market that are not occupied by competitors.

Let me now analyze the nature of the risks before proceeding to the study of specific cases.

Risk at the Research Stage. This is a low risk, because research is not expensive. However, it is extremely hard to predict the potential profit or benefit to be gained from taking this risk, and I feel that it is very dangerous to talk about the profit-earning capacity of research. An average can, of course, be worked out for a twenty-year period. It can be calculated that the research laboratory yielded X number of new processes, which brought in X amount of money. I am not completely convinced that, if this calculation were made, a chronic deficit might not be found in the profit-earning capacity of the research properly so-called.

In certain instances, notable profits would show up on the books as lucky shots. However, I am not sure that, on the average, the concept of purely financial profit-earning capacity makes it possible to cast the die in favor of research in absolute confidence. On the other hand, research does undeniably contribute something else more intangible, a contribution which cannot be expressed in figures but which is absolutely indispensable.

Firms that do not engage in research are shut off from any dialogue with scientists. They have no contact with the general technical level of their countries. Such firms are at a loss when it comes to understanding the discoveries that have been made elsewhere. They fail to sense the latters' importance, for these are things that are both perceived and analyzed with equal amounts of intuition and reasoning. Such firms find themselves isolated from today's world.

So, research is basically like a sixth sense to a firm, something that connects it with the modern universe. This sense is a factor that can hardly be conveyed by figures.

I do not believe that the reality of contact with the world around us is anything that can be assessed in terms of profit-earning capacity.

How does one go about assessing the value of sight to a blind man?

In any case, whenever a new process or a new idea has been produced by a university, by a colleague, or by a competitor, its sixth sense is the only thing that enables a firm to decide on its own policy. Failing this, minus research, minus this outlook on the future, minus this contact with the world, no modern industrial policy is possible.

Risks in the Development Stage. Let us bear in mind that the risks were low in the research stage. In the development stage, risks are high, and a strategy must be used that makes strict allowance for the financial aspect, a strategy that accurately analyzes exactly what is to be derived from a new method.

Here the money man has the floor. His arguments are sound if they are based on a farsighted and forward-looking knowledge of the markets and of civilization.

But enough has been said about generalities. Let us proceed with an examination of *typical cases*.

Once more, I beg to point out that the thoughts that I have imputed to the protagonists in these various cases have never been confirmed. I trust that the real-life characters will forgive me for having "put myself in their shoes" and imagined their reactions.

RANDOM CASE STUDIES

First, I shall attempt to "invent" the reactions of *Sir Harry Pilkington,* our glassmaking colleague in England.

In this case, the company concerned is a large glass manufacturing firm of world-wide renown. In this branch of industry, extensive scientific research is done on glass structure. This is not costly research, and may eventually lead to new and extraordinary developments in glass. However, this is not the direction in which Sir Harry's problem lay.

If you look at the surface of glass that is melting in a furnace, you will see that it constitutes a magnificent mirror, an ideally smooth surface. The idea of lifting off this molten glass surface and cooling it without having to polish it is a perfectly natural one. So natural, in fact, that it is protected by a dazzling array of patents dating from 1900-1901 through 1905.

In other words, the invention that would consist in pouring a layer of glass on a molten metal sheet, and then cooling and removing it, dates back sixty years. What was lacking in 1900 was the development possibility. Why?

In 1900, the industry was just emerging from the period of the mechanization of the hand-polishing of mirrors. There is considerable inertia in the human mental mechanisms that are responsible for scientific progress.

There are periods of inhibition, and this particular discovery had come along too soon in the early part of a phase of inhibition, which was due to the progress that had just been achieved. The Pilkington Brothers Company spend several million pounds on perfecting this process.

I will spare you the details of the technical difficulties, which were considerable.

It is to the credit of the English team to have foreseen that these difficulties could be overcome. Perhaps they had anticipated that the work would cost only a few million pounds. Perhaps it cost double that amount. Yet the team didn't allow itself to become discouraged, for as its work progressed, the certainty of success beckoned ever greater.

Here, I must draw the reader's attention to an important point, viz., at the time at which a development operation is decided on, the risk of technical failure is generally slight. It has been reduced to a minimum by preliminary investigations.

The risk of error in the financial evaluation of development costs is generally greater. Let us say that it is possible to be off by as much as one factor, or by two, perhaps by even more. There remains the business risk, and herein lies a most crucial problem.

I assume that the Pilkington Brothers Company indulged in the following calculation:

They anticipated that this process would yield a cost price reduction of $x\%$ (25%, for example), and that they would endeavor to sell the process at a price of $y\%$. On this basis, the income that might be expected would be in the range of n million pounds. Consequently, any effort carried up to $n/2$ million pounds would be a paying effort. The calculation was sound. The Pilkington Brothers Company can justifiably assume that it enjoys the prospect of recouping its initial investment with a highly comfortable multiplying factor.

This example is outstanding because it reveals technical foresight of first-rate order. This British team was able to diagnose what the stumbling-block had been in 1900, and to measure the number of negative psychological factors that had entered into the 1900 picture as an inhibiting factor. It was able to rise above all this. Now that the foregoing has been stated, we may ask whether this firm made allowance for additional considerations that would, in the event of failure, enable it to count on financial assistance. We do not, of course, know the answer. This is a clear-cut case of a risk strategy.

The second example that I propose to use from the chemical field concerns the discovery of the araldites, or of the epoxy resins, by the *CIBA Company*. This is a much simpler case.

This discovery involved a relatively simple chemical reaction applied to a well-defined family of chemical bodies. The discovery occurred at a time when the mass of scientific concepts concerning the large molecules in plastic materials was sufficiently clear to enable the intelligent minds who had grasped this scientific vision to perceive a possible new reaction, to foresee its potentialities, and to deduce the new products that could result therefrom.

I am virtually positive that the basic araldite research performed by Dr. Preiswerk and his team at CIBA hadn't been under way for more than a year before the conviction arose that here lay a vast new path for the future.

And then? All that needed to be done was to manufacture a few pounds of the product, and try them out, first as a glue, next as a surface coating, and finally as a plastifier. More products were subsequently manufactured in order for an initial market to be reached, and for the latter's potentialities to be defined. This took altogether about ten years, ten years during which the risks were really unimportant.

In the minds of the scientists, these risks were even non-existent. It is to the firm's credit to have accepted this program, and to have recognized the validity of the array of scientific knowledge possessed by Dr. Preiswerk and the members of this team. In short, it was an excellent and successful dialogue between competent chemists and capable businessmen.

In an entirely different line, there was an extremely curious product manufactured by *Dupont de Nemours,* to wit, vinyl fluoride. Dupont de Nemours devised the idea—an extremely classic one—of replacing the chlorine in vinyl chloride by fluorine, and the company launched extensive research activity in this field. In conformity with the good old American habit that is highly effective when a large market is at stake, Dupont de Nemours explored all the product's possibilities.

Dupont de Nemours accomplished an impressive amount of systematic work. I do not know the cost of this research, but judging from what I saw of the laboratories and the various published reports, I would conclude that it amounted to several million dollars.

And yet, this product was never put on the market. This is a most interesting case of development effort, because the scientific research required for discovering the large molecule was not a great effort in itself, but the effort expended for developing all the applications, including varnish, fluids, etc., was extensive, and all of it was discontinued.

This brings us to an important factor, i.e., the size of the firm.

Only an outsized firm can, without remorse, discontinue an effort that has cost x million dollars! An average-sized firm would probably feel compelled to carry through all the way to the end!

Safely ensconced in its world-wide eminence — Dupont de Nemours performs 5 percent of the world's total chemical research — this firm called a halt to its development effort, figuring that the market wasn't ripe for its product. And all the other companies in the world who had done work in this same field—to my knowledge, they are legion—believed that, since Dupont de Nemours hadn't commercialized the product, the reason was that it wasn't worth it.

Such reasoning is utterly fallacious, not to say laughable. If Dupont de Nemours didn't bother to commercialize a product, it was first of all because the firm felt sufficiently protected by a barricade of patents covering the product's applications, not the product itself! (The product itself is virtually in the public domain.) Moreover, it is quite likely that this product would have been prematurely released onto a market that as yet had no technical need for it. It would have found itself competing with others whose release hadn't yet been completely amortized. In Dupont's strategy, there was surely something deliberate and systematic, something that had been the subject of particularly exhaustive operational research. This again is merely a gratuitous interpretation by someone who has seen only the patents and a few samples.

Next, let us take up the case of the *Kodak Company*. Kodak is currently in the midst of an astounding operation. It is changing—partially, of course—the geometry of its 8 mm film.

This is an absolutely extraordinary phenomenon, considering the number of cameras in use throughout the world and considering the existing market! Kodak is changing its film perforations. For what reason? This is not an exclusively commercial operation. It is also a technical one: the investigations on the tension and on the propelling of the film were most exhaustive.

Obviously, a study and research decision had been reached before the commercial position was adopted. The two were concomitant.

This operation is tantamount to an admission that the 8 mm format is not the best one, that a surface loss occurs, as was long ago pointed out by a French firm that manufactures 9.5 mm film. Another "gap" shows up here.

It will be noted that the "gap" between R & D can be immediately followed by another yawning chasm, which can be bridged only by commercial success. Under the circumstances, the French Pathé SCI Company, which possesses what is probably the best format, has never managed to launch it successfully. In the Kodak policy of modification or improvement in the 8 mm film, Pathé sees a certain confirmation of its own position. It would have been logical for this French company to have begun tooting its own horn and shouted something like, "We told you so! Our 9.5 mm film is the best buy!" Instead, rather than launch a boisterous advertising campaign, Pathé SCI suggested a gentler solution.

This brings us to a consideration of the issue concerning commercial and advertising methods. Kodak is the only company in the world that can presently indulge itself in tampering with the format of a film, and this is one of the points that we must ponder. This topic will be returned to later, when we are wagering our bets on the success of development effort. We shall have to define what truly constitutes the success of an innovation effort. *Is it technical or is it commercial?*

WHAT ARE THE REAL PROBLEMS?

But these examples are enough. Where do the true problems lie? The primary real problem is that of ascertaining what is possible. I do not believe that any industry can engage in R & D without having a few people — not too many, a small group preferably — who possess an overall grasp of current developments in the sciences, as well as of the possibilities presently afforded by techniques and the progress that is being made in the latter.

Europeans are frequently satisfied merely with acquiring a laboratory. The head of a laboratory is very often expected to be simultaneously in charge of drawing up work programs, defending them vis-à-vis company directors — "selling" them to the management, as the Americans are fond of saying—and subsequently directing the carrying out of the programs, "orchestrating" their implementation, and preparing their successive stages. In other words, the laboratory head is overwhelmed with human responsibilities, since research is, before anything else, the creating and the continuous molding into shape of teams of human beings.

Generally speaking, European firms base their strategy on this *"one-man orchestra."*

What is the situation in the United States?

I do not know whether or not it has been represented on graphs. All I do know is that, in our laboratories, I witness the arrival of eminent men who seem to be remote from everyday routine preoccupations and whose concern it is to observe the overall "landscape," to scrutinize the scene thoroughly, to take it all in, and to ponder on it. Moreso than the mere might of American research, it is the *teams of men* themselves who are responsible for the successful choice of American scientific and development policies.

Therein lies the *first gap.*

The European firms possessing teams of observers assigned to the synthesizing of potentialities are few and far between.

It would be too easy to state that the American observers are indiscreet spies in the midst of our laboratories. Furthermore, it would be untrue!

They have come to our laboratories to observe what any university laboratory should be ready and willing to show visitors. . . and what is both willingly and kindly shown to me when I visit the United States.

These men possess an undeniable strength. They have the time to perform syntheses of scientific and technical potentialities, and they have the time to read.

Their work requires only a few qualified, well-trained men. Europe has such men, but often fails to make use of them.

EUROPE IS A TECHNICAL NECESSITY

A second point that I would like to stress is something entirely different: *the existence of a large market.* For the United States, this is a distinct advantage, a trump card. Although a Frenchman travelling in the States may occasionally deplore the fact that the food served in New York drugstores is identical with that served in the San Francisco ones, he has to admit that this homogeneous market constitutes a valuable asset.

There is no solution but to create an integral and homogeneous Europe, a scientific and technical Europe.

A unified Europe is a necessity, not a human one, of course—it is still possible for us to continue living in our present divided-up state—but a technical one. Certain elements of progress are possible only on a level above one hundred and fifty million population. Below that level, no country can effectively cover all the fields of scientific research—for the moment, we are speaking only of scientific research in the universities.

Europe is comprised of a certain number of countries ranging from some ten million to some seventy million inhabitants. All of these countries are eager to accomplish everything by means of their universities, but with a relative minimum of coordination. This strikes me as a horrendous "gap"! However, I can't help feeling that it could be readily bridged. Our unified Europe will, of course, necessarily come into being. I hope that Europe will some day acquire the equivalent of Washington's National Science

Foundation; I also hope that this European Science Foundation will have friendly links—perhaps functional ones—with its American counterpart . . . and—why not?—perhaps also with the Russian Academy of Sciences.

The above is the condition for forming a scientific Europe, the success of which will be measured by the worth of its men. Our present state of dividedness inflicts fatigue and wear-and-tear on our men. This does not mean that they are not worthy or of great capability. Europe today has a regular pool of top quality scientists, but they are separated into little bunches. I need cite only one extremely typical case, that of Professor Bauer. At long last, when he was 64, in the year before his retirement, this man finally acquired the laboratory that he had always needed. I am sure that everyone who is aware of the situation realizes that Bauer belonged to that distinguished race of the great physicists of modern times. He experienced World War I, lived through the Occupation of World War II, and coped with the small town wranglings between the University of Strasbourg and others—and not until he had reached the age of 64 did he finally get a decent laboratory in which to carry on his work.

Scientific personnel must enjoy the privilege of mobility. A closed door, a refusal from one direction must be compensated for by a welcome mat in some other place.

An American professor pursues his career while moving around to different points of the United States. A professor in France has trouble getting out of his home town, except to "go up" to Paris. And "going up" to Paris is no longer the trend.

The result is that each individual teacher wants his own working microcosm placed at his disposal on the spot. The situation is already a serious one in France, and it is even more serious on the European scale.

Our widest "gap" at present is precisely this wasting process, this wearing down of our scientific effort. Are our scientists ready for these changes . . . and exchanges? I'm not so sure about the men of my own generation, but I *am* sure as concerns the younger men in the 25-to-30-year age group. *Today's budding thesis scribblers have a true vision of tomorrow's scientific Europe as if they were already part of it.*

The third "gap" is connected with the *taking of risks*. The taking of risks of course presupposes the existence of a financial market. It presupposes that there is a dynamism of capital resources, and that there are also courage and clearsightedness. It presupposes that men have sensed and grasped the amount of trust that can be placed in scientists and technicians, that they have assessed the issues at stake, measured the risks and the chances.

It is also possible that in France today—and, in my opinion, more seriously so in Germany—we have been stricken by a deadly virus, which manifests itself in *our failure to recognize the cultural value of our technical civilization.* I myself am deeply concerned over this. I am, of course, a warm supporter of a humanism that would range from Latin through the art master-pieces in Florence via all the intermediate stages imaginable. All this not-withstanding. I would not repudiate a fascinating technical civilization, which has the value of a culture and which deserves to be lived as such.

At the present time, it isn't certain—and in saying this I am perhaps aiming a blow at our bankers—that, in the upper financial circles, in the immediately responsible echelons, there is any truly devoted attachment to our contemporary technical universe. This situation may well constitute an extremely serious gap. For, if certain American businessmen can be found fault with for a kind of cultural lack, I believe that by the same token there are also other outstanding American businessmen, who strike me as repre-sentative of a perfect synthesis between a wide culture—which is bestowed on them by their aptitude for hustling all over the planet—and an awareness of modern technical evolution, a sense of efficacity, a market sense.

Perhaps—this is only an hypothesis!—it just may be that in Europe today there is a whole set of unavowed and unconscious mental reservations which prevent us from fully entering into the game. I repeat, this is just an hypothesis, but it is nonetheless a point worth elucidating.

I come now to the subject of *government assistance.*

The United States has a staggering amount of public money at its disposal. Whether you like it or not, 60 percent of research costs and perhaps an even greater percentage of development costs are paid for by public funds in the United States, and this money is spent in the industrial laboratories.

There is nothing comparable to this in Europe.

In this connection, I hope that the motivating power for this collective effort will not be essentially a defense effort, for the word defense, in military terminology, implies simply the military field and the eventuality of warfare.

There are other, increasingly large collective efforts going on, such as the work being devoted to excavating and investigating the earth's deepest inner layers. This may easily be the most important peaceful adventure to which man has consecrated himself for quite some time now.

CONCLUSION

Now that all the foregoing has been stated, what has to be done? Our homogeneous Europe isn't going to be achieved overnight.

Each European country must devise means for assisting its industries, through research insurance, credit systems, professional cooperative mechanisms, etc. All of these are necessary.

The criteria for government aid will be extremely difficult to establish, and will almost invariably be faulty, but never mind! This will make it possible to hold out for a while at least, until our European community achieves the stature required by the present state of scientific knowledge and techniques.

I should merely like to put certain countries on their guard. I have in mind particularly my Belgian friends, who are going to enormous trouble with their I.R.C.I.A., as well as my French colleagues, who are exerting all their efforts to create assistance for development. At varying rates of speed, all of us will arrive at aid formulas that will turn out to be paying propositions when they are successful.

But what constitutes success?

Technical success? This presents no problems. If sufficient will power is brought to bear in the undertaking of a development effort, then technical success surely lies just beyond the horizon. The risk of technical failure will be slight. The criteria for success cannot, therefore, be technical—or else, it will mean that we have deliberately decided to place a technical file in the nation's archives, a new technical competence, even without an ulterior market, which is an eminently defendable thesis.

Having discarded this purely technical criterion, we come to the criterion of *commercial success.* Here, unfortunately, we are obliged to ask ourselves whether the methods set up for commercialization are sufficient to enable us to bridge this additional gap by an invention that represents the actual transition to a commercial scale of operation.

For in the successive stages of operations, including research and discovery, development, commercialization and industrialization, there are numerous gaps that can be filled in only by the use of *synthesis.*

A synthesis of scientific knowledge, technical knowledge, knowledge of market prospects and outlets, knowledge of financing possibilities, knowledge of strategies, and even, to a certain extent, knowledge of strategic patterns of development—these are the various "gaps" with which all the European countries are faced. We must adjust our mentalities to accept the modern technical world.

21

Where in the World Should We Put that Plant?

Robert B. Stobaugh, Jr.

The manager who is investigating opportunities for building foreign manufacturing facilities faces a difficult problem in selecting the "right" country for investment. He may have 50 products under his direction, and since there are more than 100 countries in the world, he faces the possibility, if he is thorough, of screening more than 5,000 potential investment situations. For the company as a whole the task can be even more intimidating: a company with upward of 1,000 products would need to explore more than 100,000 situations!

Most companies do not make use of a large scale, rational screening process to identify foreign investment opportunities. Lack of suitable methods, inadequacy of information, shortage of time, and possible cost militate against such extensive screening. So most international investments are made out of fear that a market may be lost, as a reaction to a "deal" offered by an outsider, or sometimes simply by hunch.

More managers would use rational screening methods, perhaps, if some simple and straightforward tools were available. In this article I shall discuss such a set of tools.

They are intended to aid in searching for investment opportunities in countries where the products are not made. Usually, once manufacture of a product has begun in a country, its market will be well defined, and expansion opportunities can be fairly easily ascertained.

Reprinted, with permission, from the *Harvard Business Review,* January-February (1969). Copyright© by the President and Fellows of Harvard College; all rights reserved. The author wishes to acknowledge that his research, which formed the basis for this article, was financed partially by a grant from the Ford Foundation to the Harvard Business School for a study of multinational enterprises and the nation state.

By using the methods I describe here, the manager can narrow his search to the relatively few situations where a promising foreign investment opportunity is likely to exist. Each of these will then require a detailed feasibility study; this can cost from $10,000 to $100,000. Effective screening before the feasibility-study stage obviously can save a company a lot of money and managerial time.

The tools are of two major types—those pertaining to a country and those pertaining to a product.

In the case of a particular product, the manager is interested in the expected "imitation lag" for each country, imitation lag being the lapse between commencement of commercial production in the world and commencement of commercial production in a specified country. The fact that a country with a short imitation lag begins manufacture of a product before a country with a long imitation lag can, of course, make a significant difference.

My research has shown that four *country*-related variables are important in affecting imitation lag: market size, investment climate, the availability of local technology or know-how, and distance from major producing countries.[1] (Unit wage rates are also considered to be important, but, unfortunately, no adequate measure of their effects has appeared.)

Three *product*-related variables that research has shown are significant in affecting imitation lag are freight costs, economies of scale, and consumers' need for the product.[2]

I shall discuss each of these indicators in turn, and then combine them into a matrix for screening the world for investment opportunities.

While use of some of these variables is old, the idea of applying them as a package to help the manager is new. The most extensive research into their possible use has involved the world petrochemical industry. Other research suggests that they are useful for consumer durables and plastics. While they have not been applied in this fashion to other industries, it is my belief that this approach would also be useful there.

COUNTRY-RELATED VARIABLES

First let us look at the set of factors which affect a country's imitation lag. The size of the market is generally thought of as the most important factor, and I shall dwell on it at length, with less attention to the other variables.

MARKET SIZE

Once a country's market approaches the size needed to support a profitable operation, a number of forces may push the manufacturer into building a plant, perhaps sooner than he might wish.

Freight and duty are important cost elements, but less tangible factors also are important, such as a belief that sales will increase because of greater customer confidence that the manufacturer can deliver the product on time (especially important for industrial goods), or a belief that a rival, local or foreign, might preempt the market by building a plant and thereby obtaining greater tariff protection (especially important in the less-developed countries).

Because of difficulties in making accurate estimates of market size, manufacturing costs, and capital expenditures, such investment decisions often are made on guesswork. This is especially the case with a company that has had little foreign experience.

What is needed is a measure of market size that allows the manager to anticipate when the market will approach critical size—before these other forces begin to come into play. Measuring market size, however, can be a major problem. Since detailed market data are expensive to obtain, a company needs a crude measure for rapid screening.

If the product is now being consumed in the country, the amount and expected growth of imports serve as a guide. But import statistics often are not reliable. Furthermore, consumption in that country may increase substantially once a manufacturing plant is located there.

And if the product is an intermediate (used in the manufacture of other products), it may happen that the *potential* consumption is substantial while *actual* consumption is zero because there is no manufacturing plant consuming the product.

A good example of this situation is the case of styrene and butadiene in Argentina. These chemicals are used in making synthetic rubber, which in turn is used in tires. Until recently, while large quantities of tires were used in Argentina, no styrene or butadiene was consumed there because synthetic rubber was not manufactured. Now, however, the situation has changed. When a synthetic rubber plant was built, so were plants for styrene and butadiene—all in a single project.[3]

Traditional yardsticks: The various measures of market size which companies have used—gross national product, population, and per-capita income—have serious drawbacks.

The problem in using *gross national product* (or gross domestic product) is its failure to show for some countries that a large number of people have very low incomes. Hence, a seemingly sizable GNP might nevertheless represent a small market for many U.S. goods. This measure suggests, for example, that India's market is about the same size as Canada's. But, for most U.S. manufacturers interested in foreign investment, India, of course, is not nearly as large a market as Canada.

The difficulty with *population* figures is that they do not reflect the ability of the consumer to pay; therefore they distort the relative market size more than GNP statistics do. For example, this measure indicates that India's market is about 25 times as big as Canada's.

As for *per-capita income* figures, they fail to take into account differences in population. They "show," for example, that Kuwait's market is larger than that of the United States.

Using any one of these measures as a single proxy variable clearly could be very misleading. This no doubt explains why, in interviews at many multinational U.S. corporations, I did not find any measure being employed alone in estimating market size.

If these yardsticks are to be put together in some sort of combination, the question arises as to what weight to give what factor. And, of course, the simplicity of using a single measure is lost.

One multiproduct company attempted to use a single market measure combining these and other factors, such as "share of population living in urban areas." (Weights assigned by the company were based on an arbitrary weighting of GNP, per-capita income, population, urban population, and growth of industrial production.) The results showed these market ratings:

United States	100
Japan	89
West Germany	87
France	80
India	77
Canada	70
Peru	48

Because the market ratings do not reflect the relative market sizes of these countries for most products, the company is now modifying its rating scale.

Manufacturing output: A study I made showed that a single measure, the total output of all types of manufactures, is a good proxy variable of market size for petrochemicals in a country. It showed also that manufacturing output is a major determinant of when a country begins production of a petrochemical product (i.e., of imitation lag).[4] The manufacturing output variable is also important in determining imitation lag in the world plastics industry,[5] and in many other industries can be expected to have a similar investment pattern.

The exact effect of differences in manufacturing output of various countries would depend on economies of scale in the manufacturing process and the average annual growth rates in various markets. In the case of petro-chemicals, a country whose output was twice the size of another's typically began production three to four years before the second country.

Why is manufacturing output a good proxy variable to use as an indi-cator of market size? The concept of income elasticity of demand, which is the change in the quantity of a product bought relative to a change in in-come of the buyers, can help us answer this question.

Most goods produced abroad by U.S. companies have "cross-country" income elasticities of demand substantially greater than 1—meaning that countries with high per-capita incomes spend a greater share of income on these goods than do countries with low per-capita incomes. The cross-country income elasticity of manufacturing output also is substantially greater than 1 and in some cases approximates that of the goods made abroad by U.S. corpo-rations. Therefore, using countries' manufacturing outputs as a measure of relative market sizes takes into account the effect of relative per-capita in-comes better than does the more elementary measure, GNP.

Manufacturing output figures would indicate, for example, that the size of the Indian market is about the same as Argentina's or Australia's. Such data certainly provide a more realistic market estimate for most pro-ducts the U.S. manufacturers abroad than do the measures I mentioned previously.

While manufacturing output in many cases might be a good proxy variable for relative market size, a word of caution is in order: its use to estimate the potential market for a single product rests on the assumption that the consumption patterns of all countries have identical relationships with these countries' manufacturing output. Quite obviously, this is not exactly the case; but, even so, manufacturing output is a better indicator in many cases than any other single measure.

One situation in which manufacturing output might not be a good indica-tor is in estimating for consumer products the market sizes of the few high-income agricultural countries. For example, the variable probably under-states the market size of New Zealand for consumer products.

The simple relationship between manufacturing output of various coun-tries and the dates when production of a given product starts in these countries is this: small-market countries begin production later than large-market countries, and hence have longer imitation lags.

INVESTMENT CLIMATE
The two elements underlying a country's investment climate are the willing-ness of the government to provide a good investment climate and its ability

to do so. There is often a wide gulf between the two factors. Further, they are rather abstract and thus are difficult to measure.

Exhibit 1:
A Company's Rating Scale for Determining a Country's Investment Climate

Item	Number of points
Capital repatriation allowed	0 to 12
Foreign ownership allowed	0 to 12
Discrimination and controls, foreigners versus domestic businesses	0 to 12
Stability of domestic prices	0 to 14
Political stability	0 to 12
Willingness to grant tariff protection	0 to 8
Availability of local capital	0 to 10
Currency stability	0 to 20

A readily usable measure is needed. One company has devised a measure that it has found effective. It is a 100-point rating scale in which points are subjectively assigned according to the government's policy and economic and political conditions in the country. The scale is shown in Exhibit 1.

For an example of how the company assigns points in each category, see Exhibit 2, which shows the range of points in "capital repatriation allowed."

Exhibit 2:
Range of Points in category "Capital Repatriation Allowed"

Item	Number of points
No restrictions	12
Restrictions based only on time	8
Restrictions on capital	6
Restrictions on capital and income	4
Heavy restrictions	2
No repatriation possible	0

In 1965, according to this scale, Australia and West Germany had the best investment climate, rating 94, followed by the United States at 92. In contrast, many less-developed countries were rated between 50 and 60.

This scale has proved very accurate in forecasting when countries would begin production of certain petrochemicals. After the manufacturing output of various countries was taken into account, it was found that a country with a rating of 90 began production about 10 years before a country with a rating of 50.

LOCAL TECHNOLOGY

For some industries, the availability of technology or know-how is at least as significant a variable as is size of market or investment climate. Entrepreneurs in a country where the technology is available need not wait for a foreign company to supply it (either through licensing or investing), and so they are apt to start production sooner than are those in a country lacking the technology.

In the petrochemical industry, for example, after taking into account manufacturing output and investment climate, I found that those countries that already possessed the necessary technology tended to begin production about 10 years before countries that had to import the technology.

The manager in the multinational corporation should consider the probability that a local company will possess the necessary technology to start production. Where the probability is high he may decide to move faster to invest. The relationship of investment climate and technology availability to imitation lag is shown in Exhibit 3.

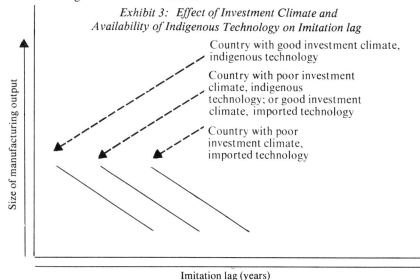

Exhibit 3:   Effect of Investment Climate and
Availability of Indigenous Technology on Imitation lag

Country with good investment climate, indigenous technology

Country with poor investment climate, indigenous technology; or good investment climate, imported technology

Country with poor investment climate, imported technology

Size of manufacturing output

Imitation lag (years)

DISTANCE FROM PRODUCERS

Obviously, the farther an importing country is from another country capable of supplying its needs, the higher the freight costs in shipping a product from one to the other. These higher costs are a factor in encouraging an earlier start-up of production in countries remote from major producing centers.

For example, I found that in the case of a variety of petrochemicals for which freight charges represented from 10 percent to 30 percent of product value, countries such as Argentina, South Africa, Australia, and Japan—which are remote from the major production centers in the United States and Europe—began production on the average four years earlier than would have been expected from an analysis of the other country-related variables.

PRODUCT-RELATED VARIABLES

Now let us look at the second set of variables that empirical tests have shown to be important—freight costs, economies of scale in the manufacturing process, and demand for products—which are product-related.

FREIGHT COSTS

Earlier, I indicated that freight costs are an important factor in determining imitation lag when comparing one country with another. They are also an important factor when considering products: high comparative freight costs for a product, in relation to its value, reduce the product's imitation lag.

A high delivered cost makes it more likely that a plant built in a consuming country will be competitive with the plant in another country originally producing the product. For example, in a representative group of petrochemicals, a product with a freight cost equivalent to 30 percent of its value was manufactured in countries using the product about four years before a product with a freight cost equivalent to 10 percent of its value.

ECONOMIES OF SCALE

Where the manufacturing process has a low economy of scale in relation to the size of the U.S. market, the result is a shorter imitation lag. For example, if Product A is made in 100 plants in the United States, one would expect it to be made in more foreign countries than another product, Product B, which is made in only 4 plants in this country. The reason is that a U.S. plant making Product A serves on the average only 1 percent of the domestic market, while a U.S. plant making Product B serves on the average 25 percent of the domestic market. More countries have a market equivalent to 1 percent than to 25 percent of the U.S. market, so the likelihood is greater that more countries are manufacturing Product A than Product B.

Note that this is a different measure from capital intensiveness. To illustrate, petroleum refining is more capital-intensive than many other manufacturing processes; yet there are about 300 petroleum refineries in the United States, and the optimum size refinery, according to one authority, is about 2 percent of the total U.S. market.[6] This low economy of scale in relation to market size is one of the main reasons why about 100 countries, many of them with small markets, have petroleum refineries.

NECESSITIES AND LUXURIES

A U.S. product considered in a foreign country to be a necessity naturally can be expected to have a shorter imitation lag than one not considered so essential.

While consumption patterns vary across national boundaries because of differences in consumer tastes, climates, and other factors, there is reason to believe that for many products U.S. data provide a good substitute for international data.[7] Because of this, and because U.S. data are more readily available, they should be adequate for use in an initial screening of foreign investment opportunities.

In attempting to measure the size of demand abroad, the manager can keep in mind that in a country in which the per-capita income is lower than that of the United States, the demand for, say, refrigerators will be greater than will be the demand for freezers, which are bought by consumers with greater discretionary income; therefore that country's market for refrigerators is larger relative to the size of the U:S. market than it is for freezers.

The manager can draw up a ranking of consumer products according to a necessity-luxury scale, using estimates from consumer surveys to find comparable consumption patterns of income groups in the United States.

I should add that an estimate of where intermediate goods would rank on such a scale is much more difficult to obtain, since their relationship to per-capita income is less definite.

COMBINING THE VARIABLES

Now let us see how the manager, in order to make better decisions on where his company should make its investment, can draw together the variables I have discussed and fashion a planning matrix. This is shown in Exhibit 4.

Here, the countries are ranked vertically by manufacturing output, with modifications according to investment climate, availability of local technology, and distance from major producing countries. (National economic data are available from the United Nation's *Yearbook of National Account Statistics.*)

The countries highest on the list are those with large manufacturing outputs, good investment climates, and indigenous technology probably available. A country remote from major producing countries is higher on the scale than it would otherwise be.

Exhibit 4: Matrix for Identifying Foreign Investment Opportunities

Countries   Products

	1	2	3	4	5	6	7	8
U.S.	X	X	X	X	X	X	X	X
A	X	X	X	X	X	X	X	
B	X	X	X	X	X			
C	X	X		X	X			
D	X	X	X	X				
E	X	X	X					
F	X	X	X					
G	X	X						
H	X	X						
I	X	X						
J	X							
K								
L								
M								

X = Product already manufactured in country.

The products are ranked horizontally by unit freight cost, with modifications according to economies of scale and expected ranking on a necessity-luxury scale. The products furthest to the left — and hence those more likely to be made in a greater number of countries — are those with high unit freight costs, those with low economies of scale relative to market size, and those considered by consumers to be necessities.

After marking the squares where the products already are manufactured, denoted by an "X" in Exhibit 4, the manager can draw a line so that all the "X"s are on the left side.

This line (which will move toward the right over time as manufacturing facilities are installed) could be called the investment "frontier." The blank spaces behind the frontier — that is, to the left of the line — identify the ripest investment opportunities.

The exact effect of the country-related and product-related variables will depend on the industry under consideration. For capital-intensive plants requiring a high level of technology, for instance, a good investment climate or the availability of local technology can reduce the required market size of a country by as much as 50 percent.

Using this as an initial guideline for the order of countries, the manager then can complete a matrix for his company's products by a trial-and-error rearrangement of the countries and products. With this matrix, he can then isolate the relatively few situations that he would want to investigate further by detailed feasibility studies. The best candidates in Exhibit 4 are C-3, B-6, D-5, E-4, and G-3.

A simple example of the use of the planning matrix for three petrochem-

Exhibit 5: Example of Matrix Identifying
Foreign Investment Opportunities for Three Petrochemicals

Countries	Products		
	Synthetic methanol	Styrene	Isoprene
U.S.	X	X	X
EEC*	X	X	X
United Kingdom	X	X	
Japan	X	X	
Canada	X	X	
Australia	X	X	
Argentina	X	X	
Mexico		X	
India	X	X	
Spain	X		
Brazil	X	X	
Austria	X	X	
South Africa	X	X	
Norway	X		
Pakistan	X		
Taiwan	X		

X = Product already manufactured in country.
*Treated as one country for purposes of this analysis.

icals — i.e., synthetic methanol, styrene, and isoprene — is shown in Exhibit 5. Synthetic methanol and styrene have about the same economies of scale relative to market size: some 15 manufacturing plants in the United States make each product. However, because freight costs in relation to product value are twice as high for synthetic methanol as for styrene, synthetic methanol is made in more countries than is styrene.

On the other hand, freight costs in relation to product value are about the same for styrene and isoprene, but the latter has much larger economies of scale relative to market size than does styrene: there are only one fourth as many isoprene plants in the United States as styrene plants. As a result, isoprene is made in far fewer countries than is styrene.

Because these are intermediate products consumed in more than one end-product, the variable involving the necessity-luxury ranking is not used in this scheme.

Several candidates emerge as prime targets for investments — i.e., synthetic methanol in Mexico, styrene in Spain, and isoprene in the United Kingdom. (Actually, these investments in Mexico and Spain have been or are about to be made by companies that saw the opportunities.)

Note that the two largest-market countries (the European Economic Community is treated as one country for this analysis) produce all three products. The countries with medium-sized markets produce only two. Among this intermediate group of countries, Austria and South Africa have the smallest markets; both, however, have very good investment climates. Finally, the three countries with the smallest markets manufacture only one product.

SUMMARY

Most companies interested in foreign expansion make so many different products, and there are so many countries, that searching for a good foreign investment opportunity represents a major effort. As a result, decisions on investments often are made in reaction to circumstances of the moment rather than as a result of a careful search for the best opportunity.

In this article I have presented a set of tools to enable the manager to screen many possible situations rapidly and pick out the few that are most likely to result in a profitable investment. These candidates should then be subjected to a detailed feasibility study.

The variables to be used by the planning manager in the screening process are of two major types—those related to the characteristics of the *country* and those related to the characteristics of the *product*.

In screening, the most important country-related variable is the size of the market. For many products the manufacturing output of a country is a good proxy for the size of its market. Three other important country-related variables are investment climate, availability of local technology, and the distance a country is from major exporting nations.

The three key product-related variables are economies of scale in the manufacturing process relative to market size, the cost of transporting the product, and the market characteristics expressed in terms of whether the product is a necessity, a discretionary product, or a luxury product.

These concepts, expressed in the form of a relatively simple planning matrix, enable the manager to pinpoint the most likely investment opportunities.

Now, I know that there will always be foreign investments made because the company president's wife likes a certain country or the chairman of the board knows the president of a country. And there will always be an undue lack of interest in some highly inflationary foreign countries because certain U.S. corporations have not yet learned how to operate profitably in an inflationary environment. Yet I hope that introducing these tools will at least make a start toward use of more rational screening methods in searching for foreign investment opportunities.

NOTES

1. *The Product Life-Cycle, U.S. Exports, and International Investment,* unpublished doctoral thesis, Harvard Business School, 1968.
2. *Ibid.* See also Louis Wells, Jr., *Product Innovation and Directions of International Trade,* unpublished doctoral thesis. Harvard Business School, 1966; an article based on Well's thesis appeared as "A Product Life Cycle for International Trade" in *The Journal of Marketing* (July 1068), p. 1.
3. See John G. McLean, "Financing Overseas Expansion," HBR (March-April 1963), p. 53.
4. The statistical results are in Stobaugh, *op.cit.*
5. Based on an analysis of data in G.C. Hufbauer, *Synthetic Materials and the Theory of International Trade* (Cambridge: Harvard University Press, 1966).
6. Joe S. Bain, "Economies of Scale, Concentration, and the Condition of Entry in Twenty Manufacturing Industries," *American Economic Review* (March 1954), p. 30.
7. See, for example, Wells, *op. cit.,* who reached this conclusion in comparing consumer durables, pp. 125,130.

A second implication is that nationalism will tend to direct economic policy toward the production of psychic income in the form of nationalistic satisfaction, at the expense of material income. If attention is confined to material income alone, a third implication is that nationalism will tend to redistribute material income from the lower class toward the middle class, and particularly toward the educated middle class; in this respect, nationalism reinforces the trend of modern society toward the establishment of a class structure based on educational attainment.[10]

This last implication relates to material income only, and does not necessarily imply that the lower classes are worse off because of nationalism when both real and psychic income are reckoned into the account. It is quite possible that the psychic enjoyment that the mass of the population derives from the collective consumption aspects of nationalism suffices to compensate them for the loss of material income imposed on them by nationalistic economic policies, so that nationalistic policies arrive at a quite acceptable result from the standpoint of maximizing satisfaction. It may even be that nationalistic policies are the cheapest and most effective way to raise real income in less developed countries;[11] in some cases, one suspects, the prospects for genuine economic growth are so bleak that nationalism is the only possible means available for raising real income.[12]

It would seem, however, from the economic analysis of government presented earlier, that the lower classes are unlikely to be net gainers from economic nationalism, due to the effects of ignorance and the costs of acquiring information in concentrating political power in the hands of pressure groups, and the general tendency for producer interests to dominate over consumer interests that results from the natural response of voters to the high cost and negligible value of acquiring political information. The tendency for the mass of the population to suffer losses from economic nationalism is probably reinforced in the new nations by the prevalence of systems of one-party government, in which the party is based largely on urban support and frequently exercises a virtual monopoly over the country's communications system.[13]

Even though nationalism may involve a substantial redistribution of real income toward the middle class at the expense of the mass of the population, this redistribution may perform a necessary function in the early stages of forming a nation, in the sense that the existence of a substantial middle class may be a prerequisite of a stable society and democratic government. In other words, an investment in the creation of a middle class, financed by resources extracted from the mass of the population by nationalistic policies, may be the essential preliminary to the construction of a viable national state. This problem, however, belongs in the spheres of history, sociology, and political science rather than economics.

NOTES

1. The model also owes something to the writer's earlier attempts to understand the origins of the particular policies recommended by Canadian nationalists in recent years; see his "Problems of Canadian Nationalism," Chap. 2 in *The Canadian Quandary* (Toronto, 1963), and "Nationalism in Canadian Economic Policy," *Lloyds Bank Review,* LXIV (1964), pp. 25-35.
2. Gary S. Becker, *The Economics of Discrimination* (Chicago, 1957).
3. Anthony Downs, "An Economic Theory of Political Action in a Democracy," *Journal of Political Economy,* LXVI (1957), pp. 135-50, and *An Economic Theory of Democracy* (New York, 1957).
4. Albert Breton, "The Economics of Nationalism," *Journal of Political Economy,* LXXII (1964), 376-86.
5. Breton makes unnecessarily heavy weather of this point.
6. Again, there may be an economic gain rather than a loss, if previously nationals were discriminated against in the employment practices of the nationalized industry.
7. I am indebted for this point to Professor A. D. Scott.
8. This consequence of the tariff has been an important factor in the exacerbation of nationalist sentiment in Canada in recent years. The formation of the European Economic Community similarly has fostered American investment within the Community's boundaries and thereby provoked nationalist complaints.
9. The emphasis on education in contemporary development tends to produce a rat-race in which a country first invests a great deal of scarce capital in educating people, and then is obliged to invest a great deal more in providing suitable employment opportunities for them, the consequence being a double waste of resources. Sometimes needs both for more education and for better jobs for the educated are urged simultaneously, despite the implicit economic contradiction.
10. It is one of the paradoxes of modern social philosophy that redistribution of income from the intellectually poor to the intellectually rich is regarded as desirable and proper whereas redistribution from the materially poor to the materially rich is regarded as utterly inequitable.
11. This point was suggested by Professor Burton Weisbrod.
12. Field research by members of the Committee for the Comparative Study of New Nations suggests that this may in fact be the case in some of the new African nations. Nationalism may itself create such a situation, nationalistic economic policies blocking economic growth so effectively that it becomes necessary to resort to ever more extreme nationalistic sentiment and policy to maintain the illusion of economic development.
13. Both dependence on urban support and control over communications media are logical consequences of the economic theory of government as applied to such countries. Dependence on urban support in turn reinforces the bias of development policy toward promotion of manufacturing, and in general fosters policies favoring the city-dweller at the expense of the agricultural population. A particular aspect of this, important especially in Latin America, is the maintenance of low urban transport rates by direct or indirect subsidization, which in its turn fosters urban population growth and increases the political importance of urban residents.

24
Nationalism
and the
Multinational
Firm

John Fayerweather

The presence of conflict between multinational firms and nationalism around the world is easy to identify, but analyzing the anatomy of the conflict is by no means easy. The nature of nationalism itself is quite difficult to describe, and the ways in which the multinational firms interact with it are complex and vary substantially from country to country. Yet the problems created by the conflict are of substantial importance. Thus the subject deserves extensive exploration.

The purpose of this paper is to outline a framework for analysis of the interaction of nationalism and the multinational firm. The framework is intended to contribute to the clarification of the problems involved and will also provide guidelines for further investigation of the subject. To establish a solid base for this analysis, it is necessary first to define the central elements of the subject. Then the interaction of the multinational firm with nationalism is discussed.

DEFINITIONS OF CENTRAL ELEMENTS

The terms "multinational firm" and "nationalism" are often used with quite varied meanings. A selection must be made among these meanings so that the use of the two terms in this discussion will be clear.

Some people feel that to be multinational a company must have a certain spread of ownership among two or more countries or that it must have a certain type of managerial or parent company outlook toward global operations. Such characteristics are pertinent to the discussion of nationalism.

339

However, for purposes of this analysis the only conditions considered essential to qualification as multinational are that a firm be participating directly in business activities in two or more countries and that it exercise a degree of central control over those activities. Thus the definition includes all of the firms which have an ownership interest accompanied by participation in decision making in foreign producing operations, sales offices, licensing arrangements, or management contracts.

"Nationalism" is an extremely complex and nebulous subject upon which one can find a number of erudite definitions.[1] A few keypoints common to these definitions are basic to the present analysis. First, nationalism is descriptive of the commitment of the members of a nation to the principles of cohesion and adherence to the nation. Implied therein is the willingness of the individual to subordinate himself to the welfare of the nation. Second, there is always found some body of shared values, ideology and other attitudinal characteristics which may be considered either part of the nationalism of a country or so intimately associated with it that the two must be considered together. This body of shared attitudes provides to a substantial degree the cement which binds the people of a nation together. Third, nationalism is a manifestation of the basic social tendency of individuals to group together for mutual security and support. This instinct found its earliest manifestation in the mating group and then the tribe and has expanded progressively into larger units including now the nation state. In this so-called "we group" relationship the individual has a natural and satisfying inclination to identify with other members of the group and an instinct for differentiation and negative reaction towards the "they" external to the national group.

In any discussion of nationalism the interests of the nation and its components are ever present considerations. The word "interests" is used here to refer to the needs and desires which individuals or groups seek to satisfy including both ultimate objectives and the means which are sought for the achievement of those objectives. It is presumed that all interests involving human activity originate with the interests of individuals. However, in the nature of modern society a large portion of *individual* interests are sought through the activity of groups, composing what may be called *collective* interests (e.g., national efforts to strengthen economic growth). This process leads in turn to the emergence of *group* interests which may be distinguished from *individual* and *collective* interests. The *group* interests are distinct in their concern with the survival of the group or the strengthening of its capacity to function through the expansion of its power or some other means (e.g., the police powers of the government). Thus, we may broadly distinguish three main types of interests: (1) the interests which the individual seeks independently; (2) the interests of the individual which are aggregated with those of other individuals and sought collectively by a group; and (3) the interests of the group in advancing its organic capabilities.

These types of interests intermingle with nationalism in several ways.

First, nationalism is a vehicle for the achievement both of collective interests and of the interests of the nation as a distinctive group (categories #2 and #3 above). The collective individual interests lie in the satisfactions and security provided by participation in the group, the "we-group" characteristic of nationalism. The group interests lie in the support of the members in various ways motivated by nationalism, which gives the nation the capacity to perpetuate itself as a group and to accomplish its objectives. The objectives themselves are often collective interests, but the power and continuity of the nation itself does not serve any particular individual; it represents a group interest.

Second, nationalism fills gaps in the national analysis of interests. Issues in which nationalism is a factor typically will involve consideration of a mixture of individual, collective, and group interests. With all of these and particularly the latter, there is a significant problem of perception and analysis for the participants. It is, for example, extremely hard even for a well informed person to determine with certainty where the national interest lies on a particular issue. Since most members of a country are relatively uninformed about a large number of public issues, their perception of interests is often incomplete and to varying degrees inaccurate. In such circumstances nationalistic attitudes provide an instinctive substitute for knowledge and thought. That is, the individual can often find among his collection of nationalistic feelings enough reactions, biases, etc. to fill the gaps in his competence to think out an issue. This factor is significant to the question of nationalism because it means that the influence of the generalized feelings associated with it is enhanced in proportion to the inadequacies of the perception of actual interest by the participants.

Third, nationalism plays a prominent part in the socio-political process by which individuals, subnational groups, and the nation seek to achieve their interests. A vital part of this process is the pattern of appeals for support by one component of the society to another and the decisions by each group or individual as to what support should be given to others.

Two general characteristics are particularly meaningful in looking at the actual response by individuals and groups to nationalistic appeals.

One is the extent to which the support giver identifies with the appeal maker by virtue of common nationalism. Presumably in a wide range of decisions, where other considerations are not of substantial weight, the presence of a sense of identification, in this instance through joint nationality, provides an adequate basis for rendering support. For example, in a large number of conflicts of American individuals or groups with foreigners the average U.S. citizen would doubtless express support for the American simply because of nationalistic feeling in the absence of significant knowledge or interest in the substance of the issue. In this case, the support is given as an instinctive response based upon a sense of solidarity as a member of a group.

A second source of favorable response lies in the explicit conclusion of the individual or group that the appeal is based on a valid component of the shared attitudes associated with nationalism. For example, some member of the national society may appeal to others for protection against an external challenge to one of the traditions of the society or one of its value standards (e.g., paternalistic job security traditions in Europe).

Fourth, there is the role of nationalism in social communications. At each stage in the communications process there are opportunities for selection, distortion, and interpretation. Nationalism influences what happens in this process. The news media provide the most conspicuous examples. Newsmen are subject to their own nationalistic feelings and to those of their readers, to whom they cater to some degree. The emotional content of nationalism fits well with the tendency of media to emphasize the sensational aspects of the news. Thus, it is common to find that stories with a high nationalistic content receive considerable attention in newspapers and other media and that nationalistic elements receive greater attention than the rational analysis of the news.

Finally, the process of change must be considered. New conditions and requirements are constantly emerging which change both the various interests involved and the content of the shared attitudes associated with nationalism. Given the difficulties of perception and communication these changes are only integrated into the system slowly and with difficulty. To cite a notable case, in retrospect, it seems apparent that the abandonment of overt military aggression as a means for achieving national goals was in the best national interest of Germany. Yet serious losses from two major wars were necessary to integrate this view into the national opinion. There is a dual learning process involved in this sort of change: first, that of acquiring adequate knowledge and perception of the changed circumstances and, second, the balancing of losses and benefits involved in any shift in views as to interests and shared attitudes.

Nationalism probably retards the learning process because of the inevitable rigidity or inertia associated with widely held common viewpoints, particularly those which have strong emotional support. Thus, in any given circumstance, nationalistic views are likely to be found supporting the *status quo*. On the other hand, nationalism places in the hands of those who seek to change public opinion a potential means for expediting change by appealing to the emotions.

INTERACTION OF THE
MULTINATIONAL FIRM AND NATIONALISM

The foregoing comments provide a general scheme of analysis into which we may now inject the various ways in which the multinational firm interacts with host country nationalism. This analysis is pursued from two directions as shown in Figure 1: the inputs of the multinational firm in the development of nationalism and the conflicts between the firm and nationalism.

The multinational corporations would appear to contribute to the formation and character of nationalism in a country in three general ways: First, they often play an indirect role by affecting the domestic socio-economic factors which contribute to the formation of nationalism. The ability and willingness of people to identify with the national group and provide support to it are affected importantly by such things as degree of literacy, distribution of income, and so forth. Through their general influence on economic development and their specific role in particular industries, multinational firms often provide a constructive influence in this direction though in some cases they undoubtedly retard the process as compared with what might take place in their absence.

Second, the existence of multinational firms as a problem confronting the nation provides a general encouragement in the direction of national unity. It is assumed here that nationalism comes into being in part as a response to the emergence of problems with which the people cannot deal effectively either on an individual basis or through subnational groups. While the importance of multinational firms as an overall national problem varies from region to region, evidence suggests that it is commonly quite significant. Its influence is most apparent in less developed countries, expressed, for example, in the prevalence of protest against "neo-economic colonialism." But it also seems to be a factor even in industrialized areas like Canada. The popularity of Servan-Schreiber's *The American Challenge*[2] suggests that it may be a primary rallying attraction in emerging pan-European nationalism.

Thirdly, collectively and individually, multinational firms have in most countries provided some of the shared attitudes which compose the content of nationalism. Indeed, in many less developed countries the anti-foreign business attitudes are among the few opinions which are almost universally held and which have strong emotional force.

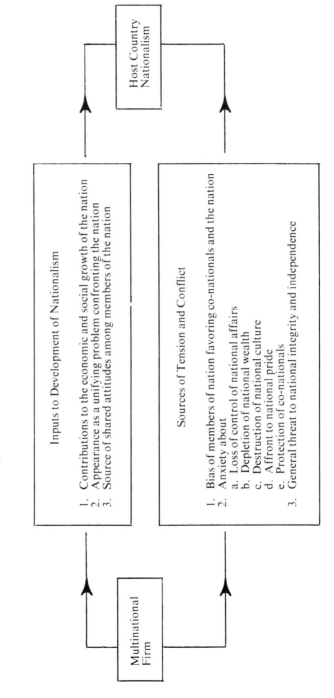

Figure 1: Nationalism and the Multinational Firm

As the second and third points are closely related, the distinction between them requires clarification. The second point is conceived as the response of the people of a nation to the multinational firm as an entity falling generically into the category of a "they," that is, as an outsider seeking to penetrate the "we-group" and thus generating instinctive cohesion to resist. This natural tendency to cohesive resistance is reinfored as specific points of conflict are recognized for which the value of the nation-state as a vehicle for pursuit of collective interests vis-à-vis the multinational firm is recognized (e.g., negotiating terms for new investments to optimize national interest benefits). The third point refers to specific facets of the reaction to the multinational firm, rather than reaction to it as an entity. The more important of these facets will be discussed later. The widespread sharing of these attitudes among the population provides specific bonds, similar in their cohesive effect to shared cultural values.

A further element of this analysis is the process by which the nationalistic attitudes toward foreign companies come into being. To be shared throughout the population, the attitudes must have been formulated at certain points and communicated effectively on a broad scale. The process presumably involves many individual contacts together with a substantial amount of communication and activity by groups and leaders in a position to aggregate and disseminate attitudes on a subnational or national basis. It is likely that the process involves also a substantial oscillation of communications between individual experiences and reinforcing communications from other sources. For example, an opinion that multinational firms are not respectful of national life may be the product of a number of individual experiences supported by views expressed by various national leaders. An individual might, for example, be personally affronted by an American supervisor; later he may read some comment in a newspaper about lack of respect shown by another company and a third unpleasant experience with an American tourist may add to these feelings. A speech by a politician attacking foreign enterprise might provide further reinforcement. By similar experiences multiplied many times throughout the population, one could visualize a given attitude evolving to broad acceptance.

PROBLEM AREAS

The problems of multinational firms which involve host country nationalism seem to fall into three main groups (as shown in Figure 1), each of a quite different character: bias, conflicts with specific nationalistic attitudes, and national struggle issues.

Bias. The tendency of members of a group to be prejudiced in favor of the viewpoint of others in the group against outsiders is well known. The extent to which bias is troublesome for the multinational firm in a given case would appear to depend upon two factors. First, there is the element of difficulty of determination of facts, issues, or other considerations in the case. Wherever there is an element of uncertainty between the position of the multinational firm and a host country national, nationalistic feeling will encourage co-nationals to accept the statements of the latter. The second factor is the breadth of involvement of host nationals. When an issue is confined to a limited number of people with whom the multinational firm can communicate directly, it can present its side of the issue and respond directly to contrary viewpoints. However, as the number of people involved broadens, their information is increasingly received by them through indirect communication channels, notably news media. The limited amount of information which can be transmitted in this manner is inevitably subject to the bias of the media, and the multinational firm has limited opportunity to counteract the bias.

These two factors are readily observed in cases where complex conflicts between a multinational company and a host nation become subjects of wide national interest. The news media in these cases give considerable space to the conflicts, but the space is never enough for a full presentation of all the background and shadings of viewpoints. To varying degrees the reporters and editors manifest their nationalistic bias by favoring the viewpoints of their co-nationals. Thus, the general populace is influenced not only by its own bias but also by the bias of the intermediary communications links, and in the appeal-support process the position of the nationals is weighted against that of the multinational firm.

Conflicts with Specific Nationalistic Attitudes. As noted already there are a number of anti-foreign business opinions among host societies which are so widely held that they are part of the shared nationalistic attitudes of the populace. The more commonly observed reactions related to these attitudes are listed in Figure 1. Some of these involve quite tangible issues of national interest, but our primary concern here is with the attitudinal aspect. The national interest aspect is important, however, because it has often been the source of the attitudes and continues to provide reinforcement for them.

1. *Control.* There is a common concern about the multinational firm as a threat to the control of the affairs of a society by its people. There is clearly substance to this feeling since as noted at the outset the multinational firm by definition seeks a degree of control over activities within the host nation. The nationalistic attitude problem, however, is not concerned with whether or not there is loss of control, but rather with the attitudes of the people to-

ward the loss. The basic nationalistic response is that any loss of control is undesirable. In reality, however, the subject is a very complex one, and it is often difficult to determine what is in the best interests of individual nationals and the host nation as a whole. On some points, like the retention of parent company quality control of pharmaceutical drug production, the loss seems clearly to the benefit of the host nation. But, most control questions are susceptible to considerable debate and the complexities of this analysis are clearly beyond the time and capacity of most people. Thus the basic negative reaction to loss of control commonly comes into play as a counter to control sought by the multinational firm.

Some reflections on history seem appropriate in considering this situation. Over the course of time individuals and groups have progressively given up greater degrees of control over their affairs to other individuals and groups and to higher orders of grouping. The process is ever accompanied by hesitation, reluctance, and worry. Only with the passage of time and the accumulation of experience are the benefits gained from giving up control assured and confidence in those to whom control has been transferred achieved. The evolution of nationalism is in itself part of this story, with the individual transferring control of much of his affairs to the nation state and achieving confidence in its ability to protect his interests.

The multinational firm is a relatively new feature in this process of evolution. There are good indications that a nation may benefit substantially in economic terms by transferring some degree of control of its industry to management organizations of worldwide scope. However, countries are still at an early stage in ascertaining what the actual costs and benefits of this process may be, in determining the degrees of control to relinquish, and, in establishing the pattern of working relations to implement the process. Thinking along these lines is still rudimentary at government levels, and it is highly underdeveloped among the general population. In the meantime, the instinctive worries about loss of control to a foreign body deter the development of the confidence in the multinational firm which is required for the transition to progress.

As the nation-state is regarded generally as the highest acceptable level of control, the idea of the transfer of some degree of control to the multinational firm external to the nation-state is resisted by nationalistic sentiment. The question of control thus becomes a point at which the basic sentiments of nationalism are themselves threatened by the multinational firm. The worries are reinforced by the observation that the multinational firm has its roots within another nation so that its decisions are responsible to a group whose interests are different and often assumed to be competing with those of the host nation.

2. *National Wealth.* Host nationals commonly believe that multinational firms take more wealth out of a country than they contribute to it in the way of benefits. This view is strongest in the countries where extractive industries are dominated by foreign firms, the physical removal of natural resources being associated in people's minds with loss of national wealth. But it is also widely held in countries where manufacturing is the main activity of multinational firms.[3] Computing with any meaningful accuracy a balance of costs and benefits from foreign investment is extremely difficult. The only statistics which are typically considered are the balance of payments effects and even in those the assessment is usually limited to comparing inflow of capital against outflow of dividends without consideration of more complex questions such as import substitution, generation of exports, and the like.

3. *Mutual Protection.* The third attitude is the tendency of members of a nation to protect each other from outsiders. The multinational firm is often believed to take unfair advantage of the members of the host society. Substance for this belief is readily found in such features as the size of the firms and their technical superiority. There are often countervailing considerations such as the difficulties of the multinational firm in staffing and organizing in a foreign environment and the unwillingness of local competitors to adopt methods which would put them more on a par with the foreign firms. But these considerations do not go directly to the point of the attitudes which give emphasis to non-rational loyalty rather than logics of competitive rules and performance. Similar attitudes may be inspired in sympathy for the position of workers employed by multinational firms, suppliers, and other nationals with whom the foreign firms have relations.

4. *Culture.* Multinational firms are often viewed as a threat to the traditional culture of the host society. They often introduce ways of doing business in such matters as industrial relations, competitive practices, and the like which conflict with the established cultural patterns. One frequently finds that the more progressive local companies are moving in similar directions. But so far as attitude formation is concerned the conspicuous identification of the multinational firm with different cultural characteristics readily creates an association in the public mind with threats to traditional ways. This sentiment is, of course, particularly significant in terms of nationalism because the traditional ways are in themselves a part of the basic nationalism. Thus the resistance along these lines as a nationalistic sentiment amounts in effect to the protection of nationalism itself.

5. *Pride.* Respect for the flag, national leaders, and other symbols of nationalism are universal. Beyond that, national self-esteem may be bound up in such varied matters as scientific achievement, political institutions, and

sports. The multinational firm is inevitably cast as a threat to national pride because its presence is based on some element of superior capability. Most commonly it possesses superior technical or managerial skills, a fact which reflects on the capabilities of the host society. This particular element does not usually appear to be strongly offensive to the pride of the host nation, presumably because possession of such skills has never been a key element in national pride or the foreign superiority has been sufficiently accepted and adjusted to in the psychology of the people. Still, it is not unlikely that it creates a small sense of loss of national pride, and reinforces specific affronts due to other actions by foreign companies.

A conceptually significant point to make about all affronts to national pride is that the role of the multinational firm as an outsider is critical in the strength of the nationalistic reaction to them. A local national could do many of them with relative impunity. He might be criticized, but usually he would not be seen as showing disrespect to the nation. The same action or words by an outsider are much more likely to trigger a defensive nationalistic feeling.

National Struggle Issues. The national struggle issues are directly related to the image of the multinational firm as a total entity confronting the national body — the "they" versus "we" role. Most of the time the negative attitudes associated with this image seem to be quite diffused and dormant. In some cases and some countries, however, they play an important part in conflicts, chiefly where major investments in small countries are involved, e.g., United Fruit Company in Central America and some of the extractive industry situations. In such instances, the impact of the foreign firm is great enough so that the host society is constantly aware of it as an overall threat to national integrity. Adverse reactions based on this feeling are readily aroused by specific events, the most dramatic being conflicts resulting in nationalizations.

But, this sort of feeling is evidently present to some degree in issues of more modest character, especially where the parent government of the multinational firm enters the picture. For example, it was a factor in a conflict between the Canadian government and the First National City Bank in 1965-67 which the author has studied.[4] Politicians and the press on a number of occasions injected exhortations to the government not to "retreat" under U.S. big business and government pressure and other phrases with combat connotations. In the latter stages, the conflict had assumed very much the character of a battle in a form of economic warfare, with feelings generically similar to those aroused by military combat being stimulated in the Canadian press. The intensity of the feelings were, of course, of a lesser order than in military warfare, but the fact that they had this character was a significant element in the conflict.

The role of the government of the parent country of the multinational firm adds a dilemma to this analysis. Except in the large company-small country situations, people of a host country do not readily see a foreign company as a serious threat to the nation as a whole. Their broadest defensive nationalistic feelings are directed at foreign nation-states, usually some neighbors and certain major world powers, the former posing specific traditional threats and the latter menacing their overall independence. Among the latter are most of the parent governments of multinational firms, including notably the United States and to a lesser degree the chief European countries and Japan.

It is not uncommon for some of this nationalistic reaction to foreign governments to become entwined with conflict relationships of multinational firms. To some degree this is a matter originating in the minds of the host nationals without reference to the realities of the particular case. There is a widespread belief, especially in less developed countries, that foreign firms act in concert with their parent governments. This feeling is due in part to the close association of government and business which is characteristic of many host societies. People growing up in such a tradition naturally assume it is common to foreign societies. And it is due in part to the few but well publicized past cases in which parent governments have intervened strongly on behalf of their foreign investors, the "gunboat" tradition.

These basic attitudes pose a problem for both firms and parent governments in the limited degree of intervention which is proper and common in current conditions. The propriety of some role for the parent government rests on the presence of its own national interest in the protection of national capital invested abroad. For the multinational firm, the intervention of the parent government may or may not be helpful. There is a trade-off between gains in the influence the parent government may be able to exert on its behalf and the negative nationalistic response which the visible involvement of the foreign nation may arouse among the host nationals.

Experts on nationalism have likened its force to that of religion, pointing out that the greatest sin a man can commit in most modern societies is treason. Thus, when the actions of the multinational firm stir people in the host society to see it as basically challenging the existence or integrity of their national body, the firm faces its most severe form of conflict with nationalism. Giving apparent reality to that image by forcing through a "victory" over the nation is an untenable solution in light of modern concepts of sovereignty and sound social and political relations. Thus the firm must find ways to either accept some symbolic "defeat" at the hands of the host nation without undue actual loss or of de-escalating the issue so that this form of nationalistic feeling ceases to be a force.

PROCESSES INVOLVING NATIONALISM AND THE MULTINATIONAL FIRM

The main elements of the processes involving multinational firms which are affected by nationalistic attitudes have already been suggested. Further comments are needed, however, to round out this part of the analysis.

First, we may consider together the questions of limited perception and the appeal-support process. The degree to which nationalism influences activities of multinational firms is determined in part by the extent to which the interests of participants are perceived. The influence increases as distance from involvement in issues increases.

In direct relations, interests of participants are usually dominant. For example, in purchasing decisions, consumers often buy goods made by multinational firms in preference to those made by national firms because of particular interests such as price or quality, even though this preference runs against their nationalistic sentiments. By the same token negotiations with union leaders, government officials, and so forth are likely to be dominated by the specific considerations of the collective interests involved. Observation of actual cases suggests, however, that the nationalistic attitudes may play a stronger role than in simple matters such as consumer buying. This may be due to at least two factors. First, the interests involved, especially in investment problems negotiated with host governments, may be complex and difficult to determine even by the leaders, so their nationalistic feelings may play a strong role. Second, they may feel under political pressure to achieve results which are satisfactory by nationalistic standards, for example, not to give up significant control to multinational firms.

In the appeal-support process, the potential support-givers not directly involved in issues are likely to have either little perception of the interests at stake or little concern with them. Thus appeal along lines of nationalism is a much stronger and often simpler process than attempting to communicate about the specific conflicts of interests involved. To a substantial degree, those in leadership positions (politicians, union officials, and the like) probably find the limited perception among non-involved countrymen satisfactory as compared to dealing with more sophisticated people to whom the niceties of issues must be explained in detail. This would suggest that there is no great effort by leaders to alter the influence of the nationalistic sentiments by injecting a greater degree of valid perception into the public mind. Improved understanding of issues comes slowly therefore through the modest efforts of multinational firms and the limited number of nationals sympathetic to them.

Second, there is the problem of nationalism in the communications process. Observation indicates that this is a major problem for multinational firms, especially in societies which do not have a tradition of objective reporting. Newsmen know that antiforeign business reports have a high reader acceptance and many of them feel considerable negative nationalistic feelings on the subject themselves. Thus there is a strong natural tendency toward nationalistically oriented processing of news. Furthermore, the multinational firm is somewhat constrained in counteracting this orientation as compared with domestic business. There are limits to the vigor with which it may state its case in public on many issues without aggravating nationalistic sensitivities, especially where conflicts of viewpoints with leading public figures are involved. The problem stated in another way is that the multinational firm cannot engage in the same range of political-public communications as a domestic firm because many actions which are acceptable by a member of the "we-group" in relations with another member will arouse nationalistic antagonism when done by an outsider.

Finally, it is worthwhile to consider the prospects for change in the nationalistic attitudes which pose problems for the multinational firm. As has been suggested in some of the points of conflict mentioned above, the nationalistic sentiments in their simple form are probably exaggerated. Action based entirely upon them may often therefore be counter to the interests of a nation. It appears that some change in them is desirable. However, this process inevitably meets substantial resistance. As noted above in two cases (the effect on culture and the question of control), elements of nationalism itself would be weakened by a greater degree of acceptance of the role of the multinational firm, and in all cases the prevailing nationalistic attitude has an inertial effect on acceptance of new viewpoints.

In the earlier discussion of change it was suggested that nationalism might be used as a general appeal by leaders seeking to deliberately expedite the process of learning new attitudes. However, only a few national leaders have urged their people to accept multinational firms using nationalistic appeals. From time to time this is done, for example, where a government is extremely anxious to bring in a new form of investment that could give a valuable lift to its economy. But the nature of that type of appeal is in such contrast to the generally held values of nationalism with respect to foreign investment that it requires strong motivation for a political leader to take the risks which it involves.

CRITICAL POINTS OF INTERACTION OF NATIONALISM AND THE MULTINATIONAL FIRM

The main components of the interaction of nationalism and the multinational firm have now been described. From this scheme a few points may be noted in which the interaction is greatest, or at least most significant, to the firm in terms of the conflicts involved and the possibilities for adaptation of policies.

First, there is the explicit incorporation of attitudes toward the firm in the body of widely held views which are a major part of the nationalism of a society. These views are the result of a complex process of learning through observation and communication with others over an extended period of time.

Second, nationalistic attitudes are a factor in the behavior of individuals and groups in face-to-face situations. On the whole, however, in such situations it would appear that the immediate and specific interests of the individuals or groups involved are of greater importance than the nationalistic sentiments.

Third, in the appeal-support process, nationalism plays a relatively greater role as compared to appeal on the basis of specific interests involved. Thus, politicians, for example, may appeal to the general public for support in conflicts with the international firm by reference to one of the relatively simplified elements of the nationalistic attitude toward the multinational corporation, such as threats to national control rather than attempting to explain in full the specific issues involved.

Finally, it is clear that the nationalistic sentiments are not of a static nature since ultimately they must be related to the individual, collective, and national group interests involved. However, the evolution of the attitudes is a complex and difficult process retarded by the basic commitment to traditionalism which is fundamental to nationalism. Thus while they may be expected to change in time, expectations of change in nationalism must be modest in terms of speed and magnitude.

NOTES

1. See, for example: Karl W. Deutsch, *Nationalism and Social Communication,* (Wiley, 1962); Carlton Hayes, *The Historical Evolution of Modern Nationalism* (Macmillan, 1931); Hans Kohn, *The Idea of Nationalism* (Macmillan, 1944) and Kalman Silvert, *Expectant Peoples* (Random House, 1963).
2. (New York: Atheneum, 1968).
3. John Fayerweather, "Attitudes of British and French Elites toward Foreign Companies," *MSU Business Topics,* Winter (1972).
4. John Fayerweather, "The Mercantile Bank Affair," *Columbia Journal of World Business,* November-December (1971).

25
Analyzing Political Risks in International Business

Franklin R. Root

International managers must plan, organize, and control business operations within and among a plurality of sovereign nation-states. This existential fact distinguishes international from uninational, domestic business. A prominent feature of national sovereignty at work today is the high level of political uncertainty that confronts the international manager, especially noticeable in the developing countries. This article explores some of the ways in which international managers can analyze political uncertainties and thereby convert them into political risks that may be rationally utilized in the decision process.

In the present context, national sovereignty means that a government has *exclusive* jurisdiction over all business entities and activities within the national territory. When an American company carries on business with or within a foreign country it is inevitably exposed to actual and potential actions on the part of the host government that may prove beneficial or detrimental to the company's interests.

It is fairly easy for a manager to evaluate the policies of a host government with respect to a particular foreign venture. It involves a straightforward collection of pertinent information. Even when such information is accurate and complete, however, it is often not a sufficient basis for business decisions involving resource commitments that extend beyond the immediate future. Informed and rational probability assessments of future host government behavior, therefore, is the key to any viable approach to the problem of political uncertainty in international business.

SOURCES OF PROBABILITY JUDGMENTS

An international manager is faced with the *possible* occurrence of a political event of any kind (such as war, revolution, coup d'etat, expropriation, taxation, devaluation, exchange control, and import restrictions) at home or abroad that can cause a loss of profit potential and/or assets in an international business operation. A "political" (as opposed to economic or social) event is one resulting from government action or is one bearing on the political authority of a nation.

An international manager judging the probability of the occurrence of a political event in a host country is actually converting a political uncertainty into a political *risk*. His judgment may be explicit or implicit, vague or precise; it may be nothing more than a belief that present conditions will persist into the future. In this sense, *any* future-oriented decision implies a probability judgment on the part of the decision-maker because he believes that the future is not random but predictable in some degree. With respect to political uncertainty, therefore, the important issues for the international manager relate to (1) the *source* of his probability judgments about future political conditions and events in a host country and (2) the utilization of such judgments as inputs in his decision process. The present article is addressed to the first issue.

The manager may derive a probability judgment from intuition, experience, information, or analysis. Only analysis meets the standards of the scientific method. *Intuition* may be defined as the sensation of knowing something without the use of reason or empirical data. The intuitive manager has a "gut feeling" that a given political event (or set of events) will or will not happen either with certainty or some likelihood. Commonly, intuition generates a conviction that a given event is *bound* to happen, that the future is known with certainty. By its very nature intuition is a subjective state of mind that can not be critically evaluated either by the manager in question or by others. This is its major weakness as a decision input.

The manager's *experience* is his memory of his own managerial performance; it is both selective and subjective. Experience alone can be a dependable guide for new decisions only if the factors that made "similiar" decisions successful in the past are present in the future. By the same token, experience is a poor guide when those factors change.

Information is data gathered for a particular purpose; it is "relevant" data. Data on a political system, government policies, administrative practices, and other factors that influence political behavior and stability constitute political information. Information may be faulty (as a result of obsolescence, incompleteness, and bias). More importantly, information as such does not indicate causal relations among political phenomena. Certain data are collected because they seem to have a bearing on political behavior, but the resulting information does not indicate which factors are independent (autonomous) or dependent (induced) or which factors are most critical to business operations.

Political *analysis* is a method of inquiry that seeks to *explain* the political behavior of a host country and its consequences for the international enterprise. It goes beyond the "what" of information to get at the "why" of change or stability, and it is directed towards the detection and measurement of causal factors and their mutual interdependence. The major tool of analysis is the *model,* a representation of reality in a conceptual form. A model identifies critical factors (variables), their mutual interdependence, and (given reliable information) the probable outcome of their interaction in specific circumstances.

Although the term "model" may strike some readers as an academic concept, it is important to understand that the international manager requires at least a subjective model to perceive and explain political circumstances and events in host countries. In a study of over one hundred international executives, this writer discovered that managers usually hold positive or negative attitudes (rather than neutral) with respect to the stability of a specific foreign government. Furthermore, their attitudes on stability correlate highly with their attitudes on the safety and profitability of investment in a given country.[1] Although not asked to do so, these managers could have rationalized their attitudes by citing certain factors, conditions, and events. In other words, they had made a model of political stability that explained the behavior of host governments.

When our models are subjective, there can be no systematic check on their congruence with outside events. Such models tend to degenerate into stereotypes. Only when explanatory models are made explicit does it become possible to examine their assumptions, logical coherence, and predictive powers. In essence, this is the value of analysis as a source of political forecasts in international business. Through analysis, international managers can also make use of intuitive insights, experience and information in ways that minimize their weaknesses.

We have gone on at some length about the merits of analyzing a given political environment because it is so seldom employed by international companies. And yet these same companies spend a great deal of time and money in formal analyses of economic and business conditions. International managers should now move to close this gap in political analysis. But to do so, they will need explicit models that explain the behavior of host governments and political systems. Are such models now available? This question is answered below.

TWO CLASSIFICATORY SCHEMES FOR POLITICAL RISKS

On a functional-descriptive level, political risks may be grouped as follows: transfer, operational, and ownership-control. *Transfer* risks are the result of uncertainty with respect to host government actions that restrict the transfer of capital, payments, products, technology, and persons into or out of the host country. Exchange controls and import restrictions (tariffs and non-tariff trade barriers) are the most notable types of transfer restrictions.

Operational risks are the result of uncertainty with respect to the policies, regulations, and administrative procedures of host governments that directly constrain the management and performance of local operations in production, marketing, finance, and other business functions. Monetary and fiscal policies, price controls, taxation, labor codes and regulations, local content requirements, and general administrative behavior fall into this category of political risk.

Ownership-control risks are the result of uncertainty about government policies and actions with respect to ownership and/or effective managerial control of the local operations of an international company. This type of risk includes possible shifts in discriminatory treatment of foreign-owned enterprises, the reservation of certain industries to local nationals, the role of state enterprise, official requirements or pressures for joint ventures with nationals (including the host government), and expropriation policies.

Although this three-way classification of political risks has descriptive value, it is not analytical. It does not attempt an explanation of changes in government behavior. To move in that direction, we offer an analytical classification that distinguishes between political/economic risks and political/social risks.

Political/economic risks are associated with the actions of a host government that are *primarily* a response to largely unanticipated internal and external changes in the national economy. Sooner or later any government must come to terms with economic realities, or it must give way to a new government that will then deal with the situation. Transfer risks tend to be political/economic in nature with the notable exception of restrictions on foreign personnel. Operations risks also tend to be political/economic although somewhat less so than transfer risks. That is to say, changes in payments restrictions or fiscal policies are ordinarily a direct response to changes in the economy.

In contrast, ownership-control risks are for the most part political/social in nature. They arise out of government responses to non-economic changes in the national society. Shifts in government policies towards joint ventures, for instance, are predominantly a response to nationalism rather than to economic forces. Expropriation is nearly always a result of political/social factors (nationalist or socialist ideologies); it can not be explained in economic terms.

Figure 1 relates the two classificatory schemes in a simple matrix. Their predominant (but by no means exclusive) relationships are indicated by X's. A detailed breakdown of the functional-descriptive categories would permit a more precise statement of these relationships.

Figure 1: Classificatory Matrix of Political Risks

	Political/Economic Risks	Political/Social Risks
Transfer Risks	X	
Operations Risks	X	
Ownership-Control Risks		X

The two analytical classes of political risk are not intended to be mutually exclusive. The emphasis is on the predominant direct cause of government action. Furthermore, it is not intended that a government be viewed as merely a passive respondent to economic and social changes. Certainly a government must respond to change in one way or another, but *how* it responds depends on the qualities of its leadership, ideology, objectives, power position, institutions, decision processes, and administrative capability. Thus a government does not respond to a given change in a predetermined manner; ordinarily there are alternatives. The course of action (or inaction) finally chosen by it may or may not have a successful outcome (slowing down inflation, for instance), but it will create a different set of political risks for the international manager. A full analysis of political uncertainty, therefore, must seek not only to detect and measure economic and social changes that will compel a response by the host government but also the government's capability to make a specific response. Figure 2 portrays the resulting analytical schemes as a simple model.

A government may, of course, seek to initiate economic and social

Figure 2: General Scheme for Political Risk Analysis

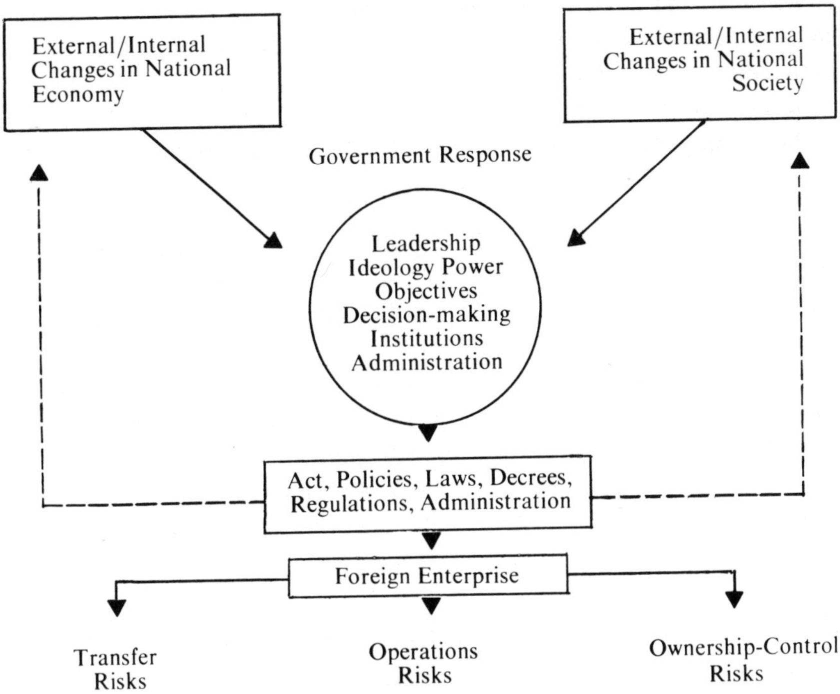

```
┌─────────────────────┐                    ┌─────────────────────┐
│ External/Internal   │                    │ External/Internal   │
│ Changes in National │                    │ Changes in National │
│ Economy             │                    │              Society│
└─────────────────────┘                    └─────────────────────┘

                    Government Response

                         ╭──────────────╮
                        │   Leadership    │
                        │ Ideology Power  │
                        │   Objectives    │
                        │ Decision-making │
                        │  Institutions   │
                        │ Administration  │
                         ╰──────────────╯

              ┌──────────────────────────────────┐
              │ Act, Policies, Laws, Decrees,     │
              │ Regulations, Administration        │
              └──────────────────────────────────┘

                   ┌──────────────────────┐
                   │  Foreign Enterprise   │
                   └──────────────────────┘

    Transfer              Operations           Ownership-Control
    Risks                 Risks                Risks
```

changes rather than simply respond to them, and a revolutionary government may try to create a new economic and social system; a reform government will strive for improvements within the existing system. A notable and common example of the government as change agent is the commitment of governments in developing countries to the goals of economic development. But in its role as change agent a government is still constrained by economic and social factors that limit or shape its possible achievements. A government is never wholly a free agent. Although recognizing the role of government as an agent of change, it is analytically most useful for international managers to view the behavior of host governments as responsive to economic and social change, mediated by their leadership, ideology, and capabilities. In any event, changes in government behavior will have repercussions on the national economy and society, as indicated by the dashed lines in Figure 2.

The distinction between political/economic and political/social uncertainties and risks is helpful in the analysis of host government behavior because two different sets of models are appropriate. The assessment of political/economic risks is primarily dependent on concepts and models drawn from economics while the assessment of political/social risks depend on concepts and models drawn from political science, sociology, and psychology. Unfortunately, the latter fields fall far short of economics in the availability of operational models that are useful to the international manager. For this reason, the forecasting of political/social risks is much less sophisticated than the forecasting of political/economic risks.

FORECASTING POLITICAL – ECONOMIC RISKS

Short-run and intermediate forecasts of political/economic risks (running up to five years or so) can make profitable use of models drawn from economics. Three kinds of models are particularly helpful: models of economic stability and instability, models of balance of payments disequilibrium and adjustment, and models of the foreign exchange market. These models may be linked (the output of one model providing the input of a second model) to build a comprehensive representation of both internal and external economic behavior. One aggregate model goes far to explain political/economic risks in host countries, especially in developing ones.

This model both starts and ends with government action, as shown in Figure 3.

Figure 3: A Political/Economic Forecasting Model

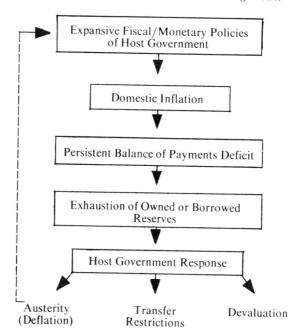

The sequential steps of the model are as follows: (1) expansive fiscal/-monetary policies of the host government cause (2) inflation that, in turn, causes (3) a persistent deficit in the balance of payments (mainly via higher imports) that compels (4) remedial government action to remove or suppress the deficit. Although this model does not forecast the specific adjustment policies of the host government, it does indicate the policy options: austerity, transfer restrictions, and devaluation. When supplied with accurate information, the international manager can use this model to make probability forecasts of the *timing* of host government action. But to forecast the probability of a specific government response, the manager must go beyond the model to an investigation of the government itself. Questions such as these are pertinent: What has the government done in similar situations in the past? Is the government committed to avoid certain courses of action (such as import quotas or exchange restrictions) through its membership in General Agreement on Tariffs and Trade (GATT) or the International Monetary Fund (IMF)? Is the government strong enough to adopt an austerity program? What is the government ideology with respect to market mechanisms as opposed to market controls? Does the government view devaluation as a loss of percentage?

How far it would pay the manager to push the analysis would depend on the sensitivity of his business operations (both actual and planned) to the particular mode of payments adjustment. If, for example, operations were very sensitive to exchange devaluation, then he should continue the analysis beyond a probability judgment of devaluation to a judgment of the degree of devaluation. For this purpose, the demand-supply model of the foreign exchange market would be a useful tool, but it would have to be supplemented by an analysis of the host government's leadership.

Models of long-run economic development and growth are less useful than short-run models. Fortunately, an international manager seldom needs to make forecasts beyond a period of five years. Long-run models, however, may help in anticipating the probable direction of shifts in government policies towards foreign trade and investment. Suffice it to say here that such shifts tend to accompany transformations of an economy as it moves through various stages of development. It is not mere chance that the high-consumption countries of North America and Western Europe follow generally liberal policies towards foreign trade and investment while the developing countries impose an array of restrictions. As Japan moves into a high-consumption economy, we can reasonably expect a liberalization of its present import and investment barriers. By the same token, most developing countries will continue to restrict imports and police the entry of foreign capital for a generation or more.

FORECASTING POLITICAL – SOCIAL RISKS

Political scientists are now turning towards an analysis of political systems to explain the forces of instability, change, and modernization in developing countries. With isolated exceptions, however, their models are conceptual and verbal rather than operational and quantitative. We offer here only a crude model that nevertheless can guide the international manager in his evaluation of the political stability of a host country.

A political system is most usefully defined for our purposes as a set of actors who perform a social function that involves "deliberation and decision-making for the purpose of providing adjustment and reconciliation of the all-prevailing aspirations."[2] Government is one of many actors in this system, but it is the key actor because only its decisions are authoritative and backed by legitimate force. Relationships among four elements of this system —decision-making, power, ideology, and institutions—make up the political process which is the transformation of conflict among interest groups into authoritative (official) decisions.

Decision-making is the most universal function of a political system. Political decisions are made by official organs of the state with the expectation they will be obeyed. In analyzing decision-making in a particular political system, questions such as these are pertinent: Who makes political decisions? How are these decision-makers selected? What is the composition of the political elite? How are decisions made? By tradition? By a charismatic leader? By rational deliberation? We may hypothesize that the long-run evolution of all political systems is toward secularization, that is to say, towards political decision-making that rests on empirical information, analysis, and a rational choice of alternative courses of action to achieve objectives which are also evaluated in rational terms. Although the political systems of the industrial West are today highly secularized, those of many developing countries fall short, with significant elements of tradition, charismatic leadership, and emotion shaping their political decisions.

Power refers to the intent and capacity of a group or individual to control or influence the behavior of others. Every political system has a power configuration, a distribution of power among organized social groups that commonly include the government (political elite), political parties, the military, the church, economic organizations (labor unions, trade associations, and the like), landowners, and intellectuals (writers, artists, journalists, professors, and students). Key questions relating to power are as follows:

What is the power configuration of the organized social groups? Is one group or coalition of groups clearly dominant? Is the power distribution stable or shifting? Answers to these and related questions will provide an understanding of the power dynamics in a particular country.

Political *ideology* denotes the patterns of thought and belief that relate to the state and the government. The social function of political ideology is to legitimize the organized force of the state. Hence the presence of conflicting or hostile ideologies in a system is one of the best indices of instability. Since ideologies generate the motivations of power groups, a study of group ideology is of critical importance in forecasting how a group will behave in the future. The international manager should raise these questions: What are the ideologies of the various actors (groups) in the political system of the host country? Are these ideologies hostile to international business? In which ways? With respect to the latter, two ideologies are particularly hostile to international business and are often shared by the same group: nationalism and Marxist socialism. Nationalism assumes many guises. When extreme, everything foreign, including foreign enterprise, becomes suspect. In developing countries, nationalism has been a major source of public support for the expropriation of foreign enterprise. Marxist socialism is opposed to all private enterprise, whether foreign or domestic, but it frequently combines with nationalism so that its force falls mainly on foreign enterprise.

Political *institutions* include both the formal organs of government and informal organs (political parties and other organized social groups) that can influence the deliberation and decision-making of government leaders. Analysis should focus on what these institutions do and how they do it. Institutions that look the same (such as legislatures and labor unions) may perform different political functions in different countries.

As shown in Figure 4, the relationships among these four aspects of political behavior constitute the political process whereby conflicts among social groups are translated into government decisions and policies.

Figure 4: The Political Process

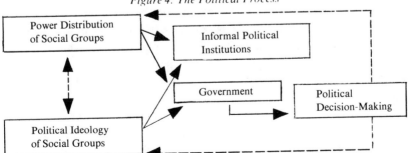

Although all the elements of this model are inter-dependent, changes in power distribution and ideology are the most common sources of political stability or instability. Shifts in power distribution (for example, the ascendancy of a political party or the military that are *not* accompanied by radical shifts in ideology will provoke non-revolutionary changes in the system. Although employing physical force, most coup d'etats fall into this category.[3] When, however, a major shift in power distribution is also accompanied by a radical shift in ideology (for example, the recent coup d'etat in Libya), a revolutionary situation is created that may transform the political system itself with a new set of political institutions. Generally speaking, changes that cause a divergence between ideology (values) and the power distribution lead to conflict. If a government fails to bring about a "synchronization" between values and the power configuration through reform, propaganda, or negotiation and it does not have the power to repress conflict, then the government will lose authority (legitimacy) and eventually collapse, either by violent or non-violent means.[4]

CONCLUSION

The international manager must learn to cope with political uncertainties both at home and abroad just as he must learn to cope with economic and market uncertainties. Frequently, however, the manager makes his forecasts of host government behavior on the basis of intuition, experience, or information, all of which have major weaknesses. This is understandable when we consider that managers ordinarily have no training for political analysis comparable to their training for economic and business analysis. But it is hardly reassuring.

This article has argued for a greater use by international managers of the analysis of political risks involving the explicit use of models as the source of probability judgments about the policies and actions of host governments. To demonstrate this approach, two models were briefly described, one for political/economic risk analysis and the other for political/social risk analysis. These were supplemented by a classificatory matrix of political risks and a general scheme for political risk analysis. Once probability judgments are derived from political analysis, managers must utilize them as decision inputs in a rational, coherent approach. Expected-value and other decision models are available for this purpose. However elaborate the decision model, its output depends on the quality of its inputs.

This article has not considered the response or strategy of international business managers with respect to political risks. A proper strategy choice may minimize both political/economic and political/social risks in host countries. Clearly the analysis of political risks is an important element in the choice of optimal strategies for international business.

NOTES

1. Franklin R. Root, "Attitudes of American Executives Towards Foreign Governments," *Economic and Business Bulletin* (January 1968).
2. Roy C. Macridis, *The Study of Comparative Government* (New York: Random House, 1955). This section is indebted to the discussion in this text.
3. Coup d'etats are much more common than elections as a means of new government formation in the developing countries. Luttwak records 88 coups d'etats (successful and unsuccessful) during the period 1945-67. Of these, only six carried out a state-directed revolutionary change (Bolivia, Cuba, Iraq, Syria, Egypt and Czechoslovakia in 1948). See Edward Luttwak, *Coup d'Etat* (Greenwich, Conn.: Fawcett Publications, Inc., 1969), pp. 204-7.
4. Along the same lines, Johnson states: "So long as a society's values and the realities with which it must deal in order to exist are in harmony with each other, the society is immune from revolution." See Chalmers Johnson, *Revolutionary Change* (Boston: Little, Brown and Company, 1966), p. 60.

Chapter Seven:
The Multinational Enterprise
and Host Governments

DEVELOPING COUNTRIES

26
International Business-Government Negotiations in Developing Countries

A. Kapoor

Governments of developing countries are playing an increasingly important role as planners, regulators, and participants in the industrialization process of their countries. Large foreign enterprises (the multinational company)[1] possess the resources (capital, technology, management, access to foreign markets) required by the developing countries. However, the willingness of developing countries to accept, and of the multinational enterprise to offer, resources will largely depend on a mutual understanding of the various forces influencing their decision-making process and approach toward negotiations.[2]

THE LITERATURE

The literature on the subject of interactions between host governments and foreign enterprise is very limited. Dr. Richard D. Robinson's *International Business Policy* explores the historical association of Western enterprise with the colonization process in developing countries, and the impact of this association on the current attitudes and policies of these countries in relation to Western enterprise. Other observers of the subject are Behrman,[3] Fayerweather,[4] Fowler,[5] Martyn,[6] Mikesell,[7] and Vernon.[8]

Literature on the more specific topic of international business negotiations is even more limited. Hanner[9] and Williams[10] have dealt with this

This paper was read at the 1971 Annual Meeting of the Association for Asian Studies, Washington, D.C., on March 29, 1971. Although this paper focuses on South Asia (India and Pakistan) and Southeast Asia (Indonesia, Singapore, Malaysia, Thailand, and the Philippines), its basic premises are applicable to the other developing nations of the world.

question, and Aharoni's penetrating study of the *Foreign Investment Decision Process* [11] brings some insight into the international business negotiation process.

The increasing importance of the subject is reflected by the research on the general subject of international business-government relations being conducted at major universities. Professor Raymond Vernon of the Harvard Business School is coordinating a project on the "Multinational Enterprise and the Nation State." An important part of the project is Professor Behrman's study tracing the sources of the tensions growing out of the development of the multinational enterprise before World War II, identifying critical events since the war, and defining the issues of jurisdictional avoidance and jurisdictional conflict that underlie the relations between business and government. Professor Behrman's work has resulted in three highly illuminating publications: *Some Patterns in the Rise of the Multinational Enterprise; National Interests and the Multinational Enterprise: Tensions Among the North Atlantic Countries;* and *U.S. International Business and Governments.*

Professor Raymond Mikesell of the University of Oregon is studying the relationships between host governments and foreign companies in the resource industries throughout the world. A key theme of the study is the types of contractual arrangements between foreign companies and host countries which seem best suited to both the expansion of resource output of the Free World and the maximum contribution to economic development.

Professor John Fayerweather of New York University is studying the conflict of nationalism and the multinational corporation with the objective of exploring ways in which conflict can be reduced. In addition, he is studying the attitudes of opinion-forming groups (labor leaders, students) in several countries toward foreign investors.

Research on the effect of private foreign investments on specific Asian countries is limited. While some information is available for South Korea,[12] Taiwan,[13] Indonesia,[14] Singapore,[15] Malaysia,[16] and India,[17] these studies do not explore the patterns of interactions between foreign enterprise and the host government.

On the general subject of international business-host government relations, Ballon,[18] Abegglen,[19] Kobyashi,[20] Glazer,[21] and Yanaga[22] have written illuminating analyses on Japan. The author of this paper has offered a detailed analysis of the dynamics of negotiation between large foreign companies and the Indian government and has suggested guidelines for international business negotiations in developing countries.[23]

NATURE OF NEGOTIATION

The term "negotiation" can be described as follows:

> ... two elements must normally be present for negotiation to take place; there must be both common interests and issues of conflict. Without common interest there is nothing to negotiate for, and without conflict there is nothing to negotiate about.[24]
>
> Moreover, negotiation can be defined in either a narrow or a broad sense. A relatively narrow definition is: Negotiation is a process in which explicit proposals are put forward ostensibly with the purpose of reaching agreement on an exchange or on the realization of a common interest where conflicting interests are present . . . It is the confrontation of explicit proposals that distinguishes negotiation . . . from tacit bargaining and other types of conflict behavior.[25]

In addition to explicit proposals, the negotiating parties make other moves—those of tacit bargaining—to strengthen their position and weaken that of the opponent or to influence the outcome in various other ways.

Negotiation does not necessarily lead to explicit agreement on all points; in fact, agreement may be reached on only some of the explicit proposals being negotiated. Even then agreements vary widely in their degree of specificity and in the extent of disagreement which remains. The outcome of negotiations is more than just an explicit agreement.

> Negotiation may change the position of the parties and their mutual relations in many . . . ways. The outcome may include, for example, tacit understanding between the parties, a clarification of the points of disagreement, a reorientation of national objectives, new commitments to third parties (allies, domestic groups, or world opinion), and propaganda effects. Many of these results may outweigh in importance whatever explicit agreement is arrived at.[26]

The negotiation process includes strategies and tactics expressed within a broader framework of interactions between groups with both common and conflicting interests. Each group has its own concept of what is "right," "reasonable," or "appropriate" in negotiations; also each group has its own expectations of the likely response of an opposing group to an issue, event, or mood. In highlighting the key characteristics of "strategy," Schelling states:

> . . . it focuses on the fact that each participant's "best" choice of action depends on what he expects the other to do, and that "strategic behavior" is concerned with influencing another's choice by working on his expectation of how one's own behavior is related to his.[27]

Schelling calls this "the theory of interdependent decision"[28] —a fundamental feature of the negotiation process.

A negotiator's expectations of the response of an opposing group are determined by his own "self-reference criterion," i.e., "the unconscious reference to one's own cultural values";[29] Aharoni emphasizes the same theme:

Foreign countries are compared to the United States, judged according to United States' standards. The larger the discrepancy in habits, culture, and business conduct between a foreign country and the United States, the stronger the subjective uncertainty.[30]

Aharoni adds that the subjective estimates of facts and payoff expectations change with time.[31] Lee concludes that "the root cause of most international business problems overseas" is the self-reference criterion of the American businessman[32]—a comment which is equally valid for businessmen and government officials from Asia and elsewhere. Therefore, in interacting with private and public groups in Asia—a non-Western social-cultural context—the Western company experiences greater uncertainty than in the Canadian, Western European, or even Latin American contexts.

A handful of host government officials and corporate executives are charged with the responsibility of initiating and negotiating foreign investment proposals with the result that international business negotiations, particularly in developing countries, are likely to be between fairly limited and well-defined groups of individuals. In addition, given the socio-cultural characteristics of developing countries, an effective relationship between two individuals, particularly when one of them is a foreigner, develops only over a period of time as a result of several interactions of a personal and professional nature. Therefore, the negotiation process is significantly affected by the nature of the relationship between the negotiators from corporations and those from the host government.[33]

International business negotiations take place within a broader framework than domestic negotiations, as observed by Williams:

The art of politics and the concepts of social science can become as important, or even more important, to the success of an investment negotiation as hard-headed technical and financial calculations or a carefully prepared legal and administrative basis for an overseas organization.[34]

OBJECTIVES AND SCOPE

The objectives of this paper are: (1) to highlight selected characteristics and to offer guidelines as the first level of generalization on international business-government negotiations in developing countries with particular emphasis on Asia; and (2) to suggest additional areas of research especially of an interdisciplinary nature. More specifically, this paper explores the effect on international business-government negotiations of: career backgrounds of government officials and corporate executives; precedent orientation of decisions; emphasis on short- versus long-term goals; concept of commitment; publicity and secrecy; association of a foreign government with a project; and role of internal and external interest groups.

NEGOTIATION CHARACTERISTICS

CAREER BACKGROUND

A very limited number of decision makers in Asian governments have a sufficient comprehension of economic/business issues largely because their career orientation has been in other areas such as politics, military, civil administration, and foreign relations.[35] Corporate executives, particularly at the most senior levels of management, have a very limited understanding of the non-economic forces influencing government actions and policies.[36] Consequently, host government officials and corporate executives experience serious problems of communication with each other.

Several reasons account for the lack of economic/business orientation of key government decision makers. First, almost exclusive emphasis on achieving political independence has resulted in promoting individuals with a strong inclination for politics. Upon achieving independence, the primary objective of the different interest groups is to consolidate their political power. Second, in several Asian countries, business activity is not viewed as an "honorable" profession, especially when compared to some form of public service such as government official, a medical doctor, a lawyer, or a member of the armed services. In many countries, businessmen are considered to be too closely associated with foreign colonial powers. Foreign enterprise largely from the former colonizing country and alien minority groups (Indians and Chinese) was accused of wanting to maintain the colonial form of government to protect their economic interests. In addition, political leaders in the forefront of independence movements and in the post-independence political consolidation period viewed indigenous business groups, especially the large business enterprises, as being too narrow in their outlook and exclusively concerned with the immediate questions of profits. Third, because of these reasons key decision makers are suspicious of the motives and methods of businessmen.

The implications of these characteristics is that the negotiation process between foreign investors and host governments in Asia is often colored by mutual distrust and suspicion. Therefore, negotiations take time, and the foreign investor has to attempt to reduce the fears of the host government decision makers.

PRECEDENT ORIENTATION OF DECISIONS

Both the host government and the foreign company consider investment proposals with reference to past proposals and expectations for the future. Host government officials pursue this approach for several reasons. First, some countries have had very limited experience with foreign investments. For example, the Indonesian government in the post-Sukarno period has been anxious to attract foreign investments. However, because of its limited experience, it has been anxious not to establish precedents (e.g., royalty terms) which would reduce its flexibility in subsequent negotiations with foreign investors. Second, governments frequently wish to implement new policies once existing policies have achieved their objectives. For example, the South Korean government is now favoring joint ventures with majority foreign ownership over wholly-owned foreign subsidiaries. Therefore, it is anxious to approve a number of projects with this feature (even if other terms of compensation such as royalty rates, technical fees, etc. are excessive) in order to create precedents for negotiations with subsequent investors. Third, in some countries, like India or Japan, a number of foreign investments have been made over a relatively long period of time. In these countries, precedents created by past investments play an important role in government decision making because a sufficiently large number of projects already exist. Even new projects with some unique characteristics are evaluated with reference to existing projects.

Government officials stress precedent orientation of decisions because such decisions are relatively safe. Officials at the ministerial and increasingly even those at the secretariat level are exposed to the broader political forces of a country. Thus, a decision on foreign investments in fertilizers is viewed as highly desirable by one political group and highly detrimental to the national interest by another political group. In addition, officials are assigned to a department of an agency for relatively short periods of time. This results in the natural tendency not to upset the apple cart. Moreover, the official does not have a full understanding of the decision making processes of his new department and is unable to effectively introduce an innovative approach. Finally, since decision-making authority is not lodged in any one department or ministry but rather shared among several ministries, any one official is unable to generate an innovative approach across ministries.

Corporate executives also stress precedent orientation in decision making because of the relative safety of such decisions. For example, executives often insist on certain terms of investment because the company has always sought these terms. Moreover, an innovative approach requires greater expenditure of time, especially at the corporate level. Often such additional expenditure of executive time is not appreciated because Asian operations contribute a very small percentage of an American company's total revenues or profits. Another explanation is that executives are assigned to foreign countries for relatively short durations of time, seldom exceeding three years. Consequently, the executive seldom wishes to make waves. The improvements he introduces might bear fruit after he is reassigned to another country.

Fourth, a precedent-oriented approach requires less time of senior decision makers. This reason is particularly important in governments where decision-making authority is concentrated in the hands of a few officials.

Other writers have noted the orientation of organizations towards weighing precedents in reaching decisions. Cyert and March state that "organizations accept precedents as binding and look at standard operating procedures as constraints in any problem-solving situation."[37] Aharoni also notes the precedent orientation of companies in the foreign investment decision process where "many previous 'policies' are taken as given and become constraints in the decision process."[38]

Negotiators view their decisions in relation to their impact on current and future negotiations. Schelling states that the advantage in negotiations "goes to the party that can persuasively point to an array of other negotiations in which its own position would be prejudiced if it made a concession in this one."[39] When the same two parties are to negotiate other topics, whether simultaneously or in the future, Schelling states that a special case of interrelated negotiation occurs:

The logic of this case is more subtle; to persuade the other that one cannot afford to recede, one says in effect, "If I conceded you here, you would revise your estimate of me in our other negotiations; to protect my reputation with you I must hold firm." The second party is simultaneously the "third party" to whom one's bargaining reputation can be pledged.[40]

It is unlikely that Asian governments will arbitrarily discard the precedents established by their decisions in the past.[41] However, their primary thrust will be to generate new precedents which are conducive to the achievement of emerging policies on foreign investments (foreign ownership, management control, use of nationals, etc.). Therefore, reference to past precedents by foreign investors is not likely to carry much weight in negotiations with host governments. New negotiation strategies by foreign companies will be necessary which recognize the precedent-generating motive of host governments in Asia.

SHORT-TERM GOALS

Do groups place greater emphasis on achieving their short-term goals rather than their long-term ones? Is agreement on terms of investment more likely if the short-term goals of groups are similar? The term "goals" as used here refers to the objectives of the different groups (actors) associated with a proposal; "means" refers to the respective preferences of the different groups (actors) on the method used to achieve these objectives; "short-term" refers to the period of time an actor — corporate executive or government official — expects to remain in a particular assignment and to the time period used to measure a group or an actor's performance.

Both government officials and corporate executives place greater weight on achieving their respective short-term objectives. The primary reason is that the performance of an official or an executive is measured largely by his achievements over the short-term. For example, the minister of foreign trade or the minister for petroleum and chemicals wishes to show an increase in exports or in fertilizer manufacturing during their stay in the particular ministry. In many cases, such positions are headed by the same minister for less than three years.

Similarly, countries often stress achievement of short-term goals. Shortly after gaining a reasonable amount of power in Indonesia, Suharto wanted to attract private foreign investments. Therefore, the government announced policies and regulations which would ensure a rapid inflow of foreign capital, at least in the form of "commitments" if not actually in the form of concrete investments. Since the primary objective was to demonstrate to the world that Indonesia was once again joining the community of nations, host government officials did not necessarily stress the long-term desirability of some of the foreign investments approved by the government.

In most cases, foreign investors and host government officials experience relatively little difficulty in agreeing on the long-term effects of a project: improved foreign investment climate; potential increase of foreign exchange earnings; generation of domestic skills. Such long-term objectives are of a sufficiently broad nature so as not to violate the specific short-term goals of the actors.

The implication for negotiations is that the foreign investor and the host government should recognize that the terms of investment sought or granted are evaluated particularly for their impact on the short-term goals of the key decision makers.

COMMITMENT

Foreign investment decisions by companies[42] and by governments are seldom made by an individual. Such decisions are almost invariably group decisions. Therefore, commitments by an official or an executive are not the same as commitments by their respective decision-making units, particularly when the size of the decision-making unit is large, contains a number of diverse interests, or when the decisions are likely to have significant economic and political effects on the host society. (The term "commitment" is aptly defined by Aharoni as representing a "state of mind, a feeling that guides action, not a legal obligation."[43])

The primary reason for group commitments versus commitments by an individual is that no one government official has the power to commit the entire decision-making unit. For example, all the Asian countries have established organizations for the specific purpose of facilitating the decision-making process on foreign investment proposals.[44] The primary function of such organizations is to encourage and cajole the various ministries concerned with foreign investments to react quickly and decisively on proposals. However, a recurrent problem, even when these investment promotion organizations have the support of key senior decision makers, is that the representative of a ministry does not wish to commit himself until he learns of the position of other ministries. The complexity of the task of coordinating decisions is revealed by the fact that in most Asian countries as many as ten different ministries or departments are involved in reacting to a foreign investment proposal. Of course, a key reason for adopting this approach is that government officials feel that a group decision is a safe decision.

For example, in India and in several other Asian countries, a project proposal above a certain level of capitalization is decided upon by the entire cabinet. While the operating ministry most directly responsible for the industry in which the project falls is still charged with the responsibility for the mechanics of negotiation, implementation, and operations, the fact that the entire cabinet makes the final decision reduces the exposure to criticism of any one minister.

In many countries (Japan, India, Indonesia) decisions are made by consensus. Japanese companies and government ministries insist on maintaining harmony in the process of decision making based largely on reaching a consensus of the various members participating in the decision-making unit.[45] In other countries (India, Indonesia) the diversity of political groups and the absence of a group acknowledged as a leader requires a consensus approach to decision making.[46]

The element of safety in group decisions is also true in the decision-making process of the American company, but the emphasis on an executive reaching decisions independently is greater than in governments. An important implication of this characteristic is that executives get very impatient with the long periods of time it takes for host governments to decide on proposals. However, host governments feel that the loss incurred through delays is far less than the benefits of achieving an appropriate expression of views made by various officials and informal groups who have an interest in the project.

PUBLICITY AND SECRECY
Foreign investment proposals are frequently accompanied by publicity.

What is the impact of such publicity on negotiations? In general, publicity tends to have an adverse effect on the negotiation process between the foreign company and the host government. Publicity is defined here as comments on a foreign investment proposal made by government officials, corporate executives, newspaper correspondents and editors, members of Parliament, and other individuals and groups and disclosed to the public largely through the press.

In many projects, especially those involving significant levels of investment, publicity tends to expose government officials to public scrutiny which is not conducive to careful consideration and private judgment of the pros and cons of a proposal. In addition, publicity tends to make a project appear more important in economic or political terms than it might be in reality. Also, economic and political interest groups in a country use newspaper reports on a proposal (incorrect as they might be) as ammunition to argue against its acceptance.

Publicity is a major tool of negotiation. Frequently, parties to a negotiation will purposely disclose confidential information to strengthen their bargaining position. Schelling observes that representatives of governments and other organizations

. . . seem often to create a bargaining position by public statements, statements calculated to arouse a public opinion that permits no concessions to be made. If a binding public opinion can be cultivated and made evident to the other side, the initial position can thereby be made visibly "final."[47]

Publicity should be avoided at least until a final agreement has been reached between the foreign investor and the host government. However, both groups should realize that, particularly in the case of large foreign investment proposals, leaks to the press cannot be completely avoided. Therefore, each negotiating unit should develop its own program for the management of communication — at what stage of negotiations, under what circumstances, and by what means information should be released to public media.

A major influence on negotiation is the ability of the different participants to keep their deliberations a secret. However, in negotiating with governments in Asia, it is very difficult if not impossible to do so. This is due to many factors. First, government officials and other local businessmen interpret the meaning of the term "secret" far differently from the American corporate executive. To Asians, a secret is a valued piece of information which should be shared with trusted friends or to those to whom one owes an obligation. In addition, claiming to know a secret tends to elevate a persons' status in the eyes of those around him. Second, a large number of officials and ministers are involved in deciding on a proposal, which facilitates the disclosure of confidential information, but at the same time makes it difficult to identify the source of the disclosure. Third, the key decision-making centers are concentrated in the capitals of Asian countries. Businessmen and government officials interact frequently resulting in disclosure of information. Fourth, government officials often wish to avoid secrets in negotiations on purpose. By keeping interested economic and political groups informed of ongoing negotiations, government officials hope to prevent charges of corruption or collusion with foreign companies.

The key implication is that a prospective investor is unable to surprise his competitors in the terms and conditions of investment he is willing to accept. Therefore, competitors can also modify their proposals so as not to be at a comparative disadvantage.

ASSOCIATION OF A FOREIGN GOVERNMENT

Investments by foreign companies can facilitate economic growth of developing countries and in this way constitute an important means by which governments can achieve their policy objectives. However, government officials or other groups in the host society are often of the view that foreign investors use the "muscle" (foreign aid, import quotas) of their home governments in negotiating investment proposals.

Governments are highly sensitive to the question of sovereignty and self-determination of national interest, particularly in Asian countries with a long colonial history. Therefore, the host country's perception of the unfair use of his home government's influence by a foreign investor is likely to transfer discussions from the relatively less sensitive and more objective plane of economic reasoning to the substantially more sensitive and subjective realm of relations between two sovereign states.

A company's tendency to use its home government's influence is largely determined by the nature of the project and the preferences of the key corporate executives. In most instances of foreign investments (which are generally small in size — less than $2 million in capitalization),[48] companies will typically refer to the embassy for introductions to government officials and to learn of the domestic political situation. However, for large projects, a company is more inclined to use the assistance of its home government, if it feels that such assistance is forthcoming in a manner which is likely to help the company's position in the country substantially.

Several observers of international business have commented on the political implications of foreign investments. Behrman notes that host governments fear that foreign investors are not truly international but rather are "under the sway of another national government."[49] He adds:

The enterprise (the foreign investor) will not be viewed (by the host government) simply in "technical and economic" terms. There is too much potential political control through the exercise of its power and too much potential interference by the parent government (of the large foreign investor) to permit governments to view the enterprise in non-political terms.[50]

Behrman concludes:

The ability of one government to impose its will, through the multinational enterprise, into another political entity or nation-state will continue to demonstrate that there are, at present, no "truly international" enterprises.[51]

Vernon, writing along the same lines, adds that the unease of host governments regarding the multinational enterprise

comes close to being pathological when the suspicion exists that the multinational group is acting in partnership with some foreign sovereign. In the less developed world, for instance, there is always the fear that the subsidiaries of U.S. parents, even though they may be nominal nationals of the host country . . . may be able to use the U.S. foreign aid program to influence the outcome of the dispute.[52]

In addition, Robinson states bluntly that

the foreign policy of at least a modern *liberal* state is very largely designed to service private international business interests that have developed — or are anticipated.[53]

Host governments are often of the opinion that senior executives of large U.S. companies have ready access to officials at the highest levels of their governments and that they attempt to promote their business objectives through official channels.[54] More direct and obvious interference by the U.S. government in the activities of U.S. companies overseas is noted by Behrman:

. . . the past and potential interference by the U.S. government in overseas business has stamped the major U.S. multinational enterprise as clearly American—potentially dominated by foreign or domestic policies of the U.S. government. The interference of the U.S. government in sales by IBM and other computer companies to the French Government drove home this subservience to American policies, undoing some of IBM's efforts to stress its local orientation in the countries of Europe.[55]

Host governments, particularly of developing countries, will continue to fear that the foreign private investor is under the sway of his national government. The governments of capital exporting countries will view private investments as a means of furthering their broader political objectives. Private investors will continue to seek the assistance of their governments in promoting and projecting their interests in foreign countries.

The critical question, therefore, is not whether control rests with the government of the foreign investor. Rather, the critical question is the extent and the manner in which such potential control is disclosed to or perceived by the host government and the wider host society. The specific course of action will vary by the particular circumstances of an investment proposal. However, as a matter of general policy, foreign investors should portray themselves to the host government as independent agents.

INTEREST GROUPS

A group attempts to promote the views and policies of its members. Such a group can be external (outside a country but having influence over its economic and political policies) or internal (indigenous to the country). In what ways do interest groups influence the negotiation process?

External groups. The primary external interest groups with significant powers over host nations are the international lending and development institutions, such as the World Bank and the International Monetary Fund. Such institutions have loaned large sums of money to Asian countries on the conditions that the recipient will accept the changes in policies and practices advocated by the lending institutions. The de facto devaluation of the Filipino peso is an example of the power of these institutions. The critical feature of the "recommendations" of such institutions is that governments are far less critical of their views than those of any individual donor country. A good example is the reaction in the Philippines if the United States had suggested or caused a de facto devaluation of the peso.

The implication for negotiations is that companies should attempt to secure the support of multilateral agencies (Asian Development Bank) in support of their position. Host government officials will be less offended by such solicitation of representation than through the use of government influence.

Internal groups. Foreign investment proposals arouse considerable interest on the part of economic and political groups in Asian countries. Therefore, the views of such groups exercise an important influence on negotiations between the foreign company and the host government.

Indigenous business interests, especially the large organizations, often fear the entry of foreign companies on the grounds that they have access to larger and better resources, and therefore create additional competition in domestic markets. Consequently, local business groups and individual businessmen constantly interact with government officials to convey their views on the desirability of an investment proposal. Government officials listen to the views of businessmen because they are contributors to political parties and because they can motivate political leaders of opposition parties to agitate over the desirability of a certain investment proposal.[56]

The implication for the foreign company, especially in the context of increasing restrictions on the entry of foreign capital in Asian countries, is to secure some form of local sponsorship, i.e., gain the collaboration or support of an indigenous group for the particular proposal. The local sponsors are far better placed to counteract the moves of other indigenous groups opposing a proposal. For example, a foreign executive, unlike an indigenous businessman, exposes himself to severe criticism if he tries to influence local political personalities.

OBSERVATIONS

The respective approaches to negotiation used by foreign companies and host governments are determined by a collectivity of issues, events, and moods engendered through and by a number of actors functioning within a complex, interrelated, and dynamic environment. Aharoni's observation on the foreign investment decision process is quite applicable to international business-government negotiation.

In summary (the negotiation process) is a very complicated social process, involving an intricate structure of attitudes and opinions, social relationships, both inside and outside the firm, and the way such attitudes, opinions, and social relations are changing. It contains various elements of individual and organizational behavior, influenced by the past and the perception of the future as well as the present. It is composed of a large number of decisions, made by different people at different points in time. The understanding of the final outcome of such a process depends on an understanding of all its stages and parts. [57]

The points explored in this paper offer at best a glimpse of some of the characteristics of international business-government negotiations. Additional research is needed on each of these (and other) characteristics. Some of the more promising approaches for research on the subject are:

1. in-depth case studies analyzing the dynamics of negotiations between foreign companies and host governments;

2. an effort to develop a conceptual framework as we gain greater understanding of the subject;

3. a determined effort to achieve an interdisciplinary approach by collaborating with scholars from other fields, such as politics, international relations, game theory, and sociology.

NOTES

1. A large number of definitions exist, depending on the set of criteria preferred by the observer.
2. For additional comments, see, A. Kapoor, "Business-Government Relations Become Respectable," *Columbia Journal of World Business* (July-August 1970).
3. Jack N. Behrman, *Some Patterns in the Rise of the Multinational Enterprise,* Research Paper no. 18 (Chapel Hill, N.C.: Graduate School of Business, 1969); see in particular pp. 118-129.

4. John Fayerweather, "19th Century Ideology and 20th Century Reality," *Columbia Journal of World Business*, Winter (1966), pp. 77-84.
5. Henry Fowler, "National Interest and Multinational Business," *California Management Review*, Fall (1965), pp. 3-12.
6. Howe Martyn, "Multinational Corporations in a Nationalistic World," *Challenge* (November-December 1965), pp. 3-16.
7. Raymomd F. Mikesell, "Healing the Breach Over Foreign Resource Exploitation," *Columbia Journal of World Business* (March, 1967), pp. 25-32.
8. As a part of the research on the project on "Multinational Enterprise and the Nation State," Raymond Vernon has published a series of articles on government business relations, stressing especially the problem of government-business relationships in developing countries. Some of Vernon's articles are: "Foreign-owned Enterprise in the Developing Countries," *Public Policy*, Vol. 15, 1966; "Multinational Enterprise and National Sovereignty," *Harvard Business Review* (March-April 1967); "Conflict and Resolution between Foreign Direct Investors and Less-Developed Countries," *Public Policy*, Vol. 17, 1968; "Economic Sovereignty at Bay," *Foreign Affairs* (October 1968), Vol. 47, No. 1, pp. 110-122.
9. F. T. Hanner, "Business Investment Negotiations in Developing Countries," *Business Horizons*, (Winter), 1965, pp. 97-103.
10. Simon Williams, "Negotiating Investments in Emerging Countries," *Harvard Business Review* (January-February 1965), pp. 89-99.
11. Yair Aharoni, *The Foreign Investment Decision Process* (Boston: Division of Research, Graduate School of Business Administration, Harvard University, 1966). Another study on the process of conflict which is of interest in a study of international business negotiations is Thomas C. Schelling, *The Strategy of Conflict* (New York: Oxford University Press, 1960).
12. Seung Hee Kim, *Foreign Capital For Economic Development: A Korean Case Study* (New York: Praeger Publisher, 1970).
13. Jordan C. Schreiber, *U.S. Corporate Investment in Taiwan* (New York: The Dunnelin Co., 1970).
14. *Doing Business in the New Indonesia,* Business International, Inc., (1968).
15. Helen Hughes and You Poh Seng, editors, *Foreign Investment and Industrialization in Singapore* (Madison, Wisconsin: The University of Wisconsin Press, 1969). See also, A. Kapoor and William Millson, "Investing in Singapore: The American Experience," *The Singapore Manager*, Vol. 4, No. 1 (June 1970).
16. V. Kannapathy, "Foreign Investment in Malaysia: Experience and Prospects," *UMBC Economic Review*, Vol. VI, No. 2 (1970), pp. 1-22; A. Kapoor and William Millson, "Investing in Malaysia: the American Experience," *Business Abroad* (April 1970); J. J. Puthuchearry, *Ownership and Control in the Malaysian Economy* (Singapore: Eastern University Press, 1960); Sumitro Djojohadikusumo, *Trade and Aid in South-East Asia — Malaysia and Singapore* (Kuala Lumpur, Malaysia: University of Malaya Cooperative Book Shop, 1969).
17. Michael Kideron, *Foreign Investments in India* (New York: Oxford University Press, 1965); see also, A. Kapoor, "Foreign Collaborations in India: Problems and Prospects," *IDEA,* Vol. 10, No. 2, Summer (1966), and Vol. 10, No. 3, Fall (1966).
18. Robert J. Ballon, ed., *Doing Business in Japan* (Rutland, Vt.: Charles E. Tuttle Company, 1967).
19. James C. Abegglen, *Business Strategies for Japan* (Tokyo, Encyclopedia Britannica, Japan, Inc., 1967).

20. T.F.M. Adams and N. Kobyashi, *The World of Japanese Business: An Authoritative Analysis* (Tokyo, Japan: Kodansha International Ltd., 1969).
21. Herbert Glazer, *The International Businessman in Japan* (Rutland, Vt.: Charles E. Tuttle Company, 1968).
22. Chitoshi Yanaga, *Big Business in Japanese Politics* (New Haven: Yale University Press, 1968).
23. A. Kapoor, *International Business Negotiations: A Study in India* (New York: New York University Press, 1970).
24. Fred C. Ikle, *How Nations Negotiate* (New York: Frederick A. Praeger, 1967), p. 2.
25. *Ibid*, pp. 3-4.
26. *Ibid*, p. 6.
27. Thomas C. Schelling, *The Strategy of Conflict* (New York: Oxford University Press, 1960), p. 15.
28. *Ibid*, p. 16.
29. James A. Lee, "Cultural Analysis in Overseas Operations," *Harvard Business Review* (March-April 1966), p. 110.
30. Aharoni, *op. cit.*, p. 94; see also A. Kapoor and Robert J. McKay, *Managing International Markets: A Survey of Training Practices and Emerging Trends* (Princeton, New Jersey: The Darwin Press, 1971).
31. *Ibid*, p. 39.
32. Lee, *op. cit.*, p. 106.
33. Referring to investments in emerging countries, Williams states that "intimate relations with government agencies, their policies, their ministers, and their staffs are an inevitable part of negotiations to invest and of day-to-day operations thereafter." See Williams, *op. cit.*, p. 96.
34. *Ibid*, p. 89.
35. For additional details, see A. Kapoor, "The Multinational Enterprise and the Nation State in Asia: The Emerging Conflicts," a paper presented at a *Research Conference on the Multinational Corporation in the Global Political System*, Wharton School of Finance and Commerce, Department of Political Science, University of Pennsylvania, April 22-23, 1971.
36. See A. Kapoor, *Columbia Journal, op. cit.*
37. See M. Cyert and James G. March, *A Behavioral Theory of the Firm* (Prentice-Hall, 1963), pp. 101-113, and "Organizational Factors in the Theory of Oligopoly," *Quarterly Journal of Economics*, Vol. 70. (1956), pp. 52ff.
38. Aharoni, *op. cit.*, p. 41.
39. Schelling, *op. cit.*, p. 30.
40. *Ibid*.
41. However, the expiration of the Laurel-Langley Act in the Philippines will result in greatly reducing the favored status of American investors.
42. Aharoni states that the decision "whether or not to invest abroad is made by a group of individuals in an organization, not by an individual." Aharoni, *op. cit.*, p. 17; see also p. 35 and p. 143.
43. Aharoni, *op. cit.*, p. 123; for greater detail, see pp. 122-141.
44. Such organizations are known by various names: Economic Planning Board (South Korea); Board of Investments (The Philippines and Thailand); Foreign Investment Board or Council (Indonesia, Malaysia, India).
45. See Yanaga, *op. cit.*
46. Michael Brecher, *Nehru's Mantle: The Politics of Succession in India* (New

York: Frederick A. Praeger, 1966), pp. 105-106; see also p. 67 and p. 92. The entire study is a fascinating account of decision making in the Indian Government. The emphasis on consensus in government decision making is demonstrated also in Japan. "Politicians and political parties do not lead. They wait, hoping for a national consensus on the issues confronting them before they are forced to act. To Westerners this way of operating may seem strange, but it is in keeping with a fundamental, perhaps subconscious Japanese drive toward agglomeration, 'clustering'"; see Carl and Shelly Mydans, "What Manner of Men are these Japanese," *Fortune* (April 1969), p. 101.

47. Schelling, *op. cit.*, p. 28. The use of the press by opposing groups to improve their respective negotiating positions is vividly demonstrated by Allan Ford, *The Anglo-Iranian Oil Dispute of 1951-1952: A Study of the Role of Law in the Relations of States* (Los Angeles: University of California Press, 1954); see pp. 64-65 and p. 107 in particular. The role of the press in favor of or against a proposal is demonstrated in the debates on the Anti-Monopoly Law in Japan; see Chitoshi Yanaga, *op. cit.;* Yanaga also discusses how the Filipino delegation used the press in negotiating the reparation settlement with Japan; see p. 219.

48. See A. Kapoor and John Elwood, "How U.S. Firms Evaluate Their Partners in India," *Business Abroad* (September 1969).

49. Behrman, *op. cit.*, p. 129.

50. *Ibid.*, p. 126; see also John Fayerweather, "19th Century Ideology and 20th Century Reality," *Columbia Journal of World Business,* Vol. 1, No. 1 (1966), pp. 77-84; Leo Model, "The Politics of Private Foreign Investment," *Foreign Affairs,* Vol. 45, No. 7 (1967), p. 639; Simon Williams, *op. cit.*, p. 98; for comments on Latin America with particular reference to Brazil, see Claude McMillan, Jr., Richard F. Gonzalez, and Leo G. Erickson, *International Enterprise in a Developing Economy: A Study of U.S. Business in Brazil* (Michigan: Bureau of Business and Economic Research, Graduate School of Business Administration, Michigan State University, 1964); Peter P. Gabriel, "Investment in the LDC," *Columbia Journal of World Business,* Summer (1966), pp. 7-16.

51. Behrman, *op. cit.*, pp. 126-127.

52. Raymond Vernon, "Multinational Enterprise and National Sovereignty," *Harvard Business Review* (March-April 1967), p. 163. See also John Fayerweather, *International Business Management: A Conceptual Framework* (New York: McGraw Hill, 1969), pp. 87-132.

53. Richard D. Robinson, *International Business Policy* (New York: Holt, Rinehart and Winston, 1964), p. vii; see also McMillan *et al; op. cit.*, p. 221.

54. Robinson, *op. cit.*, pp. 1-44 for a description of the role of business enterprise in the process of colonization; for comments on the oil industry, see Michael Tanzer, *The Political Economy of International Oil and the Underdeveloped Countries* (Boston: Beacon Press, 1969), pp. 55-56, and J. E. Hartschorn, *Politics and World Oil Economics* (New York: Frederick A. Praeger, 1962); see also Alan H. Schechter "Businessmen as Government Policy Makers," *Columbia Journal of World Business,* Vol. 3, No. 3 (May-June 1968), pp. 67-72.

55. Behrman, *op. cit.*, P. 126.

56. For a description of organized business as an interest group, see Myron Weiner, *The Politics of Scarcity: Public Pressure and Political Response in India* (Chicago: University of Chicago Press, 1962), pp. 97-129; see also Yanaga, *op. cit.*

57. Aharoni, *op. cit.*, pp. 45-46.

27
Conflict and Resolution Between Foreign Direct Investors and Less Developed Countries

Raymond Vernon

Most of the less developed countries of the world are prepared to invite foreign investors to undertake new enterprises inside their borders. Also, many foreign investors are prepared to take a serious look at the opportunities offered by the less developed countries. Yet only a small number of such arrangements are actually consummated.[1]

Debates over the obstacles usually are too general to contribute very much to understanding. Business interests usually attribute the disappointing performance to "poor climate," generated by a lack of governmental understanding of business problems. Governments, on the other hand, tend to attribute the problem to private greed or private intolerance of risk. The main theme of this paper is that although many factors contribute to the lack of direct investment, one of the major issues is the struggle between foreign business and local government over control of any proposed investment. To the extent that control is the issue, one is led to ask whether the difficulty can be bridged and whether some forms of investment are capable of providing the bridge more readily than others.

DEFINING THE CONFLICT

In a simple economic model, an investment will be attractive to the investor

Reprinted, with permission, from *Public Policy*, Vol. XVII (1968). This article is based on a study of the multinational enterprise, financed by a grant from the Ford Foundation to the Harvard Graduate School of Business Administration.

if the prospective yield to him exceeds his cost of capital and is the highest of the available alternatives; and it will be attractive to the host country if the prospective payment to the investor is lower than the social yield and the lowest of all possible alternatives.

No one doubts, however, that the questions which motivate and preoccupy both the investor and the host country are much more than questions of the price and yield on capital. [2] Although some issues can be forced into capital-price equivalents by the kind of conceptual repackaging of which economics is so fond, a few issues will persist in remaining as problems of another sort. These non-price issues have been well aired in the literature, so that only a summary introduction is needed here.

The Host Country View. To speak of a "host country view" is to do a certain violence to reality. There are many host countries, with points of view that differ in intensity and detail; and there are warring factions within host countries, eager to exploit the foreign investment issue or any other issue if it will advance their interests inside the body politic. Yet some generalizations can be made that are representative of the views prevailing in less developed countries.

One well-advertised concern of the less developed nations with respect to foreign direct investments relates to their balance-of-payment effects. In an economy that operates in accordance with the main assumptions of the classical model, every investment presumptively produces goods and services that are sufficient to pay for the factors which are used to produce them, including the foreign capital; directly or indirectly, therefore, the economy acquires the incremental resources necessary to service the foreign capital. [3] But most less developed countries are unprepared to accept some of the critical assumptions of the classical model. They assume that foreign investment cannot be counted on automatically to generate its own exchange requirements, partly because national resources cannot easily be shifted from their existing uses to uses that earn or conserve added foreign exchange, and partly for other reasons. [4] As a result, such countries sometimes turn down foreign investment proposals or insist that part of the equity should be raised from domestic sources.

The case for worrying about foreign direct investments, when based on capital-cost or balance-of-payment grounds, however, seems hardly firm enough to explain the intensity and universality of the less developed countries' reactions. In 1966, the investment of U.S. manufacturing companies in the less developed countries stood at about $3.5 billion, while the local value added annually by such companies was something over $3 billion. [5] The annual income remissions to U.S. parent companies, on the other hand, were on the order of only $200 million. Figures of this sort, taken by themselves, are not enough to gauge the effects on the economy of the investments concerned; yet neither are they of the sort that is calculated to stir expressions of concern about the cost of the balance-of-payment implications of foreign investment. Those expressions, in my view, are usually proxies for another kind of worry — the worry that such investment may lead to a dilution of a country's control over its national industries.

The motives behind the desire for national control differ according to the country and the group within the country espousing such control. As a rule, the desire for control comes most strongly out of the government sector. At times, that desire finds expression in the policy of reserving certain industries for state ownership. State ownership provides a secure and easy way to tax a specific commodity such as tobacco, or to subsidize a commodity such as fertilizer. State ownership also offers an outlet for the creative energies of the military or the civil service. Foreign ownership obviously would imperil this sort of objective.

More often, however, national control may be important to the less developed economies for other reasons. A continuous and intimate *dirigiste* relationship usually exists between governments and businessmen in such economies, especially during the industrializing phase.[6] Through that relationship, businessmen are the object of a stream of signals from government: advice to control price rises in inflation, to provide credit or materials or capital to favored enterprises, and so on. At the same time, the local entrepreneurs are themselves the originators of a series of demands on government: for protection from outside competition, for relief from the enforcement of existing tax laws or price ceilings, and much more.

There have been cases in which foreign-owned enterprises have managed successfully and unobtrusively to take their place on the national communication grid. But the presence of the foreign enterprise is usually seen by both government and the private sector as a disturbing force. It is disturbing not only because of the enterprise's assumed reluctance or inability to participate in the intimate local network of communication, but also because of its putative capability for avoiding the impact of any signals that the network issues. Because such enterprises usually have well-established bases abroad with which they constantly deal, they are assumed to be able with great facility to transfer resources into the country and out again. The relative ease with which the enterprise is thought to be able to make and implement such choices, impervious to all but the most overt commands of the local economy, is seen as a challenge to local control.

The loss of control takes a more explicit and more threatening form from the point of view of the host government when another government becomes involved in the affairs of the subsidiary. For instance, the parent company may importune its government for help in protecting the subsidiary from "unfair" treatment at the hands of the host; or the government of the parent company may relay a command to the subsidiary — a command to perform, or to desist from performing, some act inside the economy of the host government. Will the copper companies in Africa and Latin America, if controlled by U.S. parents, be prevented from shipping their product to Communist China? Will the host countries, when pressing those companies for greater output or higher taxes, be pulled up short by counterpressure exerted through the foreign aid program?

The Investor's View. A few words, now, about the obstacles as seen through the eyes of prospective investors.

If the views of such investors were to be taken at face value, the largest single obstacle to investment in the less developed countries would be the "poor climate" provided by host governments.[7] But the phrase is not very precise; and the more one tries to give it precision, the more he begins to suspect that the concept embodies a number of different elements.

At the root of the problem lies the ineluctable fact that less developed countries present a chancy environment to the prospective investor. Many businessmen are prepared to accept some uncertainties as an unavoidable element of existence, and are prepared to rely upon a capacity to shift strategies as their main defense.[8] But if they fear that they may not be allowed to make the shifts as uncertainties arise, the environment is regarded as specially hostile. Beyond that, if the government is thought to have a propensity for injecting new uncertainties into the environment, through measures such as devaluations or price freezes, the climate is said to be especially poor. The characteristic response of investors in such circumstances is either to reject the proposed investment or to tie up the government with guarantees and assurances aimed at reducing the uncertainty to tolerable levels and at regaining a certain measure of control.

Control is desired not only to deal with uncertainty but also to ensure that the operations of the subsidiary are related to those of the parent in ways that best serve the investor's total interests. To the extent that the investor is interested in profit, the relevant profit is that of the *total* network of the investor's interests, not that of the prospective subsidiary alone.[9] Even if a subsidiary investment appears to yield very little profit directly, it may yield profits that are captured in a downstream affiliate, or it may provide a captive outlet for the intermediate goods produced by the parent.[10] Or it may be providing security to the system as a whole, because it represents an offset to a move by a rival firm in an oligopolistic industry; for instance, if the rival established a beachhead in a new market or a new materials-producing area that might eventually prove important, prudence may suggest the establishment of an offsetting beachhead in the same terrain, however underdeveloped and uncertain that terrain may be.[11]

It is not only the joint objectives but also the joint resources of the whole system that may be involved in the subsidiary investment. We must bear in mind that the return which the investor is seeking to maximize may not at all be a return on finance capital; for the large multinational enterprise, the supply of finance capital at times may be almost infinitely elastic, even an embarrassment in its plentifulness. Factors other than capital may be regarded as the relatively scarce inputs, on which quasi rents can be captured. One such scarce factor — especially relevant to the prospective investor when considering whether to invest in a new source or supply — is an established market position, rendered secure by a strong distribution system or by patents. Another scarce factor is an established organization capable of performing certain relatively difficult acts, such as identifying technological needs and generating a relevant response. How to secure the maximum yield on these joint resources of the system then becomes the object of the business strategy. Such a strategy is likely to be imperiled if control over the subsidiary is uncertain.

The issue of control, therefore, emerges as a major preoccupation not only of the host government but also of the investor. The critical question for any policymaker is whether the needs of both parties can simultaneously be served.

SHAPING THE RECONCILIATION

Some Alternative Arrangements. The resulting conflict leads to a consideration of many different arrangements, infinite in their variety and detail. As a way of describing the field, however, one can think of four "pure" types, always bearing in mind that reality itself is a good deal more hybrid and more complex. The four types, in rough descending order of "foreign control," are:

1. The wholly-owned subsidiary — a corporate entity created under the local law of the host country, wholly owned and wholly managed by the foreign investor;

2. The joint venture — a corporate entity created under local law, partially owned by local private or public interests, and managed according to policies responsive in part to those local interests;

3. The co-production agreement — an agreement between a foreigner and an entity that is owned and managed by public authorities in the host coun-

try, under which (1) the entity acquires specified machinery and technology from the foreigner; (2) the entity is committed to producing specified products; and (3) the entity, over a number of years, "pays" the foreigner for the machinery and technology in kind, i.e., in specified products;[12] and

4. The technical assistance agreement — an agreement between a foreigner and an entity created under local law and owned by local public or private interests, in which the foreigner provides management services, technical information, or both, and receives payment in money.[13]

The labels of course can sometimes be misleading. One can find cases in which a parent that nominally "owns" a wholly-owned subsidiary is restrained in its power to shape the subsidiary's policies; and cases in which the foreign "manager" of a local enterprise actually has a range of powers equivalent to an unrestrained owner. But those are the exceptional cases. Generally, the four types of agreement have predictably different implications. If one is willing to accept a certain amount of oversimplification and a willingness to generalize from spotty evidence, there are a few comparative statements to be made, which are set out below in tabular form.[14] The table assumes the existence of a given project; then, holding the project itself "constant," the table purports to state the characteristic differences of the various arrangements.

In general, the table reflects in crude form a fairly clear trade-off on the part of host countries. To reduce the foreigner's control, host countries are

Table I: Resource Transfer

Form of arrangement	Capital	Foreign market access	Management and information
Wholly-owned subsidiary (WOS)	Equity portion only	Unlimited for raw materials; extremely limited for manufacturers	Unlimited
Joint venture (JV)	Less than WOS	Equal to or less than WOS	Less than WOS
Co-production agreement (CPA)	In economic equivalents, probably less than WOS or JV	Limited; but guaranteed within its limits	Less than WOS or JV
Technical assistance agreement	Less than WOS, JV or CPA	Less than WOS, JV or CPA	Less than WOS, JV or CPA

prepared to accept less in the way of valuable resources. Which of these approaches is the better "bargain," therefore, is thoroughly indeterminate; all depends on the value of what the host country forgoes by reason of not acquiring resources, measured against what is achieved by reducing the foreigner's control.

This kind of comparison, however, can easily be pushed too far. In the first place, its distinctions are much too gross; they do not allow for differences between products and differences among less-developed countries, some of which are of profound importance. In the second place, its distinctions are much too static.

The question of changing needs on the part of the host country is especially important. Such changes are usually induced by a change in the state of development of the country, or by a change in the nature of the product involved. To appreciate how these differences come about and what they imply, we must next explore three major types of foreign investment in the less developed countries: the raw-material producing facility; the facility for the production of import-substituting goods; and the facility for the production and export of manufactured goods.

Raw-Material Investments. Investments to exploit raw materials cover a wide spectrum of situations. At one end are products like oil, copper, and bauxite. In these cases, the production process is relatively capital-intensive; it requires a certain amount of organization, management, and technical skill; and it generates a product that is characteristically marketed in closed channels, by sales between affiliates. The evidence suggests that in such cases raw material investment is usually made because users prefer to control their own sources, even if such use involves the absorption of relatively high freight costs.[15]

This preference may reflect the existence of a strategy among vertically-integrated game-playing oligopolists, no one of which is willing to be at the mercy of the others in time of raw-material shortage. In some cases, it probably also reflects the technical desirability of relating a user plant to a single raw-material source because of physical variations in the raw materials drawn from different sources.

At the other end of the spectrum are investments in the production of materials such as cotton, coffee, and sugar. In these products, capital, training, and technical skill may be important in reducing costs and increasing yields. But a variety of different production functions are possible; a larger proportion of sales may be made in the open market; and the entry of new producers is relatively easy.

The classification, once articulated, suggests a great deal about the bargaining strength of foreign investors relative to host governments. Where high capital inputs, difficult management and information requirements, product differentiation, and the strategic need for a tied production source go hand in hand, the host government confronts a well-entrenched bargainer.

But no industry, however tightly organized, remains unchanged in structure over many decades. The sources of both "nonreplenishable" raw materials and the "replenishable" products of the forest and soil continue to multiply as long as they are in demand. At the same time, the smelters, refineries, and mills that are associated with the initial treatment of raw materials are constantly growing in number. Opportunities for new entrants at the processing level periodically arise; and if they do not arise as a result of market growth, they are generated artificially by governmental action. Therefore, as the number of buyers and sellers has multiplied, tight oligopoly structures have been known to show signs of raveling.

I have commented elsewhere on the rapid change in the apparent bargaining positions of investors and host governments in the field of petroleum.[16] Host governments have demanded and have managed to get increasing shares of the profits. Governments are also demanding and are beginning to acquire a voice in the management of the producing facilities; OPEC's steady pressure for involvement in the pricing and production policies of the oil companies is telling evidence of the trend. Exporting governments are even beginning to develop foreign marketing capabilities of their own, as evidenced by some of the operations of Iran's NIOC.

My interpretation of the root cause of these trends in the oil industry is the decline in the negotiating strength of the international oil companies, due to: (1) the proliferation of crude oil sources; (2) the growing availability of packaged refineries purchasable on a turnkey basis; and (3) the greater ease with which such operations can be financed, due to the appearance of new financial sources such as the World Bank institutions and the regional banks. In brief, the capacity of the international oil companies for providing markets, management, and capital, although still of major importance to foreign governments, no longer appears as utterly indispensable as it did a few decades ago.

Observe some of the implications of that interpretation, however. Raw-material-producing countries are in a stronger position to demand joint ventures or co-production agreements or management contracts, as indeed they have been doing. But these countries, while overcoming one form of dominance — the dominance of the foreign investor — are exposing themselves to another. Although the market for oil and copper is hardly likely to reach the classical atomized structure that exists for coffee, cotton, and sugar, this is the direction of its movement. The oligopoly stability that each of these countries so patently desires depends at present upon continuing the direct tie between the producing facilities in its territory and the marketing facilities with which it is linked. That tie is now provided by the multinational enterprise, whose integrated strategy aims at providing an assured market for a predictable output. In measure as the producing countries gain a voice in management prerogatives, the foreign enterprises have less incentive to try to maintain the direct link between production and marketing.

It may be that the tension this difficult position generates cannot be measurably reduced as long as there is a struggle over where the authority for major business decisions should rest. In that case, we must look for such tension to continue for a long time. For on any set of assumptions, it would be decades before the producing countries could be expected to take over the producing and marketing function for themselves.

The Import-Substituting Manufacturing Investment. The advantages that a less developed country sees in any given foreign investment in its economy tend to decline as the enterprise ages. This is a generalization that requires numerous caveats, of course. If the foreign investor rapidly alters the character of his investment after it is established — if, for instance, he turns from automobile assembly to automobile manufacture — the new activities may prove even more attractive to host governments than the original ones. On the other hand, if the general nature of the investment remains unchanged during its life, then there is a strong case of the view that its attractiveness to the host economy will decline.

It would be difficult to test the generalization with solid evidence; but it seems to follow well enough from the nature of the situation. To the extent that capital, management skill, and information are acquired, the most obvious and most valuable infusions usually take place at the beginning of the undertaking; after the first importation of capital, very little of the subsequent growth is financed through funds from outside the host country.[17] After the early transplant of technology and managerial assistance, the occult character of these contributions probably also declines in the eyes of host governments. Local businessmen arise who seem willing and able to take over the business. Accordingly, it seems safe to conclude that a foreign investment that has remained unaltered in structure and purpose over any extended period of time is less attractive to the host country in its later stages then in its beginnings.

Although the generalizations that have just been made are inherently plausible, one should be aware that they are a matter of surmise. On the other hand, some hard evidence does exist with respect to a first-cousin proposition of considerable significance: The older a given technology, the more likely that the new entrants using the technology will set up their plants free of the innovator's control. Therefore, as far as the less developed countries are concerned, the older the technology adopted, the more likely it is to be free of foreign control. This proposition has been tested so far in the plastics industry and for certain petrochemicals.[18] The results, presented in an idealized way, take the form below. The data are consistent with the view that nations manage to avoid foreign control more effectively when their new enterprises involve a long-established technology than when such enterprises are at the forefront of industrial innovation.

Table 2: Plants Classified by Years of Lag
in Establishment after First Commercial Facility

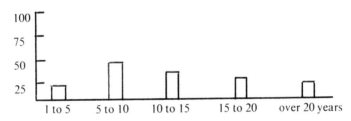

The form of enterprise, however, depends not only on the interests of the host country but also on the interests of the foreign investor. As often as not, according to the evidence, foreign investors in less developed countries make their initial investments under duress, usually under fear of exclusion from a market that had initially been developed by means of exports from the parent firm.[19] Characteristically, the initial investment has been held down to the smallest possible commitment necessary for market access, such as a packaging plant in the case of drugs and an assembly plant in the case of automobiles. Eventually, the commitment has deepened and broadened, sometimes under pressure from the host government, sometimes as a result of the development of reliable local sources for inputs.

In some of these cases, foreigners have been quite willing to accept an arrangement in which control was shared with local interests. If the initial commitment was to consist of nothing more than the processing and sale of quality-controlled and name-branded materials provided by the parent company for marketing solely in the local market, then the presence of a local partner in the venture did not seriously impair the firm's essential strategy.

If deviations from international quality or pricing practices were required for the local market, even these might be managed as a special and isolated case. True, the local partner might prove obstreperous in demanding a larger dividend pay-out and a lower rate of plough-back than the foreigner (thus incidentally behaving contrary to the hopes of his government that he might act as a restraining force in such matter). The local partner might even inquire from time to time about the formulas being used by the foreign partner to fix transfer prices or allocate central office charges (thereby performing much more in accord with his intended role). But difficulties such as these, annoying though they might be, could be managed by the foreign partner if the local facility was not vital to the structure and strategy of the multinational system.

If less developed countries were content to limit themselves to import-substituting manufactures alone, therefore, the foreign investors who had been persuaded to enter the market by way of a joint venture might well remain content with that form of investment. But the vanguard of the less developed countries is plainly moving beyond this stage. Palpable pressures are compelling the less developed countries to interest themselves in the export of manufactured products. Part of the pressure comes as a result of the anticipated strengthening of regional trade groups, notably the Latin American Free Trade Area and the Central American Common Market. Part comes as a result of the need to expand the exports of manufactures to the markets of North America and Western Europe.

When the host government becomes eager for access to export markets, the foreign investor's negotiating position usually strengthens. At the same time, however, because the output of the local subsidiary no longer is to be confined to a limited, isolated market, the foreign investor's need for control sharply increases. At that point, therefore, it is not unreasonable to anticipate that the foreign investor will feel a new and heightened interest in reacquiring total and unambiguous control. Whether his negotiating position is strong enough to sustain such a demand depends upon the individual case; but that is almost certainly the direction in which the foreigner's interests will run.

Manufacturing for Export. The exports of manufactures from the less developed countries to the markets of more advanced nations are increasing and diversifying rather rapidly.[20] But they are still quite small in total quantity; and they must increase more rapidly still if the balance-of-payment constraint on economic growth is to be relaxed very much.

The analytical work that has been done on factors that may be impeding such exports is impressive and enlightening.[21] For all the research done so far, however, there is still a considerable amount of uncertainty about the necessary and sufficient conditions for expanding the exports of manufactured goods by less developed countries.

One view—a view of which I happen to be a partisan—is that a more adequate flow of information between the less developed countries and the advanced countries concerning market demand and production capabilities would represent both the necessary and the sufficient condition for a considerable rise in exports on the part of the less developed countries. Elsewhere, I have argued that the kind of information flow needed to sell manufactured goods in the advanced countries is of a different order of detail and credibility than the information flow needed for the sale of raw materials; and that the more sophisticated the product, the more the need for a credible and effective two-way informational flow to market it.[22]

Some countries have managed to generate the needed flow—Japan, Taiwan, Hong Kong, Turkey, Israel, and Mexico are the outstanding cases. Various devices have been used to achieve these results, although the relative use of the devices is not well measured or documented. Japan has provided elaborate subsidies for market information and market contact, underwriting some of the costs not only of Japanese exporters but also of foreign importers. Hong Kong, Taiwan, and Israel have used trade channels whose efficiency may have depended in part on the special personal ties of their businessmen abroad. Many countries have relied on the relationship between local subsidiaries and foreign parents, thus internalizing the information flow within the corporate group; in such cases, company groups like Ford, IBM, Phillips, ITT, Olivetti, and others have provided the conduits to support the flow of credible information.

Would such conduits be as effective if the enterprises in the less developed countries, instead of being wholly-owned subsidiaries, were joint ventures or co-production enterprises or were simply managed under contract by a foreign manager? Although hard data on the subject are limited, my guess is that the wholly-owned subsidiary will be preferred. That preference may be weak if the sales of the enterprise are to be confined to small regional markets, outside the mainstream of the foreign parent company; but it is likely to be stronger, perhaps even controlling, if the major markets of the foreign parent are involved.

The problem that this preference presents for the less developed country is less formidable with regard to simple standardized manufactures, such as sewing machines, barbed wire, grey cloth, and frozen shrimp than it is for more advanced products. In the case of the simpler products the management and technology are not difficult, and market penetration depends primarily on price; there is accordingly no heavy dependence on the foreign enterprise.

But for more complex products, involving quality control, adaptation to market, and so on, the bargaining position of the less developed country may be very much more difficult.

ON THE AVOIDANCE OF TENSION

How can one summarize the seemingly diverse tendencies described above? Despite the diversity, there are certain main themes that stand out.

At the very onset of a foreign venture in the less developed countries, the parties confront the basic issue of the size and depth of the commitment. Surveying the possible alternatives, the prospective host country may well decide to forgo some of the control it would like to have, in order to acquire the resources offered by the foreign investor, such as added capital or overseas markets. On the other hand, if the local enterprise can be operated with some independence of the foreign investor's interests in other countries, the foreign investor may willingly accept some initial impairment of control, such as the impairment implicit in a joint venture or a co-production agreement.

Whatever the initial position of the parties may be, however, there is a strong likelihood that the interests of each will change. On the host country's side, an initial willingness to forgo control in the interest of securing needed resources is likely to be eroded. Either the foreign investor will have to provide new resources, such as more capital or technology or access to markets; or he will confront new demands by the host government for shared control; or both will occur. On the foreign investor's side, the changing character of the local operation may suggest the need for more control as well.

There are two projections commonly made as to the outcome of these changes. One projection, popular among the less developed countries, is that it is only a matter of time before foreign investors can be disposed of; another, popular among the investors, is that it is only a matter of time before foreign direct investment is accepted in the less developed countries with tolerance and appreciation. If my analysis is correct, both projections are wrong. According to the analysis, the position of the foreign investor will continually change, according to the external needs of host governments for capital, markets, and technology. Tensions will rise and fall in patterns that are partly predictable, reflecting the relative strengths of the parties concerned and the changing nature of their interests.

My guess is, however, that the tensions could be reduced measurably if (1) both parties were agreed that the initial arrangement would remain undisturbed for some fixed period of time; and (2) the termination date of the arrangement, although distant, was not remote. Agreements along these lines might well provide the investor with the prospect of the clear run necessary to justify his initial commitment, while yet providing the host government with the option of reacquiring control at some tolerable future date. Agreements of this sort, however, are not easily framed; among other things, they have to provide for the contingency that renewal negotiations, when they became due, might break down. To deal with that contingency, one would have to envisage a procedure that promised liquidation of mutual commitments on a reasonable basis. From a technical point of view, these problems can be difficult; but they are far from impossible.

But who will build the bridge? Prospective investors are understandably reluctant to initiate proposals that might demand eventual renegotiation of their undertakings, even if renegotiation should prove in their own interests. Prospective governments are often limited in their capacities to frame and negotiate the novel and complex arrangements that may be involved. Here is a neglected opportunity for institution-building in the interests of economic development.

NOTES

1. According to one survey, the total number of establishments set up or acquired by U.S. manufacturing parents in less developed countries during the six-and-one-half-year period ending December 1966 came to fewer than 100 per year; and of those established, nearly 40 percent were in Mexico. See Booz, Allen & Hamilton, *New Foreign Business Activities of U.S. Firms* (New York: Booz, Allen & Hamilton, 1967) p. 23.

2. I have summarized these considerations from the host government's point of view in "Foreign-Owned Enterprise in the Developing Countries," in John D. Montgomery and Arthur Smithies (eds.), *Public Policy*, vol. XV (Cambridge, Mass.: Harvard Graduate School of Public Administration, 1966), p. 361. For the investment process within the investing firm, and the considerations that seem relevant in the process, see Yair Aharoni, *The Foreign Investment Decision Process* (Boston: Harvard Graduate School of Business Administration, 1966,) esp. chaps. 3-7. For the results of other surveys on the motivation question in international investment, see R. S. Basi, *Determinants of United States Private Direct Investments in Foreign Countries* (Kent, Ohio: Kent State University Bureau of Economic and Business Research, 1963); National Industrial Conference Board, *U.S. Production Abroad and the Balance of Payments* (New York: NICB, 1966), p. 63; Arthur Stonehill and Leonard Nathanson, "Capital Budgeting and the Multinational Corporation," *California Management Review* (Winter 1967); R. F. Mikesell (ed.), *Private and Government Investment Abroad* (Eugene, Ore.: University of Oregon, 1962), p. 89; *Overseas Operations of U.S. Industrial Enterprises, 1960-1961* (New York: McGraw-Hill, 1960); National Planning Association, *Case Studies of U.S. Business Performance Abroad* (11 case studies; Washington, D.C.: NPA, 1955-1961); H. J. Robinson, *The Motivation and Flow of Private Foreign Investment* (Menlo Park, Calif.; Stanford Research Institute, Investment Series No. 4, 1961) p. 24; D. M. Phelps, *Migration of Industry to Latin America* (New York: McGraw-Hill, 1936), pp. 43-87; Michael

Kindron, *Foreign Investments in India* (London: Oxford University Press, 1965), pp. 253-256; B. L. Johns, "Private Overseas Investment in Australia: Profitability and Motivation," *Economic Record*, Vol. XLIII (June 1967), pp. 257-261.

3. This familiar argument is well summarized in Edith Penrose, "Foreign Investment and the Growth of the Firm," *Economic Journal*, Vol. LXVI (June 1956). pp. 220-235.

4. These alternative assumptions are incorporated formally in a two-gap model, now a fixture in development theory. An excellent summary is to be found in S. B. Linder, *Trade and Trade Policy for Development* (New York: Praeger, 1967), p. 42 *et seq.*

5. This is a crude estimate based on the fact that gross sales of U.S.-owned manufacturing enterprises located in the less developed world were about $9 billion in 1965, while the ratio of local wages, taxes, and other payments (except materials) to such sales, as last reported for such enterprises (1957), was about 33 per cent.

6. Even when businessmen in less developed countries profess a nineteenth-century brand of liberalism, as they sometimes do, they usually couple it with an expectation of intimate and continuous working relations with their governments. The point, so far as I know, has been systematically surveyed in only a few countries; see, for instance, my *Dilemma of Mexico's Development* (Cambridge, Mass.: Harvard University Press, 1963), pp. 163 *et seq.*, and the subsequent study by Arthur D. Little de Mexico, *Mexican Attitudes toward Foreign Investment* (August 1966). But its presence can be detected in studies of many countries; see, for instance, G. F. Papanek, *Pakistan's Development* (Cambridge, Mass.: Harvard University Press, 1967), p. 226 *et seq.*; and T. R. Fillol, *Social Factors in Economic Development: The Argentine Case* (Cambridge, Mass.: M.I.T. Press, 1961) p. 57 *et seq.*

7. Aharoni, *op. cit.*, p. 142 *passim;* National Industrial Conference Board, *Obstacles and Incentives to Private Foreign Investment 1962-1964* (New York: NICB, 1966), p. 39.

8. For illustrations, see M. R. Copen, *The Management of U.S. Manufacturing Subsidiaries in a Developing Nation: India* (unpublished D.B.A. thesis, Harvard Graduate School of Business Administration, May 1967), p. 110 *et seq.;* Jack Zwick, *Aspects of the Foreign Capital Rationing Procedures of Certain American Manufacturing Corporations* (unpublished D.B.A. thesis, Harvard Graduate School of Business Administration, August 1964), p. 35 *et seq.*

9. Although it hardly seems necessary to labor the point, nevertheless the persistence with which economists compile and compare yields on subsidiary investments as if they had decisive economic meaning suggests that the caution may have some point. For a systematic presentation of the size and implications of the difference in the automobile industry, see N. B. MacDonald, "A Comment: The Bladen Plan for Increased Protection for the Automobile Industry," *Canadian Journal of Economics and Political Science*, Vol. XXLX (November 1963), p. 505 *et seq.*

10. The point is not wholly neglected in the literature. See Bela Balassa, "American Direct Investment in the Common Market," *Banca Nazionale del Lavoro, Quarterly Review* (Rome), No. 77 (June 1966), p. 134; A. N. Hakam, "The Motivation to Invest and the Locational Pattern of Foreign Private Industrial Investments in Nigeria," *Economic and Social Studies*, Vol. VIII (March 1966), p. 50; D. R. Weigel, *The Relation between Governmental Economic Policy and Direct*

Investment in Developing Countries (unpublished Ph.D. thesis, Stanford University, June 1966), p.71 *et seq.*

11. This point is well reflected in the surveys cited above in footnotes 2, 7, and 8. See also the concurring view in United Nations, *The Promotion of the International Flow of Private Capital* (E/3325, February 1960), p. 12.

12. For a summary of such agreements, see Emile Benoit, "East-West Business Cooperation," *New Republic*, Vol. CLVI (February 1967), pp. 21-23, and "Business Partnerships with Communist Countries?," *World P & I Planning* (November-December 1967), p. 1 *et seq.;* also (in Spanish) Oswald Sunkel, "Politica Nacional de Desarrollo y Dependencia Externa," *Estudios Internacionales* (Santiago), I (May 1967). For details in an individual case, see Harvard Graduate School of Business Administration, "Pacific Vegetable Oil Corporation" (ICH 9G101, ICR 261, 1963, mimeographed).

13. See J. S. Pforde, *An International Trade in Managerial Skills* (Oxford, Eng.; Blackwell, 1957); also P. P. Gabriel, *The International Transfer of Corporate Skills* (Boston: Harvard Graduate School of Business Administration, 1967).

14. The table is based largely on impressionistic evidence, since systematic data on the policies of foreigners with regard to the provision of capital, markets, and technology are scarce, especially as regards the less developed areas. But see A. E. Safarian, *Foreign Ownership of Canadian Industry* (Toronto: McGraw-Hill, 1966), pp. 252, 293; Aurelio Peccei (commenting on the practices of Olivetti and of major car manufacturers), *Technology and World Trade* (National Bureau of Standards Misc., Pub. 284; Washington, D.C.: U.S. Government Printing Office, 1967), pp. 130, 131; W. P. Hogan, "British Manufacturing Subsidiaries in Australia and Export Franchises," *Economic Papers*, No. 22 (July 1966), p. 24; D. T. Brash, *American Investment in Australian Industry* (Cambridge, Mass.: Harvard University Press, 1966), pp. 93-103, 136-156, 223-266; Terutomo Ozawa, *Imitation, Innovation, and Trade: A Study of Foreign Licensing Operations in Japan* (Ann Arbor, Mich.: University Microfilms, 1966), p. 5 *passim;* M. Y. Yoshino, *The Managerial System in Japan: Tradition and Innovation* (in manuscript).

15. See the conclusion of J. E. Tilton, "The Choice of Trading Partners: An Analysis of International Trade in Aluminum, Bauxite, Copper, Lead, Tin, and Zinc," *Yale Economic Essays,* VI (Fall 1966), p. 474. Provocative but not conclusive is the extremely high proportion of international crude oil and nonferrous ore sales that take place between affiliates.

16. See my "Foreign-Owned Enterprise in the Developing Countries," cited above.

17. An analysis of the sources and uses of funds for the foreign subsidiaries of U.S. manufacturing firms outside of Europe and Canada shows the following for 1965: Of $2,244 million spent on gross asset increases, $408 million came from retained earnings, $450 million from depreciation, and $874 million from other funds obtained abroad—"abroad" in this case probably being mainly the host country itself.

18. The plastics study, thus far unpublished, is based on data originally collected by Gary Hufbauer and subsequently reanalyzed by Arthur Egendorf. The petrochemicals study was made by R. B. Stobaugh, Jr. and will appear shortly as a doctoral thesis.

19. See the studies cited above in footnote 2.

20. See, *International Trade 1966* (Geneva: GATT Secretariat, 1967), pp. 55-61.

21. See, for example, Bela Balassa, *Trade Prospects for Developing Countries* (Homewood, Ill.: Richard D. Irwin, 1964), and "Tariff Protection in Industrial

Countries: An Evaluation," *Journal of Political Economy,* Vol. LXXIII (December 1965), pp. 573-594; H. G. Johnson, *Economic Policies toward Less Developed Countries* (Washington, D.C.: Brookings Institution, 1967), pp. 78 *passim;* and UN Conference on Trade and Development, *Measures for the Expansion of Markets of the Developed Countries for Exports of Manufactures and Semi-Manufactures of the Developing Countries* (UNCTAD, E/Conf. 46/6, February 1964).

22. See my *Problems and Prospects in the Export of Manufactured Goods from the Less-Developed Countries* (UNCTAD, E/Conf. 46/P/2, March-June 1964).

DEVELOPED COUNTRIES

28
Multinational Enterprises and Nation States

John H. Dunning

INTRODUCTION

We are entering a new phase about our thinking on the role of the multinational enterprise in the world economy. At least, the questions we are asking are changing. We have got beyond the stage of asking black and white questions, like — is the multinational enterprise a good or a bad thing; is it a force for free trade and competition or an agent for economic imperialism? To start with, we now recognize that it is not very helpful to talk about *the* multinational enterprise — as if this was a homogeneous phenomenon. The most one can hope to do is to identify particular forms of multinational enterprises — according, for example, to the economic activity in which they are engaged, the size and scope of their foreign operations, and the way in which they are financed and organized — as these will greatly influence their impact on nation states of which they are part. For example, the balance of payments consequences to the U.S. of an investment by one of its petroleum companies in an oil drilling venture in the Far East may be totally different from an investment, of a similar amount, by a vehicle concern in a new car assembly plant in Brazil. To the U.K., as a host country, the effects on real income of a 100 percent takeover of a U.K. firm by a fully integrated U.S. enterprise in a high technology industry, may be quite unlike an equivalent investment, jointly financed by U.S. and French interests, to produce, say, cigarettes or cotton textiles.

Reprinted, by permission. Prepared statement read before the Subcommittee on Foreign Economic Policy of the Joint Economic Committee, Congress of the United States, Ninety-first Congress, Second Session, pp. 801-806.

Much, of course, rests on exactly how one defines the multinational enterprise. There are some economists who take a very broad view, and think of any enterprise which operates *producing* units in two or more countries (three if one wishes to be strictly correct) as being multinational. On the other hand, there are those, e.g., Professor Jack Behrman, who feel that this nomenclature should be confined to the type of company which organizes its world-wide operations in a closely integrated and harmonized way — and is strongly centralized in its decision making. While I have a certain sympathy with this latter view as it pinpoints one of the main areas which distinguishes today's international firm from its predecessors, I believe that there are other ways in which one might delineate the boundaries of the multinational enterprise which make just as much economic sense.

It depends, in part, from *which* or from *whose* viewpoint one is examining the question. At a *macro*-level, for example, there are three main interests which are likely to be affected by the operations of the multinational enterprise: the economy of the investing country, the economy of host countries, and the economy of other countries — or the world economy as a whole. At a *micro*-level, there are the interests of the investing firm, its competitors both in the investing country and in the host countries, and its suppliers and consumers. It doesn't even stop there. There are distributional and time effects to be considered. The multinational enterprise may influence the prosperity of different parts of countries in which it operates more than others — or of certain types of labor more than others — or the distribution between profits and wages. The short and long run effects of inward investment of a country's balance of payments needs to be carefully distinguished. My point here is that a lot of the discussion about the consequences of the multinational enterprise is very inconclusive simply because it fails to properly specify the particular criteria on which these consequences are to be judged.

This is particularly seen to be the case in the multinational enterprise/nation state controversy. Broadly speaking, multinational, like national, enterprises are interested only in private economic objectives. These may be quite complicated but all contain the ingredients of profitability and growth in a substantial measure. Nation states are much more complex in their goals. While the primary economic aims are fairly straightforward, viz., the maximization of gross national product (g.n.p.) and rate of growth of g.n.p., their achievement, on the one hand, implies the satisfaction of a variety of subsidiary economic goals and, on the other, is circumscribed by the need to meet certain social, cultural, or strategic targets.

In some cases, the nature of the economic system and the interpretation of the social "good" may be such as to exclude the operations of foreign owned enterprises altogether. Obvious examples are the Communist bloc countries. For similar reasons other countries may allow foreign companies to own only a limited equity of local enterprises. At the other extreme, there are nations which are politically very liberal and impose the fewest possible restrictions on either inward or outward investment. In between — as we well know — there is a vast spectrum of attitudes and policies towards the multinational enterprise. Not only do these differ between countries, but also within particular countries, depending, for example, on the extent to which foreign companies in general, or those of one nationality in particular, are likely to influence the achievement of that country's objectives.

This explains, in part, why up to the late 1950's there was very little concern about U.S. investment in Britain. After the last war, Britain (like the rest of Europe) needed all the capital and knowledge it could get. Even in 1957, U.S. firms were responsible for only 5.7 percent of the total U.K. manufacturing output and earned only 7.3 percent of the total profits. In the last decade, the rate of new American investment has risen by three times that of g.n.p. — and would have risen a great deal more had the U.K. gone into the E.E.C. Last year, U.S.-financed firms accounted for about 12 percent of the output and nearer 20 percent of the net fixed capital formation in manufacturing industry, and about one-quarter of manufacturing exports. On present trends, something like 20-25 percent of manufacturing output will be in the hands of U.S.-controlled enterprises by 1980.

Moreover, this investment is very concentrated. The largest 50 U.S. subsidiaries account for more than four-fifths of the total capital stake, and about three-quarters of the investment is concentrated in four industries, viz., oil refining, motor cars, chemicals, and electrical engineering—which also happen to be among the most research intensive industries.

It is the prospect of growing participation of foreign, and particularly U.S. capital, which is causing — in some sectors of the United Kingdom at least — some cause for concern. Though this concern — perhaps unease would be a better word — is rarely spelled out, it is in some cases little more than xenophobia. Very often it is triggered off by an isolated happening in a U.S.-controlled firm like the Roberts Arundel affair in 1967, or the transference of part of Remington Rand's production from a British factory to the Continent in 1969 — or the take-over of a technologically advanced United Kingdom firm by a U.S. firm, where some of the research and development activities are subsequently removed to the United States. In spite of these cases being rare, the possibility of their being rather more widespread in the future than in the past has led to some rethinking of the role of the foreign-owned multinational enterprises in the United Kingdom — typified best I think by the chapter devoted to this topic in the latest Trades Union Congress Economic Review.

Other reasons for the dislike of foreign investment by host countries have been well discussed in writings of Professors Harry Johnson and Charles Kindleberger, and I do not propose to reiterate these—save to agree with both these distinguished economists that, from an economic standpoint, most of these are second best arguments. The point I wish to emphasize is that attitudes towards multinational enterprises by nation states, though often formulated in economic terms, are often political at root and will differ inter alia according to the extent to which foreign participation is likely to affect the goals of domestic policy.

Here I think all the economist can do is to estimate the economic consequences of alternative attitudes and policies. Rarely are political and economic aims precisely defined. The British, for example, have as a declared policy the development of an indigenous electronics industry. What this means in terms of the extent to which foreign participation will be allowed no one knows. Presumably a 40 percent stake is acceptable but a 90 percent stake would not be. Where the proportion becomes unacceptable is a moot point and, I would have thought, could not be rationally determined a priori, without a thorough examination of costs and benefits not only of the additional foreign investment, but of its possible alternatives.

THE ECONOMIC ISSUES INVOLVED: THE HOST COUNTRY'S VIEWPOINT

For the rest of my submission, I would like to confine my remarks to the economic issues. In other words, I will assume the sole criteria of a host country's attitude towards foreign-owned multinational enterprises is whether or not they contribute more to its economic objectives than any other pattern of resource usage. I will further suppose the host country has only two aims — the maximization of real output and rate of growth of real output. The question is to what extent are the operations of the subsidiaries of foreign multinational enterprises likely to provide a first best solution in advancing these aims.

Can one formulate this question in terms which can be tested? I think one can (even though, in practice, the testing is a very difficult thing to do) *provided that,* and this is an important proviso, one makes some assumption about what would have happened in the absence of inward investment — or if it were $x\%$ less or more than it is. The proposition is — if the addition to the community's real output supplied by resources used by multinational firms (less any part of this output remitted to the investing country) is greater than those same resources could have produced, if used differently or under different ownership, then, multinational firms are advancing economic objectives.

Now, empirically, the testing of this proposition falls into two parts. The first is to measure the actual contribution of foreign firms: This, in itself, involves not only estimating their net output or value added, but the effect which their presence has had on the net output and productivity of other firms in the economy. Second, we need to estimate the net output which would have occurred in the absence of such firms — or if such firms were differently organized and/or financed, or these firms would contribute, if Government policy on institutions were different.

There is another problem. That is to isolate the contribution of foreign subsidiaries, which is due *specifically* to their multinational origin. For instance, it may be that a large U.S. subsidiary performs better than its U.K. competitor — not because it is an offshoot of a multinational company, but because it is bigger than its competitors and that, in this instance, size confers an economic advantage. If one is interested in the distinctive contributions of foreign-owned enterprises, vis-à-vis indigenous firms, then it is important to compare like with like.

Let me briefly summarize at this point. From the viewpoint of a recipient country, the contribution of *any* multinational enterprise must be judged in the light of the extent to which it assists that country in achieving its economic objectives. *Given* a particular economic policy, then this can be assessed by evaluating its contribution to net output, or growth of net output, compared with the next best use of resources (which itself may be difficult to specify). On the other hand, it may be that multinational enterprises are not contributing the most to the economic welfare of host countries because of second best economic policies or regulations. (An obvious case in point is that, in its own interests, a multinational firm will attempt to minimize its international tax burden by various devices, e.g., shifting profits from high tax to low-tax countries. As a result, high-tax countries find that their tax receipts from the multinational company fall — hence its value to the community. This, however, is not a case for restricting the flow of investment —but for tightening up loopholes in the tax regulations.)

EMPIRICAL EVIDENCE

I now turn to illustrate some of the points I have made from the viewpoint of U.S. multinational enterprises operating in the U.K.

EFFECT OF INVESTMENT ON THE U.K.'S REAL INCOME
Excluding the effects on the terms of trade, there are two main ways in which

multinational enterprises may affect the real income of host countries: first, by their effect on the level of demand for resources; second, by their effect on the allocation of these resources. As regards the first, I have elsewhere estimated[1] that U.S. firms have added about 0.3 percent to the g.n.p. of the U.K. simply by locating their activities in areas of above average unemployment (in the North East, Scotland, Wales, etc.) and using resources which would have remained unused (in spite of the Government's attempts to create full employment in these areas.) Upwards of 100,000 new jobs are being created in these areas — though admittedly some of these are possibly migrants from other parts of the country.

Most of the gain to real income arising from the presence of U.S. firms in the U.K. economy is, however, due to their beneficial impact on resource allocation. This has occurred both by the concentration of their activities in the more productive sectors of the economy and because, where they compete side by side with indigenous firms, they do better. (In 1963, for example, of 22 industrial groups, *all* foreign firms had a higher labor productivity than all producing firms in the U.K. in 17 cases.) The mean (total) productivity differential in the mid 1960's was about 20 percent—equivalent to a gain of about 0.6 percent of g.n.p. The differential is probably rather less today as such evidence we have suggests that the productivity gap is narrowing.

Equally important has been the spillover or spin off effects of inward investment, i.e., the impact on resource utilization and productivity of firms other than the investing firms, which is specifically due to their presence *and* foreign affiliations. On these questions, there is a great deal of piecemeal evidence, heresay, and casual impressions. But in general, data both in respect to the U.K. and elsewhere is impressive enough to suggest that the dissemination of knowledge and entrepreneurship by multinational firms (particularly those of American parentage) is one of the most — if not *the* most — valuable contribution they have to make to host countries.

Such a contribution may be *vertical* — e.g., know-how passed on to suppliers and customers of U.S. firms; or *horizontal* — e.g., the stimulus given to competitors — regional or industrial. More generally, information is disseminated by the mobility of personnel, by the informal interchange of ideas among executives, by the publicity of various management and administrative practices. However much it may be possible to protect innovations in product or process technology, "human technology," e.g., advances in management, marketing, labor relations, capital budgeting, and so on, are very difficult to keep quiet. In a variety of ways such as these, U.S. know-how penetrates the local economy. No less important is the added competitive stimulus afforded by these firms, the parent companies of which are likely to be among the most dynamic in the U.S.

It would be extremely difficult to attach a figure of the productivity gain to the U.K. economy of the kind just described — but my best guess is that it would be in the region of ½ percent and 1 percent of g.n.p. This would give a total (measureable) benefit to the U.K. economy resulting from the presence of U.S. firms of between 2 and 2½ percent of g.n.p. My hunch, however, is that this is on the low side.

Improvements in productivity over time largely reflect the rate at which advances in resource usage and efficiency are taking place. As we have said, such improvements may arise from a switch of resources from less to more productive sectors (or a concentration of new resources in these latter sectors) or an increased flow of resources towards more productive firms within particular sectors; or simply an increase in efficiency in any particular firm. This latter, in turn, may be brought about by the introduction of superior production or management techniques or by a better utilization of existing techniques. It may also reflect economies of large-scale production.

The share of the subsidiaries of U.S. and other foreign-controlled multinational firms in the g.n.p. of the U.K. is increasing. As we have said, in 1957, about 5 percent of the sales of the manufacturing industry were supplied by American subsidiaries. By 1966, this had risen to 10.5 percent; today the figure would be nearer 14 percent. Most of this expansion has been within U.S. affiliates already operating in 1955. Between that date and 1967, the net assets of the largest 100 American manufacturing subsidiaries in the U.K. more than doubled, while those of the leading U.K. public companies rose by only two-fifths. In the research-intensive sectors, U.S. firms grew nearly four times the rate of their indigenous competitors. In most (but not all) industries, foreign firms have maintained or expanded their share of the local market.

Our time series data are insufficient to allow us to make any *productivity* growth comparisons, but until the mid 1960's, at least, this favored American subsidiaries — even though, relative to domestic competitors, their profitability has been falling since 1955.

IS THE MULTINATIONAL ENTERPRISE
A FIRST BEST SOLUTION?

Up to this point, I have simply been concerned with giving some broad indications of the actual contribution of U.S. investment to the U.K. economy, given the environment in which it was made. But, in view of the points I raised earlier, I think host countries are now looking beyond this kind of assessment and asking whether (a) subsidiaries of multinational enterprises are contributing the most they can to the local economy and (b) whether the benefits which they confer could have been obtained other (and cheaper) ways.

Let me stress that, in an economic context at least, this is not a question of whether foreign-owned multinational enterprises are a "good" or a "bad" thing for host countries; but simply, in which conditions are they likely to be the cheapest way a country can obtain the ingredients for its prosperity. From the economist's viewpoint the question is mainly one of *price*. To give an analogy, if consumers choose to buy Spanish rather than Florida oranges — this is not to argue that Florida oranges are "bad" — simply that in relation to Spanish oranges they are thought to be too expensive. Similarly, in some instance, some nation states *may* conclude the price they are having to pay for the presence of some multinational enterprises is too high, i.e., in relation to some alternative use of resources. They then either seek ways and means of reducing the price or "buy" the benefits elsewhere.

I have illustrated some possible government policies towards subsidiaries of multinational enterprises to minimize this price or maximize the net benefits. *Such a strategy should, in no way, be interpreted as antagonistic towards foreign investment* — particularly, where it is aimed at neutralizing certain advantages which multinational enterprises may enjoy over national enterprises. It is simply an attempt by the buyer of a group of products and/ or services to obtain these as cheaply as possible. In my written statement I have sought to distinguish between various types of policies to achieve this end — particularly those which we might term unilateral and multilateral. Only multilateral policies, for example, can resolve the difficult problem of extraterritoriality.

As to the net benefits of the alternatives to foreign investment, we still know very little indeed. We do know that from the viewpoint of the investing businesses foreign direct investment is generally preferred to licensing or joint ventures as a means of exploiting overseas markets. From the host economy's viewpoint the choice is by no means as clear cut.

It may be asked, where is there a problem? Why cannot market forces decide this issue? If the government creates the right kind of economic environment, surely decisions of this kind can be left to the private sector.

I think there are three reasons why this is not the case — and all arise due to imperfections in the market. The first is the imperfection of information flows between countries and the relatively high cost of obtaining know-how. Second is the fact that at least part of the cost of producing knowledge (and we have already suggested that knowledge of one form or another is one of the most valuable contributions multinational enterprises have to offer the U.K. economy) is financed by the public sector, where market considerations may be secondary to others. Third, there are important external or social costs and benefits associated with inward investment which do not fully enter the calculations of multinational firms when deciding their investment programs. For these reasons, host countries require some kind of cost/benefit analysis of multinational enterprises and their alternatives.

In summary I would like to make three points:

1. In studying the effects of multinational enterprises on host economies, one must try and specify exactly what one's objectives are, where possible, separating the economic from the political aims. Unless one can, in some way, define one's attitude to issues such as "economic independency," "avoidance of control," and so on — it is very difficult for the economist to get even to "first base."

2. Supposing that one can specify a nation state's economic goals, then it is only possible to say much about the contribution of foreign-owned multinational enterprises if one makes some assumption about what would have happened in its absence. This means one has to make certain hypotheses about government policies and institutions.

3. The final step is to assess whether the actual contribution of multinational enterprises is the "first best solution" (from the viewpoint of the host economy). This involves both estimating whether the *net* benefits ($=$gross benefit less costs) of the multinational enterprise are as high as they might be — and an evaluation of the alternatives which might be possible.

All of these later issues involve positive and testable hypotheses. They do not involve value judgments. These come in later when one has to balance economic gains against loss of sovereignty, etc. and when there may be certain conflicts of economic objectives. Here, while the economist can try to evaluate the costs and benefits of alternative actions (e.g., the marginal net benefit, or loss, of an increased U.S. stake in the U.K. car industry from 30-45 percent, cf. 49-64 percent), in the end the final decision may have to be taken on other than economic grounds.

In our present stage of discussion of the multinational enterprise, I am not sure we are yet clear as to which of the propositions I have just mentioned we are trying to test.

NOTE

1. *The Role of American Investment in the British Economy, Political and Economic Planning*, Broadsheet No. 508 (February 1969).

29
The Multinational Enterprise and Nation States: the Shifting Balance of Power

Jack N. Behrman

The international nature of the multinational enterprise is attested by the fact that it has to be responsive in some sense to many governments simultaneously. But its purely national nature is attested, among other things, by the fact that the government of the parent has an unequal claim on the multinational enterprise and uses this claim. Just as no host government wishes to give control over part of its economic life to a foreign corporate entity, the parent government does not wish to release a corporation under its jurisdiction from certain responsibilities merely because it has become a multinational enterprise. Rather than seeing the enterprise's internationalization as a justification for releasing it from governmental control, parent governments tend to see the multinational enterprise as a potential extension of their control into international situations. And governments will not relinquish such an extension of their power unless the return for doing so is sufficiently rewarding.

Governments have asserted the right to restrict the flow of economic factors (labor, capital, goods, management, and technology) across national borders and even to control the behavior of management if citizenship or corporate ties permit. The multinational enterprise becomes a channel for con-

Reprinted by permission. This paper was presented before the Association for Education in International Business, Chicago, December 28, 1968, and is based on research made possible by a grant from The Ford Foundation to the Harvard Business School.

flicts between governments, challenging their power to control external affairs affecting them.[1]

As a result of the differences among governments, the multinational enterprise itself has the capacity to play one off against another, increasing its bargaining power. The growth of the multinational enterprise, therefore, has shifted the power positions not only among governments but also between them and the private sector. While the public sector has been gaining power over the private sector in economic affairs over the past quarter century, as Andrew Shonfield has demonstrated,[2] the multinational enterprise has been regaining some of that power and shifting the balance of remaining power among governments.

UNEQUAL POWER OF THE PARENT GOVERNMENT

The parent government of the multinational enterprise has greater control over the group of affiliates than any other government. But its power is not unlimited.

SOURCES OF POWER

The parent government derives its power over the enterprises from three situations: The headquarters company is under its legal jurisdiction; there is normally a close tie of managers of the parent to the government where the company has its headquarters; and the largest portion of assets in any one country is normally in the parent country.

The fact that the headquarters company is incorporated under the laws of the parent government gives that government the ability to compel certain actions affecting the entire multinational enterprise. It can alter the financial flows, change the trade patterns, alter the competitive relations, control the flow of technology, alter the pattern of inter-company pricing, and restrict the movement of persons. Non-compliance by affiliates brings penalties to the parent which are too serious to permit flouting the regulations.

The parent government may not have to pass laws or impose regulations to achieve its objectives because of its ties with the managers themselves. There is little question that in times of emergency the managers are loyal citizens of the parent country and will accede to the wishes of the government. But, at other times also, if high government officials request certain action on the part of the headquarters company — to be applied to foreign affiliates — the management of the multinational enterprise will generally respond. The response is out of loyalty — the historical growth of the company as "American," "Dutch," "Swiss," or whatever — out of the personal friendships of managers with government officials, and out of a desire not to affront the government.

In the United States, these ties stem partly from membership in "The Establishment," the same graduating class at a given university, the same professional fraternity, or some social business association. In France, it is a common "old-school tie" at the Ecole Polythechnique; and in Britain the same ties go back to prep-school. Consequently, some constraints on managers need be merely oral — as, for example, when denial controls were imposed extra-legally through verbal requests to U.S. companies, whose management complied even at a cut in profits of their foreign affiliates by several million dollars.

This allegiance is buttressed by the fact that there are close ties between the larger U.S. corporations — parents of the multinational enterprise — and the U.S. Government apart from personalities. These ties consist of contracts with government purchasing agencies, including most importantly the Department of Defense, research and development contracts, continuing negotiations concerning tax liabilities, and applications for government-supplied loans. Each of these relationships *could* be adversely affected by an uncooperative response to a request from U.S. officials that the parent alter the behavior of a foreign affiliate.[3] The willingness of U.S. corporate officials to respond favorably to governmental requests concerning international operations is shown by the fact that they seldom, if ever, reply that the cost of compliance is too high; rather, in discussions, cost is not a relevant factor.[4]

The fact that non-compliance exists in areas such as antitrust illustrates an important feature of governmental power. It is much greater and compelling when there is no redress and means of appeal. In the case of antitrust, the headquarters company is not dealing with requests of officials of the Executive Branch of the U.S. Government but is defending itself as to its interpretation of proper behavior under a law applying to all companies. There are different interpretations as to what "compliance" requires; many corporate officials and managers think that these particular laws are largely irrelevant to the world of today and should be changed. And there is a difference of view between corporate officials and government lawyers as to what should constitute a "substantial effect" of foreign operations on U.S. commerce.[5] Compliance to a government "request" in this area is not likely to be forthcoming, but in denial controls and balance of payments regulations, it will be.

The mere fact that the largest volume of the assets of the multinational enterprise are located within the economy of the parent country provides that government with considerable suasion. Even if the headquarters company were moved to a third country — such as Luxembourg, Panama, or Liechtenstein — the country with the largest assets of the multinational enterprise within its borders would still have considerable power over the entire complex. And, if this government were the U.S. Government, power would still exist to impose antitrust regulations on matters affecting the American affiliate *and* its relations with other affiliates or the parent (at least if the doctrine of "reciprocating partners" was applied, as attempted in the case cited earlier concerning Electric and Musical Instruments Ltd). Authority would also exist to determine denial policies of other related companies if any goods or technology flowed from the U.S. affiliate. And the U.S. Government would certainly have control over the financial flows emanating from the affiliate. The techniques of control and problems are similar to that of any host government, as discussed below, but greater because of the importance of the U.S. Government and of the greater exposure of the enterprise in the U.S. economy.

LIMITATIONS ON USE OF ITS POWER

Although the parent government may have the legal authority or the position to exercise power over the affairs of the multinational enterprise, it will not always do so. It chooses not to do so when it will not be successful in achieving its objective or because the pursuit of one objective conflicts with other objectives of the government. Or, it may be prevented from doing so by the countermoves of other governments — prevented in a legal or in a diplomatic sense.

Frustration of Objectives. Officials of multinational enterprises have argued for several years that the imposition of present U.S. antitrust regulations deters the pursuit of other foreign economic objectives of the United States which they have been asked to further: "our application of the antitrust law has proved a significant deterrent to the achievement of important American foreign economic objectives."[6] At the White House Conference on Export Expansion in the fall of 1963, corporate officials asserted that the antitrust laws had hampered the expansion of exports and the gaining of additional revenue from licensing and other foreign transactions to help ease the U.S. payments deficit.[7] Mr. David Sarnoff stated at the Conference that —
"The basic difficulty with the U.S. antitrust laws imposed on American business abroad is that they do not permit us to compete on equal terms with foreign business. American companies encounter obstacles under our antitrust laws if they participate with other American companies in joint research, development or marketing programs abroad, or in the allocation of

foreign marketing areas with such companies. Foreign companies are not faced with these obstacles. The net result is that foreign revenues, which American companies could obtain, go to foreign competition.[8]

Similar arguments have been made by corporate officials concerning the impact of balance of payments controls over foreign investment. Managers of multinational enterprises consider that U.S. Government officials do not understand the complex relationships within such an enterprise and treat its various functions as separable parts — readily controlled for divergent objectives. They have argued that the imposition of controls would only "buy time" to make corrections in economic policies which could redress the payments position and that the continuation of controls, for any length of time, would be self-defeating — costing more than was gained. This argument is based on the view that investment abroad is a necessary means of expanding exports and is a net earner of exchange in a few years.

Corporate executives also have argued that limitations on direct investment in the developed countries have a direct impact on reducing investment in the less-developed countries, where the U.S. Government has been trying to expand private outflows. Not only are investments in less developed countries fed from earnings in advanced countries — sometimes directly (avoiding U.S. taxes) but restriction of outlays to 110 percent of past investments eliminates some potential investors with no "base" under the regulations. Also, if one company does not use its quota, no provision is made to shift it to another which would like to invest more. The controls, therefore, limit the outflow even more than allegedly intended.[9]

The U.S. Government has not responded favorably to the recommendations of corporate executives in the areas of antitrust and constraints over capital flows. This negative response indicates either that the government does not agree with their analysis of the contradictory impacts, or that the losses in one area are considered less than the gains in other objectives, or that U.S. Government officials operating the various individual programs do not attempt to coordinate their effort to assess the costs of one on another. If it is the latter, each program would be operated as though it need not be limited by conflicting objectives.

In the area of export control the existence of the multinational enterprise itself and its methods of doing business are a limitation on the exercise of these controls. One of the objectives of the denial controls is to engage in economic warfare by relaxing them when there is a "thaw" in the Cold War and "building bridges" to the East — then tightening them if there is further "freezing" and "burning the bridges" at least slightly. But this "on-again, off-again" permission to trade is quite disruptive of commercial contacts with Soviet countries, with whom long negotiations are necessary to complete a contract and who like to stick to repeat orders once a supplier is found satisfactory. U.S. companies find the cost of long negotiations — possibly to be made fruitless by government denials of export licenses — simply too great. Therefore, when there is a thawing in the controls, they expand their contacts with Soviet countries through their European affiliates.[10] If they are able to supply the goods wanted, eventually, without the use of U.S. components or technology, they are able to continue the commercial contacts developed regardless of U.S. controls. In effect, therefore, the multinational enterprise does limit the capability of the U.S. Government to impose the types of restrictions it would like to impose on trade with Soviet countries, eventually frustrating those controls.[11] Such frustration is not possible in the case of the Treasury controls over "trading with the enemy," for these extend to *any* financial transaction to all U.S. Persons; thus, exports from an affiliate to China and other proscribed destinations are not possible.

Conflict with Other Governments. The potential generation of a conflict with another government becomes a limitation on the power of the parent government to exercise authority which its own laws may provide it. The American Bar Association used this probability of conflict to argue that the U.S. Government should not exercise the authority it had in the antitrust area. This judgment is not for an outsider to make, however. It is the responsibility of government officials to decide the degree to which a potential or actual conflict with other governments should ameliorate any given constraint on the operations of the multinational enterprise.

There appear to be relatively few cases in which "too costly" a price in terms of diplomatic concessions restrained the U.S. Government from imposing either antitrust or export control regulations on multinational enterprises headquartered within its borders. Only one significant intervention by the State Department (and White House) in favor of a violation of antitrust regulations comes to mind — that concerning an oil consortium in the Middle East. Repeated proposals that the Department of State be given a "foreign policy" veto over antitrust proceedings affecting foreign activities of multinational enterprises have gone unheeded by the Government.

In the field of export control, the resentment and pressure of foreign governments has produced some limitations of U.S. denial controls. The suspension of one aspect of the technology regulations and the removal of controls over computer sales to France were taken as a result of diplomatic pressures.[12] The fact that the U.S. Government has tried, and failed, to get all major Western governments to agree with it on the level and importance of such controls leads to the conclusion that its exercise of denial controls over foreign affiliates and licensees of U.S. companies is an attempt to achieve through the private sector what it cannot gain diplomatically. Such a tactic increases the resentment and raises in the minds of foreign officials the possibility of foreign control through economic penetration. This is not a view which the U.S. Government accepts, but the multinational enterprise feels the pressure of its intermediary position.

In a sense, the U.S. Executive Branch is also caught in an intermediary position. Even if U.S. Government officials might like to relieve the multinational enterprise of its pain, it cannot do so at present. Congress has repeatedly shown its interest in maintaining tight controls. To remove them, the Executive Branch would have to admit to a growing inability to control effectively the outflow of U.S. technology and exports and their use by affiliates abroad. The admission that the U.S. Government cannot implement these controls effectively because of frustration by the multinational enterprise and its foreign-based competitors would demonstrate that the U.S. Government is not fully a sovereign, even over foreign assets owned by U.S. companies. Such an admission is difficult for the Administration to make and for Congress to accept.

Some admission of a lack of omnipotence exists in the consultative procedure with Canada on export controls and on antitrust matters.

Under the export control procedures in determining whether to permit a Canadian subsidiary of a U.S. company to fill an order requiring a validated license, the U.S. Government has tended to lay stress on whether the export involved is significant to the Canadian economy (reflecting the degree of pressure applied by that government) and whether the order can be filled from Canada *only* by the U.S. subsidiary. If the answer is positive to these questions, the license is more likely to be granted than not. Kingman Brewster concluded that "the more indispensable the source and the more economically significant the sale, the greater the willingness to permit it."[13] However, such permission tends to undercut the purpose of the controls themselves, which is to deny to Cuba or China whatever it is within the power of the U.S. Government to deny.

In the antitrust area, the U.S. Government was required to retreat when the order of the U.S. Court of Imperial Chemical Industry was disallowed in the British courts. And, in the Swiss Watch case, the Swiss government protested that "international law forbids the suppression of agreements between Switzerland and third country consumers."[14] The Swiss Government further protested that the antitrust indictment by the U.S. Government was a direct attack on the legislation and policy of a sovereign foreign government. A cost to the U.S. Government existed in the fact that the Swiss Watch case remained as an unpleasant background against which the negotiations on U.S. tariffs on watches were played out over a number of years prior to the Kennedy Round (concluded in 1967).

In the area of investment controls, the U.S. Government did accede to the pressures from Canada and Britain to make exceptions in their cases, because of their own balance of payments problems. The concessions to Canada were a mixture of self-defense as well as an effort not to embarrass Canada. The ensuing pressure on the Canadian dollar threatened the U.S. dollar itself. In order to prevent this backwash, the U.S. Treasury reversed its request to repatriate earnings and other funds and even "urged" U.S. companies *not* to bring funds from Canada, despite the fact that the weakness of the Canadian dollar would normally be a signal for a corporate financial officer to protect the company's interest. The U.S. Treasury Secretary went so far as to explain that the new mandatory control on U.S. capital flows "does not call for and is not intended to have the effect of causing abnormal transfers of earnings or withdrawals of capital" from Canada; rather, he said, "U.S. corporations are expected to act as good corporate citizens in Canada." But nothing was conceded to Australia and Japan despite concerns expressed by their governments.

The effectiveness of the capital controls is limited further by the willingness of countries with surpluses in their international payments to let them work. Unless foreign governments permit borrowing on the Euro-dollar market at feasible rates of interest, the foreign borrowing which occurred in early 1968 — in volumes even larger than in 1967, i.e., from a level of $500 million in 1967 to $700 million in the first four months of 1968 — could not have taken the pressure off of the multinational enterprises. As a means of constraining the outflow of funds from Canada after the U.S. guidelines were imposed in 1965, Canadian banks (without any forewarning) demanded that U.S. borrowers carry compensating balances in the lending banks *or* pay off the loans; this action was taken on some loans 18 months old.[15] In addition, some countries have regulations against borrowing by a company to remit dividends abroad — which is the effect of the controls in some instances. The U.S. Government would then have had a still more difficult decision because it would have faced the likelihood of constraining even further the growth of the multinational enterprise and potential exports. In addition, the repatriation of short-term funds, of earnings, and loans could have been stopped by the host governments. That these flows were not interdicted means that other governments were sufficiently in agreement with the objectives and techniques of the U.S. controls — including the discrimination among countries — to permit them to be effective.

In sum, though the U.S. Government holds unequal power over the multinational enterprises which are headquartered within its borders, it does not hold absolute power over them. In fact, the mere existence of the multinational enterprise tends to dilute that power and frustrate some U.S. foreign economic policies. Though all governments lose some power to the multinational enterprise, the loss of power by one government may also increase that of other governments.

POWER OF THE HOST GOVERNMENTS

The fact that the parent government has power to sway economic developments in the host countries becomes the basis of a fear of economic and political domination. The Canadian Task Force concluded that "an elaborate legal and administrative apparatus" had been created by the American Government "to implement their legislation abroad in regard to American goods, technology and the actions of subsidiaries" and that this network was "capable to being turned to any objective in foreign policy or to meet any future stringency, such as a further deterioration of the American balance of payments position. This poses for Canada a basic political problem, namely, that for an uncertain future the 'elbow room,' or decision-making power of the Canadian Government has been reduced in regard to economic relations involving American subsidiaries. The essence of the extraterritorial issue is not the economic costs — and in the interacting network of Canada-United State relations, there may even be economic benefits from Canadian compliance — but rather the potential loss of control over an important segment of Canadian economic life."[16]

Despite this challenge to the sovereignty of host governments, these same governments hold some elements of power themselves. They derive this power from the fact that they hold some assets of the multinational enterprise, have incorporated one or more affiliates of the enterprise, and hold some bargaining power with the parent government itself. Even if there is no legal basis for interference with affairs of the related affiliates or the foreign-incorporated headquarters company, the existence of substantial assets within any country provides a leverage on the part of that government. The mere threat of adverse legislation or of administrative actions can bring considerable compliance with governmental wishes.

The Canadian tariff rebates on auto exports of American-owned affiliates was an effort to alter the pattern of trade in automobiles and parts and to induce larger investment in Canada to increase local production and raise efficiency; though the final techniques were different, the initiative succeeded, and the parent companies in the United States had responded favorably even prior to negotiations between the U.S. and Canadian governments, further investment in Canada was induced in 1964 and 1965 — only to be hampered by the urging in 1965 of "voluntary restraint" on U.S. capital outflows.

The Philippine Government exercised its power through the threat of the Retail Nationalization Law which would have nationalized the outlets of Singer and the petroleum companies. The power was exercised not only against the companies to gain some modifications of behavior but also was a bargaining tool in negotiations with the U.S. Government in the extension of preferences under the Laurel-Langley economic treaty.

The existence of substantial assets within their borders provides the opportunity to the host government for a type of "blackmail." And the fact that the multinational enterprises are tending to integrate their affiliates' operations with each other and with the parent increases the "spoiler capacity" of any one government. Any one government can influence the entire multinational enterprise by hampering a key function in the interlocked process of production and sale. The host government is not, therefore, without the ability to alter the operations of the multinational enterprise — subject to the ability of the enterprise to reduce its exposure to the government over time as it expands and contracts operations.

Governments may also seek to increase their bargaining position by introducing legislation countering the impact of U.S. (or other parent) Government regulations. Several governments passed legislation prohibiting compliance with U.S. requests for information in antitrust cases. And the Canadian Task Force recommended the formation of a special corporation to handle Canadian trade with Soviet and Chinese countries so as to reverse the government's position of "tacitly accepting the principle of extraterritoriality."[17] The new corporation would be informed of any requests for goods coming from the prohibited destinations under U.S. law and then make certain that these orders were filled if it was in the Canadian national interest to do so — regardless of the wishes of the U.S. Government. This, and other recommendations, were directed toward "strengthening Canadian law and administrative machinery to countervail extraterritorial operations of American law and administrative machinery."[18]

But the host government is also limited in its capacity to control the multinational enterprise by the diplomatic power of the parent government or that of other host governments.[19] Canadian Government officials sometimes feel they must have "money in the bank" in Washington — such as having contributed to "neutral inspection teams," troops in Cyprus, etc. — in order to be able to "win a point" on economic matters such as treatment of U.S. subsidiaries.

The conflicts described above illustrate the problems with the parent government; and, as the Fruehauf case in France demonstrates, the parent government does not always win. In addition, the host government frequently has other current negotiations with the parent government which can be used to trade off concessions against its desired controls over the multinational enterprise — such as trade negotiations, contributions to international economic assistance programs, contributions to joint military-support efforts, etc. Conversely, it may give up efforts to control the multinational enterprise to gain favorable conditions in these other areas. For example, the Canadian Task Force accepted "as necessary" the special arrangements with the United States on export control enforcement because of "the pervasive trade ties between Canada and the United States" and the desirability of keeping an "open border."[20] The trade-offs need not be expressed by officials or precisely balanced; they merely form part of the day-to-day bargaining and milieu in which diplomacy is carried out.

An increasingly important limitation on European governments is the fact that they are beginning to obtain significant foreign-affiliates of their own multinational enterprises. If the U.S.-based multinational enterprise were the only such complex in existence, host governments might treat it more cavalierly. But — as with the Dutch and the Swiss, particularly — the existence of important multinational enterprises based in their countries and having significant affiliates in foreign countries prevents them from attempting to control foreign-owned affiliates in their own country too strictly. They prefer a freer hand with their own affiliates overseas than a tighter control over foreign affiliates within their own borders.[21]

These observations point up the fact that the multinational enterprise is tying economics and policies of the advanced countries more closely together, restricting their means of maneuvering against each other, while increasing the number of tensions and areas of conflict.

POSITION OF THE MULTINATIONAL ENTERPRISE

The situations which the multinational enterprise faces as far as governmental regulations are concerned can be classified into four different sets of constraints: (1) both (or all) governments require the same (or similar) action by the enterprise and its affiliates; (2) governments are in disagreement as to what is desired from the enterprise, but there is no compulsion from any government; (3) governments are in disagreement and some are attempting to compel particular behavior, while others are not; (4) governments are in disagreement or conflict and all are attempting to compel a particular behavior. In some of these situations, the power of the multinational enterprise to circumvent governmental policy is increased; in others it is nearly voided.

In the first situation, the enterprise retains little choice, for the same response or action is required by all—such as a minimum capital equity contribution in the formation of a company in each country. The second and third situations provide the maximum leeway to the multinational enterprise and an ability to "cut and weave" through the regulations or requests of several governments. There are many instances of these two types of situations and they frequently give rise to tensions.

The multinational enterprise can, in the situation where there is disagreement but no compulsion by governments, choose the tactic or activity which gains the most for its own objectives—and it tends to do so. The more it exercises this choice, the more it will be able to dictate the next step for government, for it has already taken the first steps in setting the pattern of economic and commercial behavior. The governments then tend to enter as "reactors" rather than initiators or controllers.

In the event that one or more government (but not all) impose regulations in a given functional area, the multinational enterprise has the choice of limiting its exposure to the governments which impose such regulations. This has been the response of many to the regulations imposed in the developing countries—simply to stay out of those economies. This response is especially evident on the part of many of the potential multinational companies of Europe, which have made a policy decision to expand in Europe and in a few, carefully-selected foreign countries, avoiding those with a propensity to interference.

But there are other sources of power for the multinational enterprise in this third situation. One is the fact that governmental policies tend not to be carefully coordinated, while there is a comparatively greater likelihood of communication throughout relevant parts of the multinational enterprise. The latter can, therefore, choose the areas of compliance and direct its negotiations with governments to those agencies or ministers where their compliance will be most noticed, avoiding those where they are not complying. They may also select the particular officials with which to communicate, knowing that there is frequently a division within the government on a particular policy.

The multinational enterprise also obtains some power from the fact that it normally plans its activities from 10 to 15 years ahead, while governments tend to plan for only a few years, if at all. Consequently, multinational enterprises view government demands as short-term and secondary to their long-term objectives. Also, the fact that government ministers and their plans are limited by their terms of office means that the economic objectives of the public sector may well change. Multinational enterprises tend to see the host government—party or officials—as impermanent: "We will be here long after this government has passed on; the next may see it our way." They find it easier to stick to their own projections, thereby limiting the effectiveness of governmental requests.

In the fourth situation, when the various governments concerned are explicit in their requirement and they are in conflict—the multinational enterprise also tends to lose its bargaining position, but only if the conflict of interests is raised to the diplomatic level. In this event, corporate officials may make representations, but the resolution of the differences is at the hands of governmental authorities—as with export control procedures. If the governments impose restrictions, but leave the decision to the corporate officials—as might be the case in a conflict of tax or antitrust laws—the multinational enterprise may find a way through the labyrinth, avoiding penalties in either country. But it may also find itself in violation. It is this uncertainty which causes corporate officials to complain most bitterly concerning these regulations. But, so far, governments show no propensity to remove the burden from the multinational enterprise—probably as a reflection of its exercising power through controlling certain areas of uncertainty facing the multinational enterprise.

In sum, the multinational enterprise is changing the degree of sovereignty which governments have over their national and international economic policies and positions. These shifts also alter the abilities of governments to affect policies of other governments and tend to raise some issues to the diplomatic level. The enterprise is therefore, a new and distinct element in international economic affairs changing not only traditional patterns of trade and investment but also power relationships.

NOTES

1. The Canadian Task Force concluded that "from the perspective of the host country, if the country of origin insists on the primacy of its jurisdiction, and regards subsidiaries as proper instruments for the exercise of its policies, economic and otherwise, problems are created that are too serious to be ignored and often too intractable to be fully resolved, short of outlawing foreign ownership." *(Foreign*

Ownership and The Structure of Canadian Industry, Privy Council Office, 1967, pp. 310-311.)

2. *Modern Capitalism* (New York: Oxford University Press, 1965, *passim.*)

3. In all interviews, corporate officials were asked if they had ever felt any of the pressures enumerated. Without exception none had actually received word from a Government official that lack of action to one request would jeopardize its position in another negotiation. But, equally, they emphasized that they didn't *need* to hear the word so clearly, or didn't want to risk hearing it.

4. In the Fruehauf case on sales to China, the cost to the French company and the U.S. parent of $750,000 (relative to an order valued at only $350,000) was not argued by Fruehauf as too heavy a penalty. Nor is there any provision for indemnification of a U.S. company because of necessity to comply with the controls; rather, there are criminal penalties for violation.

   In one case concerning electronic connectors, the amount of business that could have been lost was 35 times the value of the shipment under denial. Exceptionally, it *appeared* that the Government was willing to accept the fact that denial in this instance was not worth the disruption of business.

5. See, for example, the speech of Ray R. Eppert, Chairman of Burroughs Corporation, before the National Industrial Conference Board Conference, March 3, 1966, New York, on "The Competitiveness of American Business in World Markets."

6. James A. Loughran, "Global Aspects of Antitrust Laws on Trade and Business Activities," *The Magazine of Wall Street,* May 6, 1961, p. 194.

7. For example, one U.S. chemical company reported that its affiliate in Belgium faced the combined marketing effort of all Belgium-owned companies, who are permitted to join in an export cartel, which the U.S. affiliate was prohibited from joining, thus cutting its earnings and the remittances to the parent.

   Another company reported that Japanese companies are encouraged to cartellize under laws promoting specific industries, but American companies are not permitted to participate, making it effectively impossible for them to operate in certain industries.

8. Reported in *American Metal Market,* October 2, 1963. Former Attorney General Herbert Brownell, in a speech before the National Industrial Conference Board on May 16, 1962, argued that the U.S. objective of economic growth was hampered by antitrust policies: "The public interest requires that our expanding U.S. economy continue to expand its manufacturing and marketing activities in Western Europe. The governmental policies that tend to discourage this expansion are contrary to our national interest. Tariff and tax policies must recognize this. Antitrust policies which would apply our domestic antitrust laws indiscriminately to the international business of our U.S. companies are not appropriate to Western Europe which now has its own antitrust regulation. Modernization of our antitrust policies in this area is urgently needed to encourage our expanding economy."

9. Corporate officials involved have felt that the priorities of the Departments of Commerce and Treasury in correcting the payments deficit were being given predominance over those of the Department of State and the Agency for International Development to raise the flow of private funds to developing countries.

10. This tactic also removes the possibility of customer reaction in the United States which might arise from a widely advertised charge that the company was "shipping goods to the Soviets," as was apparently the reason for the pull-back of Firestone on its deal with Rumania after long and successful negotiations, de-

spite the fact that there was a "high policy" determination by the U.S. Government that such trade would be desirable.

11. Kingman Brewster, in his Canadian essay, asserts that "the most important reason for applying the boycott policy to sales by foreign companies is not the strategic significance of the sale but an effort to be sure that U.S. citizens who happen to have foreign plants do not profit by trade which is prohibited for their domestic U.S. competitors." ("Law and United States Business in Canada," Canadian-American Committee, 1960, p. 26.)

12. The technology controls require that technical data (broadly defined and including knowledge carried in a man's head) may not be transferred to a foreign company without an assurance that neither it nor its first product will be shipped to prohibited destinations without prior approval of the U.S. Government. Where such assurances cannot be obtained, the U.S. company must obtain a validated license from the proper officials before transferring the technology. This requirement was distasteful to many countries, who did not like to see their hands bound in promoting trade with whatever countries they might wish.

    In order to assuage foreign governments *and* to permit U.S. companies to pursue legitimate and desirable opportunities abroad (urged by the U.S. Government under its export promotion program), these regulations were temporarily suspended—in September 1964—and remain so today. The intention of the denial policy to interdict transfers of technology is, therefore, circumvented because of the practical impossibility of implementation.

13. *Loc. cit.*

14. American Bar Association Report, *op. cit.,* p. 19.

15. The threat to financial stability in Canada is illustrated by the fact that U.S. investments and long-term loans in Canada (not counting short-term loans of several billion dollars) amount to over half its G.N.P. Reportedly, one U.S. insurance company holds a portfolio in Canada larger than the official monetary reserves of the Canadian Government.

16. *Op. cit.,* p. 339.

17. *Op. cit.,* p. 321 ff.

18. *Op. cit.,* p. 345.

19. In conversations in Canada, it was made clear to me that more extreme measures against the First National City Bank purchase of the Mercantile Bank were rejected because of a fear that "too harsh" treatment would generate retaliation on the part of the U.S. Government, which might force the Canadian officials to do *nothing* to stop the partial take-over.

20. *Op. cit.,* p. 316.

21. A further example of this trade-off is the decision of the Dutch Government not to limit exploration of off-shore oil reserved to Dutch companies—for fear of retaliation similarly by other governments in oil exploration by Royal-Dutch Shell.

30
Issues Between the Multinational Corporation and Host Governments: the European Case

J. Boddewyn

Europe is now America's favorite investment spot, after slightly overtaking Canada in 1969. Some $22 billion, or thirty percent, of U.S. direct investments are in Europe, and American firms control from 5 to 10 percent of the industrial production of most major Western European countries. This growing presence is bound to generate some friction, although conflict is still minimal and will probably remain so. However, in order to keep frictions at a minimum, American investors will have to keep abreast of current conflictual issues and understand and deal wisely with Western European governments.

THE ROLE OF GOVERNMENT

Public authorities everywhere are charged with preserving the independence of their nation and with guiding it towards the achievement of its goals. They are in a way "management" of the entire land; and, like managers, governments are responsible for expliciting goals and mobilizing resources (natural, financial, technological, moral) towards their achievement. While some governments are totalitarian and control all of their country's resources, most delegate much of this managerial task to private individuals and groups, including business firms.

In the United States, the government's role has been restricted by various historical phenomena: belief in a supreme natural law rather than in expediency; a minimum of social conflict; a general acceptance of change; and a good deal of separation of powers among the legislative, executive, and judiciary branches. Elsewhere, however, governments have played a much more active role as the main modernizing agent concerned with unifying the country, fighting social and economic privileges, and championing the notion of change. We see this phenomenon not only in the new nations of Asia and Africa as well as in Latin America, but also in old ones like France and the United Kingdom in which economic and social planning was developed in the postwar period to help transform the economy and society. Even the business-oriented governments of Belgium, West Germany, and Switzerland now play a role in developing new industries and regions; and in the United States, government has not hesitated to step in when consensus was low, conflict high, and performance poor.

Public authorities abroad usually have a lot of power to back up their aims for they own firms, are major purchasers of goods and services, and/or have extensive regulatory authority as well as significant control of credit and capital.[1] They have not found any philosopher's stone in devising good plans and in turning them into realities, but they keep trying out new reforms.

This then is the first thing to remember about foreign governments: they are frequently modernizing agents rather than a mere bunch of meddlers; they consider themselves to be good guys on the side of what is right; they usually take this role very seriously; and, typically, they have many ways of forcing and/or inducing people and organizations to help them in achieving their modernizing goals, even though their choice of objectives and instruments often falls short of perfection.

Yet, it must be immediately realized that this powerful role of government does not at all rule out a powerful role for business. After all, private enterprise still controls about two-thirds of the national income, and it generates at least three-fourths of the gross national product in practically all Western European nations. Besides, business is intimately brought into the making and application of public policy. Not only do certain individual businessmen or firms exert a good deal of influence—with industries lobbying singly and collectively—but business itself is represented on many top-level advisory bodies and drawn into economic planning. Furthermore, Western European governments are discovering more and more that there are limits to what they can do. Hence, they have to turn to business in order to obtain the information they need and to achieve the goals they have set. This situation gives business a good deal of leverage; as a result, Western European economies often resemble much more an American regulatory commission such as the Securities and Exchange Commission where business is quite influential than the superfirm represented by Russia, Inc.

CONFLICTUAL ISSUES

It is in this kind of environment that American subsidiaries and affiliates operate in Europe. In order to be effective there, American investors have not only to understand the role of government but also must fit into its current concerns and avoid a clash. The point here is that dealing with European governments presents not only risks but also opportunities, and the wise international manager takes advantage of the latter. The following analysis attempts to show both aspects of business-government relations in Europe in the context of current issues which center on matters of national interest, national sovereignty, and national feelings.

NATIONAL INTERESTS

At any particular time, European governments pursue a series of inter-related aims or objectives through an assortment of *instruments* which make up its economic policy whose content is outlined in the following table[2] (p. 429).

GOALS AND INSTRUMENTS MATTER

It is obvious that the national interest of a particular country, *as presently conceived,* must be ascertained and considered by the American investor at all times. Some goals may rule out any foreign investment as when matters of national defense or other crucial "commanding heights" industries are involved (e.g., armaments, banking and mining in Sweden); and the benefits for the corporation of contributing to national objectives may not be worth the trouble. Furthermore, some governmental instruments may conflict with the policies of the multinational firm in such matters as ownership and logistics or simply with its preferences and prejudices. Thus, the Swedish government is presently urging foreign investors to enter into joint ventures with local partners and/or even with its new state holding of industrial firms. Combustion Engineering has found it possible and apparently profitable to form just such a tripartite company with a Swedish private firm and with the state holding, but other American companies may shirk from such arrangements. It remains, however, that a foreign firm can only acquire legitimacy abroad if it fits into the host country's current objectives and instruments, however difficult it may be to perceive and reconcile them.

While no international firm shall fail to ascertain first if there is a profitable market—private or public—for their foreign endeavors, it is quite evident that governmental priorities and incentives create opportunities which are quite legitimate and not any riskier than markets that can go sour or production plans that may turn out to be inefficient.

Major Goals	Major Instruments

1. FULL EMPLOYMENT
  a. In the short run: reducing cyclical unemployment
  b. In the long run: reducing structural and frictional unemployment
	a. Governement investment and subsidies
	b. Bank-rate manipulation
	c. Prices and wages controls
	d. Control of operations

2. PRICE STABILITY	a. Prices and wages controls b. Taxes c. Foreign-trade and investment controls

3. IMPROVEMENT IN THE BALANCE OF TRADE AND OF PAYMENTS
  a. In the short term: protecting gold and foreign exchange reserves
  b. In the long term: achieving structural changes in the proportion of imports and exports, and in their composition
	a. Foreign-trade and capital controls
	b. Bank-rate manipulation
	c. Devaluation-revaluation of currency
	d. Participation in international institutions (GATT, EEC, OECD, etc.)

4. EXPANSION OF PRODUCTION	a. Government investment and subsidies b. Tax credits and allowances

5. IMPROVEMENT IN THE ALLOCATION OF THE FACTORS OF PRODUCTION
  a. Promotion of internal competition
  b. Promotion of coordination to avoid waste
  c. Increase in the mobility of labor
  d. Increase of the mobility of capital
  e. Promotion of the international division of labor
	a. Antitrust measures
	b. Participation in international institutions
	c. Foreign trade and investment controls

6. SATISFACTION OF COLLECTIVE NEEDS
  a. General administration
  b. Defense
  c. International affairs
  d. Education
  e. Culture
  f. Science
	a. Government expenditures
	b. Participation in international institutions

7. IMPROVEMENT IN THE DISTRIBUTION OF INCOME AND WEALTH	a. Taxes b. Transfer payments c. Incomes controls
8. PROTECTION AND PRIORITIES TO CERTAIN REGIONS OR INDUSTRIES	a. Government subsidies b. Foreign trade and investment controls
9. IMPROVEMENT IN THE PATTERN OF PRIVATE CONSUMPTION	a. Quality controls and standards b. Subsidies and controls
10. SECURITY OF SUPPLY	a. Foreign-trade and investment controls b. Control of operations

*Adapted from: E.S. Kirschen *et al.*, *Economic Policy in Our Time* (Chicago: Rand Mc-Nally & Co., 1964).

The proper perspective here is one of a joint endeavor with foreign governments in the sense that the international company identifies with the current notion of what is in the national interest. This can be an "arms' length" relationship for a definite period of time — just like contracts with suppliers, customers, and other partners, which do not bind forever but certainly restrict the parties' freedom for a while. When discussing the multinational firm's desire and capability to produce, sell, hire, raise capital, and license abroad, we tend to overlook this long-term commitment element as if firms could and do frequently pull out stakes on very short notice. A more realistic view is that firms are usually bound for shorter or longer periods of time as a result of contractual agreements and of the need for time to appraise any new venture and (hopefully) to bring it to fruition. A commitment to a foreign government is not essentially different in this respect from a private contract if adequate safeguards (which are never completely foolproof in any contractual agreement) have been provided before moving in or expanding abroad. For that matter, firms usually insist for protection on capital and income repatriation guarantees, but there are many other ways of protecting one's position overseas against sudden changes in public policies (e.g., by borrowing locally as most American companies have done in Europe).

PRIORITIES CHANGE

European governments pursue a variety of goals simultaneously, but the foreign investor must realize that their priorities change. Thus, during the 1960's, the Belgian government was particularly interested in (1) eliminating pockets of structural unemployment in declining or underdeveloped regions; and (2) maintaining a favorable balance of trade on account of Belgian's dependence on exports in order to absorb the output of large modern plants and in order to pay for the imports essential for a country poor in resources. Hence, the first two questions asked of a potential American investor were: (1) How many jobs will you create?; and (2) How much will you export?[3] The available incentives (capital grants and loans, training subsidies, tax holidays, and free sites) were given to those who could answer these questions satisfactorily. Today, however, unemployment is no longer a major problem, and the Belgian Government is much more interested in upgrading the technological level of industry so that the favored investor is the one that brings in advanced processes and products and does research and development work in the country.

Besides, success in attracting foreign investors (and a few abuses by the latter) is making the Belgian authorities more demanding. Consequently, the prospective investor or reinvestor must commit himself much more formally to his obligations, and can no longer promise something for the future and receive the incentives immediately. Instead, he must enter into a "progress-contract" that spells out the respective rights and obligations of the firm and the authorities; the incentives are given to him in proportion to the fulfillment of his commitments.

It follows that the American investor must recognize that priorities and instruments change, identify the contemporary ones, and adopt his behavior to whatever objectives and instruments are current. For a company to have created 300 low-skilled jobs five years ago when unemployment was an important public issue no longer earns it any public gratitude when another concern (such as technological upgrading of industry) becomes uppermost—not to mention the fact that governments have short memories and quickly take for granted a particular contribution. As they say in organizational psychology: "A satisfied need does not motivate anymore."

GOALS CAN CONFLICT

In general, governmental goals are fairly obvious, and their change is not too difficult to anticipate. At times, however, government may not be in agreement about what needs to be done and how. Thus, the French Committee on Foreign Investments, which passes on applications for investment permits, groups the delegates of various ministries and has to reconcile their varied interests. The Ministry of Industry wants technologically advanced firms and is concerned with developing a few strong native industries. Just creating more jobs does not interest this ministry; it is concerned, however, about American takeovers or even about new ventures which upset the regrouping of a particular industrial sector. The Ministry of Finances, on the other hand, wants the foreign investor to bring in new capital from abroad in order to improve the French balance of payments and to avoid upsetting the local capital market. If a takeover is involved, it wants to make sure that the French seller has been adequately compensated and that the monetary compensation does not flee the country. Matters of employment or of "industrial policy" concern this ministry much less. Now enters DATAR, the quasi-ministry concerned with land-use planning and regional development, wanting new jobs, preferably in the provinces, in which France experiences serious unemployment problems; and it controls most of the incentives available to the appropriate investor. DATAR is much less concerned with developing strong industries or improving the balance of payments; and takeovers do not interest it since they usually do not involve new employment. The story does not stop there either because other ministries may be involved; because regions and cities have their own views of what is good for them and have some incentives of their own to offer; because the European Economic Community and the Organization for Economic Cooperation and Development are looking askance at some of the French controls and incentives; and because France's Treaty of Establishment with the United States is supposed to let American firms enter the country freely. Behind these ministries, various French interest groups also push and pull in different directions.

The lesson for the American investor or reinvestor is that he has to know where power currently lies. Some investments will please practically everybody, but the success of most requires careful planning to make them acceptable to a majority. Sometimes it is a matter of patience, as when General Electric finally obtained permission to buy more shares than it had asked for, in the "Machines Bull" case. On the other hand, Westinghouse has had pretty much to give up its original plans for acquiring Jeumont-Schneider.

NATIONAL SOVEREIGNTY

The multinational enterprise serves more than one master, and experience has taught that such a situation creates trouble. In fact, practically everyone has to live and operate under such multiple-mastership situations, notwithstanding organization principles to the contrary. Besides, most firms manage to do it without encountering major difficulties, but others do, more or less frequently.

Issues of national sovereignty revolve around the fact that European nations are the masters and want to remain so in their own house, unless they choose to relinquish some of their sovereign rights in the context of regional (e.g., the European Economic Community, and the European Free Trade Association) groupings and international agreements (e.g., the Organization for Economic Cooperation and Development, and the International Monetary Fund).

Governments do of course sin against the national sovereignty of other nations by violating agreements or slyly cheating on them; and it is very difficult to make them abide by their engagements unless they agree to accept the decision of some ruling or arbitrating body. Thus, in November 1969, the Common Market Commission took France to the EEC Court of Justice for an alleged infraction of the Rome Treaty by compelling all foreign companies investing in France (including companies incorporated in other EEC countries) to apply for authorization from the French Ministry of Finances. The incriminated French law of January 1967 was aimed at preventing back-door investments in France by U.S. companies via their subsidiaries in other EEC countries. Paris assured the EEC Commission that "genuine" EEC companies would not be refused authorization, but the Commission considered this French assurance insufficiently binding juridically, and it disagreed with France's definition of "community companies." This matter has now been settled.

American multinational enterprises are, of course, in trouble when U.S. interests and regulations conflict openly with those of European nations. Problems here usually center on the extraterritorial application of American laws bearing on antitrust matters and on the export of capital, strategic products, and technology.[4] The U.S. government has its own views about what is in the American interest and even of what is good for other nations, but the latter do not always agree.

It is obvious that the better part of wisdom for governments consists in minimizing such conflicts of national sovereignty. The Nixon Administration has apparently taken a more conciliatory position in this respect by not rattling sabers too much in Latin America and by letting foreign subsidiaries sell nonstrategic goods to Red China. Besides, there is some slow evolution towards developing mechanisms for international arbitration and for the supranational control of multinational corporations.[5] Still, conflicts will remain, whether latently or openly.

The American subsidiary abroad cannot therefore avoid problems in this area as it has to comply with a multiple set of objectives and regulations, and to act as the direct agent of several governments all interested in improving their balance of payment, in strengthening their industries, and in thwarting their enemies (not necessarily the same).

The only immediately possible courses of action consist of avoiding clear-cut situations of conflict (e.g., by not going to a country that insists that the American subsidiary sells its strategic product to "enemy" countries); and of shifting the problem to third countries (e.g., by borrowing on the Eurobond market, if France and the United States object to the use of either French or American capital). There are of course slier ways of extricating oneself from issues of sovereignty, as when companies go ahead in the hope that the relevant governments will look the other way, or when they can show that they *had* to comply with one government's requirements as this usually settles the issue. However, such ploys do not really resolve the issue nor do they help the multinational firm prove that it has the national interest at heart.

NATIONAL FEELINGS

"National interests" and "national sovereignty" are fairly objective concepts, but "national feelings" is much more subjective. Such "nationalism" is usually used to refer to the attitude of a government or its people that object to, resist, or combat the coming or presence of a foreign company simply because it is "foreign"—irrespective of any violation of national interests or of the extra-territorial application of foreign laws. The issue no longer centers on *legality* of behavior but on: (1) *loyalty* to the interests of the host country as defined by the host government ("In a pinch, they will rally around their flag!"); (2) *empathy* with the ways of the local culture ("They are different and do not understand our ways"); and (3) *solidarity* of one group against another ("It is us against them"). Nationalism boils down here to a feeling of participation in a national struggle against foreigners in order to protect one's way of life, pride, and independence; of a bias in favor of compatriots; and of concern over their welfare.[6]

Nationalistic feelings can be subtle or crude but they are always latent, and they can be triggered by anything. Thus, when the British Petroleum Company's attempt to acquire Standard Oil of Ohio was temporarily challenged by the U.S. Department of Justice, there was the *feeling* in Europe that this represented some sort of discrimination against foreign companies trying to get a strong foothold in the American market. This was denied by the American authorities who stressed that this was in fact proof that the British company was treated like any other local monopolistic firm; but few Europeans believed it.

Some nationalistic feelings are purely irrational, and they reflect frustration, a search for scapegoats, or demagoguery on the part of politicians. However, much nationalistic feeling is healthy and simply reflects a desire for self-determination and identity. Besides, some nationalistic reactions have been unnecessarily triggered by ill-conceived or thoughtless violation of natural interests, sensitivities, and sovereignty. Thus, Dun & Bradstreet was roundly criticized in Sweden when it went ahead and acquired a second Swedish credit-information company although it knew that the government and certain important segments of public opinion were very much concerned about its first acquisition. Some Swedes were already uneasy about private firms controlling information about the credit-worthiness of individual persons and companies—they considered it an invasion of privacy—but letting a foreigner monopolize it was too much.

The multinational enterprise must also thread its way carefully between complying with local traditions and contributing something new to its new home country. Too much change or too much haste can stir up nationalistic reactions and reinforce negative feelings about American ways—particularly when they fail. Thus, when the Schlitz Brewing Company withdrew precipitously from Belgium after only two years of unprofitable operations, apparently as a result of a faulty reading of market demand, it was felt that not only had it jeopardized Belgian national goals by threatening several hundred jobs, but that its sudden declaration of bankruptcy was an improper way of getting out, only too representative of American "financial mentality" and lack of consideration for employees, suppliers, and customers. The Belgian way would have been to smooth over things with government subsidies in one way or the other in order to tide Schlitz over, or to facilitate the selling of the brewery to another interest. The American company may still have left Belgium, but without stirring up as much resentment, for which other U.S. companies in Belgium will have to pay.

CONCLUSION

American companies operating in Europe are faced with various issues which can be summarized as follows:

	HOST COUNTRY criticizes:	AMERICAN COMPANIES criticize:
ISSUE* OF NATIONAL INTEREST	The behavior of foreign companies that is inconsistent with, or goes against, the economic and social goals of the host country.	The behavior of host governments that amounts to a mistaken or unclear notion of the national interest, or to the faulty implementation of economic and social goals.
ISSUE* OF NATIONAL SOVEREIGNTY	The use (or at least the abuse) of foreign companies as instruments of their home-governments, and the extra-territorial application of foreign laws.	The refusal of host governments to accept supra national agreements regarding the handling of disputes, or to abide by such international agreements.
ISSUE* OF NATIONALISM	The lack of loyalty of foreign companies to the interests of the host country, as well as their lack of understanding and concern for local desires to be independent and different.	The discrimination by host governments against foreign companies simply because the latter are foreign.
*Issues = "Matters in dispute."		

However, each one of these issues also offers opportunities for operating profitably in Europe because the American company which does contribute to the achievement of national goals, and does it without clashing too much or too often with local sovereignties and feelings, can thereby augment (or at least preserve) the market gains that attracted it there in the first place.

NOTES

1. This modernizing role of government and its larger power has been excellently analyzed for a number of Western European countries by Andrew Shonfield in *Modern Capitalism: The Changing Balance of Public and Private Power* (New York: Oxford University Press, 1965).
2. Governments also have social, political, and cultural policies often related to their economic policies. E. S. Kirschen *et al.* define "policy" as "action taken by the Government in pursuit of certain aims," with "economic policy" representing the economic aspect of government policy in general. To put their economic policies into effect, governments either alter certain economic quantities (such as tax rates) or make changes in the economic structure (e.g., through nationalization). These economic quantities which governments can change or the types of intervention in the economic structure are their "instruments." *Economic Policy in Our Time, in General Theory,* Vol. 1 (Chicago: Rand McNally & Co., 1964), pp. 3-4.
3. J. Boddewyn, "Don't Take Belgium for Granted," *Worldwide P & I Planning* (November-December 1969), pp. 34-48.
4. For an excellent analysis, see: Jack N. Behrman, *National Interests and the Multinational Enterprise: Tensions Among the North Atlantic Countries* (Englewood Cliffs, N.J.: Prentice-Hall, 1970).
5. For a discussion of these solutions, see: Behrman, *op. cit.* and Charles P. Kindleberger, *American Business Abroad* (New Haven, Conn.: Yale University Press, 1969). Lecture 6.
6. These concepts have been elaborated by John Fayerweather in the context of his current multinational study of nationalistic attitudes among various economic and political elites.

Chapter Eight:
Evolution

31

The Multinational Corporation and Uneven Development

Stephen Hymer

SUMMARY

1. The multinational corporation, because of its great power to plan economic activity, represents an important step forward over previous methods of organizing international exchange. It demonstrates the social nature of production on a global scale, and as it eliminates the anarchy of international markets and brings about a more extensive and productive international division of labor, it releases great sources of latent energy.

2. But the multinational corporation is still a private institution with a partial outlook and represents only an imperfect solution to the problem of international cooperation. It creates hierarchy rather than equality, and it spreads its benefits unequally. As it crosses international boundaries, it pulls and tears at the social and political fabric and erodes the cohesiveness of national states.

3. Whether one likes this or not, it is probably a tendency that cannot be stopped. Through its propensity to nestle everywhere, settle everywhere, and establish connections everywhere, the multinational corporation destroys the possibility of national seclusion and self-sufficiency and creates a universal interdependence.

4. This applies to the United States as well as to other countries. Continued growth of U.S. direct foreign investment at its present rate of 10 percent per year implies an increased cleavage between international and national interests, i.e., more dependence upon the world economy, greater difficulty

Reprinted by permission. Prepared statement read before the Subcommittee on Foreign Economic Policy of the Joint Economic Committee, Congress of the United States, Ninety-first Congress, Second Session, pp. 906-910.

in controlling large corporations, and greater involvement in maintaining law and order to protect international private property.

5. However, in proportion to its success, the multinational corporation leads other groups, particularly labor and government to mobilize their power; it creates counterforces in the form of conflicts within major centers, between major centers, and between the major centers and the hinterland.

6. The present crisis may well be more profound than most of us imagine, and the West may find it impossible to restructure the international economy on a workable basis. One could easily argue that the age of the Multinational Corporation is at its end rather than at its beginning. The present hearings may be the epitaph of the American attempt to sustain the old international economy, and not the herald of a new era of international cooperation.

THE COMING CRISIS OF THE MULTINATIONAL CORPORATION

Since the beginning of the Industrial Revolution, there has been a tendency for the representative firm to increase in size from the *workshop* to the *factory* to the *national corporation* to the *multidivisional corporation* and now to the *multinational corporation*.

Until recently, most multinational corporations have been from the United States. Now European corporations, as a by-product of increased size, and as a reaction to the American invasion of Europe, are also shifting attention from national to global production and beginning to "see the world as their oyster." If present trends continue, multinationalization is likely to increase greatly in the next decade as giants from both sides of the Atlantic (though still mainly from the U.S.) strive to penetrate each other's markets and to establish bases in underdeveloped countries, where there are few indigenous concentrations of capital sufficiently large to operate on a world scale. This rivalry may be intense at first but will probably abate through time and turn into collusion as firms approach some kind of oligopolistic equilibrium. A new structure of international industrial organization and a new international division of labor will have been born.

So profound a change in economic structure will require correspondingly radical changes in the legal, political, and ideological framework. At present "practice is ahead of theory and policy," as John Powers, president of the Charles Pfizer Corporation, has put it. Multinational corporations, through their everyday business practice, are creating a new world environment, but policy makers (and theoreticians) are lagging behind.

In other words, the situation is a dynamic one, moving dialectically. Right now, we seem to be in the midst of a major revolution in international relationships as modern science establishes the technological basis for a major advance in the conquest of the material world and the beginnings of truly cosmopolitan production. Multinational corporations are in the vanguard of this revolution, because of their great financial and administrative strength and their close contact with the new technology. Governments (outside the military) are far behind, because of their narrower horizons and perspectives, as are labor organizations and most non-business institutions and associations. Therefore, in the first round, multinational corporations are likely to have a certain degree of success in organizing markets, decision-making, and the spread of information in their own interest. However, their very success will create important tensions and conflicts which will lead to reactions by other groups.

Thus, whether foreign investment can continue to grow at 10 percent per year, as it has for the past twenty years, with drastic implications such an expansion has for world order, is an open question. Economic factors, in the sense of an expanding world market, are favorable. Political factors are a different matter. Since economic power cannot long be out of phase with political power, multinational corporations must mobilize political power, or they will not be able to create the new world economic order we hear so much about.

UNEVEN DEVELOPMENT

Suppose giant multinational corporations (say 300 from the U.S. and 200 from Europe and Japan) succeed in establishing themselves as the dominant form of international enterprise and come to control a significant share of industry (especially modern industry) in each country. The world economy will resemble more and more the United States economy, where each of the large corporations tends to spread over the entire continent and to penetrate almost every nook and cranny. What would be the effect of a world industrial organization, decentralization and centralization. On the one hand, the come distribution? To what extent would it perpetuate the present system of uneven development, i.e., the tendency of the system to produce poverty as well as wealth, underdevelopment as well as development?

The growth of firms involves a double movement: differentiation and organization, decentralizational and centralization. On the one hand, the multinational corporation because of its power to command capital and technology and its ability to rationalize their use on a global scale, will probably spread production more evenly over the world's surface than now is the case. At the same time, it will tend to centralize strategic decisions in regional coordinating centers and in corporate headquarters. Horizontal expansion of corporations through the world will be accompanied by a vertical differentiation of levels of command (symbolized by the corporate skyscraper) and a stratification of employees from operatives to executives, with wide differences in authority, status, remuneration, horizons, mobility, mental demands, and development.

The spatial or geographic implication of the corporate structure lies in the close correspondence between the centralization of control within the corporation and centralization of control within the international economy. A system of North Atlantic Multinational Corporations would tend to produce a hierarchal division of labor between geographical regions corresponding to the vertical division of labor within the firm. It would tend to centralize high-level decision-making occupations in a few key cities in the advanced countries, surrounded by a number of regional sub-capitals, and confine the rest of the world to lower levels of activity and income, i.e., to the status of towns and villages in a new Imperial System. Income, status, authority, and consumption patterns would radiate out from these centers along a declining curve, and the existing pattern of inequality and dependency would be perpetuated. The pattern would be complex, just as the structure of the corporation is complex, but the basic relationship between different countries would be one of superior and subordinate, head office and branch plant.

One would expect to find the highest offices of the multinational corporations concentrated in the world's major cities—New York, London, Paris, Hamburg, Tokyo. These along with Moscow and perhaps Peking, will be the major centers of high-level strategic planning. Lesser cities throughout the world will deal with the day-to-day operations of specific local problems. These in turn will be arranged in a hierarchal fashion: the larger and more important ones will contain regional corporate headquarters, while the smaller ones will be confined to lower level activities. Since business is usually the core of the city, geographical specialization will come to reflect the hierarchy of corporate decision-making, and the occupational distribution of labor in a city or region will depend upon its function in the international economic system. The best and most highly paid administrators, doctors, lawyers, scientists, educators, government officials, actors, servants, and hairdressers, will tend to concentrate in or near the major centers.

The new economy will be characterized by a division of labor based on nationality. Even within the United States, ethnic homogeneity increases as one goes up the corporate hierarchy; the lower levels contain a wide variety of nationalities, the higher levels become successively more pure. A similar phenomenon will probably develop on a world scale as firms try to balance the need for adaptation to local customs and circumstances with a centralized strategic point of view.

Day-to-day management in each country will be left to the nationals of that country who, being intimately familiar with local conditions and practices, are able to deal with local problems and local government. These nationals remain rooted in one spot, while above them is a layer of people who move around from country to country, as bees among flowers, transmitting information from one subsidiary to another and from the lower levels to the general office at the apex of the corporate structure. In the nature of things, these people (reticulators) for the most part will be citizens of the country of the parent corporation (and will be drawn from a small culturally homogeneous group within the advanced world), since they will need to have the confidence of their superiors and be able to move easily in the higher management circles. Latin Americans, Asians, and Africans will at best be able to aspire to a management position in the intermediate coordinating centers at the continental level. Very few will be able to get much higher than this, for the closer one gets to the top, the more important is "a common cultural heritage."

The multinational corporate system thus does not seem to offer the world national independence or equality. Instead it would keep many countries as branch plant countries, not only with reference to their economic functions but throughout the whole gamut of social, political, and cultural roles. The subsidiaries of multinational corporations tend to be among the largest companies in the country of their operations; and their top executives play an influential role in the political, social, and cultural life of the host country.

Yet these people, whatever their title, occupy at best a medium position in the corporate structure and are restricted in authority and horizons to a lower level of decision making. The governments with whom they deal tend to take on the same middle management outlook, since this is the only range of information and ideas to which they are exposed. In this sense, one can hardly expect such a country to bring forth the creative imagination needed to apply science and technology to the problems of degrading poverty.

CORPORATIONS AND NATIONS

"For a worldwide enterprise, national boundaries are drawn in fading ink," wrote *Business Week* (February 17, 1968), as a headline with reference to George Ball's now famous argument that corporations are modern institutions and nation states are old fashioned institutions rooted in archaic concepts. What does this mean in particular for the United States, the most powerful national state of all?

In the first place, one should note that the conflict is not really between corporations and nation states, but between groups of people within corporations and nation states struggling over who decides what and who gets what, i.e., between big multinational corporations over the share of the world market, between big business which is internationally mobile and small business and labor which are not; between the middle class of different countries over managerial positions, between high wage labor in one country and low wage labor in another; and between excluded groups and elites within each country over the direction development is to take.

The importance of these conflicts depends upon the scale of foreign investment. The rapid growth of U.S. foreign investment over the last twenty years has already revealed certain cleavages between the interests of international investors and the rest of the domestic economy over taxation, balance of payments, extraterritoriality, and foreign aid. For example, multinational corporations have pressed for relief from taxation on foreign income and from regulation by antitrust and other laws. They would like the United States to adjust its balance of payments by deflating the economy or controlling imports rather than controlling foreign investment. At the same time, they would like freedom to produce where costs are lowest, unhampered by tariffs and trade. On these issues they conflict with other domestic taxpayers who wish equal taxation for foreign income; firms who cannot meet the challenge of foreign competition through investment but must rely on exports or on the domestic market; and certain classes of labor threatened by foreign competition.

These types of problems will grow as foreign investment continues to grow. Three major types of complications are likely to emerge.

First, the United States will become increasingly interdependent with the world economy. The multinational corporation is a medium by which laws, politics, foreign policy, and culture of one country intrude into one another. Already United States antitrust laws and balance of payments controls quickly feed into other countries via multinational corporations and then quickly react back on the United States Government. More of this can be expected in the future, as the multinational corporation acts as a viaduct for transmitting pressure from one country to another, thus reducing the sovereignty of all nations and requiring the building of supranational institutions to coordinate policy and reduce conflicts. To many, this is its most positive feature.

Second, the ability to control large corporations will be reduced. Multinational corporations because of their worldwide horizons and scope of operations have a certain flexibility for reducing the control of any one country over them. This applies to monetary policy, fiscal policy, and a host of others, and is perhaps best illustrated by tax questions. In an environment of free capital movements and free trade, a government's ability to tax multinational corporations is limited by the ability of those corporations to manipulate transfer prices and to move their productive facilities from country to country. Countries become like cities competing for branch plants.

Third, because the multinational corporation is associated with world stratification and inequality in property, power, and income, it creates a goal in those lower down the hierarchy to try to change it. This tendency is dampened to the extent that the system provides continuous improvement and opportunity for everybody. The multinational corporation, because of its dynamic qualities, has a certain stabilizing effect in this regard. But the available evidence indicates that it can provide some degree of participation for at most one third of the world's population. The remaining two thirds, who get only one third of income, gain little. And, along with the many dissatisfied of the upper third, present a continuous challenge. The United States, because of its special position, pays the largest part of the cost of maintaining the system in face of these challenges. The costs have been rising rapidly and may easily come to exceed any benefits the nation as a whole is alleged to gain from them (as opposed to the substantial gains accruing to the limited sector directly involved in foreign investment). At any rate, this is what happened to the British Empire.

32
How to Divest in Latin America and Why

Albert O. Hirschman

The dispute between Peru and the United States over the expropriation of the International Petroleum Company is only one of a monotonously long list of incidents and conflicts which call into serious question the wisdom of present institutional arrangements concerning private international investment. This paper will discuss the principal weaknesses of these arrangements, with particular emphasis on political economy rather than on economics proper, and will then survey a number of ways in which current institutions and practices could be restructured. It is written against the backdrop of rising nationalism and militancy in the developing countries, particularly in Latin America, and of an astounding complacency, inertia, and lack of institutional imagination on the part of the rich countries.

The basic position adopted here with respect to foreign private investment is that it shares to a very high degree the ambiguity of most human inventions and institutions: it has considerable potential for both good and evil. On the one hand, there are the celebrated and undoubted contributions of private international investment to development: the bringing in of capital, entrepreneurship, technology, management and other skills, and of international market connections, all of which are either wholly lacking in the poor countries, or are in inadequate supply given the opportunities and programs for economic development. On the other hand, foreign investment brings not only the dangers of economic plunder and political domination which are the stock-in-trade of the various theories of imperialism, but a number of other,

Reprinted, with permission, from *Essays in International Finance,* No. 76 (November 1969). Copyright © 1969 by the International Finance Section, Department of Economics, Princeton, New Jersey.

more subtle, yet serious effects and side-effects which can handicap the development efforts of countries placing prolonged and substantial reliance on private investment from abroad. The picture that has sometimes been painted of the career of foreign investment is that at one time, long ago, the negative aspects predominated: there was sheer exploitation of human and natural resources as well as crude power play in the early free-wheeling days, when capital followed the flag or was, on the contrary, the "cat's paw of empire"; but this unfortunate phase has been outgrown, so it is widely thought, with decolonization, with the world-wide assertion of national sovereign states and their taxing powers, and with the desire, on the part of modern foreign investors, to perform as "good corporate citizens" of the host country and as "partners in progress." Unfortunately, this edifying story of human progress is incomplete and one-sided. It can, in fact, be argued that certain negative aspects of foreign investment do not only continue to coexist with the positive ones, but typically tend to predominate over them as development proceeds, at least up to some point. These are the just-mentioned "more subtle" effects and side-effects that will now be briefly explained.

PRIVATE FOREIGN INVESTMENT: AN INCREASINGLY MIXED BLESSING

The positive contribution of foreign investment to an economy can be of various kinds. In the first place, it can supply one of several *missing* factors of production (capital, entrepreneurship, management, and so forth), factors, that is, which are simply and indisputably not to be found in the country receiving the investment. This is the situation often prevailing in the earliest stages of development of a poor country. More generally, foreign investment can make it possible for output to increase sharply, because it provides the recipient economy with a larger *quantity* of comparatively scarce (if not entirely missing) inputs.

Another contribution of foreign investment, conspicuous in relations among advanced industrial countries and inviting often a two-way flow, is of a rather different nature: it can have a teaching function and serve to improve the *quality* of the local factors of production. By on-the-spot example and through competitive pressures, foreign investment can act as a spur to the general efficiency of local enterprise. This effect is likely to be particularly important in economic sectors which are sheltered from the competition of merchandise imports from abroad. Such sectors (services, industries with strong locational advantages) appear to expand rapidly at advanced stages of economic development. If foreign investment is successful in enhancing the quality of local enterprise, then its inflow will be providentially self-limiting:

once the local business community achieves greater efficiency, there will be fewer openings for the demonstration of superior foreign techniques, management, and know-how. But what if local businessmen, faced with overwhelming advantages of their foreign competitors, do not respond with adequate vigor and, instead, deteriorate further or sell out? This is, of course, the nub of recent European fears of the "American challenge." I cannot deal here with this problem, but the fact that it exists has interesting implications for the topic at hand.

If foreign investment can fail to improve and may even harm the *quality* of local factors of production, then the question arises whether it may also, under certain circumstances, lead to a decrease in the *quantity* of local inputs available to an economy. In other words, could the inflow of foreign investment stunt what might otherwise be vigorous local development of the so-called missing or scarce factors of production?

This question has been little discussed. (Important exceptions are the article by J. Knapp "Capital Exports and Growth," *Economic Journal,* September 1957, and the paper by Felipe Pazos cited below.) The reason for the neglect lies in the intellectual tradition which treats international investment under the rubric "export of capital." As long as one thinks in terms of this single factor of production being exported to a capital-poor country, it is natural to view it as highly complementary to various local factors—such as natural resources and labor—that are available in abundance and are only waiting to be combined with the "missing factor" to yield large additional outputs. But, for a long time now, foreign investors have prided themselves on contributing "not just capital," but a whole bundle of other valuable inputs. In counterpart to these claims, however, the doubt might have arisen that some components of the bundle will no longer be purely complementary to local factors, but will be competitive with them and could cause them to wither or retard and even prevent their growth.

The possibility, and indeed likelihood, that international *trade* will lead to the shrinkage and possibly to the disappearance of certain lines of local production as a result of cheaper imports has been at the root of international-trade theory since Adam Smith and Ricardo. This effect of trade has been celebrated by free traders through such terms as "international specialization" and "efficient reallocation of resources." The opponents of free trade have often pointed out that for a variety of reasons it is imprudent and harmful for a country to become specialized along certain product lines in accordance with the dictates of comparative advantage. Whatever the merit of these critical arguments, they would certainly acquire overwhelming weight if the question arose whether a country should allow itself to become specialized not just along certain commodity lines, but along factor-of-production lines. Very few countries would ever consciously wish to specialize in unskilled labor, while foreigners with a comparative advantage in entrepreneurship, management, skilled labor, and capital took over these functions, replacing inferior "local talent." But this is precisely the direction in which events can move when international investment, proudly bringing in its bundle of factors, has unimpeded access to developing countries. (In the fine paradoxical formulation of Felipe Pazos: "The main weakness of direct investment as a development agent is a consequence of the complete character of its contribution." (See his paper "The Role of International Movements of Private Capital in Promoting Development," in John H. Adler, ed., *Capital Movements and Economic Development,* 1967, p. 196.)

The displacement of local factors and stunting of local abilities which can occur in the wake of international investment is sometimes absolute, as when local banks or businesses are bought out by foreign capital; this has in fact been happening recently with increasing frequency in Latin America. But the more common and perhaps more dangerous, because less noticeable, stunting effect is relative to what might have happened in the absence of the investment.

As already mentioned, foreign investment can be at its creative best by bringing in "missing" factors of production, complementary to those available locally, in the early stages of development of a poor country. The possibility that it will play a stunting role arises later on, when the poor country has begun to generate, to a large extent no doubt because of the prior injection of foreign investment, its own entrepreneurs, technicians, and savers and could now do even more along these lines if it were not for the institutional inertia that makes for a continued importing of so-called scarce factors of production which have become potentially dispensable. It is, of course, exceedingly difficult to judge at what point in time foreign investment changes in this fashion from a stimulant of development into a retarding influence, particularly since during the latter stage its contribution is still ostensibly positive—for example, the foreign capital that comes in is visible and measurable, in contrast to the domestic capital that might have been generated in its stead. One can never be certain, moreover, that restrictions against foreign investment will in fact call forth the local entrepreneurial, managerial, technological, and saving performances which are believed to be held back and waiting in the wings to take over from the foreign investors. Nevertheless, a considerable body of evidence, brought forth less by design than by accidents such as wars, depressions, nationalist expropriations, and international sanctions, suggests strongly that, after an initial period of development, the domestic supply of

routinely imported factors of production is far more elastic than is ever suspected under business-as-usual conditions. If this is so, then the "climate for
foreign investment" ought to turn from attractive at an early stage of development to much less inviting in some middle stretch—in which most of Latin
America finds itself at the present time.

The preceding argument is the principal economic reason for anticipating increasing conflict between the goals of national development and the
foreign-investment community, even after the latter has thoroughly purged
itself of the excesses that marred its early career. The argument is strengthened by related considerations pertaining to economic policy-making, a "factor of production" not often taken into account by economists, but which
nevertheless has an essential role to play. In the course of industrialization,
resources for complementary investment in education and overhead capital
must be generated through taxation, the opening up of new domestic and
foreign markets must be made attractive, institutions hampering growth must
be reformed, and powerful social groups that are antagonistic to development
must be neutralized. The achievement of these tasks is considerably facilitated
if the new industrialists are able to speak with a strong, influential, and even
militant voice. But the emergence of such a voice is most unlikely if a large
portion of the more dynamic new industries is in foreign hands. This is a
somewhat novel reproach to foreign capital, which has normally been taken
to task for being unduly interfering, wire-pulling, and domineering. Whatever the truth about these accusations in the past, the principal failing of the
managers of today's foreign-held branch plants and subsidiaries may well be
the opposite. Given their position as "guests" in a "host country," their behavior is far too restrained and inhibited. The trouble with the foreign investor may well be not that he is so meddlesome, but that he is so mousy! It is
the foreign investor's mousiness which deprives the policy-makers of the
guidance, pressures, and support they badly need to push through critically
required development decisions and policies amid a welter of conflicting
and antagonistic interests.

The situation is in fact even worse. Not only does policy-making fail to
be invigorated by the influence normally emanating from a strong, confident,
and assertive group of industrialists; more directly, the presence of a strong
foreign element in the dynamically expanding sectors of the economy is likely
to have a debilitating and corroding effect on the rationality of official economic policy-making for development. For, when newly arising investment
opportunities are largely or predominantly seized upon by foreign firms, the
national policy-makers face in effect a dilemma: more development means at
the same time less autonomy. In a situation in which many key points of the

economy are occupied by foreigners while economic policy is made by nationals it is only too likely that these nationals will not excel in "rational" policy-making for economic development; for, a good portion of the fruits of such rationality would accrue to non-nationals and would strengthen their position. (For some interesting remarks along these lines, see Hans O. Schmitt, "Foreign Capital and Social Conflict in Indonesia," *Economic Development and Social Change,* April 1962.) On the other hand, the role and importance of national economic policy-making for development increases steadily as the array of available policy instruments widens, and as more group demands are articulated. Hence the *scope* for "irrationality" actually expands as development gains momentum. That its *incidence* increases also could probably be demonstrated by a historical survey of tax, exchange-rate, utility-rate and similar policies that were aimed directly or indirectly at "squeezing" or administering pin pricks to the foreigner, but managed, at the same time, to slow down economic growth.

The preceding pages have said next to nothing about the direct cost to the capital-importing country of private international investment nor about the related question of the balance-of-payments drain such investment may occasion. While these matters have long been vigorously debated, with the critics charging exploitation and the defenders denying it, the outcome of the discussion seems to me highly inconclusive. Moreover, undue fascination with the dollar-and-cents aspects of international investment has led to the neglect of the topics here considered, which, I submit, raise issues of at least equal importance and suggest a simple conclusion: strictly from the point of view of development, private foreign investment is a mixed blessing, and the mixture is likely to become more noxious at the intermediate stage of development which characterizes much of present-day Latin America.

Hence, if the broadly conceived national interest of the United States is served by the development of Latin America, then this interest enters into conflict with a continuing expansion and even with the maintenance of the present position of private investors from the United States. Purely political arguments lend strong support to this proposition. Internal disputes over the appropriate treatment of the foreign investor have gravely weakened, or helped to topple, some of the more progressive and democratic governments which have held power in recent years in such countries as Brazil, Chile, and Peru. Frictions between private investors from the United States and host governments have an inevitable repercussion on United States-Latin American relations. In a number of cases such disputes have been responsible for a wholly disproportionate deterioration of bilateral relations. The continued presence and expansion of our private-investment position and our insistence on a "favorable investment climate" decisively undermined, from the outset, the credibility of our Alliance for Progress proposals. Land reform and income redistribution through taxation are so obviously incompatible, in the short run, with the maintenance of a favorable investment climate for private capital that insistence on both could only be interpreted to signify that we did not really mean those fine phrases about achieving social justice through land and tax reform.

If these political arguments are added to those pertaining to economics and political economy, one thing becomes clear: a policy of selective liquidation and withdrawal of foreign private investments is in the best mutual interests of Latin America and the United States. Such a policy can be selective with respect to countries and to economic sectors and it ought to be combined with a policy of encouraging new capital outflows, also on a selective basis and with some safeguards.

THE "LOST ART" OF LIQUIDATING AND NATIONALIZING FOREIGN INVESTMENTS

Before the possible elements of such a policy are examined, it is worth noting that liquidation of foreign investment has frequently happened in the history of capital movements. But, as a result of convergent developments, such liquidation has strangely become a lost art. Worse, this art has not been properly recorded by economic historians. In part, this is so because economic historians, like both the advocates of foreign investment and its critics, have been far more interested in the tides of capital flow than in its occasional ebbs. Moreover, the tides have been more regular and easier to detect and measure.

Some of the "mechanisms" which in the past permitted partial liquidation of foreign investment have been the unintended side-effects of such large-scale, sporadic, and wholly unedifying happenings as wars and depressions. The two World Wars led to a substantial decline in both the absolute and the relative importance of foreign investment in the national economies of Latin America. In the first place, with most Latin American countries joining the Allies, German investments, a not unimportant portion of the total (think of all those prosperous breweries!), were expropriated. Secondly, the British were forced in both World Wars to liquidate a good portion of their security holdings, in order to pay for vitally needed food, materials, and munitions. Some of these securities were acquired by the citizens of the countries for which they had originally been issued. Thirdly, Latin American countries acquired large holdings of gold and foreign currencies during the wars, as they continued to export their primary products, but were unable to obtain industrial goods from the belligerents. These accumulated holdings made it possible for them to buy out some foreign investments in the immediate postwar period. The most conspicuous, but by no means the only, instance of this sort of operation was the purchase from their British shareholders of the Argentine railways by the Peron government in 1946. Finally, the wars led to a complete interruption of capital inflow. Since, at the same time, Latin America's industrial growth was strongly stimulated, the relative importance of activities controlled by foreign capital declined substantially.

The depressions which periodically afflicted the centers of capitalist development until the Second World War had similar results. Again, capital inflow would stop for a while during periods in which the Latin American economies frequently received growth impulses because, with foreign-exchange receipts low, imports had to be throttled, giving domestic industrial production a fillip. Moreover, when overextended corporations based in the United States and Europe fell on hard times, a sound management reaction was frequently to retrench and consolidate. In the process, foreign branch plants and subsidiaries were sold off to local buyers, a process which has been well documented in the case of American investments in Canada during the depression of the thirties. (See H. Marshall, F. A. Southard Jr., and V. W. Taylor, *Canadian-American Industry,* 1936, pp. 252-262.) Sometimes, especially in the case of European firms, these transfers took the form of ownership and control passing into the hands of the parent company's local managers who, while of foreign origin, would eventually become integrated into the local economy. Finally, of course, there were cases of outright bankruptcy and forced liquidation.

The quantitative importance of these various factors remains to be established. But, in the aggregate, they must have had a substantial limiting effect on the foreign-investment position in Latin America during the first half of the 20th century.

Actually, a less cruel mechanism permitting the nationalization of foreign investment was also at work before the "good old days" of portfolio investment had been eclipsed by direct investment. While those days were of course by no means wholly good, portfolio investment, which took primarily the form of fixed-interest bond issues, did have several advantages for the capital-importing country. Among these, the lower cost and the existence of a termination date have been mentioned most frequently. There is, however, one further property of portfolio investment which is of particular interest in the context of the present essay. This is the fact that nationalization of portfolio investment could take place at the option of the borrowing country and its citizens, who were free to purchase in the international capital markets securities that were originally issued and underwritten in London or Paris. I have collected (and hope eventually to publish) considerable evidence that these so-called "repurchases" of securities by nationals of the borrowing countries took place on a large scale in such countries as the United States, Italy, Spain, Sweden, and Japan in the late 19th and early 20th centuries. They also occurred in much poorer countries, such as Brazil, and were in general so widespread that the phenomenon is referred to in one source as "the well-known *Heimweh* (homesickness) of oversea issued securities." (J. F. Normano, *Brazil: A Study of Economic Types,* 1935, p. 157.) As a result of this *Heimweh,* then, an increasing portion of maturing bond issues often came to be owned by the nationals of the borrowing country, so that payment at maturity did not occasion any balance-of-payments problem.

This is not the place to speculate on the reasons for which the bonds issued abroad became so often a preferred medium of investment for national capitalists; suffice it to say that patriotism or nationalism on the part of local investors probably has little if anything to do with it. Whatever the reason, it appears that international investment, as formerly practiced, permitted the gradual transfer, via anonymous market transactions, of foreign-held assets to nationals, entirely in accordance with the capabilities and wishes of the borrowing country's own savers.

Today's arrangements are totally different, of course. Transfer to local ownership and control of foreign-held subsidiaries requires either an initiative on the part of the parent company or a decision to expropriate on the part of the host government. A valuable mechanism of smooth, gradual, and peaceful transfer has become lost in the shuffle from portfolio to direct investment.

Up to this point, it has been established (1) that progressive liquidation and nationalization of foreign private investments is likely to become desirable in the course of economic development, and (2) that mechanisms to this end functioned, if unwittingly and irregularly, in the 19th and through the first half of the 20th century, but have no longer been available over the past 25 years or so.

The purpose of recalling these mechanisms was to sharpen our institutional imagination and perception for substitute mechanisms which it may be desirable to put into place at the present time. An open and far-ranging discussion of various possible alternatives is obviously desirable. The following pages are meant as a contribution to such a discussion, rather than as a fixed set of proposals.

A SURVEY OF POSSIBLE DIVESTMENT MECHANISMS

An attempt will now be made to sketch possible answers to the following questions.

1. What arrangements should be made to permit the transfer of local ownership and control of existing foreign-held investments?

2. What arrangements should exist for this transfer in the case of new foreign investments?

3. To what extent should devices that are designed for the purpose just indicated be modified in the light of other important objectives of the developing countries, such as the export of manufactures and the promotion of local centers of technological research and innovation?

These questions will be taken up in order, although there is considerable overlap between the answers to the first two questions.

AN INTER-AMERICAN DIVESTMENT CORPORATION

In the light of the above considerations, partial liquidation of *existing* foreign investment in Latin America is outstandingly important. The book value of direct investments by the United States in Latin America amounted to 11.9 billion dollars at the end of 1967, while the annual outflow of fresh capital from the United States (outside of reinvested profits) never reached 500 million dollars during the past five years, even on a gross basis. The steady increase in book values is, moreover, due more to the reinvestment of profits than to fresh funds newly invested. In other words, if the quantitative and qualitative role of foreign-controlled enterprise in Latin America is judged to be excessive, something must be done about the existing foreign firms operating in the area, rather than only about those that may conceivably establish operations there in the future.

Vital as it is, this subject has received much less attention than the desirable regime for new foreign investments. It is of course the politically most delicate part of the operation here contemplated. Also, from the economic point of view, the use of any capital and, worse, foreign-exchange resources for the purchase of property rights over assets already located and functioning within the territories of the developing countries seems perverse to those who remain basically convinced that the pace of economic development is conditioned on little else than the availability of capital and foreign exchange. Those who are not so convinced and who take seriously the economic and political arguments developed earlier would see nothing fatally wrong in allocating a portion of the country's savings and foreign-exchange resources to the purchase of foreign investments already in their midst. From the purely financial point of view, moreover, expenditure of foreign exchange for the purchase of existing foreign assets could in a number of cases be preferable to the indefinite servicing of these assets (depending on one's estimate of the applicable discount rate and of future earnings and remittance patterns). The trouble is that the recipient countries do not generally have the financial resources to seize these opportunities nor have they in fact been able to borrow or to use aid funds for this purpose. Moreover, even when local resources are available there may be difficulties in bringing seller and buyer together, because the foreign owners may be ready to sell at a time when the local investors are not quite ready to purchase or because the two parties have difficulty in agreeing on the value of the assets to be transferred, without a mutually-trusted third party.

A need exists, then, for a financial intermediary, an agency, that is, which has resources of its own enabling it to acquire foreign-owned assets and to hold them until such time as it can place them with local investors. Dr. Raul Prebisch earlier this year proposed that such an agency should be established within the Inter-American Development Bank. This course may well be preferable, because of the special urgency of the Latin American situation, to a suggestion I made as early as 1961, but with total lack of success, to the International Finance Corporation (IFC) that it devote a portion of its resources to this task.

The proposed agency—I shall call it the Inter-American Divestment Corporation—would engage in several distinct types of operations. In some cases it could limit its role to that of arbitrator and guarantor. As just noted, it could help set the fair price of the assets to be transferred from the foreign to the domestic owners and, if payment is to be made over a period of years, it could guarantee the debtor's obligation and, to some extent perhaps, the convertibility of his currency into that of the creditor. One can imagine situations in which the purchaser would have to be granted longer terms than can or should be imposed on the seller, as is common in some agrarian-reform operations. In this case, the Corporation would need to supply funds of its own to bridge the gap between the two sets of credit terms. The most usual type of operation would presumably consist in the outright acquisition by the Corporation of a controlling block of shares of the firm to be divested, without any fixed schedule of repurchase by local investors.

As in any foreign-aid project, some contribution should be forthcoming from the local government as an earnest that it judges the particular divestment enough for it to commit some resources of its own. As the Divestment

Corporation acquires experience, it should be able to attract additional resources from the private-investment-banking community, much as is done by the IFC in connection with new ventures.

Which foreign-owned firms should be eligible for divestment assistance on the part of the Corporation? In deciding this crucial matter, the Corporation should probably take its principal cues from the governments of the host countries. Just as the doctor asks the patient where it hurts, so the Corporation could periodically inquire among governments which are the firms where foreign ownership is felt to be irksome. In many cases there will be a history of conflict which will clearly point to the main trouble spots. One can also easily imagine situations in which governments are reluctant to point a finger at specific firms. For this and other reasons, it should be possible for private parties in the host country, for the foreign investors, and for the Corporation itself to take the initiative in the divestment process which, in the end, will require the agreement of the host government as long as it is expected to contribute some of its own resources to each divestment operation.

An interesting question arises with respect to the eventual disposition of the equity which will be acquired by the Corporation. One objection will surely be levied against the operation: Is it really desirable to transfer presently foreign-owned firms to local ownership when the new owners cannot but be drawn from the very small clique of already too powerfully entrenched local capitalists? History issues a warning here, for this very sort of thing happened in the second half of the 19th century when liberal parties came to power in a number of Latin American countries. The newly installed, anticlerical governments expropriated the sizable lands owned by the Catholic Church—and then proceeded to sell them at bargain prices to the landed elite. As a result, the concentration of landholdings became far more pronounced.

At the present time, the weight of concern over a similar development in case of nationalization of foreign investment varies no doubt from country to country, as well as from industry to industry within each country. Moreover, the Corporation could make a deliberate attempt to broaden the basis of industrial ownership when it sells its portfolio. This should, in fact, be one of its principal functions. If foreign-owned assets were to be sold directly to local investors, it would be impossible not to sell to the few and the powerful. But, if an intermediary stands ready to hold the divested assets for some time, the outcome may be quite different. One attractive possibility is that the agency would sell, on the installment plan, a substantial portion, and perhaps a majority, of the equity of the erstwhile foreign firms to white- and blue-collar workers, with first choice being given to those who are employed in such firms. This would be a method of tapping entirely new sources of capital formation. Moreover, in this manner, the liquidation of foreign ownership would become the occasion for effectuating, by the same stroke, a more equitable distribution of income and wealth within the host country. As in the case of the Mexican *ejido,* special safeguards may then have to be established to protect the new asset-holders against the temptation to sell out right away.

Those who have stressed the advantage of a late start have usually had in mind the technological windfalls accruing to the newcomers and their freedom from a declining industrial plant based on some previous but now passé phase of industrial expansion. For various reasons, these advantages have been more in evidence for Germany and Japan than for countries whose industrialization was much more tardy; but the latter could perhaps attempt some social leapfrogging, as, for example, in the manner just indicated.

It is quite conceivable, moreover, that the foreign investors themselves would take a more benign view of divestment if they knew that their assets were to be transferred to their workers and employees rather than to their local competitors or to some public agency.

The projected divestment operations via a financial intermediary could be made to serve another objective that is particularly important within the present Latin American setting. It could help create financial and, hence, managerial ties among firms located in several Latin American countries. In this form a foundation would be laid for truly Latin American multi-national corporations. The absence of such corporations, combined with the ever alert presence throughout Latin America, of United States-controlled multi-national corporations, accounts for much of the timidity with which Latin Americans have moved so far in the direction of a Common Market. Thus, the proposed divestment, combined with a measure of "Latinamericanization," rather than mere nationalization, of the divestment enterprises could impart a much needed momentum to the integration movement.

By now, I hope to have convinced the reader that it is worthwhile to raise funds for the Corporation. In part, such funds should simply be taken from the general pool of foreign-aid monies. For the reasons indicated, the use of aid funds for this purpose could be eminently "productive," using this term in a wide and realistic meaning. The question what fraction of the total should be allocated to this purpose is no doubt difficult to resolve; but it is not more so than many other allocation decisions that are constantly made in practice without the guidance or availability of precise "cost-effectiveness" criteria.

Nevertheless, the nature of the proposed operation may point to special sources of finance that are not available for other purposes, so that the Corporation would not have to compete for general-purpose aid funds. A first thought that comes to mind in this connection is that the opposition in the United States Congress to appropriations for foreign aid is now motivated, to an increasing extent, by apprehension over the way in which aid and its administration makes for uncontrollable and possibly escalating involvements by the United States in foreign countries. A program of financial assistance which would have disengagement as its principal objective might therefore gather more public support at this point than the conventional aid program. In fact, if such a program were presented separately from conventional aid, a new political coalition might get behind it so that in the political sense the funds accruing for our purpose could become truly additional. Appropriation for the Corporation might also have other appeals. Aid for divestment is unexceptionable from the points of view of both balance-of-payments and inflationary impacts. The dollars disbursed by the agency would immediately return in full to the divesting country, such as the United States, but they would not enter directly into that country's spending stream.

The program may be opposed on the ground that the taxpayer of the United States should not be asked to "bail out" its corporations that have engaged in foreign operations at their own risk. In reply it may be argued that a large part of the risk of recent foreign investments has already been taken over by the taxpayer, through the investment-guaranty program. Moreover, the Divestment Corporation should be in a good position to minimize the "bail-out" aspect of its operations: one of its principal tasks would be to negotiate a fair price for the assets and to convince the foreign investors that are being bought out to accept deferred payment for a substantial portion of their claim.

In a search for special sources of finance, it is natural to eye those parties which stand to gain from the proposed operations. The beneficiaries, in a sense, are the foreign investors themselves. In the first place, they will receive a valuable new option—to sell out at a fair price—as a result of the contemplated arrangements. The proposed agency would in effect administer a program whose purpose is to *prevent* the confiscation of foreign-held assets by timely transfers of these assets. Obviously not all foreign-owned firms will be able to exercise the option. But the orderly liquidation of foreign ownership in the cases where it is particularly objectionable to the host country cannot help but be a boon to the remaining foreign-controlled firms. The presence in a country of foreign interests that are felt as irritants poses a danger for the prosperity and, indeed, the life of *all* foreign firms, no matter how constructive and popular they may be. Hence a contribution from all corporations with foreign assets can be justified. As long as firms are willing to pay a premium which insures them against the risks of actual confiscation, there is no reason why they should not contribute something toward a program which materially decreases these risks.

Another possible source of special finance for the divestment agency should be briefly mentioned. The agency may well be the ideal beneficiary of the much discussed "link" between the new monetary reserves created as a result of the Rio Agreement (the Special Drawing Rights) and the developing countries. The principal objection against any such link has been that the reserve creation should not become a mechanism for effecting permanent transfers of real resources from one set of countries to another. This objection would be largely met if the industrial countries used part of their allocation of Special Drawing Rights for the subscription of capital or bond issues of the Divestment Corporation. The partial use of the new reserves for the repatriation of foreign-held assets could not have an adverse effect on the intended increase in world liquidity, for the simple reason that this use, unlike others that have been proposed, would not entail any real transfer of goods and service.

BUILT-IN DIVESTMENT: A GARLAND OF SCHEMES

Considering the mass of foreign investment, the Divestment Corporation will be able to operate only on a highly selective, *ad hoc* basis. The question arises, therefore, whether the institutional framework within which foreign investment is conducted should be modified with a view toward building into it a mechanism making for eventual divestment. This question is best discussed in considering desirable regimes for *new* investments. Whether any such regime could or should be extended to existing foreign-owned firms can be considered subsequently.

The topic has given rise to a considerable literature and to several proposals. For example, the desirability for foreign capital to become associated with local capital in joint ventures has been exhaustively canvassed. Whatever the merits of this device, its usefulness is now recognized to be limited. In many situations, particularly those involving the transfer of new and complex technology, complete foreign control and ownership is said to be required or desirable at the outset. For this reason, increased attention has been given—by such authors as Paul Rosenstein-Rodan, Paul Streeten, and Raymond Vernon—to the possibility of a gradual transfer of all or the majority of the new firm's capital to local ownership, in accordance with a fixed schedule.

This is a fruitful idea which should be spelled out in full institutional detail. Consideration should, for example, be given to the granting of fiscal incentives to firms electing this option. In the capital-exporting countries, the parent company committing itself to gradual divestment of its foreign assets over a stated number of years could be given a credit against its income-tax liability for some portion of its foreign-capital outlays; alternatively or additionally, the firm could be exempted from all capital-gains taxation on profits made in selling its foreign assets to local investors. The capital-importing country could facilitate divestment by allowing the foreign-owned company to pay income taxes in stock in lieu of cash. Such an arrangement would probably have to be restricted to economic sectors in which foreign enterprise is not competing with domestic enterprises. Where there is actual or potential competition, the arrangement would give an unfair cash-flow advantage to the foreign firm.

Gradual divestment over a given number of years normally means expenditure of scarce foreign exchange. It also requires the finding of local partners. The difficulties here are, first, that such partners are not always easy to come by. It would be necessary to designate some public agency of the host country, perhaps acting in cooperation with the Inter-American Divestment Corporation, as a residual buyer of the stock to be transferred from the original owners in accordance with a fixed schedule and a prearranged price formula. Another drawback of a direct sale of assets from the foreign owners to nationals has already been mentioned. The local buyers that would be found most readily may not be the most desirable, if advantage is to be taken of the unique opportunity afforded by divestment for diffusing ownership more widely than before. Finally, in most situations, there will be a need to agree on a "fair price" of the assets: the potential for conflict over this issue is almost as great as that over the actual presence of foreign investment.

These problems of a scheduled gradual sale of equity from foreigners to nationals point toward a simpler and more radical arrangement: namely, that a firm established with foreign capital be given a term of x years, at the end of which all or the major portion of foreign ownership would simply be vacated, without any compensation. Some of the ideas already discussed in connection with the Divestment Corporation can be utilized in deciding on the parties on which ownership should be bestowed at the end of the term. Up to a certain percentage, the foreign owners could distribute the stock directly to their employees and workers, or to their favorite local charity or foundation, and another portion would be handed over to the Inter-American Divestment Corporation for the purpose of fostering industrial integration.

The new owners would be free to negotiate a management contract with the former owner-operators.

Arrangements which set a time limit on ownership have long existed in concession contracts. The major drawback of such arrangements has also long been known: they encourage early depletion and discourage keeping up with technical progress during the years immediately prior to expiration. In manufacturing, the former danger would be rather smaller than in mining, and the latter would be reduced if the divesting firm is scheduled to maintain a minority equity position and is interested in a continuing relationship with its erstwhile foreign branch through management contracts and other technical-assistance services. Also, if the foreign owners know that they will be handing a substantial portion of the equity over to their workers and employees or to their favorite charity or foundation in the host country, they will presumably be more reluctant to squeeze their property dry in the last years than they might be if it were to be handed to the government. Nevertheless, the objection to fixed termination date is serious enough to prompt consideration of yet another institutional design.

Limiting ownership of a firm to a certain time period, at the end of which that ownership lapses or "expires" automatically, is tantamount to setting a ceiling on the profits the firm can remit to its parent. Why not make explicit this implicit ceiling on profit remittances? Instead of specifying the number of years a firm may remain in foreign hands, it would, in other words, be conceivable to limit the total amount of profits a subsidiary could remit to its parent. This amount would be related to the capital originally committed to the project, as well as to any fresh funds brought in subsequently over and above reinvested profits. Such a regime for divestment would have incentive effects directly opposite to those of the traditional concession. Since the firm can make the pleasure of control and ownership last by remitting as little as possible, that is, by reinvesting all of its profits, the incentive to deplete and milk the subsidiary would be replaced by the incentive to reinvest (on the assumption that management, control, and growth are important motivating forces for the modern corporation).

It may be useful to pick a number for illustrative purposes. Suppose that the ceiling on remittances is 200 percent of the originally invested capital. This could mean, for example, that a parent company would lose ownership of its subsidiary after it had received a 10 percent dividend on invested capital for 20 years. The internal rate of return of such a financial result would be just short of 8 percent. In other words, if a rate higher than 8 percent were appropriate as a discount rate in the particular environment where the subsidiary operates, a financial situation in which 10 percent would be earned for 20 years would be superior to one in which 8 percent would be earned in perpetuity. Hence, the perishable nature of the investment need not impair decisively its rentability, particularly in the frequently encountered situations where the applicable discount rate is fairly high.

Consideration could be given to the question whether, in computing the aggregate "allowable" profit, some discount rate should apply to the dividend remittances themselves. If this were done, payments made at a later date would contribute less heavily to the eventual extinction of ownership than payments made in the first years of the new enterprise, and the incentive to postpone and hold down profit remittances might be further strengthened. The arguments against any such complication are: first, that it is a complication; and, second, that the real burden of profit remittances for the host country does not depend so much on the country's national product, which can be expected to be larger in later years, as on its balance of payments, which could well be in a more critical position ten years *after* the initial investment than at the time at which the investment is made.

The last point highlights an important advantage of the scheme under discussion. One of the major complaints with respect to foreign investment has been that because of reinvestment of profits—which in turn are made possible in part through local borrowing—the book value of the foreign-owned firms is likely to grow apace during an initial period, so that eventual dividend remittances may be a multiple of the capital originally brought into the country. While the scheme here discussed encourages reinvestment of profits, it averts the threatening prospect of huge remittances which might be made once the firm's growth slowed down, when they could represent an unacceptable burden for the country's balance of payments.

In all fairness, so it may well be asked, if cumulative profits are subject to a ceiling should they not be granted a floor in compensation? No doubt, such a floor could make the scheme much more attractive to the capital-exporting firms. The floor should obviously be at most 100 percent of the initially invested capital and probably rather less, so as to preserve an adequate degree of risk. Suppose a payback of 50 percent of the invested capital is to be guaranteed as a consideration for the 200 percent ceiling that is imposed on profit remittances. The capital-exporting country could provide such a guarantee simply by permitting the parent company a tax credit against its income-tax liability up to 50 percent of the capital invested. As was pointed out before, such a tax credit may be desirable in any event in order to encourage firms that invest abroad to take advantage of the divestment options.

Once some of the divestment arrangements sketched out here become available for *new* investments, it will be desirable for *existing* investments to be able to participate in them. Existing foreign firms should, of course, be eligible to operate under one of the several divestment options that will be offered to new firms. Once again, fiscal incentives granted by the capital-exporting or capital-importing country, or by both, could be used to make participation attractive. There is no particular difficulty in adapting to existing firms the options calling for gradual sale of equity or for outright divestment after a certain number of years. Problems are more likely to arise with respect to the option terminating foreign ownership after remittance of profits in some multiple of the originally invested capital. Applying this rule to the original capital of the existing firms may be too restrictive, yet taking the present book value as a yardstick may be too generous. Some middle ground between these two solutions may have to be found.

To what extent would the existence of the Inter-American Divestment Corporation keep existing firms from electing to convert to some of the automatic divestment procedures here advocated? If a firm could be sure that it would become an object of the tender mercies of the Divestment Corporation, it might well prefer that course to any automatic divestment arrangement (other than gradual sale of equity), since it would be paid for its assets instead of losing them outright after a certain lapse of time. Actually, this sort of "competition" from the Divestment Corporation is not a serious danger. In the first place, the Corporation will not have sufficiently large funds to make acquisition a likely prospect for the average foreign-owned firm. Secondly, given its limited resources, the Corporation will generally acquire the assets of existing firms under medium- and long-term credit arrangements instead of paying cash. In these circumstances, foreign firms may often decide that they can do better under divestment schemes which allow them to manage their affairs and earn profits for a number of years ahead.

COMBINING DIVESTMENT WITH OTHER OBJECTIVES

The purpose of the preceding pages was to present, in bare outline, a variety of possible institutional arrangements for divestment. It is now necessary to consider how these arrangements could be modified if divestment conflicts with other important objectives of the developing countries.

It has, for example, been pointed out by Raymond Vernon that foreign-owned firms have a special aptitude for contributing to the exports of manufactures from the developing countries. In many cases, of course, foreign branch plants have been criticized for exactly the opposite tendency, namely for the determination to confine themselves to the local market and to reserve all exporting to the parent company. Nevertheless, this is no necessary and permanent failing; the multinational corporation in particular is obviously able to establish an integrated network of manufacturing facilities and commercial operations which could insert its individual producing units in different countries into a world-wide pattern of specialized production and internal exchange.

It looks, therefore, as though in some sectors some developing countries are likely to face a dilemma: continued foreign ownership or no exports. But in reality there is no need to make so difficult a choice. The dilemma can be transformed into a trade-off situation where both objectives are pursued simultaneously and one of them is only marginally given up for the sake of achieving a limited gain for the other. The schemes already put forward can easily be adapted to this end. Take the scheme under which a majority ownership ceases automatically at the end of x years. It would be relatively easy to introduce a variant such that a firm achieving exports of z percent of its total output by the time the x years are up, would retain majority ownership for another y years. In this or some similar fashion, the built-in divestment provisions can actually serve to provide incentives for the achievement of other desirable objectives.

The same argument applies to other objectives, namely, promotion of regional integration and of establishment by foreign firms of centers of applied technological research. In these cases it is, of course, difficult to quantify performance. Nevertheless, an independent expert commission could be created with the task of appraising whether in any individual case the contribution of a foreign firm to, say, the implanting of technological research and innovation warrants a slowing down of the divestment schedule.

In the end, therefore, a developing country may spell out for foreign investors several distinct mixes of objectives, among which divestment would be only one; and each foreign investor could elect the particular mix that corresponds most closely to his taste and capabilities.

CONCLUSION

Rapid and incomplete as it is, the preceding survey of conceivable divestment arrangements will have given the reader a sense of the sizable alteration in the institutional environment for foreign private investment that is advocated here. Several questions are raised in consequence: (1) what would happen to the outflow of private investment funds if some of the arrangements spelled out were actually adopted as national policy by the developing countries of Latin America as well as by the capital exporters such as the United States? Would that outflow slow down to a trickle or come to a full stop? And (2) if the latter occurred would considerable damage be done to economic development in Latin America?

To answer the last question first, it is my belief that the larger countries of Latin America are today in a quite favorable bargaining position to insist on substantial institutional changes of the kind here indicated. The damage that would be inflicted on them if international capital took offense and stopped flowing to them is no longer what it might have been 100, 50, or even 25 years ago. Most literature and official reports about Latin America stress the continent's continuing poverty and problems. These laments have hidden from view the very real economic progress that has been accomplished over the last 25 years. With a per capita income of around 500 dollars and a population of 250 million people, the Latin American continent is now well supplied with both "light" and "basic" industries. Countries such as Brazil, Mexico, and Argentina produce a large and constantly increasing portion of the capital goods needed by their industrial establishment. A boycott of Latin America by international investment capital might reveal the strength and resilience and ability to *fare da sé* in a great number of areas which the Latin American industrial establishment has acquired, in much the same way in which the two World Wars permitted its then fledgling industries to take vigorous steps forward. Perhaps Latin America really needs at this point a sort of "economic equivalent of war," a measure of insulation, that is, from the advanced economies that would permit it fully to deploy the potential for entrepreneurship, skills, and capital formation which it has accumulated over the past 25 years of continuing intimate contact. In other words, it is quite conceivable that a temporary suspension of the flow of private capital toward Latin America would be beneficial rather than calamitous for the area's growth. That Latin Americans can afford to make "demands" from a position of strength was perhaps sensed when their official representatives started to speak in quite a new voice to the United States at the Viña del Mar Conference of May 1969.

The question remains whether a boycott by private capital would necessarily result from a Latin American attempt to change the rules by which the game of international investment is being played. This is not at all certain. There are at least some signs that a number of private investors may be willing to operate in a substantially altered institutional environment. In the first place, they know how to bend with the wind—an example is the "Chilenization" of Kennecott and now also of Anaconda. Some farther-sighted corporations in mining and telecommunications are no longer waiting for pressures from the host countries to provide for "-ization" of substantial equity in their concession contracts. A few scattered experiments in divestment are also going forward under the auspices of IFC, ADELA, and of the AID guaranty program. Furthermore, where official ideology proscribes "private ownership of the means of production" altogether, private companies located in Western Europe and the United States have been able to do business via so-called "co-production agreements" through which capital goods, technology, and skills are transferred, with repayment scheduled often in kind, on a medium- or long-term basis. As a result, Western business firms find themselves in the ironical position of granting a better deal to their ideological foes than to their friends. Finally, a few small experiments in bringing manufacturing operations into an area and then turning them over to community ownership and control are now being tried out in the United States in some of the black ghettos; corporations such as Xerox and Aerojet have been pioneering in this field.

It may well turn out, then, that the corporation will once again justify its reputation for flexibility. The radical nature of the changes required should nevertheless be clearly visualized. If the corporation is celebrated as an institution, this is so to a large extent because it has permitted business to be carried on *sub specie aeternitatis,* by an organization, that is, whose life span has become as unlimited as that of older permanent institutions such as the nation-state and the church. It is here suggested that, in some of its foreign operations, the corporation ought to institutionalize its own demise. Having achieved deathlessness, it must rediscover how to die.

Putting it less brusquely, the corporation must learn how to plan for selective impermanence. Perhaps it would do so more cheerfully once it realizes that the same need exists increasingly for other institutions proud of their permanence, such as the nation-state. So, why not be a trail blazer?

33
International Divestment: Panacea or Pitfall?

Jack N. Behrman

The idea that forced divestiture of foreign-owned affiliates is an answer to the tensions between private direct investment and developing countries has been given renewed impetus by Professor Albert O. Hirschman and Dr. Raul Prebisch.[1] Both have written with Latin America specifically in mind, but their proposal is applicable in other developing countries as well, if it is suitable at all. Recommendations that divestment *be required* by host governments are gaining supporters among their advisers and in some academic circles. The Andean Pact countries (Chile, Peru, Colombia, Bolivia, Ecuador) have recently proposed to require divestment in a period of between 10-15 years. The Organization of American States has supported the proposal on the grounds that the alternative is more frequent expropriation of foreign affiliates and that divestment raises fewer problems. This article is a critical assessment of the proposal and its implications.

THE PROPOSAL

The technique proposed is that foreign companies owning affiliates in a developing country be required to sell to local nationals the majority or totality of ownership within a stipulated period, which is expected to be no less than 7 and no more than 20 years.

The proponents seek to shift further investment away from ownership and

Reprinted, with permission, from *Looking Ahead,* November/December 1970 (Washington, D.C.: National Planning Association), pp. 1-12.

more toward contributing a flow of skills and technology. The alternative of purchasing these skills and technology outright is, they believe, less satisfactory than obtaining them as part of a package including capital inflow and *initial* foreign ownership.

Although the proponents recognize that it is easier to apply the procedure to new investment, obtaining agreement to divestment during the negotiation on entry, they generally would like to apply it also to existing investment. They make no distinction among the different industrial or commercial sectors which would be appropriately covered by the requirement; the Andean Pact would apparently apply to all new foreign investment.

The implicit or expressed procedures for divestment range from sale on the open market of shares of the affiliate, with purchases by any ready buyer, to arranged sale to a government agency. The government agency would be either a "purchaser of last resort" or the only permitted purchaser. The funds are expected to come either from domestic savings or from special international agreements or institutions—such as an Inter-American Divestment Corporation—relying primarily on contributions from governments of capital-exporting countries. The government agencies, in turn, would be expected to sell the stock in the enterprises to local entities or to companies in neighboring countries—i.e., to "Latin Americanize" an industrial sector, restructuring ownership regionally rather than nationally.

The proposal is hardly more detailed than this. Any further refinements are offered to meet supposed objections and are, therefore, characterized as "possibilities" or "responses." These elaborations are not deemed to improve the proposal, but to be necessary modifications if pressures arise. To determine their usefulness, we must assess the proposal in some detail, analyzing the different situations in which it might be applied and the results which could be expected.

ASSESSMENT

This assessment ranges from a critique of the objectives sought under the proposal to an evaluation of the details of implementation. In all of the aspects examined, the proposal has serious difficulties and expensive trade-offs. This is not to say that host governments will not opt for the proposal, but simply to caution that the cost in development terms would appear to be quite high.

OBJECTIVES

The proponents do not argue that foreign direct investment is bad or undesirable; they argue that the "cost" in terms of returns is too high. Hence, their objective is not to alter significantly the *behavior* of foreign affiliates.

The only *economic* objective is a cessation of capital outflow in the form of dividends and other returns.

If the objective were to alter behavior, economically or commercially, it could be accomplished better by direct means than through a change in ownership. In fact, such a change is not calculated to improve *any* of the economic or commercial activities of the affiliate, save the outflow of funds. Local owners would undoubtedly behave as similarly as possible to the owners (if the enterprise had been successful). And they may transfer or retain abroad even larger funds than the former foreign owners were allowed to remit as profits.

If the new owner were the host government, what evidence is there that the operations of the affiliate would be improved? State enterprises have not distinguished themselves in making their activities more efficient than those in the private sector, and no one has argued that the results would be better from the standpoint of economic growth.

The objectives, therefore, are either political or psychological, or both. Their achievement might well necessitate a change of ownership. More fundamentally, however, these objectives require government control, whether through public ownership or through regulation of private enterprise. Unless the government is willing to take the necessary steps to gain control, it is merely shifting the economic influences from the hands of foreigners to the hands of nationals, who may be less effective in promoting economic growth. Admittedly, whatever the result it would then be the responsibility of nationals, though, if unsuccessful, they might still argue that their "plight" was the result of past "sins" on the part of the foreign owners. Disputes over the condition of the assets transferred and the "going concern" value of the company would undoubtedly arise, for they will affect the calculation of the "efficiency" of the new managers/owners. (The problem of valuation is discussed later.)

An implicit objective of the proposal, though unexpressed by any proponent, is the disintegrating of the host economies from the world economy— that is, national separatism. This consequence is implicitly recognized by Professor Hirschman in his suggestion that buying up foreign-owned affiliates could lead to their "Latin Americanization" through the merging of these companies across national boundaries. Obversely, if they are not so merged, the result could only be their "national-ization" and withdrawal from the new world of international production.

If international economic integration is recognized as no longer simply a matter of trade flows, but, more importantly, as a matter of international production, the separation of foreign-owned affiliates from ties with international integration. Of course, many of these affiliates, particularly in the manufacturing sector, have not been effectively integrated because of existing governmental constraints.[2] What does not exist can hardly be destroyed. So, admittedly, divestment in the developing countries hardly affects integration in manufacturing simply because it is seldom found there. Integration does exist, however, in the extractive sector and would probably be lost.

A move to retie the purchased affiliates regionally would, of course, be an integrating move. But the prescription presupposes that the Latin American governments would be more eager to integrate industry across regional national boundaries than to permit such integration with the world economy or that of the United States. Based on discussions during a recent trip through Latin America, it seems unlikely to me that the more advanced countries would seek that option; rather, each insisted that *if* it were to integrate externally, it would prefer to do so *with* the United States, not to its exclusion! This is probably less an indication of positive willingness to integrate with the United States than a measure of the reluctance to integrate regionally in Latin America.

But even if the Latin American governments were willing to integrate the purchased companies regionally, it would be difficult to do so without some coordinated policies concerning divestment. The coordination would have to be accomplished in several directions. First, similar divestment policies would be required, applying to the same types of industries, or else the integration could not take place over the entire region. Second, the terms of purchase would have to be similar so that valuations of the various parts could be made comparable and exchange or purchase of shares realistic; otherwise, it would be too easy to "overcharge" for any given affiliate, especially the last one to be required. Third, the rules of affiliation would have to facilitate integration. However, the proposed Andean Pact code requires a foreign affiliate to be joined with a *national* investor in the host country and not with any *local* investor in the Andean region, making integration more difficult.

In sum, no clear economic growth objective is served by the proposal, and it is by no means certain that regional integration would be accelerated by it.

The proposal's application is presumably to *all* sectors of industry and to existing as well as new investment. Problems arise in each area of application, however. Imposition of divestment in the extractive industries raises more problems than in manufacturing and, in any case, the objective of terminating the investment is better served by the concession arrangement. Concessions can simply be limited in time, reverting to the government as it desires. Extractive enterprises have long been used to this arrangement, and the market pressures of competition for resources will regulate the term of the arrangement—being as short as the competition will allow.

From the standpoint of the host government, the proposal is very impractical in the extractive area if, at the time of the initial investment, a firn agreement is to be made on the purchase price based on the investment by the foreign enterprise. Governments do not want to buy back unproductive oil fields or mines. Alternatively, if the sites were productive, a negotiated repurchase prior to the termination of the concession may be tantamount to expropriation, especially if conducted under the threat of expropriation. Of course, if expropriation is to occur, the foreign investors would prefer to have the valuation procedures agreed upon in advance. But there is no assurance that these procedures would be followed under the political conditions dictating expropriation. In the heated atmosphere of a negotiation under duress, determination of procedures for valuation is the problem that gives rise to the greatest conflict.

Evidence that the more likely procedure in the extractive field would be expropriation rather than divestment can be found in the experience in Latin America. Each expropriation over the past years *could* have been undertaken through the repurchase route, with independent evaluators or assessors determining the value of the property or remaining concession. Although some properties were offered for sale to the governments, in only a few instances was the take-over accomplished in a commercial bargaining setting. Some public utilities were offered to the Chilean Government by foreign investors, but President Frei refused to purchase, not wanting the headaches which the company was facing. The present government appears to seek nationalization. In the case of the Chilean copper mines, the principal companies have in effect given a majority of the shares in some mines to the government, reducing their holdings to less than 50 percent, an act that should have been considered directly in line with divestment and thus wholly satisfactory from that standpoint. But the Allende Government promises to take over the remaining shares—under expropriation proceedings.

In the service industries, the proposal is also hardly applicable. The international hotels are tied together more through common holding of "concessions" or management contracts than through ownership, making it useless to "national-ize" them. With respect to advertising and accounting, foreign-owned firms would lose their clients in many instances if they were sold off, and it is relatively easy to start an independent local firm.

Some of the problems in the banking area are similar to those in the extractive industries. Again, valuation is the critical problem. It would be easy to control the banks simply by imposing a "licensing" requirement, which would permit operation for a number of years, letting the market determine whether it was worth coming in under these conditions. The licensing procedure would lend itself to market determination of the value of any remaining "assets and good-will," if nationals wished to enter the banking business. If the government were the purchaser, the proceedings might again take on the coloration of expropriation, and the foreign investor would keep up the assets and value of the operation in direct proportion to his expectations of "fair valuation" by the government. (We will return to the problem of valuation later.)

These comments restrict the sectoral scope of the proposal to retailing and manufacturing—areas in which little expropriation has occurred. In fact, there is no significant case of expropriation of a manufacturing enterprise outside the Cuban experience. These activities do not create the same political problems as do the extractive industries and are not subject to the same widespread insistence on "national-ization." The foregoing discussion indicates that it is these areas, however, to which the proposal for divestment would be most applicable. Divestment in either retailing or manufacturing is feasible, but the trade-offs will be different within each activity and among companies. Less will be lost, for example, by taking over a low-technology operation than a high-technology one. The following assessment is confined to the problems arising in these sectors. Before examining the impacts, however, some general problems of application should be noted.

The question arises as to whether it is equitable to apply the proposal only to new activities. Discrimination among different enterprises according to when they arrived on the scene is an age-old problem of regulation. It is inhibited, however, by the desire not to impose *post-hoc* changes in the conditions under which foreigners have invested in the country. Given the opposing moral considerations, there is no clear answer as to whether such regulations should be imposed on existing as well as new enterprises. Some adjustment in the time period might be made as appropriate compensation for imposing the requirement on already existing affiliates.

Foreign ownership is generally not felt to be a problem until it reaches a certain percentage of control in a given sector. It is conceivable, therefore, that, if there is any economic gain from continuing foreign ownership, governments might decide to impose divestment only on enterprises which raise the percentage of penetration above a critical level. For example, it would not make economic sense to impose divestment on an enterprise which was the only foreign-owned one in the industry and held less than, say, 10 percent of the market; nor would political pressures be likely to occur—unless a sentiment arose to eject all foreigners. Hence, it is possible that governments might decide to impose the requirement only on new enterprises and only after they raised the penetration above a certain (announced) level or on the most recently entering investors if they had raised the penetration above the critical level.

However, this approach is no panacea, either. The critical level is not an objectively determined cut-off, but one set by changing political winds. Under this approach it is unlikely that any investor could feel that his permission to continue in possession would be safe from arbitrary change. The imposition of divestment would tend to turn on the rate of expansion of foreign investment compared to that of domestic enterprises in a given industry and on the political sensitiveness (including the power of pressure groups) of that sector. It might even happen that in a given sector domestically-owned companies would grow much faster than foreign-owned ones, making prior agreements to divest unnecessary or undesirable from the standpoint of the government.

This temporal nature of the proposal is recognized by Dr. Prebisch, who compares Latin America to Japan at an earlier stage of development. He notes that Japan has recently moved to liberalize foreign ownership of its industry and expects that Latin America would not require divestment after it had reached a comparable stage of development—creating its own technology and entering foreign markets through direct investment. The situation, then, becomes one of turning the clock back and slowing down the pace of the hands. In the eyes of some company officials, this might put a premium on waiting for a more receptive climate before committing themselves to investment in Latin America.

REACTION OF DIRECT INVESTORS

Foreign direct investors will react in two ways to the imposition of a requirement to divest within a certain period: one is to decide against the investment (if a new investment is being contemplated); the other is to modify their existing operations to reduce the cost and risk of the requirement. What is the likelihood of rejection? And what are the likely patterns of behavior under the requirement? These responses depend, of course, on the precise form of the regulation, but some reactions can be anticipated.

The probability of rejection is correlated with the assessment of alternative opportunities elsewhere in the world and those which might exist later in the country under a less severe policy. In turn, this assessment depends on the nature of the industry, the company's objectives, the marketing pattern, and the expectation of the investor of fair valuation of the assets upon divestment.

Opportunities available to the investing enterprise occur both geographically and through time. The geographical opportunities mean that the developing countries must compete for investment with the industrialized world. In the past two decades, the competition has not been resoundingly successful. Only when developing countries have sought to draw private direct investment (Brazil) or have had an attractive market (Mexico) have they gained substantial inflows in the manufacturing sector. There are few countries economically significant enough to attract foreign companies in the face of constraints. Japan, because of its large internal market, has been successful also in attracting licensing arrangements in preference to direct investment, in fostering joint ventures over wholly-owned affiliations, and in obtaining portfolio capital.

In the case of Latin America, apart from Brazil and Mexico, a large internal market can be created only by the formation of a regionally integrated market. Foreign direct investors would clamor for entry and might well accede to some rather stringent terms in order to get into such a market. But to create it is not easy, and Dr. Prebisch insists that it cannot be done effectively without the aid of foreign investors, who are needed to accelerate growth, foster the spread of industrialization, and provide foreign exchange. If such a common market is to be created, coordination of policies on foreign investment will be necessary as it is recognized under the Andean Pact, for it would be impossible for one country to require divestment and another not to do so. The existence of a common market would frustrate the ability of one to impose such a constraint by itself. In sum, for Latin America to be *able* to impose such constraints, it has to have the economic attractiveness needed to induce investment despite the requirement of divestment.

If, as Dr. Prebisch suggests, economic growth in the developing countries would relieve the need for and desirability of divestment, it is likely that a number of companies will hold off on investment until they can retain ownership. It would make little sense to create a competitor during one decade and then attempt to enter once again in the next. Since no company could gain an advantage by coming in under the divestment procedure, there would be no competitive pressure to enter early. For the requirement to be successful, the expectation of business must be that it will *not* be removed within any relevant planning period.

The assessment of alternative opportunities is affected by the nature of the industry and the competitive structure. If, for example, the normal payout period for a new investment in the industry is 20 years, the planning period is longer, taking longer for capital "turn around." It would probably require a period of ownership of more than 20 years to induce investment under a divestment procedure. But it would also not necessarily pay such an enterprise to wait for a more receptive governmental policy if that was expected to be 20 years off; if only 10 years away, it would definitely be advantageous to wait.

On the contrary, if the pay-out period were normally 5 years and the industry was highly competitive, the potential investor might well consider the opportunity worth taking—coming in again later under more propitious circumstances. These assessments will vary the further away the industry is from pure retailing and the more it involves heavy investment in fixed equipment or complex production structures.

Company objectives will also alter the assessment, with those enterprises more oriented toward quick returns willing to take the risks of divestment. Thus, the policy is likely to attract the higher-profit per turnover industries rather than the lower-profit ones; whether this is what the host government wants will, of course, depend on its own industrial policy or attitude toward its growth needs. A potential investor that is interested in long-term growth and in building a base for a strong multinational enterprise is likely to reject the opportunity to invest if it involves divestment.

Similarly, a company that sees the market of the affiliate as wholly within the boundaries of the host economy is much more likely to invest under this constraint than one that perceives the market as including exports also. Why should a potential investor establish a competitor for itself in the world market? This is a dilemma faced by companies providing foreign licenses covered by patents, trademarks, or know-how. In the main there is an effort to prevent the licensee from exporting into markets covered by the licensor or other licensees, which is, of course, legal so long as the arrangement is covered by a patent or trademark. It seems unlikely that potential investors would find it profitable to establish an affiliate with full access to its know-how, introducing its products into the world market, only to give up that affiliate within a matter of years. Therefore, with the requirement of divestment, companies which might take the risk would be particularly those that do not intend to export from the affiliate.

All of the above assessments are affected by the possibility that the host government will move to expropriate the property rather than purchase for fair value at the time of divestment, a subject discussed later.

But suppose that investors do enter under the divestment constraint. What changes can be expected in their mode of operation as a result of such a requirement? Consider first the impact on exports. As indicated above, no company will want to create an export competitor. To offset this reaction, Professor Hirschman proposes that the investor be permitted to continue as owner for a longer period if he succeeds in getting exports up to a certain percentage of total sales. However, divestment would be required at the end of the longer period. What this accomplishes is a *certainty* that there will be a competitor at the end of the period — one having an established entree into the market. *Or,* alternatively, the exports would have been *through* the marketing organization of the parent, which would then be closed to the divested affiliate. Or the exports might have been to the parent company itself, which may or may not find it desirable to continue the relationship. If, as a consequence of the divestment, the exports are cut off, the potential buyer will certainly put this into his valuation, and if the buyer is the government, it will undoubtedly feel cheated of its objectives.

The proposal of Professor Hirschman to extend the period of ownership is couched in terms of an acceptable "trade-off" between exports and ownership. Foreign ownership is not even, in his eyes, always less desirable than some contribution to economic growth — in this case an increase in exports. But the desired behavior can be gained without a threat of divestment, as shown by the conditions imposed by some European governments on entry of new firms. However, if the exports achieved are to the parent company or through its marketing organization, Professor Hirschman's trade-off results in greater dependence of the host country on the international company. Therefore, exports are bought at the cost of no reduction in foreign ownership and greater dependence on foreign markets held by the parent.

The investor faced with divestment is also unlikely to build up local research and development (R & D) facilities; yet, creation of an R & D capability is one of the major reasons why Dr. Prebisch considers direct investment necessary.

The creation of R & D facilities will depend on the availability of personnel, the ability to sub-divide research among affiliates of the parent, the cost of particular projects in the host country, and the payout period anticipated. If the parent company believes it worthwhile to set up R & D facilities — that is, if these can pay out within the period prior to divestment — *or* if it anticipates getting fair valuation of the facilities and on-going projects, it might well create them. But then it would do so without the divestment constraint, which adds risks that militate against establishing the facilities.

One of the major reasons for permitting foreign ownership of local enterprises is to obtain top management for them. If this is not forthcoming, the advantage of foreign ownership is lessened. Divestment almost certainly reduces the willingness of top management to spend valuable time on the affiliate's development and problems. Rather, the likelihood is that junior management will be given the task as an "exercise in entrepreneurship" to do the best it can. Top management will reserve its time for the most significant foreign operations — namely those which are essential to other aspects of the total company interest. Only if the affiliate to be divested were a major proportion of the total enterprise would top management be deeply concerned with it, but it is unlikely that top management will commit so much of the company's resources to a single, short-term investment — except in the extractive field. Therefore, we may conclude that the advantage of expert managerial talent will be substantially diminished by divestment requirements.

In addition, it is doubtful that the parent company will feel that the commitment of the most capable junior managers to this particular affiliate is worth the time spent in the learning curve. It requires substantial time to become familiar with a country's customs and to become effective in a foreign environment, and one of the pay-outs of this training period is that the individual brings back expertise on the country that will be useful to the parent in its continuing investment there. If the investment must be terminated, what is the pay-out of the learning process? There is a significant one only if the company can have a continuing presence in the country. Again, alternative opportunities will affect the investor's assessment.

Similarly, efforts to train local managers as replacements would not be so intensive or complete as they would be if the parent company had a continuing interest. And whatever interest was created in the early years would wane as the date for divestment approached. The same lack of interest would arise in the area of technology transfer. No foreign investor facing divestment will commit himself to provide "all relevant technology" to the foreign affiliate; the license providing for such transfers will be carefully circumscribed, and the developments of the later years will undoubtedly be withheld.

Attention to the development of the local market will also wane in the later years since the profit return on such expenditures would accrue increasingly to the owner after divestment. How should such expenditures and their future returns be valued in the negotiated sale? Or sales and price policies may shift to exacting the largest possible profit in the remaining time (short-run versus long-run profit policies), to the detriment of future development of the market. And, finally, the affiliate may be de-capitalized by the large return of dividends and repayment of loaned capital. In fact, the affiliate is likely to be capitalized in such a way that a substantial payback is possible within the period of ownership; this can be accomplished by small capital stock and large loans from the parent. Professor Hirschman recognizes the possibility of fast pay-out of dividends, leaving little for expansion, and proposes extending the period of ownership in direct proportion to retention of earnings (for an unspecified period, but presumably zero dividends would elicit retention indefinitely). Alternatively, he suggests that dividends might simply be limited over the life of the project. Supposedly, if the term of ownership were extended indefinitely with zero dividends, an affiliate that had no earnings and was in no position to remit dividends would be retained by its foreign owners.

The use of a ceiling on remittances over the life of ownership raises the question of whether the return allowed is commensurate with the risk. Professor Hirschman proposes to guarantee *some* return (through a tax credit on capital outflow by the U.S. government!) in exchange for a limit on the total return (which of course prevents the U.S. Government from recouping on the successful ventures what it might lose on the unsuccessful ones).

As Professor Hirschman recognizes, the real burden of dividends is not their remittance to shareholders, but their transfer through the exchanges to a *foreign* owner. Since the burden on the exchanges has no relationship to the earnings percentage or the proportion of earnings retained, it is nearly impossible to set a limit on remittance that takes into account future balance-of-payments problems.

VALUATION AND TERMS OF SALE

The reaction of the investor faced with a divestment requirement depends significantly on his expectations of a fair valuation of the enterprise at the future date. Rather than examine the excruciating problems of determining "going-concern value" and the equitable price of shares owned by the foreign investor, Professor Hirschman concludes that there are two appropriate alternatives: one is the creation of a Latin-American Divestment Corporation to buy the shares under an "international" negotiation, avoiding the problems of dealing with a government; the other is simply to require the owner to abandon the shares at the end of the agreed period. The first does not, of course, finesse the problem of valuation. And the second declares them to have a value of zero to the foreign owner. To ease the pain of such a declaration, Professor Hirschman proposes that the shares be given to the workers or to a charity or foundation chosen by the foreign owner. This donation would have the salutary effect of making the owners "more reluctant to squeeze the property dry in the last few years than they might be if it were to be handed to the government."

Speaking to the quoted sentiment first, it is a naive presumption that foreign enterprises are going to take all the time and trouble involved in a foreign operation in order to give a donation to a foreign charity, much less to create a form of syndicalism with workers owning the enterprise abandoned. Would the owner obtain a tax credit in the United States, for example, for his donation to a charity? — to the workers? Or would he write it off as a "loss"? In either event an evaluation of the assets donated or lost is necessary. The problem of valuation will not go away.

As Professor Hirschman implies, the problem of valuation is intimately related to who is buying the affiliate. At one extreme, the valuation is zero — the investment is treated as a concession, terminating with no value at the end of a given period. At the other, the valuation would be left to a free market, but there is hardly an adequate capital market in any less-developed country. In between, there are a variety of negotiations possible, ranging from purchase by an international agency, to purchase by a government, to purchase by a private consortium or individual enterprise.

Except for the concession-type arrangement, there is no certainty to the divestor regarding the future price — not even how it will be determined. Will the terms of sale be settled at the time of investment — or at least the *means* of determining the price and to whom the sale will be made? About all that could be decided initially is whether the government or private enterprise will be the purchaser; and even this cannot be firmly fixed 10 to 20 years in advance, given the changes in governments. Any attempt to set the method of valuation would also be subject to change at the time of sale.

The only good approximation to equitable negotiation would be to establish an independent tribunal to assess the value of the company. If a private buyer did not come forward, the government would agree to purchase at the assessed price. Given the unwillingness of less-developed country governments to accept the World Bank as an adjudicator of disputes over expropriation, it is questionable whether they would accept it as an impartial agency to assess valuations. But it is the only one that comes anywhere near to meeting the needs of a private investor.

The foreign investor will be calculating the alternative returns to the various factors at his disposal — capital, management, technology. He will expect an adequate pay-out on each, or at least on the package. The divestment requirement cuts substantially the potential returns to both management and technology, and the sale price would have to reflect this loss of future returns on past inputs, plus return to capital.

The valuation problem includes the question of the means of payment

— local currency, foreign exchange, debentures, etc. If the payment is in local currency, the presumption is that the divestor is expected to reinvest in another enterprise in the host country. Is this also to be under future divestment regulations? Or is his only alternative to make some type of portfolio investment?

If the payment is in debentures of the government, their future value is sufficiently in doubt to make the actual valuation quite uncertain.

If payment is in foreign exchange, the question of exchange drain arises, to which Professor Hirschman and Dr. Prebisch reply that the funds must come from international financial sources. It is unlikely that any investor would consider satisfactory any procedure which did not include prompt payment in foreign exchange for the affiliate. This could be guaranteed only by an international agency with sufficient funds. Professor Hirschman suggests that these funds could come out of the aid programs. Whether or not governments would be willing to see funds for this purpose is assessed in a following section.

If valuation is to be determined at the time of divestment, a critical element in the negotiation is adjudication of disputes. Are the governments of the investors to be permitted to become involved? Since it is expected that these governments will not only provide funds for the divestment, but also extend tax concessions to induce the investment initially, it would appear that a position prohibiting their intervention would be highly arbitrary, to say the least. Under these conditions the effort to obtain acceptance of the Latin American Calvo Doctrine — which says no foreign investor shall call on his own government for protection — would seem to be counter to concepts of equal representation.

If the parent government is to be excluded, then it would appear that the host government should also be excluded, leaving both the determination of valuation and any disputes among parties to be resolved by third-party arbitration. Given the strong expressions by Dr. Prebisch and others in Latin America that these nations must no longer take dictation from international organizations and must eliminate the "foreign strangulation" of their economies, it would appear that this arrangement would be unacceptable.

Clearly, the proponents of the divestment approach have much more work to do to devise a mechanism of valuation and sale that has a chance of being acceptable to both parties. One means of achieving the transfer without raising these problems is to encourage (*not* require) the gradual transfer of ownership through sale of equities of the local affiliate to national investors, as further capital is needed for expansion.[3] In this manner Bell Telephone's affiliate in Canada has become almost wholly Canadian-owned. Local capital is thereby substituted for foreign capital, reducing the foreign inflow. Alternatively, if local capital had already been borrowed by the foreign investor, a shift to local ownership might not increase the call on local capital, as equity would be substituted for debentures.

LOSS OF CONTRIBUTIONS

Given the objections noted above, it is likely that a policy of forced divestment will simply dry up the flow of private foreign direct investment to the country adopting it. Such a result would not be desirable in Dr. Prebisch's view, but it does not bother Professor Hirschman. He argues that it may be a blessing in disguise if direct investment dries up, leaving the Latin Americans to proceed on their own, which he thinks they are now more ready and able to do than they will admit to themselves. They have much of the infrastructure for industry and a good foothold in light manufacturing as well as in some heavy industries, leaving only the need for them to take the initiative and forge ahead. (One is reminded of the counseling of Professor E. Kemmerer, who helped several Latin American countries into bankruptcy by advising them to return to the gold standard in the interwar period.)

Dr. Prebisch thinks otherwise. He considers it absolutely necessary that the Latin economies have several more infusions of management techniques and technology before they can expect to move ahead on their own. And he argues that what is needed above all in direct investment are affiliates which are export oriented. This means extensive marketing organizations abroad with technical service agencies if the more technically advanced products are to be exported—viz., Sony's efforts throughout the world. The quickest way for Latin American countries to obtain such outlets is through the multinational enterprises. But to date the affiliates in Latin America have generally been unable to produce at prices competitive in the world market, and costs are raised by continued protection of inefficient local suppliers (e.g., autos).

If the Latin Americans are interested in producing the latest and more technically advanced products, as Dr. Prebisch argues they should be, they will require a couple of decades, as did the Japanese in the postwar period, to get into a viable position. In the meantime they will need the training which foreign technology provides. The Japanese were able to obtain and use effectively a large inflow of technical assistance under foreign licenses. The patent rights and know-how received were used not only to produce locally and gain experience, but also to build a base for indigenous R & D.

Whether Latin American countries have a similar orientation to indigenous research is as yet unproven, but it is even more questionable that they could obtain licenses of proprietary rights in the absence of direct investment. Although there is a flow of technology into Latin America apart from direct investment, it is not large or significant compared to that which flows with direct investment. Even though it shut out direct investment, Japan was able to succeed because it had a sufficiently large and dynamic internal market for many U.S. companies to feel that they had to have *some* foothold in it which they could expand later when the country liberalized its restrictions on foreign investment. But Latin American countries — with the possible exceptions of Mexico and Brazil — are neither as magnetic nor moving toward greater liberalization. Only after creation of effective regional integration can such magnetism be developed and know-how gained outside of direct investment.

Similarly, it will remain difficult to obtain management skills outside of direct investment. Although there are management consultant companies that could provide training, they are not yet adequate in number. Nor do they have the "management teams" necessary to solve all the production and technical problems involved, as well as those of "top management," such as finance and direction. But the main limitation is that there is little for these groups to manage simply because the capital and technology are not available outside of direct investment.

Proposals such as those of Professor Rosenstein-Rodan to overcome the lack of capital by recreating large flows of portfolio capital to Latin America and other less-developed countries have fallen on rocky ground. The sources of such capital are much more ready to release it to or through a U.S. or European company investing directly abroad than to lend it directly to indigenous companies in less-developed countries. Nor are foreign investors generally willing to take minority positions in affiliates abroad if there are attractive alternatives for their capital.

If it is true, as Dr. Prebisch argues, that Latin America needs the infusions of capital, management and technology which direct investment brings, then it is shortsighted to propose a policy that will stifle those flows — *unless* they can be obtained by means other than direct investment. This does not appear to be the case. For there simply are no adequate incentives to those who hold the necessary management and technical skills and capital to make them available separately on the terms envisaged by the proponents of divestment. Therefore, it would appear that the divestment approach will result in a damaging decline or drying up of direct investment.

COMPETITIVE STANDARD

Moreover, the damage will be compounded by the loss of a competitive influence within the host countries brought by the foreign-owned affiliates. Purchasers in the host country are likely to be those already in the industry; or, if a monoply merely changes hands, the pressure to raise efficiency which comes from belonging to a multinational enterprise is removed. The development of competition within their economies and in exports to the rest of the world is considered a vital need for less-developed countries, and Dr. Prebisch stresses this need in his recent exhortation entitled *Transformación y Desarrollo*, written for the Inter-American Development Bank (IADB). He argues that substantial transformations are required before Latin America is in a position to be competitive both with potential imports and in the world market. To generate the pressures needed to produce a competitive response, a reduction of import barriers is needed, within Latin America at least, he asserts.

Even with a reduction of intra-Latin American barriers, it is possible to keep out competitive pressures in many areas, and no guidelines exist on how to become competitive, especially in the world market. In Latin America and other less-developed countries, foreign-owned affiliates, operated under foreign techniques and advanced technology, are crucial in providing the standard both for internal marketing and for exporting. Without these enterprises a major stimulus to competitiveness will be removed.

As many have observed, transformations do not occur readily nor without the continuing pressures needed to sustain them. The existence of the foreign-owned enterprises helps to generate competitive pressures — one result being improvement of the capabilities of the domestically-owned sectors, which in turn diminishes the significance of the foreign-owned affiliates. This pressure should be permitted to operate throughout the economy, and care should be taken that the foreign affiliates themselves are induced to operate at optimum efficiency through subjecting them to import competition and encouraging them to export.

These competitive standards would be useful in activities ranging from pure retailing (e.g., Sears and supermarkets) to extractive industries. Without these companies as competitors or "standards" in the market, it is likely that the newly acquired (divested) enterprises would be conducted in traditional management patterns, which have been, in Latin America at least, more monopolistically oriented than competitive.

CAPITAL MOBILIZATION

There are three aspects of the question of capital mobilization in developing countries which should be examined: Is the purchase of existing assets the best use of available capital? Will additional capital resources be available for this purpose, either internally or through international agencies or foreign governments? Will the funds put in the hands of divesting companies remain within the host economy? If the answer to all three questions is "no," then the proposal for divestment should be avoided. But a "yes" to any one of them might, from the standpoint of capital formation, justify the approach. That is, the purchase of existing affiliates may not be the best use of capital available and additional funds might not be made available especially for this purpose, but if the funds given to the foreign investor could be redirected into the host economy, ownership would have been shifted and other effective uses made of the same capital.

There seems to be little to justify the view that purchasing existing assets of foreign-owned affiliates is the best use of local capital in a host country. If the capital so used flows out of the country, there is a net loss without any offsetting gain in capital formation. How such a move can be justified òn the part of capital-scarce countries, which in turn are asking others to extend capital grants for development, is hard to see. The consequence of Peron's purchase of the Argentine railways from British owners at the cost of nearly $1 billion in foreign exchange is too well known to merit more than this mention of it as an example of inappropriate use of capital in a less-developed country. In fact, this purchase was cited by President Frei as a reason for his refusal to buy foreign-owned public utilities in Chile.

The drain would, of course, be relieved if *additional* foreign funds would be made available *because* they were to be used for the purpose of divestment. But can such funds be expected? It is highly unlikely that the U.S. Congress or European Parliaments would vote funds to buy out the investments of their corporate citizens, especially when these legislatures are trying to encourage the spread of private enterprise and the likely new owners will be less-developed country governments. Even if such funds were voted, the "coup de grace" would be given to appropriations for future years, once serious inequities arose in valuations, and they are likely to occur in *any* negotiation in which one party is under duress.

But suppose that funds were made available by the United States and other governments. It is not likely that they would be given to less-developed country governments to enable *them* to purchase the affiliates; the funds would undoubtedly go to an international agency. And it is unlikely that they would be loaned rather than given to it, and in turn loaned by that agency to potential buyers or used by it to purchase equities for later sale at its convenience. This is, in fact, the proposal for a Latin-American Divestment Corporation. It would make the actual purchases, selling its assets as it saw fit at a later date.

The consequence for the less-developed country governments is that control through private equity ownership is superseded by control held by an international organization. What is it likely to do with the shares it holds? Will it pursue regional integration policies not acceptable to individual governments? Suppose it holds control over a number of affiliates in a single industry. Would it not soon become a supranational industrial corporation? Is this what is desired by less-developed country governments and by the proponents of the divestment proposal?

To avoid this, host governments, in turn, would have to borrow the funds from the international agency to purchase the affiliates. It would then substitute a balance-of-payments liability to an international agency for the liability under private equity ownership. Whether the potential or actual drain on foreign exchange under one was more than under the other is a matter of the terms and practices. Professor Rosenstein-Rodan is firmly convinced that the portfolio liability is preferable to that under equities. However, the evidence is not clear. And the balance may be tipped by a potential loss of foreign exchange as the divested enterprise loses former exports to or through the former parent company.

Given the lack of any clear evidence that the economic results of divestment would be an improvement over the situation under foreign ownership, the strong likelihood of a lower level of efficiency and of foreign exchange earnings, and the drastic policy reversal that parliaments in donor countries would have to accept, it seems unlikely that the proposal to create additional funds for divestment through an international agency will be readily accepted.

In the absence of capital contributions or loans to pay for it, the divestment proposal could be supported if local capital were used to purchase the foreign affiliate and the latter then reinvested the proceeds in the host economy in the most useful opportunity for economic growth. There is some reason to believe that foreign investors might be able to pick such opportunities better than local entrepreneurs, especially if the objective is to accelerate exports. But is there reason to expect that such a roll-over would occur? If it is required from the beginning of negotiations on investment, the original investment is unlikely to be made. If the roll-over is required at the time of purchase, it is unlikely that other private investments will flow in. Therefore, the only policy alternative is to make the reinvestment attractive. This can be done either by removing the divestment requirement *or* by making the prior settlement so fair and equitable that subsequent divestment and roll-over seem attractive compared to other opportunities. Can one expect such perfect harmony in negotiations which are so difficult and fraught with political pressures?

In sum, the reply to all three questions is much more likely to be a "no" than a "yes" for any one of them. And there seems little justification for using local capital for this purpose other than attempting to assuage a fear of the foreigner (however valid that fear may be). It is understandable that such a fear might exist as a result of attitudes inherited from the colonial period, the scarcity of "socially conscious" examples on the part of local enterprises, undesirable practices of some foreign investors in earlier decades, and the general lack of information regarding the beneficial effects of most foreign affiliates today. However, this fear could be better relieved by other means.

REACTION OF LOCAL ENTREPRENEURS

In his recent study of Latin American development for the IADB, noted above, Dr. Prebisch comes to the conclusion that one of the most effective means may be simply to stimulate domestic private enterprise. Does divestment of foreign affiliates contribute to this end? In one sense it could. If it did hand over (sooner or later, depending on the procedure) a going concern to the indigenous private sector, local entrepreneurs would get a valuable boost in serving the market efficiently. But unless the valuation is quite fair, local competitors of the new local owners would have a legitimate complaint that the latter received a subsidy.

If the less-developed country government is the final purchaser, it is doubtful that local entrepreneurs will welcome the incursion of state-owned enterprises into the various industrial sectors formerly occupied by the foreigners. The government could retain ownership and control, for a variety of reasons, putting pressure on domestic entrepreneurs — a competitive pressure that would certainly be considered "unfair," being backed by the tax revenues of the government. Or the government could sell the enterprises to accomplish particular objectives — such as industrial integration across national boundaries, permitting entrepreneurs of other Latin American countries to buy the companies. Local entrepreneurs would have reason to complain about this approach also. Despite the potentially highly desirable results from the standpoint of economic growth, there is little evidence that private entrepreneurs in the less-developed countries are willing to support schemes which pass ownership outside the nation to other less-developed countries. This is particularly true of the local managers of the affiliates being sold; they would almost always prefer a tie to an American or European company than to one in another less-developed country.

In sum, the only local entrepreneurs who are likely to support the approach of divestment are those who feel assured that the sales are to be made to private enterprises within the host country and who stand to gain additional economic power thereby. If they see it as a means of expanding governmental influence, they will undoubtedly not support the scheme. And, from the standpoint of Dr. Prebisch's belief that a prime means of growth would be to encourage indigenous private enterprise, it is questionable whether the way in which divestment is likely to work would do so.

A REMEDY FOR SYMPTOMS?

There is a major difficulty with "solutions" that are concerned with the *ownership* of industry: they are not addressed to the real issues of economic growth or of political and economic power. The real issues concern who controls and how, and whose interests are served? The objective is transformation and development, as Dr. Prebisch says. Yet, it is also participation — participation by each nation in the fruits of industrial and economic growth and political independence, and participation by each group (and person) within the national society in the transformation and development process and its benefits. To be *given* largesse is one thing; to have the opportunity to participate in creating the wealth, which all share, is quite another.

Ownership is one facet of participation, but to satisfy this desire does not require that *all* the resources available to the society be owned within that country. Since the government itself has final control, what is necessary is to promulgate measures to produce the desired transformation and development plus participation. Mere change of ownership will not produce these results automatically, and most of the desired benefits can be gained without the cost of changing ownership.

Divestment will not necessarily produce either transformation or development — other than symptomatically — and may even lessen both, since it might pass economic power to less energetic and enterprising groups. Nor is an increase in participation necessarily best achieved by transferring ownership. A better combination of transformation, development and participation will be achieved by expanding the economy and making certain that it serves the objective of the society. In this way the impact of foreign-owned affiliates is reduced proportionately, and the concern for or fear of the foreigner is reduced, putting his role in a better perspective. This, I take it, is the thrust of Dr. Prebisch's thesis, but he has made his objective more, rather than less, difficult to attain by his proposal on divestment.

If local participation in specific industrial, commercial, or financial sectors needs to be assured, these sectors can be closed (temporarily or permanently) to foreigners — as the Japanese have done. Or they can be opened on specified terms which limit penetration by the foreigner. Even this should be done only when it is clear that domestic entrepreneurs will come forward — with or without government support. Development is more important than who *owns* the processes *so long as* there is reasonable control by the host society, and so long as its members have the *opportunity* to participate fully in the processes and the allocation of the results.

What is needed to put foreign investment in proper perspective is to accelerate and expand the new opportunities for domestic private activity. Moreover, there are ways other than forced divestment of using foreign investment to advantage while minimizing the concerns arising from foreign control. If, however, nations insist that *ownership* is more important than *behavior,* and redistribution of ownership more important than expansion of investment, then they probably should be left to develop only at the rate which their own efforts can produce — without foreign investment or foreign governmental assistance. The divestment approach would take them a long way toward this state of splendid isolation.

NOTES

1. Albert O. Hirschman, "How to Divest in Latin America, and Why," *Essays in International Finance* (Princeton University International Finance Section, November 1969); Raul Prebisch, "The Role of Foreign Private Investment in the Development of Latin America," Sixth Annual Meeting of the IA-ECOSOC (June 1969). OEA/Ser. H/X14, and in "La Marcha de la Integración," *Boletín de la Integración,* INTAL (March 1970), no. 51.
2. For an exposition of the nature of these affiliates in relation to international integration, see my article on "The Multinational Enterprise: A Challenge of Private Power," *European Business* (January 1971).
3. This suggestion repeats a proposal I made 10 years ago in my study of "Private Foreign Direct Investment" in Raymond F. Mikesell (ed.), *U.S. Private and Government Investment Abroad* (Eugene: University of Oregon Books, 1962), pp. 181-83.

34
The Future of International Management

Richard D. Robinson

It is said that one evening a guide in the employ of the famous Lewis and Clark expedition to the Pacific Northwest announced to the explorers that he had two bits of news for them, one good, one bad. "The good news," he announced, "is that we are making excellent progress. We are well ahead of schedule. The bad news is that we are lost."

I feel fairly strongly that we in the international management field stand in somewhat the same position — great progress, but to what end? It was this uncertainty in the future of international management that I had in mind when proposing the subject.

I should first define my terms. By "international management" I mean simply the generation and control of flows of funds, goods, people, and information across national political frontiers.

To build some plan into this analysis, let me suggest some possible alternative dimensions. It seems to me that ten, twenty, or more years hence, international management could conceivably take a variety of forms along several dimensions. I shall dwell on six.

1. International management could be predominantly of a private commercial nature (i.e., internal profit maximizing) *or* of a public political nature (i.e., external policy satisfying). In between, of course, is the mixed case.

2. It could be predominantly justified for its effect on economic growth (which is defined in terms of aggregate world consumption) *or* on redistribution of consumption among and within societies. Note: I would hold that it is the effect on consumption rather than production which is important.

3. It could be predominantly related to the generation and control of goods

Reprinted, with permission, from "The Future of International Management," *Journal of International Business Studies,* Spring, 1971.

(capital, raw materials, intermediates, or consumer) *or* of funds (debt or equity) *or* of people (labor, technicians, or managers) *or* legal rights *or* of pure information. Note that the continuum runs from the more to the less tangible.

4. It could be predominantly fragmented in terms of control *or* centralized to the extent, as some have predicted, that perhaps 200 to 400 giant entities will control (if not own) two-thirds to three-fourths of the world's fixed industrial assets.

5. It could be predominantly found in a more highly concentrated *or* in a less concentrated business structure.

6. It could be predominantly managed in less or a more participative style.

These dimensions can be reduced to six interrelated but distinctive continuua, which may be abbreviated as follows:

1. **Internal purpose:** from profit maximization to political policy satisfaction (or political gain)

2. **External justification:** from economic growth to redistribution of consumption

3. **Substance:** from the tangible to the intangible

4. **Control:** from greater centralization to less

5. **Structure:** from a higher degree of concentration to a lesser one

6. **Managerial style:** from less participative to more.

Admittedly, one might talk of other dimensions, but these strike me as possibly the most significant.

INTERNAL PURPOSE

One cannot automatically equate profit maximization for stockholders in Country A with the welfare of consumers in Country B, wherein the operations of a firm owned by Country A nationals is located. One speaks not only of imperfections of the market but also of differing priorities of national values as translated into national policy objectives. For example, one might cite environmental integrity versus exploitation of the environment; international integration versus national autarky; maximum personal consumption for some versus personal security for all at a lower consumption level — to mention just a few. I suggest that there is no objective function establishing one set of values as better than another in any universally valid sense. So what may be profitable for the stockholders in Country A may not be perceived as generating the greatest benefits in Country B.

It is also quite clear that private business has not constituted a force closing the gap between poor and rich society, nor even between poor and rich within societies. Rather, the evidence indicates that the reverse is happening despite rapid increases in international trade and investment. The profit-motivated flow of goods and services would appear to be associated with a widening of the welfare gaps. Obviously, investment does not flow into the poorer countries at the same rate that it flows among the richer nations. The former are relatively capital-poor by definition — whether the capital be embodied in capital equipment or skilled people. Hence, returns should be relatively high on such capital-intensive goods and skills in the poorer countries.

The problem is that these returns are seen by the investor as subject to high risk. Therefore, the present discounted value of the expected flow of returns is perceived to equate with a significantly lower flow of returns in the more developed — less risky — societies. So, capital flow is inadequate to equate *real* returns between rich and poor nations. As the gaps widen, expectations in the poor countries, or within the poorer sections of a society, are increasingly frustrated. The frustrations are aggravated, of course, by the improvement in information which exposes increasing numbers to the consumption model of the affluent. The situation is thus likely to become even more violent and uncertain, and the discount rate applied by the investor rises still further. In the absence of an adequate flow of capital-intensive inputs from the richer to the poorer societies, the gaps widen still more. So it goes on and on, and I see no limits.

In this situation, I suggest that international business will feel compelled to seek increasing support and protection from its own governments in order to protect its stream of earnings. Hence, I see an increasingly politicalization of international business. With this rising politicalization business will become more responsive to national political policy objectives.

And precisely because the political and social objectives of a society committed to an accelerated, catch-up rate of development may not best be served by a private enterprise system (in part because of the short time horizon of the subsistence-plus consumer), one can anticipate a growing role of government in industry and commerce in the poorer countries. We already see that process at work. Hence, I can anticipate an emerging pattern of more highly politicized North American, European, and Japanese business interests engaged in enterprises and activities with government entities throughout the world.

It is my impression—and we have been doing some research in this area at the Sloan School in collaboration with others — that generally speaking

U.S.-based corporations are ideologically and psychologically less prepared to deal realistically with this situation than are many Europeans and Japanese. For example, I found it significant that Renault, last July, accepted the condition that the government of Colombia have a half share in a Medellin assembly plant. Renault won the assembly plant deal in competition with a number of firms, including General Motors, Ford, Chrysler, and American Motors, which looked upon this condition as "nonsensical."[1]

EXTERNAL JUSTIFICATION

Turning now to the matter of external justification, I would direct attention to the fact that many have assumed that the private business system would stimulate maximum world economic growth. As we have seen, one might well quarrel with that contention simply on the basis of recent historical evidence, given the obviously widening consumption gaps between and within nation states, between the richer and the poorer. But even if it were true that private international business were justified on the grounds that it stimulated world economic growth at a maximum pace, is economic growth in an aggregate world sense desirable?

For some months now a group of scientists from a number of nations—the so-called Rome Club—has been working on a computerized model of the world. It purports to interrelate the mutual effects of population, the fraction of capital directed to agriculture, pollution, natural resources, and something called "quality of life." The latter is itself a function of environmental pollution, population density (i.e., per capita space), food consumption, and health. The point is that obviously we live within a global life support system that is finite. The problem was—and is—on the basis of the best scientific inputs, how to achieve and maintain equilibrium with our limited life support system. As one of the principal spokesmen for the group has written, "It is certain that resource shortage, pollution, crowding, food failure, or some other equally powerful force will limit population and industrialization if persuasion and psychological factors do not. Exponential growth cannot continue forever. Our greatest immediate challenge is how we guide the transition from growth to equilibrium."[2] In other words, more and more people cannot continue to consume more and more, which, incidentally, makes economic growth theory clearly wrong in that there may be an absolute ceiling in an aggregate world sense unless we develop ways of recycling virtually all output. That in itself would revolutionize price structures.

But how soon and under what conditions do we hit a real crisis? That the problem is already grave is supported by the possibility that during the past 50 years we may have killed 50 percent of all life in all oceans. If we are so unfortunate that technology removes the natural resource restraint on industrialization, the crisis begins about 30 to 40 years out, the computer model predicts—well within the lifetimes of our students, if not some of us. The following is a summary statement of the issues raised by the preliminary investigation undertaken by the Rome Club. This quotation is part of a statement made before Subcommittee on Urban Growth of the House Committee on Banking and Currency in October.[3]

1. Industrialization may be a more fundamental disturbing force in world ecology than is population. In fact, the population explosion is perhaps best viewed as a result of technology and industrialization. I include medicine and public health as a part of industrialization.

2. Within the next century, man may be facing choices from a four-pronged dilemma—suppression of modern industrial society by a natural resource shortage, collapse of world population from changes wrought by pollution, population limitation by food shortage, or population control by war, disease, and social stresses caused by physical and psychological crowding.

3. We may now be living in a "golden age" where, in spite of the worldwide feeling of malaise, the quality of life is, on the average, higher than ever before in history and higher now than the future offers.

4. Efforts for direct population control may be inherently self-defeating. If population control begins to result as hoped in higher per capita food supply and material standard of living, these very improvements can generate forces to trigger a resurgence of population growth.

5. The high standard of living of modern industrial societies seems to result from a production of food and material goods that has been able to outrun the rising population. But, as agriculture reaches a space limit, as industrialization reaches a natural-resource limit, and as both reach a pollution limit, population tends to catch up. Population then grows until the "quality of life" falls far enough to generate sufficiently large pressures to stabilize population.

6. There may be no realistic hope for the present underdeveloped countries reaching the standard of living demonstrated by the present industrialized nations. The pollution and natural resource load placed on the world environmental system by each person in an advanced country is probably 20 to 50 times greater than the load now generated by a person in an underdeveloped country. With four times as much population in underdeveloped countries as in the present developed countries, their rising to the economic level of the United States could mean an increase of 200 times in the natural resource

and pollution load on the world environment. Noting the destruction that has already occurred on land, in the air, and especially in the oceans, no capability appears to exist for handling such a rise in standard of living for the present total population of the world.

7. A society with a high level of industrialization may be nonsustainable. It may be self-extinguishing if it exhausts the natural resources on which it depends. Or, if unending substitution for declining natural resources is possible, the international strife over "pollution and environmental rights" may pull the average world-wide standard of living back to the level of a century ago.

8. From the long view of a hundred years hence, the present efforts of underdeveloped countries to industrialize along Western patterns may be unwise. They may now be closer to the ultimate equilibrium with the environment than are the industrialized nations. The present underdeveloped countries may be in a better condition for surviving the forthcoming world-wide environmental and economic pressures than are the advanced countries. When one of the several forces materializes that is strong enough to cause a collapse in world population, the advanced countries may suffer far more than their share of the decline.

It is very possible that our students, as they reach full managerial maturity, will be concerned more with problems of redistribution than economic growth in the usual sense. The private international business system is viable in such a world only if—by taxation or other means—we can give the redistributive process a profit motive—that is, a financial reward internal to the firm—and by the same token equate any net increase in production with internal financial loss to the extent that the increased output is not recycled.

SUBSTANCE

In respect to the substance of international business transactions, it seems to me that because of the pressures on the international business system—some of which have already been suggested—one can, with considerable reason, anticipate that international commerce in intangibles will become of overwhelming relative importance. There is already some statistical evidence in the United States and Japan suggesting a trend in this direction, but more important is the evidence of rising national resistance in the poorer nations to the unlimited external ownership of domestic assets.

Most recently the Andean Group (Colombia, Ecuador, Peru, Bolivia, and Chile) is reported as considering a foreign investment pact which would require at least 51 percent ownership by local nationals within ten years, subject to some exceptions. Indonesia already has a 20-30 year limit on foreign ownership rights, subject to extension by agreement. India has toyed with a similar policy, and so have Argentina and Brazil. To what extent the Japanese model has influenced this restrictive trend is difficult to know. But the fact of Japan's dramatic economic growth, coupled with highly restricted entry for direct foreign investment, is widely known. Would Japan's growth have been even more rapid with a more liberal entry policy? I doubt it. Without restrictions, many U.S. and European firms would not have sold their technology, but rather would have exploited it themselves via wholly-owned or majority-owned subsidiaries in Japan. One of the explanations often cited for Japan's growth is its acquisition of foreign technology at bargain basement prices. The lesson is surely not lost on others. As markets—perhaps regional, as in the Andean case—become attractive, they are likely to restrict foreign ownership and thereby encourage separate flows of technology at controlled prices. Whether the strategy in fact works is another matter, although I have a feeling that it will if and when the protected market becomes attractive.

CONTROL

As you realize, I have already spoken of control. There is no reason to believe that as markets broaden and deepen the poorer countries cannot force the separation of ownership and control from technology—which is embodied in machines, people, and documentation. An element of control remains, of course, in the debt instrument or in the license or technical assistance contract, but it is restricted to such matters as use in third markets, quality and repayment schedules, and extension to new technology. One has to admit that such elements of control are very much more limited than the control normally associated with the ownership of fixed industrial assets and operation of same.

STRUCTURE

Some have suggested that a limited number of giant international firms will, by the year 2000 or so, own the larger share of the world's fixed industrial assets. But, as Professor Farmer has pointed out in a recent article, if one assumes a 20 percent growth rate for a firm with present sales of a billion dollars, and a 6 percent *world* growth rate—not too unreasonable—by the year 2035 or so, the firm's sales will exceed the world's GNP.[4] Indeed, if you reflect on what the Rome Club has said about the irresistible nature of the forces driving us toward an equilibrium with our life support system, you can see that the same principle applies here. For the large firms, growth is undoubtedly a short-run phenomenon. Obviously, there are limits, and, once the limit has been reached, then it will not be the large firms which will grow, but the smaller ones. It is entirely possible, if not likely, that many of the super-firms of the near future will break up because they will be unable to attract resources (particularly skilled people) at the same price as the smaller, more rapidly growing firms.

Quite apart from that consideration, it seems to me clear that there is evidence of rising public concern about the extranational power wielded by these giant firms. As yet, society has been unable or unwilling — possibly the same thing—to develop international agencies with the power to regulate international corporate activity. But it will come. We may soon get such authority in the space and seabed areas and perhaps on a regional basis in Europe. Therefore, after a certain level, concentration will be restricted by national, regional, and eventually international, regulatory bodies. The prevailing opinion in Europe and Japan seems to be that concentration is a good thing so long as it can be demonstrated that the public welfare is served by such concentration. There comes a point, however, at which either such a demonstration cannot be made, or, if it can, the proposed concentration loses its value to the participating firms. If economies of scale cannot be internalized, why move to a larger scale? In any event, there would appear to be many diseconomies of scale. Projecting the recent past into the future is an exceedingly hazardous business. And I would emphasize the singular brevity of history—hardly the basis for valid generalization in respect to the future.

Furthermore, if national or regional restrictions among the less developed countries on entry do in fact increase, these giant firms will reach a growth ceiling sooner rather than later. After all, by the year 2000 or before, three-fourths to four-fifths of the world's population will probably be living within the Third World.

Therefore, I find predictions of high levels of concentration made by some to be unrealistic and naive. Professor Farmer speculates that "the real winners in the past twenty years may not be the real winners in the next twenty years . . . . This suggests a certain kind of discontinuity, a certain significant difference from what has been observed in the past twenty-five years. If so, much of what has been studied, discussed, taught, and warned about may prove in the end to have been wrong.[5]

MANAGERIAL STYLE

Personally, I would extend Professor Farmer's comment to managerial style. The biggest shocker of the last 25 years in this area is not that Japan has risen to the position of the world's third-ranked economic power—and threatens to exceed our per capita GNP in another 15 years—but that Japan has done so with a managerial system that is obviously "inferior." Though slight changes are reported, expert observers—and Japanese executives themselves—tell me that the Japanese managerial system is still overwhelmingly characterized by life-time employment, seniority-based advancement, very low inter-company mobility, the *ringi-sho* (group consensus) system of decision making. Furthermore, there is a very high debt-equity ratio, a high level of personal savings, and a close working relationship between government and business. Could it just be that given the complex modern technology and the anomie of modern urban living in a congested, compacted world such a system is the most creative and productive—i.e., both personally and socially satisfying—yet developed?

Consider a *debt-based* system as opposed to equity-based. The former is less sensitive to the pressure for profit maximization in the short-run, internal financial sense. And concentration need *not* lead to monopolistic practices—i.e., restriction of output in order to maximize monopolistic profits—for the *pressure for growth* is very great in a permanent employment and debt-based system. Therefore, one can enjoy economies of scale without onerous government controls. Even a monopolist tends to be pushed to the point of competitive equilibrium. (Build in a debt-based economic and permanent employment, and micro-economic theory changes.) One result is that hostility between government and business tends to be less.

A lifetime employment system places on a firm many welfare functions that in other countries are the responsibility of government. And these functions are not diluted by an undue syphoning off of profit. Thus, there is more of a common interest between the private and public sectors, and it is in the interest of the government that the firms continue to pay for and administer the welfare programs; it is in the interest of the firms that the government not compete in this area. And the labor unions, not concerned with the issue of unemployment, are inclined to identify their interests more with the well-being of the firm. The seniority system and year-end bonus system, plus the fact that only a small share of company earnings are distributed as dividends, tends to bind union and firm. Needless to say, union members need not fear innovation; no one will lose job or seniority because of a change in assignment. And, anticipating an employee's life-long commitment, the firm can afford extensive re-training if necessary. The average pay-off period will be long.

But what is important at the managerial level is that lifetime employment and seniority-based promotion mean that one lives his professional life in a relatively stable group. Competition is not on an interpersonal basis;

it is on a group basis. Hence, communication within the group should be relatively good. One does not fear his colleague in the next office. Influence and status is enlarged by demonstrated capability and informal recognition of such by one's peer group, but direct economic reward is largely restricted to seniority. So likewise is change in formal title and authority. One suspects that such an economically and socially secure system may provide an optimum environment for maximum creativity, particularly in respect to more complex problems requiring coordinated group effort. And the need to rise to the top of the system is not as great because of the decision-making by consensus, at least down to and including the upper-level middle management. This system reduces the authority of the man at the apex. One can be important and not be president.

The system also is more responsive to the inputs of younger men, precisely the men bearing the new technology and new ideas.

Quite apart from the influence which the Japanese model is likely to have, I would draw attention to the rather startling success of participative management in Yugoslavia via the workers' communities. They are not figments of imagination; they are real and they are working with surprising efficiency. Admittedly, participation there — as in Germany and France — is of a different nature than that of the Japanese. In general, however, one can reasonably doubt that our more hierarchical, competitive, individually based, profit-driven system is inherently inferior in a complex, socially dense world. It is not very satisfying to the individual and it does not provide an environment conducive to high levels of creativity. Perhaps that is what a lot of our youth are trying to tell us. It is significant to note that William F. May, Chairman of American Can, is quoted recently as having predicted that the traditional organizational pyramid will become more of a participative structure.[6] I would suggest, however, that participative management cannot be really effective without some of the complimentary social-political attributes of the Japanese (or possibly Yugoslav) systems. Otherwise participative management merely reduces the age and seniority requirements for entry into corporate power politics.

But in saying these things I have fallen back to the traditional assumptions underlying conventional wisdoms, that is, that economic growth (i.e., higher consumption) is good—or, indeed, possible. Perhaps precisely because our managerial system appears to be *less* productive, it is superior to a more participative system of the Japanese style. Managerial style, however, is not limited to the private, internal profit-maximizing organization—even though profit may be defined differently in some cases so as to *include* the wage bill. It may just be that the first industrial societies to make the adjustments in objectives discussed earlier—i.e., from growth in consumption to equilibrium with the life support system and redistribution of consumption— will be those such as the Japanese. It may be no accident that Datsun is the first automotive company to commit itself to the production of the virtually pollution-free, freon-powered vehicle, a U.S. invention. Perhaps a more participative managerial style produces an industrial structure more sensitive to costs and benefits external to the firm. Such sensitivity also requires close cooperation between business and government both in defining objectives and in devising ways of moving toward them.

By way of conclusion I should call for increased wariness in extending the past into the future. Such extensions, first, assume no limits—when we know perfectly well we live within a finite system. And, second, they assume that history has been long enough to set a trend line, which I most seriously doubt. All of written history is but the sum of the lifetimes of 50 individuals. The history of modern business scales but two lifetimes. The corollary danger is that of meshing our educational and research efforts too closely with the contemporary market, matching those efforts too closely with the views and experience of the practicing international manager. We need more speculation as to the nature of our social system 10, 20, 30 years hence, when those now in professional management schools will be in positions of authority. To employ an overworked word but one for which there seems no substitute: Is what we are doing really "relevant"?

NOTES

1. New York *Times,* July 20, 1970, p. 37.
2. Jay W. Forrester, "Counterintuitive Behavior of Social Systems," Testimony for the Subcommittee on Urban Growth of the Committee on Banking and Currency, House of Representatives, Washington, D.C., October 7, 1970 (printed privately, copyright 1970, Jay W. Forrester), p. 12.
3. *Ibid.,* pp. 22-23.
4. Richard N. Farmer, "Where Does Business Go From Here?" *Economic and Business Bulletin,* Vol. 23, No. 1, Fall 1970, p. 24.
5. *Ibid.,* p. 27.
6. *Business Abroad* (October 1970).

INDEX

Accounting, 233, 234, 242, 255, 260
   financial statements, 261, 262, 263, 264
   "fiscal ethnocentrism," 235, 236, 256, 257
   in international firms, 238, 239
   nationalistic restrictions, 239, 240, 241, 242, 256, 257
   principles, 243, 244, 248, 249, 252, 253, 254
      "accounting thought," 259
      economic-business environment, 247, 248, 249, 250, 251, 257, 258
      education, 258
      inflation, 259
      tax, 258
      technology, 258, 259
   taxation, 258
   transfer agents, 237
   transfer of skills, 234, 235, 236, 237
Advertising, international, 174, 175, 176, 182, 183, 184, 185
   appeals in, 177, 178, 179
   copy, 180, 181, 182
   illustration and layout in, 179, 180
   symbols in, 176, 177
Affiliates. *See* Subsidiaries
Andean Group. *See* Andean Pact Countries
Andean Pact Countries (Chile, Peru, Colombia, Bolivia, Ecuador), 467, 470, 494

Balance of Payments, 70, 71, 72, 73

Calvo Doctrine, 480
Canada, 417, 418, 419, 420, 421, 481
Chile, 471, 484
Corporate management orientation, 13
Currency, salaries in foreign, 153, 154

Decision-makers, national composition of, 8
Devaluation, 270, 271
   and exchange controls, 277
      equity, 278
      goods and services, 278
      loans, 278
   policies against, 276, 277
   pricing strategy in, 273, 274
   tabulating, 271, 272, 273
   and working capital defences, 274
Divesting, 445, 463, 464, 467, 468, 469, 470, 471, 472, 473, 476, 477, 479, 480, 481, 482, 483, 484, 485, 486, 487, 488
   in Latin America, 445, 446, 454, 455, 456, 457, 458, 459, 460, 461, 462, 463, 465, 466, 468, 469, 470, 471, 472, 473, 478, 481, 482, 483, 486

Economic barriers, 69, 70
Environment, world economic-business, 244, 245, 246, 247
   and accounting, 247, 248, 249, 250, 251, 257, 258
"Environmentalism," 167, 168, 169, 170

EPG, 60, 61, 62
  profile, 60
Ethnocentrism, 57, 58, 62, 63, 64,
    65, 66
Executives, compensation of, 53, 54,
    55, 57, 59, 66, 144, 145. *See
    also* Management; Managers

Financial statements, 261, 262, 263,
    264. *See also* Accounting

Geocentrism, 60, 61, 62, 63, 64, 65,
    66
Government, 367, 370, 411, 412, 413,
    414. *See also* Nationalism
  conflict with, 416, 417, 418
  of developing countries, 367, 368
  in Europe and the Middle East,
    426, 427, 428, 435, 436
  negotiation with, 369, 371, 372,
    374, 375, 376, 377, 378, 379,
    380
  power of host, 419, 420, 421

Hirschman, Albert O., 467, 469, 476,
    478, 479, 480, 481

Industrial competition, types of, 282
Industries, classification of, 110, 111,
    112, 113
Inflation, 259
Inter-American Divestment Corp-
    oration, 454, 455, 456, 457,
    458, 459, 460, 463, 468, 478,
    484, 485
International affiliates. *See* Sub-
    sidiaries
International business. *See also*
    Multinational enterprise
  and host governments, 367, 368,

369, 370, 371, 372, 373, 374,
    376, 378, 380
  size of, 92
International management. *See*
    Management, international
International marketing, *See* Market-
    ing, multinational
Investing, 292, 293, 303, 304, 305,
    306, 374, 375, 376, 377, 378,
    379, 380, 384, 385, 386, 387,
    390, 391, 392, 393, 394, 395,
    396, 397, 405, 406, 407, 408,
    446, 447, 448, 449, 450, 451,
    452, 453, 454, 468, 491
  changing patterns, 95, 96
  "climate," 296, 297, 298, 383
  and distance from producers, 299
  in Latin America, 450, 451, 474,
    475, 476, 477, 478
  and local technology, 298
  market size, 293, 294, 295, 296
  and nationalization, 451, 452, 453,
    454. *See also* Divesting
  product-related variables, 299,
    300, 301, 302
    economies of scale, 299
    freight costs, 299
Investment, 24, 25, 26, 27, 69, 70,
    84, 85, 87, 88, 89, 93, 94, 95,
    96, 111, 115
  and multinationalization, 26, 27,
    28
Investors, direct, 473, 474, 475, 476,
    477, 478

Joint ventures, 5, 7, 30

Management, international, 8, 28, 29,
    137, 138, 139, 140, 141, 142,
    143
  corporate policies, 46, 47

future of, 489, 490, 491, 492, 493, 494, 495, 496, 497, 498, 499
nationality of, 8
overcentralization of, 41, 42
Managerial concepts, 119, 120, 121, 122, 123, 124, 125, 128, 129, 130, 131, 132, 133, 134, 135, 136, 140, 141, 142, 496, 497, 498, 499
Managers, 28, 29, 107, 108, 109, 110, 120, 121, 122, 124, 134, 140, 142, 143, 157, 158, 159, 300, 354, 355, 356, 357, 361, 364, 477
allowances and bonuses, 147, 148, 149, 150, 151, 152, 153
base salary of, 146, 147, 153, 154
compensation of, 145, 158, 159, 160, 161
fringe benefits, 156, 157
marketing, 164
relocation expenditures, 155, 156
tax liability of, 154, 155
Manufacturing, for export, 394, 395, 396
import-substituting, 392, 393, 394
Marketing, multinational, 164, 170, 171, 172, 204, 205, 222, 223
as a social process, 166, 167
barriers, 213
in industry, 216, 217, 218
legal restrictions, 221, 222
market characteristics, 216, 217, 218
marketing institutions, 220, 221
market size, 293, 294, 295, 296, 312
comparative, 165, 168, 169, 170
definition, 165, 166, 172, 173
standardization of, 205, 206, 207, 208, 209, 212, 213
consistency, 209, 210, 211
cost savings, 206, 207, 208, 209
improved planning and control, 211, 212
Multinational cluster, 17
Multinational corporation. See Multinational enterprise
Multinational enterprise, 3, 4, 438, 439, 440
behavioral characteristics of, 13, 14, 15, 16
classification of, 17, 18, 388, 389, 421, 422, 423
commitments of, 11
and control of world trade, 3
in crisis, 439, 440
definition of, 3, 4, 17, 22, 23, 339, 340, 403, 404
de-nationalized, 6
de-politicization of, 45, 46
effects on Communist countries, 35, 36, 37
effects on developed host countries, 33, 34, 35
effects on international and transnational institutions, 43, 44
effects on international relations, 38, 39, 40, 41, 42, 43
effects on investing countries, 37, 38
effects on less developed host countries, 30, 31, 32, 33
European, 3
factors affecting development of, 16
and host governments, 367, 368, 369, 370, 371, 372, 373, 374, 376, 378, 380, 426, 427, 428, 430, 431, 435, 436

Multinational enterprise *(Continued)*
Japanese, 3
and nationalism, 343, 345, 346, 347, 348, 349, 350, 351, 352, 353
and national policies, 47, 48
and nation states, 3, 31, 402, 403, 404, 405, 406, 407, 408, 409, 410, 411, 412, 413, 414, 415, 416, 417, 418, 419, 420, 421, 442, 443, 444
organizational forms, 29
organizational structures of, 9, 105, 106, 107, 108, 109, 110, 111, 112, 113, 116, 117
ownership of, 4, 7
problems in, 6
rise of, 23, 24, 25, 26
size of, 91, 92, 97, 98, 99, 100
stages of development, 23
subsidiaries, 139, 140
supranational, 16
U.S. based, 3
and world economic development, 440, 441, 442
Multinational firm. *See* Multinational enterprise

National feelings, 433, 434, 435
Nationalism, 6, 325, 326, 327, 330, 331, 332, 334, 335, 336, 337, 338, 339, 340, 341, 342, 343.
and accounting, 239, 240, 241, 242
as economic program, 333, 334
and the multinational enterprise, 343, 345, 346, 347, 348, 349, 350, 351, 352, 353
as political ideology, 332, 333
theoretical models of, 327, 328, 329

Nationalistic sentiment, 28
Nationalization, of foreign investments in Latin America, 451, 452, 453, 454, 469, 470
National sovereignty, 432, 433

Occupational mobility, 126, 127
Operations, integration of foreign and domestic, 138, 139

Organization of American States (OAS), 467
Ownership, sole, 30

Performance characteristics, 10
Personnel, selection of, 125, 126, 127, 128
structure, 312, 313, 315, 316, 317, 318
training of, 306
Political risks, 354, 355, 356, 359, 365
classification of, 357, 358, 359, 360
forecasting, 360, 361, 362, 363, 364
Polycentrism, 58, 59, 60, 62, 63, 64
Prebisch, Raul, 467, 473, 474, 476, 480, 481, 482, 483, 486, 487
Production, 89, 90, 91, 97, 98, 99, 305, 306
integration of, 306, 307
internationalization of, 68, 73, 74, 75, 76, 77, 78, 79, 80
patterns in, 398, 309
nature of product, 310, 311
parent company, 308, 309
scope, 309
Product planning, 224, 231
market analysis, 229, 230
adaptation costs, 230, 231

company analysis, 230
strategies, 224, 225, 226, 227, 228, 229
choice of, 229
Products, standardization of, 307, 308

R & D, 280, 281, 283, 290, 291
case studies in, 283, 284, 285, 286, 287
in Europe, 288, 289, 290
in Latin America, 476, 481
problems in, 287, 288
and types of industrial competition, 282
Retailing, 187, 188, 189, 192, 193, 194, 195
control and consistency in, 197, 198, 199
diversity, 195
impact, 201
information and advice, 190, 191
internationalization of, 191, 192
limited advantages, 197

luxury merchandise, 189
merchandise, 195, 196, 197
and the middle class, 200, 201
ownership, 189, 190
profitability, 195, 196

Rome Club, 492, 493, 495

Sales, transfer pricing, 11
unit of measurement, 12
Statistics, international business, 84, 85, 86, 87, 91, 92, 97
Subsidiaries, 139, 140

Taxation, accounting and, 258
financing and, 268
policies, 266, 267, 268, 269
Trade, 81, 82, 83
Trading companies, 24

World-wide company. *See* World-wide corporation
World-wide corporation, 3, 17